D0630842

HYPNOSIS AND EXPERIENCE:
The Exploration of Phenomena and Process

HYPNOSIS AND EXPERIENCE:
The Exploration of Phenomena and Process

Peter W. Sheehan
University of Queensland

Kevin M. McConkey
*The Institute of Pennsylvania Hospital
and University of Pennsylvania*

LEA LAWRENCE ERLBAUM ASSOCIATES, PUBLISHERS
1982   Hillsdale, New Jersey   London

Copyright © 1982 by Lawrence Erlbaum Associates, Inc.
All rights reserved. No part of this book may be reproduced in
any form, by photostat, microform, retrieval system, or any other
means, without the prior written permission of the publisher.

Lawrence Erlbaum Associates, Inc., Publishers
365 Broadway
Hillsdale, New Jersey 07642

Library of Congress Cataloging in Publication Data

Sheehan, Peter W.
  Hypnosis and experience.

  Bibliography: p.
  Includes index.
  1. Hypnotism.   I. McConkey, Kevin M.   II. Title.
[DNLM: 1. Hypnosis.   BF 1141 S541h]
RC495.S5   154.7′7   82-2486
ISBN 0-89859-195-3   AACR2

Printed in the United States of America

To Isolde

A portion of the meaning of hypnosis

Contents

Preface

Hypnosis today continues to fascinate and intrigue. The layperson marvels at how easily experiences can be manipulated or changed in hypnosis, and the student of hypnotic behavior cannot fail to appreciate the challenge the field presents for the understanding of the processes that underlie behavior and the intricacies of human consciousness. The apparent ease with which suggestion achieves its effects, however, is more illusory than real. Hypnotic responsiveness, as we observe it in the laboratory or in the clinical setting, produces behaviors that are evidence that the susceptible person is actively at work. The hypnotic subject thinks, feels, is driven, and behaves as a person in a specific context in which the hypnotic situation operates conjointly with subject skills and capacities to determine the final outcomes that we observe. Hypnotic response is complex, variable and idiosyncratic in character, and defies simple description and explanation. The danger we face is the temptation to overgeneralize in theory before the phenomena are really in hand; thus, it is our purpose in this book to explore the phenomena that do exist in as much detail as possible.

The phenomena of hypnosis range from simple tasks involving ideomotor response to more complex tasks involving substantial distortions of perceived reality, such as age regression, hallucination, and amnesia. The techniques of assessment that we have to tap these phenomena are many and varied, and there is a resurgence of interest in the field today in modes of measurement that attempt to embrace multifaceted dimensions of hypnotic response. We survey the modes of assessment that are available to the researcher and to the clinician and then adopt the framework of a particular mode of assessment, which is phenomenologically based, in order to explore the meaning of both phenomena and process. Most of us would agree that the experience of the hypnotic subject provides us with prime data about the meaning of hypnotic phenomena.

This book differs from other books on hypnosis not only in the overall framework of thinking that it adopts, but also in its style and content. We do not survey the field at large and evaluate the full range of existing theories about hypnosis. Rather, we choose to adopt a specific point of view with the aim of illustrating the nature of hypnotic phenomena; this, in turn, enables us to appreciate the relevance of a variety of specific explanations.

During the course of our explorations, implications for the understanding of hypnotic process arise, and we invariably take up the gauntlet by emphasizing the role that individual differences among hypnotic subjects play in accounting for the phenomena at hand. We find it useful, for instance, to appeal to individual cognitive modes or styles of responding to delineate subjects' preferred ways of hypnotic response and to pointedly illustrate the variability of hypnotic reactions. We use the concept of cognitive style to categorize what appear to us to be meaningful differences in behavior and reported experience; we also use it as a process variable that assists us in explaining the underlying regularities that exist in hypnotic performance. In presenting our point of view, however, we have tried to integrate our discussions around a wide body of data, much of which has been collected for the specific purpose of writing this text.

In this book, our focus is less on subjects' success in responding hypnotically than on subjects' differing perceptions of the communications that they receive and the cognitive techniques that they adopt in moving toward successful response as they perceive it. It is this type of response that primarily concerns us, and it is the idiosyncratic character of susceptible subjects' reactions to suggestion to which we are most oriented. The book is thus heavily subject focused. We have virtually nothing to say, for example, about the skills of the hypnotist, although we recognize that hypnotist variables are a legitimate and important area of concern. The book is also cognitively oriented. We view the hypnotic subject, for instance, as a cognitively active participant in the events of trance. He or she is an individual who actively processes the information received, often in a sophisticated and skilled way, in order to arrive at a response that satisfies the demands of the hypnotic setting. In emphasizing the cognitive features of response, however, we have tried to avoid compartmentalizing the hypnotic subject and are always mindful of the hypnotic subject as a whole functioning person who feels, thinks, and strives to respond in a social situation that itself has considerable complexity.

The book is divided into 10 chapters. Chapter 1 discusses the notion of altered state of consciousness and evaluates its usefulness for the study of hypnosis; we find the notion of altered state useful because it orients us to look for qualitative differences in subjects' preferred ways of responding. The chapter also considers the value of verbal reports because the testimonies of hypnotic subjects provide us with such a central part of the body of data that shapes our theorizing. This chapter paves the way for the specific study of hypnotic phenomena in the chapters that follow. Chapter 2 attempts to provide a comprehensive overview of the assessment procedures that are available to both the researcher and the clinician; it also states the case for adopting the phenomenological mode of assessment as a relevant and important means of inquiry with which to study hypnosis. Chapter 3 sets out in some detail the development of a new technique of phenomenologically oriented inquiry, which we have labeled the Experiential Analysis Technique (EAT). Having briefly reported on this technique elsewhere (Sheehan, McConkey, & Cross, 1978), we now attempt to define the method, outline its assumptions, and discuss its relevance as a specific mode of measurement that can assist us in the analysis of individual differences in hypnotic responsiveness. We have found it to be a technique that is highly sensitive to the measurement of the richness of subjects' experience and, accordingly, we have used it to explore specific phenomena in the chapters that follow. These include the study of ideomotor response (Chapter 4), age regression and tolerance of incongruity (Chapter 5), hypnotic dreams and hallucinations (Chapter 6), posthypnotic amnesia (Chapter 7), and finally, a phenomenon that picks up in a special way the individual nature of hypnotic response—cognitive persistence (Chapter 8). For the most part, in Chapters 4–8 we study in detail data collected from highly susceptible subjects whom, in our experience, provide the most useful data for explaining the nature of hypnotic response. Throughout the book (e.g., Chapters 5, 6, and 9), we discuss data that we have collected from nonhypnotic subjects, but our primary emphasis is on the responsiveness of hypnotic subjects themselves.

In structuring the book in this way, we have attempted not only to highlight the nature of hypnotic phenomena, but have also tried to argue the potential relevance of specific techniques and procedures of inquiry to the pursuit of both research and clinical goals. Accordingly, Chapter 8 sets out ways in which the EAT can be used in the laboratory-research context to explore the meaning of hypnotic phenomena (in this instance, amnesia), and Chapter 9 explicitly addresses itself to ways in which the EAT can be adapted or modified for use in the clinical setting. Specifically, Chapter 9 presents potentially useful modifications of the standard procedures for the EAT, set out in Chapter 3, and evaluates these modifications for particular clinical and experimental purposes.

In Chapter 10, we isolate the major themes studied throughout the book and discuss these in relation to the overall position or framework of thinking that we have adopted. For instance, this final chapter includes a discussion of the essential diversity and complexity of hypnotic response and the notion of the hypnotic subject as an active processor of the events of hypnosis. In this chapter, we also hypothesize about some of the patterns that have occurred in the data we collected and suggest, in particular, the value of interpreting the performance of the hypnotic subject in terms of the skills of attention. Here, as in Chapter 8, we are most explicit about the relevance of the individuality of the hypnotic subject (together with the assessment of these individual differences) to theorizing about hypnotic process. We also review the limitations of verbal reports and point to future research directions in which investigators might move in order to resolve some of the major issues that have been raised.

Although this book leans heavily on the data we ourselves have collected, each chapter aims at presenting relevant literature on the phenomena being discussed and attempts to reflect changing directions in the field. In this sense, the text tries to be representative rather than comprehensive. We consider, for instance, the emergence of more flexible modes of assessment that suit the purposes of the clinician (Chapters 2 and 9), trance logic as a potential defining feature of hypnosis (Chapter 5), and amnesia as a durable and persistent phenomenon (Chapter 7). Other hypnotic phenomena exist but we consider that, for the most part, the processes that underlie them are similar to those that underlie the representative phenomena that we discuss.

We hope this book is of value to researchers, clinicians, and all serious students of hypnosis. Its aim is to foster a deep appreciation of the richness and essential variety of hypnotic phenomena and to facilitate understanding of the processes that underlie them. There are aspects of the experiences of hypnotic subjects that are highlighted by the procedures we have developed, which may well be familiar to those who have worked clinically with many patients or clients. Our aim, however, is to subject these experiences to detailed empirical analysis and to focus on their relevance. In writing the book, we have come to learn just how much is yet to be accomplished in the field, but it is our hope that the book communicates to others a portion of the meaning of hypnosis as we came to understand it.

We owe thanks to many who assisted in the book's preparation. We would like to thank Lawrence Erlbaum for his enthusiasm concerning the enterprise and for his faith in a new type of venture. We wish also to thank the students of hypnosis at the University of Queensland for their discussion of many of the notions presented in this book. Particular thanks go to Darryl Cross who offered his skills in helping us collect much of the data that we present here and to Leonard Eron for use of his aggression instructions in Chapter 5. We are grateful to our colleagues at the Unit for Experimental Psychiatry, The Institute of Pennsylvania Hospital, for their de facto evaluation of many of the ideas that we have presented. Our thanks go also to Margaret Gnepp, Mary Lavercombe, Fern Liebman, Mary Murphy, and Colleen Wilson for their help in preparing the manuscript.

Finally, most of the research presented here was supported by grants from the Australian Research Grants Committee and the University of Queensland to the first author. During the preparation of the manuscript the second author was supported in part by grant #MH 19156–10 from the National Institute of Mental Health. We are grateful for that support.

Peter W. Sheehan
Kevin M. McConkey

HYPNOSIS
AND EXPERIENCE:
The Exploration of Phenomena and Process

1

Consciousness and Altered Awareness

INTRODUCTION

In this book we aim to analyze the meaning of the experience of the hypnotized individual. Because hypnotized individuals feel and experience events in a way that frequently suggests they are experiencing some considerable degree of alteration in their normal state of awareness, it is important to come to grips with the notion of consciousness in studying hypnosis in both its clinical and experimental applications. Initially, however, if we are to understand the differences that exist between people in the nature of their hypnotic experiences, it is essential to understand the general nature of consciousness and altered awareness in the broad context of psychology.

The psychology of today has very much returned to consciousness, and the era of narrow behaviorism has passed (E. R. Hilgard, 1980; McKeachie, 1976). The discipline is now firmly demarcated by cognitive approaches to psychological phenomena, and exploration of how cognitions are formed, regulated, and changed has become an integral part of its study. It is now eminently respectable, for instance, to talk about the behavioral manifestation of consciousness while at the same time asserting the value and meaning of the subjective concomitants of that behavior.

Consciousness derives from the interaction of an organism with his or her environment (Pribram, 1976a), but where explanations of human behavior were previously couched in terms of a limited set of determinants, personal and environmental influences are viewed by contemporary psychology as being interdependent. A person's environment is no longer considered an autonomous force that orchestrates his or her behavior; rather, as Bandura (1978) notes:

1

"psychological functioning involves a continuous reciprocal interaction between behavioral, cognitive, and environmental influences [p. 345]." By our own social and cognitive actions we play an active role in creating the environment that influences us.

Contemporary theorizing in personality has seen a steady progression through unidirectional accounts of the interaction between people and their environment, where persons and situations are treated as independent entities that combine to produce behavior, to more complicated bidirectional accounts emphasizing reciprocal interactions, where behavior, internal personal and cognitive factors, and environmental influences mutually operate as interlocking determinants of each other (Bandura, 1978). Internal personal factors including our conceptions, beliefs, and self-perceptions have come to be seen as important to the explanation of the type of behavior that we display; our efficacy and outcome expectations, for example, strongly influence how we behave, and the environmental effects created by our actions in turn alter our expectations (Bandura, 1977).

There is a wide variety of theories that attempt to come to grips with the existence and properties of consciousness. Personality theories of functioning are coming to acknowledge and primarily stress the human capacity for conscious judgment and intention (see, Cantor & Kihlstrom, 1981). Much of cognitive theory, however, has accepted a more materialistic position that attempts to explain consciousness and its properties in terms of detailed information-processing accounts of cognition. These stress concepts such as the organized nature of conscious experience, its limited capacity, and its control function (Shallice, 1978). Viewed in this way, Atkinson and Shriffrin (1971), for example, regard consciousness as corresponding to the contents of a short-term memory system of quite limited capacity; alternative limited-capacity approaches have been adopted by others (e.g., Posner & Klein, 1973; Posner & Snyder, 1975) in similar fashion.

Information-processing accounts of cognition, however, have themselves recently taken a more subjective turn, and this is especially evident in the emergence of the field of social cognition where script theory (Abelson, 1976, 1981), for example, is viewed as an alternative way of thinking about behavior. Abelson (1976) defines a script as a: "coherent sequence of events expected by the individual, involving him either as a participant or as an observer [p. 33]." According to this view, our acts are firmly embedded in a network of our prior experience, which is concrete, idiosyncratic, and often imageable (Taylor, 1976).

Social psychologists are also returning to the position that one of the best ways to find out what people are doing is to ask them, thus emphasizing the essential role that verbal processes play in defining the operations of our conscious experience. This role is an especially critical one for those interested in understanding the nature of hypnotic phenomena. We turn now to consider the general nature of consciousness as it has been conceptualized by contemporary psychology.

THE MEANING OF CONSCIOUSNESS

Basically, the term "consciousness" has been used in three distinct ways (Battista, 1978). First, it is used as a theoretical construct denoting the system by which an individual becomes aware; second, it refers to reflective awareness— our awareness of being aware; and third, it is frequently used as a general term that encompasses all forms of awareness and is relevant across diverse fields of psychological inquiry. One can, in fact, look on the interested, attending, and conscious person as someone who heeds his or her surroundings (Pribram, 1976a). Viewed in this way, a wide variety of characteristics emerges as important, suggesting the need to explain how we see, look, remember, and even talk. The approach to consciousness that we are taking here is necessarily broad in scope. A brief review of the different uses to which the term can be put illustrates the utility of arguing for a generalist orientation and sets the stage, as it were, for addressing the inherent complexity of hypnotic consciousness.

Battista (1978) argues that the use of consciousness just as a theoretical construct is limiting because the term is commonly used to refer to experience rather than provide us with the means of explaining it. Similarly, restricting the term to reflective awareness creates problems because it may fail to incorporate experiences that occur before the development of such awareness (as in childhood) and also experiences that take place without reflective awareness (e.g., dreaming). Consciousness seems better employed as a general term that allows us to refer to many different forms of experience or awareness that can shift or alter gradually (or dramatically) in response to internal as well as external conditions of stimulation. Referencing consciousness in this way emphasizes the fact that the events of consciousness are complex and varied; they incorporate, for instance, images in a variety of sensory modalities and in every degree of believability, vividness, and realism, including hallucinations, reveries, inner dialogue, and dreamlike sequences (Klinger, 1978).

If a single definition of consciousness fails to reach consensus, it is even more difficult to define the notion of an altered state of consciousness. As Marsh (1977) indicates, certain changed states are easy to index and are enough a part of our everyday experience that they can be readily accepted and defined as altered or alternate states (e.g., drug intoxication and sleep states can be regarded in this way). The demarcating features of an altered state of consciousness begin to blur, however, when we consider daydreaming and certain states of reflection and meditation. Argument can then be made as to whether the differences among the alternate states are a matter of degree (E. R. Hilgard, 1979a; Singer, 1977) or whether they, in fact, reflect obvious discreteness (Tart, 1976). For instance, Marsh (1977) points out that it is difficult to know just where: "deep contemplation in a usual state of consciousness become(s) a meditative alternate state [p. 9]." The problem is especially apparent when one considers the extent of redundancy in the information presented to the senses. In this respect, Singer (1977) argues that the absent-mindedness or seeming distraction of the creative scientist or artist may indicate less of a shift to an altered state of consciousness than a finely honed capacity for assigning high priority to concentrating on private, ongoing streams of thought.

The term "altered state" requires special discussion. The notion of "altered state of consciousness" has come to be rejected by some in the consciousness literature as an inappropriate way of classifying changed awareness. Zinberg (1977), for instance, objects to the word "altered" because it conveys the implication that such states represent a departure from the way consciousness should be. Zinberg (1977) prefers the term "alternate" because it more clearly conveys that: "different states of consciousness prevail at different times for different reasons and that no one state is considered standard [p. 1]." Viewed in this way, our usual state of consciousness is simply classified as one specific instance of the category "alternate" state. Whatever the choice of term, there is no basis for the assumption that our ordinary state of consciousness represents the way that consciousness ought to be. Many of the phenomena that we experience in our usual state of consciousness are unusual, but because they are so familiar to us, we simply do not attend to them a great deal (Tart, 1980).

The essential emphasis of definitions of altered (or alternate) states is usually on the qualitative features of subjects' shifts in consciousness (Sheehan, 1979c). Taking hypnosis as an example, it is not simply a matter of people experiencing more imagery, or forgetfulness, or anesthesia; rather, the claim is that the nature of the mental processes themselves is altered. A person does not just fail to remember what he or she is told if amnesic, for instance; the person cannot remember despite the effort that is spent in recalling. It is as if a barrier is present to prevent the memories coming to awareness, although this barrier may be reversed with the appropriate signal. Gill (1972) argues that the notion of altered state should explicitly convey the fact of reversibility. Persons experiencing an alternate state of consciousness experience a transient or temporary, rather than permanent, reorganization of psychological functioning.

It is important to recognize that altered or alternate states of consciousness should not be defined in terms of the content of consciousness; rather, appeal should be to structure. Hallucinations, for instance, do not simply occur in hypnosis. They can and do occur across a variety of states of consciousness including those resulting from meditation, drug intoxication, and psychopathology. The most distinctive feature of states of consciousness lies clearly in their overall organization (Pribram, 1976a, 1976b; Rappaport, 1957; Tart, 1975). The same elements, for example, exist in hypnosis as may exist in a dream or even in routine awareness. Tart (1972b, 1975, 1980) places considerable emphasis on this distinction between process and content, arguing that states of consciousness result from the interaction of different subsystems (e.g., perception and memory); it is the modes of organization involving these subsystems that constitute the distinctiveness of the state in question, and the pattern of interaction among the subsystems gives the state of consciousness its recognizable identity. States of consciousness, for example, are not demarcated in terms of specific memories that are forgotten or objects that are hallucinated, but in terms of the changes in interaction or altered configuration among the subsystems that result in the modified organization. This distinction between process and content explicitly acknowledges the important fact that changes in process are critical to the definition of an alternate state, not variation in content.

Just as qualitative changes in the patterning or organization of consciousness denote the presence of an alternate state, quantitative changes in patterning usually indicate a shift in the depth of consciousness. Tart (1975) captures the distinction in an analogy regarding the differences between boats, cars, trains, and planes. Depth of consciousness is more like the miles per hour measurements within each of these modes of transportation being considered rather than differences in the modes of transport themselves. However, a problem exists with respect to the degree to which qualitative (as opposed to quantitative) features may change with the concept still retaining its meaning. Let us illustrate the point again with respect to hypnosis.

The next chapter looks at hypnotic abilities in some detail, but at the outset hypnosis can be said to tap the following range of skills: the capacity to combine thought and action in an imaginary way (as in hand lowering or arm levitation); the capacity to experience suggestions where the hypnotist challenges the subject to be able to respond (as in fingerlock or arm immobilization); and the capacity to distort reality and cognitively experience events that have no basis in the real world (as in hallucination or amnesia). As one proceeds from ideomotor performance to cognitive-delusory performance on standard hypnotic test scales, it is difficult not to reserve the term ''state of hypnosis'' for performance on the more difficult items—those that appear, at least, to represent more marked changes in quality of awareness and experience. The hypnotized person who hallucinates and is amnesic normally interests investigators most in hypnosis, not the person who can hold his or her arm out and feel it heavy as it begins to fall down with the weight of an imagined object.

Although the changes in organization or patterning that occur in alternate states of awareness are qualitative rather than quantitative, it is nevertheless important to recognize that states of consciousness themselves may vary over time. This variation contributes to alterations in the depth or degree of the state concerned, and such variation can also occur from one alternate state to another. As Marsh (1977) states the point: ''Within each state . . . the ceaseless change and variability fall within ranges of tempo, imagery, and intensity [p. 22].'' Although the essential elements of one state may equally pertain to alternate states, it is the changes in the way in which the elements are organized or patterned that most likely will lead to the awareness of the experiencing person that the state is somehow different.

Not always, however, is awareness of the usual state lost in alternate states of consciousness, and knowledge of this fact is important in any attempt to understand hypnotic consciousness. In daydreaming, for example, the dream frequently occurs in a context where we know that we are daydreaming. Similarly, in hypnosis, persons never completely lose touch with their ordinary everyday frame of reference and at times may not even be aware that consciousness has changed. A subject who is fully amnesic for the events of trance, for instance, may be irritated at what seems to be a puzzling "lapse" of memory.

The ways in which reality features of the environment are processed by the hypnotized person are, in fact, more complicated than assumed in the current literature. Our understanding of that processing underscores the inherent complexity of hypnotic consciousness and helps us to understand the appreciable differences that exist in such consciousness among highly susceptible persons themselves. The subject in hypnosis who reports not hearing anything relies on some contact with reality to recognize auditorily the hypnotist's command: "Now you can hear again." The implicit conflict in that situation may be resolved in a variety of ways by susceptible subjects, as we see in the chapters to follow.

Behavior that indicates at one and the same time that a subject cannot hear (when the hypnotist tests for deafness) and can hear (when the hypnotist verbally instructs the subject to hear) has been labeled paradoxical, and there is much that is apparently incongruous about such hypnotic responses. The paradoxes in question, however, express the fact that simultaneous registration of suggested and real events characterizes many so-called alternate states of awareness, not just hypnosis.

When noting the significance of reality processing, it is important to recognize that the structure or patterning of consciousness that characterizes waking may have altered in the changed state but rarely fades completely. It does fade enough, however, so that experiencing subjects can frequently be aware of a disruption in their usual waking consciousness. Insistence on the presence of a dramatic qualitative change in consciousness as the yardstick for judging hypnosis or any other altered state of awareness is misleading. Change can be gradual rather than dramatic, and sometimes it seems that the changes occurring in hypnosis appear to reflect alterations of monitoring and control processes rather than changes in the quality of consciousness per se. As E. R. Hilgard (1979a) notes, a hypnotic subject who is hallucinating somebody, but who also acknowledges the real person as present, may report that the two persons being seen look completely alike. In this instance, the quality of consciousness appears the same; the alteration is more in the way the presentations are monitored and controlled by the hypnotized person. Perhaps the most compelling evidence to support the relevance of altered monitoring functions to the understanding of hypnosis is the evidence available on the hidden observer phenomenon that has been collected by E. R. Hilgard (1976, 1977) and his associates. Some hypnotized persons (but not all, and not all who are highly susceptible) indicate through automatic writing or talking that pain is being experienced even though neither pain nor suffering is indicated in the analgesic state by the normal method of verbal report. It may well be, then, that hypnosis involves us in talking about different kinds of altered or alternate states of awareness for different kinds of persons, even those who are highly susceptible. This is a theme that we return to often in the chapters to follow.

Normally speaking, states of consciousness have specifiable sets of characteristics that define them, and certain common features can be delineated that are relevant to their study, hypnosis included. Generally speaking, alternate states of consciousness lead to modifications in thinking that may incorporate impairment of reality testing, loss of volition, perceptual distortions, and increased susceptibility to accept and respond to statements as they are suggested (Ludwig, 1969). This last feature appears to be a special characteristic of hypnosis where argument is made that responsiveness to suggestion occurs in a context where the subject typically demonstrates a redistribution of attention, a heightened ability for fantasy production, and an appreciable reduction in reality testing (E. R. Hilgard, 1965).

Shor's (1959, 1962) notion of loss of generalized reality orientation theoretically captures the statelike features of hypnosis in this regard. Shor argues that in hypnosis our everyday waking orientation fades into the background so that experiencing the present comes to be detached or isolated from our ordinary frame of reference. This fading is accompanied by an increase in primary process levels of mentation and psychological functioning, the processes being involved leading to a reduction in alertness and critical thinking and a facilitation of imagery-based forms of cognitive activity. Secondary characteristics are reported as well. Gill and Brenman (1961), for example, discuss split-second hesitations, frozen postures, memory lapses, and alterations in body movement where hypnotized persons may indicate shifts in bodily awareness, even in the absence of specific instructions by the hypnotist. Although a number of theorists in the field of hypnosis tend to agree in a descriptive sense about the different features of hypnosis that are implied by the terms "altered state" (see E. R. Hilgard, 1965, 1969; Orne, 1959), they nevertheless differ appreciably in the processes that they associate with the state characteristics that they recognize and the theoretical frameworks in which they prefer to embed them. Gill (1972), for example, talks of changes in reflective awareness, voluntariness, and diminution in reality testing as "regression in the service of the ego."

E. R. Hilgard (1976, 1977) and others (e.g., Bowers, 1976) focus on the significance of the process of "dissociation"; Orne (1974) emphasizes the relevance of "delusion" as the most important intrapsychic process for understanding hypnotic phenomena; and Sarbin and Coe (1979) choose to appeal to more socially defined processes of explanation such as the concept of "self-deception."

MIND-BODY RELATIONSHIPS

Discussion of consciousness and its alternate forms demands at least some general comment on the models of the mind implied by the term consciousness and how the data bear upon the different positions that can be taken. There are three main approaches to consciousness (Battista, 1978): dualistic, monistic, and holistic. Dualistic approaches stress that physical and mental states are separate; monistic accounts assert that only one or the other state exists; and holistic frameworks consider that physical and mental states are simply different levels of a unified reality.

Each of the main approaches can be subdivided into further theoretical positions. For example, there are relativistic, emergent, and informational approaches to holism. Emergent theories, for instance, consider that consciousness develops from physical interactions. Sperry's (1976) work illustrates this approach in that he views consciousness as a higher-order, molar property of the brain that controls lower-order neurophysiological phenomena. Other representatives of the position that mind is an emergent property are Pribram (1976b) and John (1976). Pribram considers alternate states of consciousness as due to alternate control processes exercised by the brain on sensory and physiological stimulus invariants and on the memory store. John talks of multiple levels of information processing in the brain that correspond to sensations, perceptions, subjective experience, and self-awareness.

The work of these and other neurophysiologists represents the most important body of current data on what constitutes the content of consciousness, and the reader is referred elsewhere for reviews of the substantial body of evidence that bears upon the different positions (see Globus, Maxwell, & Savodnik, 1976; Schwartz & Shapiro, 1976). How best to decide among these different views of consciousness is beyond the scope of our discussion. E. R. Hilgard (1979a) notes that there is little reason to expect to be wiser than others before us at the metaphysical level. Most practical discussions of consciousness are served adequately by the use of a double language—both the language of physiology and the language of mental functions appear to be justified by the data on consciousness.

ASSESSMENT OF CONSCIOUSNESS
AND VERBAL REPORTS

We now consider the role assessment plays in the way we incorporate consciousness into our frameworks of thinking and, in particular, the status of verbal reports of experience. In later chapters, we detail particular assessment procedures in relation to hypnosis and how they make specific use of verbal reports.

Our approach emphasizes the primary role that statements about experiences have to play and rejects the position that reduces all mental events to observable reactions. If consciousness were exclusively objective, all one would need to do would be to study the associations that take place between what happens on the stimulus side and specific neurophysiological events.

This is not to ignore the importance of the associations that are observed, however. Our knowledge about transitory states of consciousness between waking and sleep, for example, has been significantly enhanced by the work that demonstrated that the period just prior to Stage 1 sleep is accompanied by slow, rolling eye movements and a slowing of the alpha rhythm (see Foulkes & Vogel, 1965). In this instance, the distinctiveness of the hypnagogic state can be reliably indexed in terms of publicly observable brain-wave and eye-movement patterns, thus overcoming the limiting nature of the privacy of people's verbal testimonies concerning their experiences.

Particular ways of conceptualizing consciousness are heavily tied to techniques or modes of assessment. Consider, for example, the impetus toward consciousness captured by the movement in personality theorizing called interactionism. This movement recognizes specifically the influence of the person in context rather than the person or environment considered alone. There are varying ways in which we might formulate the interaction at issue (see Bandura, 1978; Mischel, 1979), but all explicitly acknowledge the role the individual plays as a sentient, cognizing, and interpreting organism.

Individuals are not to be seen as mechanically influenced by the environments in which they are placed; rather, they change and, in turn, are changed by their contexts. The modifications that take place frequently require effort and occur in an active and cognitive fashion, thereby implicating the processes of consciousness. As Ekehammer (1974) indicated, psychology is simply making an about-face to recognize the significance of what had been said in other contexts and by other theorists many years ago. Angyal's (1941) biosphere conception, Lewin's (1951) field theory, and Sullivan's (1953) interpersonal theory reflect only some of the theories influential in the past that have essentially depended on interactionist (and hence cognitive) assumptions.

A particular problem in grappling with changes in the Zeitgeist within the discipline of psychology comes from isolating modes of assessment that are consistent with or flow specifically from particular theoretical assumptions. For example, Sullivan's (1953) interpersonal theory implicates the two-person interview situation, and Freudian theory depends heavily on the modes of assessment known as free-association and projective testing. The interactionist view, however, despite its current major emphasis on cognition and modes of consciousness, has no special techniques of assessment to reinforce the validity of its account. The assessment procedures that have emerged to date are inadequate for the task. Emphasis may be placed, for example, on factorial designs in which the behavior of individuals is measured in different contexts of testing. The results are then analyzed so as to isolate the extent of variance in behavior due to situations, persons, and joint (i.e., situation X person) effects.

Researchers argue about which of the components—persons, situations, or person X context—accounts for most of the variance in behavior. As Bandura (1978) states, when one considers the interlocking, reciprocal interaction of persons, situations, and behavior, the factorial approach is clearly ill-equipped for the task. A person's conscious judgment of a situation in which he or she is placed may affect behavior, but the behavior in turn can equally affect that person's cognitions. The interdependent aspects of person, situation, and behavior and the role consciousness plays in relation to this interdependence are complex. We inevitably come to rely on persons' verbal reports of their behavior, especially in the absence of well-delineated modes of assessment that are tied to particular interactionist assumptions.

The interactionist stance is clearly relevant to the study of hypnosis. In hypnosis, persons with distinctive aptitudes and skills (collectively labeled "susceptibility") bring these talents to bear on their attempts to satisfy the demands of the hypnotist. The final outcome of their attempts as expressed in terms of their behavior and experience undoubtedly reflects the influence of the overall context and conditions of testing.

If we are sentient, apprehending persons in the contexts in which we are placed, then the active nature of our imagery and fantasy is a particularly important part of psychological functioning to explore. Many salient characteristics of our mental activity fail to be captured by objective procedures of assessment, the problem being that processes of consciousness (e.g., imaging) are inherently difficult to index. As Bugelski (1970) asserts, we instruct people to image objects, and they tell us that they have done so. Experimenters tend to fall back on using their instructions as operational definitions of the process when all they have to consider is the person's description of what he or she is doing. The status of verbal reports as data clearly represents a major issue in the study of consciousness. We now consider current views on the status of such reports and some of the factors that may affect our acceptance of their validity.

Nisbett and Wilson (1977) provide a searching critique of subjective reports that has important implications for the study of alternate states of consciousness. They offer the radical thesis that persons report falsely rather than truthfully most of the time and that if correct reports do happen to occur then they do so incidentally because the subjects correctly employ a priori causal theories about the behavior they have just shown. According to this view, subjects work to formulate appropriate theories to explain their actions and, more often than not, they fail to formulate the correct ones.

Subjects in dissonance studies, for instance, often cannot report correctly about the existence of motivational responses produced by the complex manipulations of the experimenter. The danger—especially where increased suggestibility exists, as in alternate states of consciousness—is that subjects can formulate with relative ease conceptions about explaining their behavior similar to those held by the experimenter who is testing them. The implications of experiencing an altered state of consciousness can be readily apprehended by subject and investigator alike in circumstances where both participants have come to expect discontinuities in experience.

Recently, Ericsson and Simon (1980) have argued that Nisbett and Wilson (1977) go too far in their attack on verbal reports and claim that conditions can, in fact, be isolated in which verbal reports can be a valuable and thoroughly reliable source of information about cognitive events. Nevertheless, Nisbett and Wilson present some useful guidelines for checking the veracity of verbal reports. For instance, there ought to be regularities concerning the conditions that give rise to subjects' introspective certainty about their cognitive processes. If Nisbett and Wilson are correct in their thesis, then subjects' reports about their higher mental processes should be neither more nor less accurate in general than the predictions about such processes that observers who are not actually experiencing the treatments can make. If observers of hypnotic induction procedures could indicate exactly the same reports as subjects who were actually administered induction, then one could very legitimately question the accuracy of what the hypnotized subjects said they experienced. In essence, the problem is to adopt procedures that will specify which types of reports can be termed accurate and which can be termed inaccurate, regardless of subjects' apparent conviction of what they purport to be true. We return to this problem in Chapter 10.

The most significant difficulty for assessment with respect to verbal reports is that we are tempted to rely on their veracity when it might not be justified. Yet, when considering hypnosis, the study of the behavioral consequences of suggestion is insufficient if one argues, as we do, that strong appeal to the internal processing of the organism is essential if one is to understand fully what suggestion achieves. If hypnosis is invoked as an alternate state of consciousness, we can at best admit that it is a hypothetical construct indexed in an imperfect way by subjects' verbal reports and the behavior that accompanies them. We can perhaps be comforted, however, by Kety's (1960) admonition that: "Nature is an elusive quarry and it is foolhardy to pursue her with one eye closed and one foot hobbled [p. 1862]."

The message is that because states of consciousness are difficult to measure we should not restrict our field of vision unnecessarily. For example, the state of dreaming can be corroborated by subjects' verbal reports of dreaming and other public observable indices of response such as EEG activity; in a similar way, hypnotized persons' reports of their trance experience can be usefully corroborated in convergent fashion by reaching agreement across different measures. Just as the concept of dreaming is strengthened by the presence of associations between periods of rapid eye movement and reports of dreaming (see Stoyva & Kamiya, 1968), so the concept of hypnosis as a particular state of consciousness is strengthened by the consistent associations between subjects' verbal reports of an alternate state and behavioral indications of shifts in perceptual and memorial functioning. When verbal reports are gathered together with other indices of behavior, it is possible to check the consistency of the verbal reports with that behavior and so establish some of the different types of processes that underlie hypnotized individuals' cognitions about the environment in which they are placed.

In discussing the status of verbal reports, it is important to emphasize that empirical data do exist that attest to their utility and that verbal reports are useful data (Ericsson & Simon, 1980; Smith & Miller, 1978). One of the most important indications of the need to study subjects' testimonies of trance is that verbal reports may be either in or out of phase, as it were, with the objective concomitants of suggestion.

Subjective and objective scores following hypnotic induction normally correlate highly together with one score replicating the other, but verbal reports of hypnosis can at times correct or rectify assessments made on the basis of objective data (E. R. Hilgard, 1973; Ruch, Morgan & Hilgard, 1974). For instance, objective scores can be influenced unduly by pressures for compliance (Bowers, 1967; Sheehan & Dolby, 1974) and may be modified when the experimenter specifically requests subjects to give honest and truthful reports (Spanos & Barber, 1968). Also, at times test conditions can show appreciable inconsistencies in the effect of hypnotic treatments while subjective evidence demonstrates near-perfect stability (Connors & Sheehan, 1978). It is clear that items failed objectively are not necessarily failed subjectively; subjects may have very genuine feelings of responsiveness, even though the motor action indicating conformity to the suggestion is not actually demonstrated (Ruch et al., 1974). Despite the argument made by Nisbett and Wilson (1977), the extent to which subjective scores may correct objective scores indexes their primary and significant nature in a strictly empirical sense.

Up to this point, this chapter has adopted a broad general definition of consciousness that rejects the reduction of mental events to statements about physical states. The characteristics of alternate states of consciousness have been outlined, and the validity of verbal reports, in particular—as one useful indicant of such states—has been analyzed in some detail. Furthermore, the claim is recognized that verbal reports necessarily emphasize the close and integral relationship that exists between measurement and the nature of the theory at issue. We now examine the extent to which statements regarding consciousness, and hypnotic consciousness in particular, may provide a quite legitimate framework for explanation.

STATUS OF STATEMENTS ABOUT CONSCIOUSNESS

Psychologists inevitably reject the notion of altered state of consciousness as a viable explanatory construct on the ground of its limited parsimony and testability. The concept is also regarded as one that incurs risks in terms of its circularity of argument. And finally, subjective reports per se—the essential data for state theory—are often considered basically unreliable and essentially untrustworthy in what they index.

Certainly, explanation of hypnotic events in terms of subjects' expectancies and attitudes (see Barber, 1972) offers a more parsimonious account of hypnotic phenomena than the notion of alternate state, but contemporary research in hypnosis indicates that explanations of a purely social kind are too simplistic in themselves to explain adequately the full range of hypnotic phenomena. It is for this reason, perhaps, that theorists in general have come to focus upon the internal processes of the organism so as to emphasize more directly the importance of subjects' experiences. Appeal to parsimony alone, however, appears to be an insufficient reason to reject the alternate state account.

Although many theorists in the field of hypnosis argue that appeal to the construct of hypnosis is essentially circular (see Barber, 1969; Sarbin & Coe, 1972), the argument need not be circular. Strictly speaking, a sophisticated theorist would not assert that subjects were hypnotized because they passed the test suggestions that were administered; the subjects could be regarded as "hypnotized" even if they had not been tested. The causality in question really concerns our knowing that the subject is experiencing hypnosis.

Two kinds of causal events are implicated, and three (not two) terms are relevant: the subjects passing the suggestion tests is one term, their being hypnotized is another, and our knowing that they are hypnotized constitutes the third. It might be legitimate to say that hypnosis causes passing the tests, but it is entirely illegitimate to argue in circular fashion that passing the tests causes being hypnotized. Rather, the passing of the tests determines our knowing that the subject is in trance. The effect then really lies with our awareness or cognition that the subject is hypnotized—an effect similar to knowing or recognizing that someone is intelligent, immature, or depressed. Consciousness itself helps to resolve the problem of the apparent circularity.

The testability of the concept of hypnosis as a state of consciousness is perhaps the most difficult criterion to satisfy because it is very hard to index mental processes in an unequivocal way. One could, for instance, look for measurable psychophysiological changes in the hypnotized person or behavioral increments (or decrements) in performances, as well as taking first-hand reports indicating that experience in hypnosis is somehow different from what it is out of trance. Unfortunately, neither distinctive physiological indices of hypnosis (Sarbin & Slagle, 1972), nor unique behaviors or performance enhancements exist. The main reason for utilizing the state construct is that it appears to classify the reported experiences of hypnotized subjects usefully, and it acknowledges explicitly that the departure from normal experience may involve important qualitative shifts in awareness and alterations in the structure of consciousness.

There are definite risks, however, in the breadth of explanatory power of the concept of consciousness when it is forced to rely too integrally on the accuracy of what subjects report. There are also difficulties in establishing the limits of the concept in an operational sense. Waking suggestions of a certain kind, for example, are as much a part of the domain of hypnosis as suggestions given following trance induction (E. R. Hilgard, 1973), and if hypnosis is to be considered in terms of the events of consciousness, then the limits of the waking consciousness must eventually be demarcated from the boundaries of the hypnotic domain.

There is probably little argument that the label "altered state of consciousness" is a meaningful description for the apparent effects flowing from the application of consciousness-arousing agents such as drugs, stimulus deprivation, and verbal suggestion. The term "sleep," for example, can be used to describe a person's radical change in psychological (and physiological) functioning just as the term "hypnosis" can be used to describe the impact of the hypnotist's communications to the subject, especially if those communications lead to gross alterations in perceived reality such as hallucination and posthypnotic response. But, descriptive analogy does not constitute scientific explanation. The psychoanalytic theory of consciousness, for example, is rejected by many because the concept of psychic energy on which it rests is vitalistic and totally incompatible with physical energy (Holt, 1967). The point is not so much that vitalistic thinking is false, but rather that it constitutes a metaphor or descriptive analogy instead of a scientific explanation (Battista, 1978). Scientific explanations require specific predictions that are testable in terms of the subject's measurable reactions.

State and nonstate theories of hypnosis emphasize different variables and processes of influence, and these differences are often subtle. State theories (see E. R. Hilgard, 1965, 1977; Orne, 1959, 1974) tend to emphasize that the abilities or person characteristics of the hypnotized subject reflect a radical alteration in psychological functioning due to the operation of the state in question. On the other hand, nonstate theories (see Barber, 1969, 1972; Sarbin & Coe, 1972, 1979) argue that social psychological and situational variables determine the behaviors and reports of experience that we observe. Contemporary formulations of state and nonstate theory have merged together, however, in that both now emphasize the importance of internal, intrapsychic processes in explaining hypnotic events (see Spanos & Barber, 1974). Even so, differences between the two accounts can still be discerned. State theorists, for example, assert that hypnosis results directly in a substantial alteration of subjective experience. They tend to argue that cognitive processes play a critical part in determining the nature of the experience, whereas nonstate theorists consider that cognitive processes are relevant to the experience but that the experience results essentially from the impact of the situation in which the hypnotized subject is placed. Both viewpoints tend to underemphasize the complexity of the interaction between the person attributes of the susceptible individual and the situational impact of the hypnotic context.

When scientific statements involving consciousness and its alternate states are at issue, it becomes especially important to review the available empirical evidence. For example, the state of awareness labeled "hypnosis" is clearly an inferred process, and the empirical basis for that inference needs to be established.

There is a natural bias in altered state conceptions to ask whether people in the altered state perform better (Sheehan & Perry, 1976). There has been a failure, however, to find consistent superiority of hypnotized over unhypnotized subjects or to find unique effects, and these findings can be generalized to other alternate states as well. The search for state effects has shifted over the years to focus on subtler differences (e.g., variations in behavior), which relate to qualitative shifts in performance such as the subject's increased tolerance for logical incongruity (Orne, 1959; see Chapter 5 for a detailed discussion of this phenomenon). The hypnotized subject, for example, is said to behave paradoxically: Two people are reported as present (the real and the hallucinated person) when it appears to us as observers that no such state of affairs could possibly exist "logically." This phenomenon, together with data on "hidden observer" reactions to subjects' reports of pain following suggestions of anesthesia (E. R. Hilgard, 1976, 1977, Knox, Morgan, & Hilgard, 1974), appears to implicate the coexistence of different levels of consciousness. In these several instances, the simultaneity of seemingly contrary reactions expresses the essential character of much hypnotic behavior and highlights the particular importance of understanding the ways in which stimulus events are registered in conscious or unconscious fashion.

Frequently, behavior in an alternate state implicates specific internal processes. Tolerance of incongruity, for example, is said to be explained by the process of delusion (Orne & Hammer, 1974). It is argued that a subject irrational enough to admit seeing a real person at the same time as responding to a hallucinated one must be deluded about what is happening. There appears to be no simple relation, however, between behavioral events and the internal processes that are claimed to explain them. Tolerance of incongruity (see, Obstoj & Sheehan, 1977; Orne, 1959; Sheehan, Obstoj, & McConkey, 1976) does not necessarily implicate the process of delusion, though the literature has tended to argue that way. Traditionally, subjects' capacity to tolerate incongruous behavior has been argued as a nonsuggested attribute of hypnotic behavior—a quality of consciousness unrelated either to situation characteristics or to cues from other sources.

The data, however, are consistent with an interactionist stance for the explanation of hypnotic phenomena. Some waking imagination subjects as well as hypnotized subjects may manifest incongruity response, but in a fashion that indicates both types of subjects will assess the cue implications of the test suggestions that they receive. Obstoj and Sheehan (1977) found that some subjects who behaved incongruously did so in ways that were compatible with the total stimulus nexus operating at the time; they gave an incongruous response to a hallucinated object, but it was compatible with the kind of features that characterized their particular hallucinations of the object in the first instance. In other circumstances, both hypnotized and unhypnotized subjects gave seemingly paradoxical responses but in ways indicating that stimulus-reality information was being actively, cognitively assimilated with the nature of the hypnotist's suggestion. For instance, subjects reported seeing an object as transparent during the course of responding to a suggestion that it should disappear. For the incongruously behaving subjects (those showing the transparency response), it appears that the relevant stimulus was not just simply blocked out; selective inattention appeared to be accompanied by a gradual cognitive construction of the absence of the stimulus, the transparent report indicating that partial blocking behavior was taking place.

If subjects were deluded in this instance, then the nature of their delusion was clearly affected by the particular stimulus situation that existed at the time. This example also serves to emphasize the important distinction between the sensitive or receptive aspects of consciousness and its active or productive aspects (E. R. Hilgard, 1979a). Much of hypnotic consciousness appears to be active, where that activity implies the initiation of action to overcome difficulties or the exerting of control when decisions have to be made. As Hilgard states, these two aspects characterize normal consciousness. The study of hypnotic experience, however, appears to have very much underemphasized the assessment of the more active aspects of hypnotic consciousness at work.

CONCLUSION

Strictly speaking, the status of an altered state conception of hypnosis is that it poses a useful alternative account of phenomena, albeit one that is imperfectly indexed by subjects' verbal reports. Its special usefulness, however, is precisely in the extent to which it orients us to search for distinctive (rather than unique) variations in response between persons claiming to experience the state and those claiming they are not (especially as those differences are themselves linked with qualitative shifts in experience among the persons concerned). When such an account is invoked, it is important to stress that the state of awareness of the subjects who are involved will necessarily reflect the influence of situational factors adhering to the hypnotic setting and their interaction with the person characteristics of the experiencing individual. Moreover, the state of consciousness displayed by one subject may be quite different from that displayed by another subject. The simple presence of a positive response to hypnotic induction offers no guarantee that the quality of consciousness or alterations in its monitoring or controlling functions that may occur will be comparable from one person to another. Differences will doubtlessly exist in the nature of consciousness among hypnotic subjects, and these differences are a major focus of our assessment of hypnotic experience in the chapters to follow.

In pursuit of this goal, this book presents (in Chapter 3) the development of a new technique that is geared to the assessment of subjective experience underlying hypnotic events and recognizes the value and significance of verbal reports as data. We discuss data gathered from the application of this Experiential Analysis Technique (Sheehan, McConkey, & Cross, 1978) in order to illustrate a range of hypnotic phenomena and to draw inferences about some of the processes that we think may be responsible for them. But before discussing the technique itself, we need to argue the relevance of our approach within the context of the other currently available modes of assessment. Chapter 2 thus reviews the techniques of hypnotic assessment that are routinely available for the researcher and the clinician and establishes the framework of measurement within which we discuss the phenomena of hypnosis in the chapters that follow.

2

The Assessment of Hypnosis: A Survey of Measuring Instruments

INTRODUCTION

Regardless of how one defines the term hypnosis (and there is much debate), few would argue about the relevance or importance of measuring hypnotizability. The term hypnotizability or susceptibility to hypnosis reflects a trait characteristic of the individual and denotes the ability of that individual to respond to suggested events. Vivid experiences accompany that response; for example, the suggested events appear real or are responded to in an involuntary way and reflect the trait in operation. Hypnotizable persons have cognitive abilities suitable for eliciting a range of phenomena, and these are defined primarily in terms of the experiences that they evoke. There is no theory of hypnosis discounted by the abilities in question being manifest in the waking state, although some theories would assert that certain abilities are enhanced when an individual enters hypnosis. When imagery is aroused by a suggestion to imagine that a cold wind is blowing, for example, it has been argued that the imagery is stronger in hypnosis than out of it.

Individuals differ in the extent to which they respond to hypnotic suggestion, and this fact is fundamental to an understanding of hypnosis. There is evidence for a normally distributed trait of hypnotizability (E. R. Hilgard, 1965), at least as it is measured in the laboratory (as opposed to the clinical) setting. But hypnotic abilities themselves have a certain degree of specificity and, as Tellegen (1978-1979) states, subjects tend to demonstrate different relative levels of responsiveness to varying suggestions. This is perhaps best understood by viewing for a moment the inherent complexity of the hypnotic situation.

symptoms illustrating the different stages of depth. Two features of the scale were that it lacked specificity in relation to induction techniques and did not use any precise scheme for quantifying response. Davis and Husband obviously made the assumption that a wide variety of inductions lead to similar distributions of hypnotic response, and evidence supports the claim to some extent. Banyai and Hilgard (1976), for example, found that an active alert induction (subject riding a stationary bicycle) led to comparable results for a standard eye closure form of relaxation induction. The standardization of induction procedures, however, became a departure point for later scales, as did the development of more precise scoring criteria for assessing positive response.

The Friedlander and Sarbin Scale (1938) became the major precursor for the tests of hypnosis emanating from Stanford University in the 1960s. It employed a strictly standard method of trance induction (visual fixation) and developed far more precise scoring criteria for items that were essentially a composite collection of tasks on the two earlier tests, the Davis and Husband (1931) Scale and the Barry, MacKinnon, and Murray (1931) Scale. The ceiling was raised in comparison with the other scales, and the score range was simpler and more truncated. Norms for all of the early scales were generally inadequate and less comprehensive than for the modern scales. The Eysenck and Furneaux Scale (1945), for instance, was standardized on 60 hospital patients where procedures were presented to the participating subjects as methods suitable for use in relaxation, and stronger conclusions were drawn than were warranted from the data at hand (e.g., amnesia is a natural accompaniment of hypnosis). But for the most part, the early scales attempted to measure feeling states accompanying objective responses and so produced a relatively comprehensive look at hypnotic phenomena that many of the more modern scales miss.

Modern hypnotic testing in standardized format essentially began with the development of the Stanford Hypnotic Susceptibility Scale, Forms A and B (SHSS:A & SHSS:B) (Weitzenhoffer & Hilgard, 1959). These scales attempted to define their domain of concern far more precisely than their predecessors and applied strict quantitative criteria for successful responses that were based on an extensive body of normative data. The development of the Stanford scales was, in fact, a milestone in the history of the assessment of hypnosis, which actually opened the path for the construction of future scales developed to meet a rich variety of uses. For example, scales later emerged that were especially suited to the assessment of children's hypnotizability and to use in the clinical as opposed to the laboratory context. Most were dependent in some way on the development of the Stanford instruments. More recently, however, the swing to quantitative systems of scoring has shifted, and test constructors have come to recognize the influence of cognitive events much more explicitly than before. One modern scale, the Creative Imagination Scale (CIS) recently constructed by Wilson and Barber (1978), adopts a scoring scheme based entirely on the experiences of the subjects taking the test and makes no attempt to measure behavior in any way.

TABLE 2.1

Major Precursors to Modern Scales

Scale	Description	Special Features	Relevant References
1. Bernheim's Depth Scale	9-pt. scale varying from 1st degree (torpor) to 9th degree (ability to hallucinate) depth.	Scale assumed to be unidimensional. Emphasizes amnesia in relation to deep hypnosis.	Bernheim (1888). See Hilgard (1965) for review.
2. Liebeault's Depth Scale	6-pt. scale; 4 pts. characterize light sleep and 2 pts. characterize deep or somnambulistic sleep.	Scale assumed to be unidimensional. Emphasizes amnesia in relation to deep hypnosis.	Liebeault (1889). See Hilgard (1965) for review.
3. Barry, MacKinnon, & Murray Scale	Single 5-pt. scale (graded 0-3) rated in relation to five negative suggestions (inability to open eyes, raise arm, bend arm, separate interlocking fingers, and speak name). Sixth item is suggested amnesia scored on 4-pt. graded scale (0-2).	Single rating score covers multiple items.	Barry, MacKinnon, & Murray (1931). Correlation between attitudes and hypnotizability reported by White (1937). Evidence of low ceiling for scale (see Friedlander & Sarbin, 1938).
4. Davis & Husband Scale	Depth scale varying from insusceptible to somnambulistic trance (5 stages). Objective symptoms of depth rated; score range, 0-30. Items range from relaxation (0), to closing of eyes at hypnoidal stage (4), through to bizarre posthypnotic suggestions (23), and negative auditory hallucinations at somnambulistic stage (29).	Lacks specificity in relation to induction techniques and quantification of response.	Davis & Husband (1931).

		Weighting of items has experimental basis.	Friedlander & Sarbin (1938).
5. Friedlander & Sarbin Scale	Strictly standardized trance induction procedure (by visual fixation method). Main precursor to Stanford Scales. Composite of earlier scales. Items: eye closure, 5 challenge suggestions of Barry et al. (1931), posthypnotic voice hallucination from Davis & Husband (1931) scale, and amnesia item adapted also from Barry et al. (1931). Score range 0-5 on four major types of items. Possible range, 0-20.	Scoring criteria quite precise (e.g., scores allocated for extent of response to particular item). Combination of scales argued to overcome the limitations of separate scales. Ceiling specifically higher than for Barry et al. (1931) test.	
6. Eysenck & Furneaux Scale	21-item scale incorporating feelings (e.g., eyes tired, complete relaxation) and objective response (e.g., arm stiffness, arm heaviness). Items involve ideomotor response, challenge, distortion of reality (e.g., negative auditory hallucination), and unsuggested amnesia. Items are weighted with items weighted more where few persons respond positively. Special scoring method for amnesia (see Eysenck & Furneaux, 1945). Separate scores also for hypnosis and for posthypnosis suggestibility (3 items). Score range, 0-51.	Sample on which scale was standardized was 60 patients from hospital for nervous disorders. Procedure was presented as method oriented to teach them how to relax; patients not told they were being hypnotized. Tentative conclusion drawn from results that amnesia is natural accompaniment of hypnosis. Primary suggestibility ("ideomotor") correlated highly with hypnotizability; secondary suggestibility ("indirection") did not. Trait of hypnotizability shown to be distributed continuously, not dichotomously.	For full discussion of hypnosis scale and the relationship of items in it to selected items measuring suggestibility, see Eysenck & Furneaux (1945).

Note. For detailed review of nineteenth century scales, see Bramwell (1903), Hilgard (1965) and Loewenfeld (1901).

The CIS perhaps represents the most obvious manifestation of the cognitive trend in placing primary emphasis on the experiencing of subjects in that it replaces previous attempts to quantify suggestibility behavior in a thoroughly precise way (see Barber, 1969, for a discussion of the Barber Suggestibility Scale; BSS).

Another major factor in the development of assessment procedures in the field of hypnosis has been the growing recognition of the importance of measuring the specialized talents of individual hypnotic subjects, a theme that we illustrate and extend in this book. The need to study the selective skills of good hypnotic subjects first emerged with the construction of the Stanford Profile Scales, Forms I and II (SPS:I & SPS:II) (Weitzenhoffer & Hilgard, 1963), which provided the major impetus behind the thrust to develop clinical scales of assessment. Tests were obviously needed that were more flexibly attuned to tapping the hypnotic potential of the persons being assessed.

Tables 2.2–2.6 begin with the Stanford scales and trace the development of modern tests of hypnosis from the early 1960s to the late 1970s. These tests represent what we judge to be the most influential scales for measuring hypnosis in use at the present time. Further, our selection of tests does not attempt to include a review of strategies that have been developed for conducting interviews of clients or subjects posthypnotically, which have been shown to be useful (e.g., J. R. Hilgard, 1970), nor does it cover the measurement of self-hypnosis (see Johnson, 1979; Ruch, 1975; Shor & Easton, 1973, for attempts at such measurement; see Orne & McConkey, 1981, for an analysis of current inquiry into self-hypnosis). The major body of tests reviewed clearly represents the measurement of hypnotizability among adults, and here, for the most part, the scoring procedures that are adopted are objective and behavioral rather than subjective or experience based.

A number of scales for measuring suggestibility are also reviewed because they are frequently discussed (and used) in the literature as scales of hypnotic responsiveness; classification is separate for these tests, however, because we respect the intent of the persons who constructed them to label the tests in a way that make no necessary assumptions about the existence of a state labeled as hypnosis. Scales are also classified separately for the clinical assessment of hypnosis among both adults and children. Experienced-based scales are also reviewed, including those tests that are based on the measurement of hypnotic depth reached through subjects' self-report judgments and phenomenological assessment procedures involving judgment by an independent assessor about subjects' experiences. This last approach (phenomenological assessment) parallels in principle the technique of measurement that we have developed and outline in the next chapter; the application of this technique to study and evaluate a range of hypnotic phenomena is set out in Chapters 4–8.

The classification of tests as behavioral, clinical, or experience based, as reflected in the tables, differs from the scheme adopted for purposes of classification by Shor (1979). Shor sets out four types of assessment methods: behavioral,

clinical, subjective, and phenomenological; for the purpose of the present review, however, phenomenological assessment is subsumed under the category
"experience-based." For the most part, our review describes each scale briefly,
states whether a specific induction procedure is indicated, describes the major
items or types of items on the test, outlines the scoring procedure associated with
the measurement procedures, and states whether norm data are available and
whether there are special features of the test or references that a potential user
should note.

Behavioral Hypnotic Scales (Adults)

Table 2.2 sets out the eight major tests of hypnotic susceptibility of adults. The
tests are explicitly labeled "hypnotic" and emphasize subjects' behavior in the
scoring of their items.

*The Stanford Hypnotic Susceptibility Scale, Form A and Form B (SHSS:A &
B) (Weitzenhoffer & Hilgard, 1959).* Using a standard eye-closure induction
technique, this test presents parallel forms of a battery of hypnotic test tasks
involving 12 items ranging from simple ideomotor items (e.g., hand lowering)
through positive hallucination, to amnesia and posthypnotic suggestion. It is the
first of the Stanford scales and is essentially a restandardization of the Friedlander and Sarbin scale (see Table 2.1); the items have been altered to produce a less
skewed distribution of scores and aim to measure (E. R. Hilgard, 1978-1979):
"what by common consent are the behaviors and experiences typical of hypnotized subjects [p. 69]." The scale places less emphasis than subsequent scales
from the Stanford laboratory on complex, cognitive-delusory skills and the
capacity to distort reality. It has been criticized by Barber (1969) for its emphasis
on the motor aspects of hypnotic performance, and by Curran and Gibson (1974)
for the extent to which its factorial structure changes with deviation in set procedure. It has also been criticized by Reyher (1977) for its inconsistency of phras-
ing, variation in whether the desired effect is presented through weak or strong
suggestions, and variation in the degree to which imaginal props are employed.
Although less frequently used than the Stanford Hypnotic Susceptibility Scale,
Form C (SHSS:C) (Weitzenhoffer & Hilgard, 1962) for work with individual
subjects, this measuring instrument is historically influential and is still used
widely. It represents the culmination of attempts by earlier scales to reach toward
a standard format, and it aims to be psychometrically definitive by focusing
exclusively on objective behavior. It has the further advantage over preceding
scales that the suggestions given on the test are personally nonintrusive.

*Stanford Hypnotic Susceptibility Scale, Form C (SHSS:C) (Weitzenhoffer &
Hilgard, 1962).* Where the SHSS:A and SHSS:B scales are weighted with the
measurement of motor functions (either movement suggested directly or inhibi-

TABLE 2.2

Behavioral Hypnotic Scales (Adult)

Scale	Description	Induction	Items	Scoring	Norm Data	Special Features	Relevant References
1. Stanford Hypnotic Susceptibility Scale, Form A (SHSS:A) and 2. Stanford Hypnotic Susceptibility Scale, Form B (SHSS:B)	Restandardization of Friedlander & Sarbin (1938) Scale. Measures phenomena said to be typical for hypnotized subjects. Items heavily motoric in nature.	Eye closure, built into test.	1. Postural sway 2. Eye closure 3. Hand lowering, left (right) 4. Arm immobilization, right (left) 5. Finger lock (overhead) 6. Arm rigidity, left (right) 7. Moving hands together (apart) 8. Verbal inhibition, name (town) 9. Hallucination, fly (mosquito) 10. Eye catalepsy 11. Posthypnotic suggestion, changing chairs (standing up) 12. Amnesia	Items scored pass or fail. Maximum score = 12. Scoring based on observation of behavior of subject	Available; see Weitzenhoffer & Hilgard (1959). Additional data in Hilgard, Weitzenhoffer, Landes, & Moore (1961), and Hilgard (1962).	SHSS:A and SHSS:B are parallel forms. Alternative wording on items preserves face validity for unresponsive subjects.	For critique see Curran & Gibson (1974). For review see Frankel (1978-1979), and Hilgard (1965, 1978-1979). For general critique of these and other scales, see Weitzenhoffer (1980) and for a reply see Hilgard (1981).

3. Stanford Hypnotic Susceptibility Scale, Form C (SHSS:C)	Aimed as extension from motor emphasis of SHSS:A and SHSS:B to better represent fantasy and cognitive distortion in its test items. Items derived in part from 17-pt. scale of Weitzenhoffer & Sjoberg (1961). Argued to be the best available criterion of hypnotic responsiveness (Hilgard & Hilgard, 1979).	Eye closure, built into test.	1. Hand lowering, right 2. Moving hands apart 3. Mosquito hallucination 4. Taste hallucination 5. Arm rigidity, right 6. Dream 7. Age regression 8. Arm immobilization, left 9. Anosmia to ammonia 10. Hallucinated voice 11. Negative visual hallucination (3 boxes) 12. Posthypnotic amnesia	Items scored pass or fail. Maximum score = 12. Scoring based on mixture of behavioral and experiential criteria, the latter via the subject's report.	Available; see Weitzenhoffer & Hilgard (1962).	Alternative wording on items preserves face validity for unresponsive subjects. Personality correlates relate more obviously to SHSS:C than to SHSS:A.	See Tart (1970) for discussion of experiential score (range, 0-116) derived for SHSS:C; score based on rated intensity of experience and automaticity in relation to each of major suggested effects.
4. Stanford Hypnotic Susceptibility Scale, Form C (Tailored Version)	One of original items of SHSS:C is replaced with task suitable for specific purpose of investigation.	Eye closure, built into test	As for SHSS:C except for replacement of "specific purpose" item.	As for SHSS:C (excluding special item)	Available; see Hilgard, Crawford, Bowers & Kihlstrom (1979).	Considers individual differences of susceptible subjects on particular hypnotic tasks.	For full discussion of test and its purpose, see Hilgard et al. (1979).

(continued)

TABLE 2.2 (Continued)

Scale	Description	Induction	Items	Scoring	Norm Data	Special Features	Relevant References
SHSS:C (Tailored)	Argued that essential character of SHSS:C is retained.					More convenient and less time consuming test for achieving some aims of SPS:I and SPS:II (see entries 5 and 6, this table).	
5. Stanford Profile Scale of Hypnotic Susceptibility, Form I (SPS:I)	More advanced for measuring particular hypnotic abilities. Suitable for tapping the idiosyncrasies of good hypnotic subjects. Items heavily cognitive in nature. Scale normally limited to subjects scoring 4 or higher on SHSS:A.	Arm levitation, built into scale.	1. Hand analgesia 2. Music hallucination (positive) 3. Anosmia to ammonia 4. Recall of meal (hypermnesia) 5. Hallucinated light (positive) 6. Dream 7. Agnosia (house) 8. Arithmetic impairment 9. Posthypnotic verbal compulsion.	Nine items scored on scale, 0-3. Maximum score = 27. Scoring based on mixture of behavioral and experiential criteria. Subscales may be used incorporating items from SPS:I and SPS: II. Extended profile scale can be used to include motor and amnesia items of SHSS:A.	Available; see Weitzenhoffer & Hilgard (1963, 1967); see also Hilgard, Lauer, & Morgan (1963). Norms assume prior testing on SHSS:A and are based on sample curtailed at lower end of susceptibility continuum.	SPS:I and SPS II are not strictly parallel forms, but are clearly related. Tests should be used to supplement each other, and complete test requires administration of both forms. Alternative wording for unresponsive subjects. Comparability of self scoring and observer scoring	Test restandardized; see Weitzenhoffer & Hilgard (1967). For summary evaluation of scale, see Hilgard (1978-1979). For report of a scale, related to the structure of the SPS:I and SPS:II, and which aims to meet similar objectives, see Sutcliffe, Perry, Sheehan, Jones, & Bristow (1963).

6. Stanford Profile Scale of Hypnotic Susceptibility, Form II (SPS:II)	As for SPS:I.	Hand lowering, built into scale.	1. Heat hallucination 2. Selective deafness 3. Hallucinated ammonia 4. Regression to birthday 5. Missing watch hand	As for SPS:I	Six major sub-scales associated with profile. These are: ag nosia and cognitive distortion; hallucinations positive; hallucinations negative; dreams and regressions; amnesia and poshypnotic compulsions; and loss of motor control. Deviations on any sub-scale considered from mean of all six sub-scale scores.	As for SPS:I	As for SPS:I	(see Hilgard, 1965)

(continued)

TABLE 2.2 (Continued)

Scale	Description	Induction	Items	Scoring	Norm Data	Special Features	Relevant References
			6. Dream (about hypnosis) 7. Agnosia (scissors) 8. Personality alteration 9. Posthypnotic automatic writing				
7. Harvard Group Scale of Hypnotic Susceptibility, Form A (HGSHS:A) and	Test is group adaptation of SHSS:A(B). Nine of 12 items are same as SHSS:A(B) and others are designed to test similar functions. Suited most for hypnotic screening, and taps wide range of hypnotic tasks.	Eye closure, built into scale.	1. Head falling 2. Eye closure 3. Hand lowering, left (right) 4. Arm immobilization, right (left) 5. Finger lock (overhead) 6. Arm rigidity, left (right) 7. Hands moving together 8. Communication inhibition	Items 1-11 scored by subjects taking test; subjects asked about their behavior. Item 12 scored independently.	Available: see Shor & Orne (1963). Australian norms available also; see Sheehan & McConkey (1979).	Only hypnotic tests available that have been constructed especially for group administration and scoring.	See McConkey, Sheehan, & Law (1980) for detailed analysis of scale's structure.
8. Harvard Group Scale of Hypnotic Susceptibility, Form B (HGSHS:B)						HGSHS:A and HGSHS:B are parallel forms. The HGSHS:B form, however, is not widely used. Scale has been	

Scale	Description	Content	Scoring	Availability	Comments	Reference
		9. Hallucination, fly (mosquito) 10. Eye catalepsy 11. Posthypnotic suggestion, touching left ankle (touching left shoe) 12. Posthypnotic amnesia.			adapted for measurement of self hypnosis (Shor, 1978), and has been revised to give more weight to experience (Tellegen & Atkinson, 1976).	
9. Stanford Hypnotic Arm Levitation Induction and Test (SHALIT)	Test designed for short induction and measurement of hypnotic responsivity. Motoric in nature and suited most for brief hypnotic screening. Arm levitation serves both as focus for induction and hypnotic testing.	Arm levitation only.	Scored for actual arm levitation achieved over short period of time. Scoring based on initial rapidity, and number of promptings needed to achieve arm raising. Self report of depth scored on scale 0-10, and self report of involuntariness scored on scale of 1-5.	Available; see Hilgard, Crawford, & Wert (1979).	Test takes only 6 minutes to administer, and is convenient. Test correlates appreciably with both SHSS: A (.63) and SHSS:C (.52). Does not sample a wide range of hypnotic behavior, as do other scales.	Hilgard, et al. (1979).

tion of movement), this scale is aimed far more directly at tapping cognitive distortion. It is similar to the earlier forms in that it has an eye-closure induction built into the scale and measures responsiveness on 12 distinct items. The test differs from the earlier scales not only in its greater emphasis on cognitive function but also in using a mixture of behavior and experiences by which to assess success or failure on its tasks. On the anosmia to ammonia item, for example, a pass on the item requires that the odor of ammonia be denied as well as the absence of overt signs of smelling, and the dream item is judged entirely on the basis of self-report. The scale also presents its items in ascending order of difficulty, a feature not emphasized in the earlier forms.

The test is reliable ($r = .85$); it correlates highly ($r = .72$) with SHSS:A, and analysis shows that despite the new items on the scale it appears to be measuring basically the same dimension(s) as SHSS:A. Data further show that personality correlates relate more obviously to the SHSS:C than to the SHSS:A, presumably because of the cognitive items that the new scale adds to the battery of test tasks (E. R. Hilgard, 1978-1979). An experience score has been derived for the scale by Tart (see Tart, 1972a), but it is used independently of the standard format developed by the test's authors. The disadvantages of SHSS:C are that it is lengthy for clinical application, and its challenge items are considered clinically awkward (Frankel, 1978-1979), the worry being that the therapeutic context could be inhibited if items are failed. The sleep metaphor on which this scale, SHSS:A, and SHSS:B are constructed is also reported as clinically unpopular because it emphasizes the scientific rather than therapeutic goal of testing (Frankel, 1978-1979). Although critical comment has been made about this and other Stanford scales (Weitzenhoffer, 1980; see E. R. Hilgard, 1981, for a reply), its norms are adequate and well researched, and the SHSS:C probably represents the best measuring instrument available for assessing individual responsiveness to hypnosis in the laboratory setting.

A tailored version of the SHSS:C has been recently constructed (Hilgard, Crawford, Bowers, & Kihlstrom, 1979; see Table 2.2), which aims to overcome problems created by the length of the test in clinical practice and to render the scale somewhat more flexible to suit individual investigators' or clinicians' needs. In this version of the SHSS:C, one or two items given prior to the final amnesia item may be replaced by special items serving an investigator's specific objective. Argument is made that the retained items carry sufficient burden for the additional items to have only a minimal effect on the test scores. If an investigation is concerned with the analysis of logical incongruity, for example, an item measuring this facet of responsiveness (e.g., test of double hallucination or missing watch hand) can be substituted for, say, the scale's hallucinated voice item. The impetus for development of the tailored scale has largely come from the concern that has grown for more individualized forms of assessment and the perceived need to increase the flexibility of the more standard, quantitative assessment tests. Its disadvantage, as Tellegen (1978-1979) states, is that the scale is really investigator-tailored, rather than subject-tailored. It is perhaps difficult to make the claim that any items can replace existing test tasks on the SHSS:C without making substantial difference in the reliability or validity of the longer scale; more research needs to be done to document the generality of such a claim. The tailored version, however, does indicate that it is possible to vary the format of the SHSS:C at least in a limited way or to adapt or modify the SHSS:C so as to render it suitable for a broader range of test purposes.

The Stanford Profile Scale of Hypnotic Susceptibility, Form I and Form II (SPS:I & II) (Weitzenhoffer & Hilgard, 1963). Following the development of the earlier Stanford scales, there was a need for detailed assessment of responsiveness among those persons with at least a moderate degree of aptitude for hypnosis. With this sample, a more sensitive test was required for differentiating special aptitudes or abilities so as to diagnose susceptibility to hypnosis more exactly. The profile scales challenge the assumption of previously constructed tests that subjects who are highly susceptible to hypnosis will demonstrate a uniform pattern of test data and achieve in a limited way the major goal of the profile scales, this being to render less difficult the identification of subjects with special abilities while at the same time assessing general responsiveness to hypnosis. The profile scales are heavily cognitive in character, more so, in fact, than the SHSS:C or its tailored version. Although the scale has two forms, they are not strictly parallel; rather, they supplement each other. Forms I and II employ nine items each, and these can be grouped into major subscales (see Table 2.2) that provide distinctive profile patterns of hypnotic responsiveness. The norms have been constructed on a sample that is necessarily curtailed at the lower end of the susceptibility continuum, and the scale is more difficult than the SHSS:A and SHSS:C, but it appears to tap personal idiosyncrasy (e.g., subjects scoring alike on the scale often do not pass and fail the same test items).

E. R. Hilgard (1965) reports that high positive correlations exist between the profile scales (both forms) and the SHSS:A and SHSS:C despite differences in test content, altered induction procedures, changing hypnotists, and time between tests. Results for subjects tested on the SHSS:A, SHSS:B, and SHSS:C, however, show that subjects with the same general level of hypnotizability indicate varying patterns of scores on the profile test (E. R. Hilgard, 1978–1979). The weakness of the test is that, because it is geared toward selected subjects on the hypnotic continuum, it is limited as a general measure of hypnotic responsiveness. The test also assumes prior testing on an individualized scale, which is not always possible. Perhaps for these reasons, the subscales on the test are not widely researched in the hypnotic literature. More clinical in its intent than the earlier Stanford scales, however, it offers us a sensitive standardized instrument for measuring personalized response to hypnotic suggestions, and it correlates sufficiently well with other hypnotic scales that it provides an alternative means for validating scores on other test scales.

Harvard Group Scale of Hypnotic Susceptibility, Form A (HGSHS:A) (Shor & Orne, 1962). This test is essentially an adaptation of the SHSS:A for the purpose of group administration. It is self-scored, and the sleep metaphor is again used to present the scale to subjects. Viewed as a very useful screening instrument, it is equipped to select subjects for individual testing and can be used to test hypnotic responsiveness in groups as large as 30–40. Its efficiency in this respect makes it an especially appropriate test to adopt when large numbers of subjects have to be tested in order to select diagnostically distinct subgroups of the hypnotic population that are required for further testing or investigation. Although its scoring is largely by self-report after the test items have been administered (by tape recording), self-report scoring and scoring by an external observer correlate highly together, and the test correlates well with other measures of hypnosis, especially the SHSS:A (Bentler & Roberts, 1963).

Its major advantages are the efficiency and economy of effort that result when large numbers of subjects have to be tested. Its major disadvantages are the problems created by response sets that can readily occur with self-scored questionnaires and the fact that susceptibility test scores on the scale may be influenced by situational factors adhering to the group testing situation. Further, the time for the test (approximately 60 minutes) may be considered impractical by some. The scale, however, represents the best standardized test that is available for when group assessment is the major purpose of testing. There are other tests that can be administered to groups (e.g., the Creative Imagination Scale), but these have usually been constructed primarily for assessment of individual responsiveness.

The Stanford Hypnotic Arm Levitation Induction and Test (SHALIT) (Hilgard, Crawford, & Wert, 1979). This final test, as illustrated in Table 2.2, reflects the emerging trend in the literature toward the development of tests that briefly assess hypnotizability. Designed subsequent to development and construction of the Hypnotic Induction Profile (HIP) (see Spiegel & Spiegel, 1978), the test aims for the similar goals of clinical utility and economy of measurement. It limits the analysis of hypnotic responsiveness to the study of a single item and like the HIP relies on arm levitation for its focus. The data available on the test demonstrate reliability for the scale ($r = .88$ for a 6-week interval of testing) and evidence of stability of the test's predictiveness over elapsed time between tests. It correlates less highly with the SHSS:C than with the SHSS:A, however, possibly because of the latter scale's more obvious dependence on ideomotor items. It shares the major disadvantages of all single-item scales of hypnotic responsiveness. As the authors of the test acknowledge, the scale fails to sample a sufficiently wide range of hypnotic behavior as illustrated by the low correlation ($r = .40$) with the longer, more representative scales of hypnosis that tap complex cognitive function. Like the HGSHS:A, it is suited for screening, but because of its inherent limitations the test's authors argue that low scores on the scale should not be used to reject patients from therapy. Further, the scale is limited in the amount of qualitative information that it can reveal about hypnotic experience. This is a general criticism that can be made about all of the standard scales and highlights the potential value and significance of phenomenologically oriented assessment.

Behavioral Scales of Suggestibility

Two additional major scales for measuring responsiveness to suggestion are illustrated in Table 2.3. These are the Barber Suggestibility Scale (BSS) (Barber, 1969) and the Creative Imagination Scale (CIS) (Wilson & Barber, 1978). Both scales are designed to be flexible instruments in the sense that they may or may not be used with hypnotic induction instructions; in fact, a range of instructions can be used for orienting subjects differently to the test suggestions.

The Barber Suggestibility Scale (BSS) (Barber, 1969). This eight-item scale utilizes a range of tasks designed to tap the trait of responsiveness to suggestion or suggestibility. The test does not label performance on the test tasks as hypnotic in character. Items on the test yield both a behavioral and a subjective score that can be used independently in investigations of suggestibility and its correlates. The wording of the test is more authoritarian than the Stanford scales, and argument is made that the test is a reliable homogeneous scale. Data show that the test is relatively stable over time (test-retest correlations range from .80–.88), and normative data are interpreted to suggest that items all load highly on an initial general factor (Barber, 1965). However, more recent data challenge the claim that its sister instrument, the CIS, is unifactorial in structure (Hilgard, Sheehan, Monteiro, & Macdonald, 1981). Although flexible in the sense that it can be used with or without hypnotic induction, it has no alternative wording for unresponsive subjects, and past evidence suggests that the scale is characterized by a degree of social pressure or behavioral constraint (Sheehan & Dolby, 1974) that may artificially enhance responsiveness. Data with the BSS, more than with any other scale, have substantiated the claim that hypnotic behavior is not unique, with results for the scale demonstrating in a consistent and powerful way that subjects performing without induction are comparable in the level of their suggestibility response to subjects performing with induction. The reasons for that comparability, however, are not entirely clear; the factors responsible for the performance in both groups may well be quite distinct (Sheehan & Perry, 1976).

The Creative Imagination Scale (CIS) (Wilson & Barber, 1978). This scale was designed for use in both the laboratory and the clinic and was first introduced by Barber and Wilson (1977). The CIS aims to correct the authoritarian nature of the wording of the BSS and adopts a form of instruction in which suggestions guide, rather than direct, subjects or clients toward utilizing their own creative imagination so as to produce phenomena as suggested. Heavily cognitive in

TABLE 2.3
Behavioral Standard "Suggestibility" Scales

Scale	Description	Induction	Items	Scoring	Norm Data	Special Features	Relevant References
1. Barber Suggestibility Scale (BSS)	Items selected tap representative range of hypnotic-like behaviors without necessity for prior induction of hypnosis.	Not formally associated with scale, but may be added to test.	1. Arm lowering, right 2. Arm levitation, left 3. Hand lock 4. Thirst hallucination 5. Verbal inhibition 6. Body immobility 7. Posthypnotic-like response, coughing 8. Selective amnesia	Scored either objectively, or subjectively. Maximum objective score = 8. Maximum subjective score = 24; subjective items scored on 3-pt. scale. Original method of subjective scoring was for subject to report on experience. Revised method has subject respond to written questionnaire.	Available; see Barber (1965). Also, Barber (1969), and Barber & Calverley (1963). Norms for revised subjective scores reported by Wilson & Barber (1978).	Designed for use with or without hypnotic induction. Used both to measure responsiveness to suggestion, and as a classification scale prior to experimental manipulation. Correlates appreciably with Stanford hypnotic test scales.	For review of use of scale, see Wilson & Barber (1978); see also Barber & Ham (1974), and Barber, Spanos & Chaves (1974).
2. Creative Imagination Scale (CIS)	Test suitable for clinical practice as well as for laboratory use, and for group or individual testing. Range of items guiding subjects' own thinking to	Not formally associated with test.	1. Arm heaviness, left 2. Hand levitation, right 3. Finger anesthesia 4. Water "hallucination" 5. Olfactory-	Each item self scored on 5-pt. scale by subject taking test. Scale exclusively focuses on experience. Maximum score = 40.	Available; see Barber & Wilson (1978-1979), and Wilson & Barber (1978).	Versatile instrument conveying a permissive orientation to subjects not conveyed by BSS. May be used with or without induction.	For discussion of processes tapped by scale see Kiddoo (1977), McConkey, Sheehan, & White (1979), and Sheehan, McConkey, & Law (1978). For initial discus-

	Description	Items / Content	Normative data	Scoring	Comments	References
	creative imagining. Includes both motoric and cognitive items, but heavily cognitive in character.	gustatory "hallucination" 6. Music "hallucination" 7. Temperature "hallucination" 8. Time distortion 9. Age regression 10. Mind-body relaxation	Not reported.		Used with special set of "think-with" instructions (see Wilson & Barber 1978; Barber & Wilson, 1978-1979).	sion of data relevant to the scale, see also Barber & Wilson (1977). For use of the scale with a clinical population, see Straus (1980).
3. Waking - Suggestion Test	Range of representative items requesting subject to produce miniature hypnotic-like effects in himself or herself.	12 items, 4 items developed in each of following areas: (a) involuntary movement (e.g., arm extension); (b) difficulty in making a movement (e.g., in opening mouth or extending fingers); and (c) ability to produce sensory imagery (e.g., warmth, heaviness).	Not relevant.	Scored by subject both objectively and subjectively. Subjective scoring is on 7-pt. scale.	Focuses on subject imagining effects happening.	For description of test see Field (1966).

character, its scores are derived solely by subjects rating their own experience. The test is considerably more flexible than the BSS and aims at providing a nonthreatening, permissive method for assessing responsiveness to suggestion. It is briefer and more easily administered than the BSS and may be adapted easily for group administration. With the exception of the arm-heaviness and hand-levitation items, the scale is entirely cognitive in character, not even requiring any communicative action on the part of the subject until after all of the suggestions have been administered.

Data demonstrate that experimental as well as control subjects are as responsive on the scale as those exposed to standardized hypnotic induction, and special instructions (e.g., "think-with instructions") are equally effective in enhancing scores on the scale above the control level. The scale also correlates with absorption and imagery or imagining (Sheehan, McConkey, & Law, 1978), is as reliable as the BSS (the test-retest correlation approximates .82), and capitalizes more directly than its predecessor on the imaginative resourcefulness of the subject taking the test. The scale's disadvantages are that it relies solely on subjective response rather than attempting to integrate subjective and behavioral estimates of responsiveness, and it makes assumptions about the kinds of mental processes that accompany positive experience, which may not be borne out in fact (McConkey, Sheehan, & White, 1979). Tellegen (1978–1979) notes that the CIS relies negligibly on the inventiveness of the subject by providing explicit imagery that the subject may not accept.

Argument can also be raised about the nature of the scale's factorial structure; for example, whether it primarily measures responsiveness to suggestion or the capacity to image or involve oneself in imaginative events or both (Hilgard et al., 1981; Monteiro, Macdonald, & Hilgard, 1980; Sheehan, McConkey, & Law, 1978). Data suggest (see Straus, 1980) that similarities exist in the way subjects perform on the CIS in the laboratory and clinical settings, and research is needed to determine whether this is equally true for the other scales that we have reviewed.

There are other measures of suggestibility, and Table 2.3 lists one such test constructed by Field (1966) for measuring waking suggestion in particular. Designed to request response from the subject, it is scored both objectively and subjectively but focuses primarily on the subject imagining effects as they are happening. But its appearance in the literature is infrequent, as the major tests of suggestibility are the BSS and CIS.

We now consider clinical scales of hypnosis that have been constructed especially for the assessment of hypnotizability among adults. Some of the scales we have already reviewed have been used for clinical purposes (e.g., SHALIT, Tailored SHSS:C, and CIS), but they have not been constructed especially for clinical use; rather, they are instruments that can be readily adapted for clinical purposes. Table 2.4 sets out the three main clinical instruments: (1) the Hypnotic Induction Profile (HIP) (Spiegel, 1974; Spiegel & Bridger, 1970; Spiegel &

Spiegel, 1978); (2) the Diagnostic Rating Scale (DRS) (Orne & O'Connell, 1967); (3) the Stanford Hypnotic Clinical Scale for Adults (SHCS:Adult) (Morgan & Hilgard, 1978–1979a). Before proceeding to a discussion of these tests, however, it is relevant to outline the main functions of clinical instruments for the assessment of hypnotizability.

Clinical Scales of Assessment

The question of how susceptible a client is who is anticipating therapy or currently in a therapy program is an important one for the practitioner to answer. Clinicians, in particular, want to know about the special abilities of the clients they see and how those abilities may relate to therapeutic progress. However, there is some reluctance among clinicians about whether to assess hypnotizability (especially using standard measures of responsiveness). The reason for this appears to be that the relationship between hypnotizability and positive outcome in the therapeutic setting is not entirely clear-cut. It is well known, for instance, that a higher rate of positive response to hypnotic suggestion exists in the clinical as compared to the laboratory setting. But, uncertainty stems from not knowing what factors are responsible for the difference in response. The therapeutic context is a very complex one involving both the client and the practitioner in a network of feelings, motivations, and attitudes about change. Behaving in the way that the therapist asks may be quite different from cooperating with the laboratory researcher; in the laboratory context, for example, compliance with suggestion usually means far less to the subject personally. Another worry that clinicians face (Frankel, 1978–1979) is that the assessment of trance capacity in the clinical setting, especially by means of standardized instruments developed in the laboratory, may interfere with the level of hypnotic response in the clinical context; assessment is basically required that will in no way interfere with therapeutic goals.

Clearly needed are specific instruments for assessment that have been designed particularly for use in the clinic setting, which allow the practitioner to answer whether clients have special hypnotic skills and whether these skills can be utilized meaningfully in a particular therapeutic program. As Hilgard and Hilgard (1979) state: "The only satisfactory way to arrive at firm answers about the extent to which hypnotic talent is stable or modifiable, or the relationship between hypnotic ability and therapeutic outcome, is to have available, and to use, appropriate instruments of measurement [p. 139]." To a large extent, the achievement of this goal depends on resolution of the debate concerning the frequency with which high aptitude for hypnosis appears in the clinical population. Some practitioners argue that everyone is hypnotizable in the clinical context, the problem being only to isolate the most appropriate method for inducing trance. Individual differences in susceptibility, however, do appear to persist in the clinical setting (Bowers, 1976; Perry, Gelfand, & Marcovitch, 1979), and there is sufficient evidence to suggest that probability of positive outcome increases the more hypnotizable a patient is (Collison, 1978), at least for some categories of pathology or symptom disorders. If such is the case, then there is special value in collecting observations on the degree of aptitude that patients may have (Sheehan, 1979a).

When evaluating clinical instruments of assessment, a number of important guidelines can be formulated for judging their utility. Time, for example, should be provided to judge whether a client has achieved his or her maximum capacity; the employment of time periods for assessing standardized response would seem to have far less a place in the clinical context than in the laboratory setting. If the therapist is interested in collecting data on the client's aptitudes, the role of an investigator is an appropriate one (Sheehan, 1979a), but the methods used should not be too obtrusive. The clinical scale must also be primarily oriented to revealing special abilities and talents that can actually be used in therapy. For instance, skills at regression may usefully indicate the special appropriateness of using regression in the therapeutic program; ability to be amnesic (and to recover quickly) may also be a relevant talent when emotionally laden material has to be recovered and perhaps forgotten quickly until the client is better able to incorporate the material into awareness.

In the therapeutic context, it is also important that items are not threatening to clients and do not interfere with the rapport that has been established between client and therapist. At the same time, however, the test that is used must satisfy the basic requirements of good reliability and validity and also maintain considerable flexibility; the scoring must be simple, yet objective, wherever possible; and the test should be oriented toward detecting qualitative observations pertinent to the accurate diagnosis of the propensities of the client. The criteria for adequacy of a good clinical test of hypnotizability are thus especially demanding.

Although there are many differences between the laboratory and clinical contexts of testing, it is important to recognize that hypnosis as practiced in the clinical setting must bear some relationship to phenomena observed in the laboratory. Otherwise, as Frankel (1978–1979) argues clinical hypnosis can be seen as nothing more than transference, relaxation and placebo effects. Nevertheless, it is equally important to acknowledge that the clinical setting is a special context that is idiosyncratic enough to render generalization from the norms of standard laboratory tests (that are typically established on samples of student volunteers) quite inappropriate. Finally, it should be stressed that although it is often useful and sometimes necessary to know the special talents of research subjects tested in the laboratory, the differentiation of particular talents and skills in the clinical context is mandatory.

We now consider three major scales of assessment designed especially to measure the hypnotizability and special talents of adult clients in the clinical setting. The scales considered are listed in Table 2.4. They may be used with subjects in the laboratory setting but should be judged primarily by the degree to which they satisfy the criteria for adequate assessment in the clinical context.

TABLE 2.4
Clinical Hypnotic Scales (Adult)

Scale	Description	Induction	Items	Scoring	Norm Data	Special Features	Relevant References
1. Hypnotic Induction Profile (HIP)	Developed in clinic, scale aims to provide information for screening purposes to aid in diagnosis of psychopathology, and to assess broad personality styles. Combines Eye-Roll sign (ER) with an induction procedure built around Arm Levitation (LEV).	Arm levitation, integral part of test	1. Eye-Roll Sign (ER) 2. Dissociation 3. Signaled Arm levitation (LEV) 4. Control Differential (CD) 5. Cut-off 6. Float	During eye closure, subject is rated for eye-roll and squint, yielding ER score. ER alone is not held to be measure of hypnotizability, but rather of presumed capacity to experience hypnosis. Major test scores are: (a) Induction score (IND)—this is sum of five arm levitation items (corresponds most directly with measurement on Stanford scales):	Available; see Stern, Spiegel, & Nee (1978-1979) and Spiegel & Spiegel (1978).	Test takes 5-10 minutes to administer, is very convenient, and unobtrusive. Dissociation and Control Differential items are not instructed, but occur spontaneously or not at all. ER and IND scores are reliable, but correlate in mixed fashion with SHSS:A and SHSS:C (Hilgard, 1978-1979).	Detailed instructions for administration and explanation of IND, and profile scoring methodology reported by Spiegel & Spiegel (1978). For full discussion of conflicting data on validity of scale, see Orne, Hilgard, Spiegel, Spiegel, Crawford, Evans, Orne & Frischholz (1979), and Frischholz et al. (1980). Original manual (Spiegel & Bridger, 1970) revised twice (see Spiegel, 1974; Spiegel & Spiegel, 1978).

(continued)

TABLE 2.4 (Continued)

Scale	Description	Induction	Items	Scoring	Norm Data	Special Features	Relevant References
				and (b) Profile pattern falling into categories of intact, nonintact, and zero–associated with subtypes in each category.			
2. Diagnostic Rating Scale (DRS)	Graded 5-pt. rating scale derived from clinical practice and aimed at assessing maximum depth of hypnosis measured under the most favorable conditions of testing. Classified as "an	None specified.	Rating 1: Unhypnotizable (no response). Rating 2: Very light (ideomotor response) Rating 3: Light (challenge response with subjective involvement)	Subject rated on response and stated experience according to criteria (listed) for each point of scale. Points on scale also rated "+" or "−" in each category, according to degree of automaticity for score	No norms available but approximate norms cited by Hilgard (1979b).	If subject shows resistance, no rating is given, and tentative rating only given to subject who shifts from one category to another. Evaluation of depth conducted both during hypnosis and post-hypnosis and post-	For analysis of relationships to SHSS: A and SHSS: B, see Shor, Orne, & O'Connell (1966).

achievement test after practice, rather than a work sample under standard conditions" (Orne & O'Connell, 1967, p.126).		Rating 4: Medium (hallucinatory response) Rating 5: Deep (amnesia and true posthypnotic response)	of 2, reality of experience for categories 3, 4, and 5.		experimental inquiry.	
3. Stanford Hypnotic Clinical Scale for Adults (SHCS: Adult) Items are modified from items on SHSS: A, B and C, and aim to tap the kinds of processes most likely used in therapy. Aims also to tap subjects' special cognitive abilities	Relaxation instructions (through counting).	1. Moving hands together (hand lowering as alternative) 2. Dream 3. Age regression 4. Posthypnotic suggestion (clearing throat or cough) 5. Amnesia.	Items scored pass or fail. Maximum score of 5. Scoring based on assessment of behavior and experience. Subjective rating made on items 3 (5-pt. scale) and 4 (4-pt. scale) at the end of session.	Available; Hilgard & Hilgard (1975); see also, Morgan & Hilgard (1978-1979a).	Special instructions for correcting difficulties when necessary (e.g., difficulty in restoring alertness or persistence of cough). Relatively brief time to administer (20 minutes).	Scale described in full by Hilgard & Hilgard (1975) and by Morgan & Hilgard (1978-1979a). Reviewed also by Frankel (1978-1979). For discussion of adequacy as clinical instrument in relation to single item scales (HIP and SHALIT), see Hilgard & Hilgard (1979).

The Hypnotic Induction Profile (HIP) (Spiegel, 1974; Spiegel & Bridger, 1970; Spiegel & Spiegel, 1978).   This test is perhaps the most controversial instrument for clinical assessment appearing in the literature. The controversy revolves largely around debate concerning what the scale measures. The test was developed in the clinic and was designed to provide diagnostic information with regard to both hypnotic ability and psychopathology. The scale meets the clinician's demands for an instrument that is brief and easy to administer, and it fits unobtrusively into the clinical setting. The hypnotist first administers a simple test of eye roll to establish the client's potential for hypnosis and then gives an arm-levitation suggestion that is an integral part of the scale as a whole. The test bears a considerable relationship in its focus on arm levitation to the SHALIT scale (see Table 2.2)—both are motor scales of hypnotic responsiveness and do not tap the more complex cognitive functions measured by the longer, standardized scales; they say little, for instance, about the skills involved in visual and auditory hallucinations, analgesia, amnesia, or age regression. But the formats of the HIP and SHALIT differ in important respects. Whereas in the HIP the hypnotist insists on the arm levitating, in the SHALIT the suggestions for arm levitation are continued without the hypnotist's insistence that the arm actually move.

There are six main scores on the HIP scale; five of these are associated with arm-levitation instruction (see Table 2.4). The eye-roll test yields an eye-roll score, but it is not held to be a measure of hypnotizability; rather it is viewed as a measure of the client's presumed capacity to experience hypnosis. The data associated with the test are complex. For example, results varied quite substantially across different samples of testing when the validity of the test was investigated by correlating data from the HIP with those from Stanford hypnotic test scales (Orne, Hilgard, Spiegel, Spiegel, Crawford, Evans, Orne, & Frischholz, 1979). Data also support the claim that the eye-roll test contributes a separate factor that is unrelated to overt hypnotizability, with results for the eye roll being essentially independent of scale scores based on arm levitation. Correlation of the eye-roll scores with other tests of hypnotizability are near zero, whereas correlations of the induction (IND) scores with other test scales (e.g., the Stanford scales) are mixed. The IND score (see Table 2.4) correlated .34 with the combined total SHSS scores, for example; aggregating the data across the samples that were considered, results suggested a low positive correlation with the test scales overall. The reliability for the scale is high (for a summary of the data see Stern, Spiegel, & Nee, 1978–1979). Even though HIP scores are stable and the test's factor structure replicates (see Debetz & Stern, 1979), the major question for the test is the precise nature of the dimensions that underlie it and the test's relationships with other existing scales. The aggregate relationship in the Orne et al. (1979) study shows a positive relationship, but substantial differences in subsample data were found that need to be resolved before the claims for the test can be fully supported. It is not clear, for example, why the correlations of the

HIP induction score with SHSS:A and SHSS:C were .32 and .45 for a sample tested at the University of Pennsylvania, and only .22 and .20 for samples tested at Stanford University. This discrepancy is puzzling, although attempts have been made to explain it in terms of differences in motivational set existing across subject samples (Frischholz, Tryon, Fisher, Maruffi, Vellios, & Spiegel, 1980).

Diagnostic Rating Scale (DRS) (Orne & O'Connell, 1967).   The aim of this test, which can be used in the experimental and clinical settings, is to diagnose, in clinical fashion, aptitude for trance. When used in the laboratory setting, it aims primarily to validate standardized scales of hypnotic susceptibility and to provide an independent instrument for assessment of hypnotic skill. It involves the application of a simple 5-point rating scale where the categories employed are divided into + and − depending on the quality of response that the subject or client conveys. It is a flexible instrument and an excellent backup test where additional assessment is required. However, it involves administration by a trained practitioner or researcher who has to make an informed interpretive judgment about the quality of the response that is being indicated. Its structure bears some degree of relationship to the major divisions made in the Davis–Husband Scale (see Table 2.1). Although norms have not been provided on the test for an unselected population, some estimates have been made (E. R. Hilgard, 1978-1979). When administered as intended, the correlation of the test with existing scales is both positive and high; for instance, Shor, Orne, and O'Connell (1966) found in a study of 25 subjects specially selected to overrepresent highs and lows in hypnotizability a correlation of .75 between initial SHSS:A score and diagnostic rating scale score before a steady (plateau) level of hypnosis had been reached, and a correlation of .93 for SHSS:B after plateau level had been achieved.

Stanford Hypnotic Clinical Scale for Adults (SHCS:Adult) (Morgan & Hilgard, 1978-1979a).   This test was designed primarily to detect special abilities likely to relate to therapeutic programs beneficial to clients selected for therapy. Abilities considered potentially relevant are the availability of imagery, the ability to enjoy age regression, and posthypnotic responsiveness. Its five items have been selected from existing Stanford scales (see Tables 2.2 and 2.4), but there is a greater dependence on what the client reports as his or her own experience for this scale as compared with the earlier ones. The assumption of the test is that clients with the same average scores may require quite different approaches to therapeutic treatment. If the scale is to be used for prediction, the preferred procedure is to use the predictive scale first, followed after a period of time by the criterion scale or the one that is predicted (Hilgard & Hilgard, 1979). Data for the validity of the test show that the shorter SHCS:Adult score correlates as highly with the longer SHSS:C ($r = .72$) as the longer SHSS:A does with the SHSS:C. The scale, however, is said to be a test that points usefully toward therapeutic orientations that the practitioner may take when the time to employ longer, more predictive scales is not available. Brief scales also can communicate partial and misleading information and may omit relevant qualitative information provided by those tests that sample the skills of clients in a more representative fashion.

We now consider published scales for the assessment of hypnotic susceptibility of children. Three major tests are listed in Table 2.5. The scales that are illustrated are the Childrens' Hypnotic Susceptibility Scale (CHSS) (London, 1963), and the Stanford Hypnotic Clinical Scale for Children (SHCS:Children) (Morgan & Hilgard, 1978–1979b), Forms A and B.

Children's Hypnotic Susceptibility Scale (CHSS) (London, 1963). This is a test constructed and standardized by London (1963) with norms provided by London and Cooper (1969). It is constructed in two parts: Part I is based on SHSS:A and SHSS:B; Part II is adapted from items on SHSS:A, SPS:I, and SPS:II. One of its most distinctive features is its scoring system. It employs an objective score, a separate subjective score, and a total score that combines these two measures. It is reliable; test-retest reliability is .92, and interscorer reliabilities for the objective score, subjective score, and total score are .97, .88, and .94, respectively. The weighted combination of the objective and subjective score (see Table 2.5) is taken as approximating the impressions that a hypnotist might have of a subject or client viewed under clinical conditions where judgments regarding both overt behavior and accompanying subjective involvement are made simultaneously. It correlates positively and in a moderate fashion with SHSS:A ($r = .67$) and is suited for use with children at either a young (5–12) or adolescent (13–16) age. The scale is lengthy but represents a rich assortment of motor and cognitive items.

The Stanford Hypnotic Clinical Scale for Children, Forms A and B (SHCS: Children) (Morgan & Hilgard, 1978–1979b). This scale represents a brief test that is especially suited for the clinical administration of hypnotic test tasks to children. It is shorter than the CHSS and explicitly varies its induction procedure for the testing of small children. With the young age group (Form B is suited for the testing of children aged 4–8), no formal induction procedure is, in fact, administered; rather, imagination instructions are employed to introduce the tests of suggestion. It is regarded by its authors as directly relevant to choice of therapeutic technique, and the scale is said to be particularly sensitive to the test requirements of anxious and less mature children. For instance, both forms allow the testing of children with eyes open rather than closed. The authors found that very young children, in particular, preferred an eyes-open, shared-fantasy situation to one employing standard eye-closure, relaxation instructions. Preliminary data suggest that the scale correlates well with existing hypnosis tests; the relationship, for example, between the SHSS:A and the childrens' scale was .67, the

TABLE 2.5

Hypnotic Scales for Children

Scale	Description	Induction	Items	Scoring	Norm Data	Special Features	Relevant References
1. Children's Hypnotic Susceptibility Scale (CHSS)	Specific measure of responsiveness of children to hypnotic suggestions; involves a standardized induction procedure and wide range of selected test items. Test is in two parts. Part I consists of 12 items and Part II of 10 items. Items are taken from SHSS: A and B, and SPS: I and II.	Eye closure, integrated into scale.	Part I: 1. Postural sway 2. Eye closure 3. Hand lowering 4. Arm immobilization 5. Finger lock 6. Arm rigidity 7. Hands together 8. Verbal inhibition (name) 9. Auditory hallucination (fly) 10. Eye catalepsy 11. Posthypnotic suggestion (standing up) 12. Amnesia	Three major scores: (a) Overt Behavior (OB) score emphasizing behavior only, on pass/fail basis or 4-pt. continuum. (b) Subjective involvement (SI) score, on 3-pt. scale, aiming to distinguish between "true" response and role-playing. (c) Total (T) score that is weighted combination of OB	Available; see London & Cooper (1969) and Cooper & London (1971).	Scale can be used over wide age range. Two forms exist: one for ages 5-11, and one for older children, ages 13-16. Forms differ in the wording of some of the instructions.	Scale reviewed by Moss (1970), Watkins (1970), and Weitzenhoffer (1963). For detailed account of scale, see London (1963) and for account of scale and summary of supporting data, see Cooper & London (1978-1979).

(continued)

TABLE 2.5 (Continued)

Scale	Description	Induction	Items	Scoring	Norm Data	Special Features	Relevant References
			Part II:	and SI (sum of products of OB x SI scores).			
			13. Posthypnotic suggestion (re-induction)				
			14. Visual and auditory hallucination (television)				
			15. Cold hallucination				
			16. Anesthesia				
			17. Taste hallucination				
			18. Smell hallucination				
			19. Visual hallucination (rabbit)				
			20. Age regression				
			21. Dream				
			22. Awakening and posthypnotic suggestion				

Scale	Description	Induction	Items	Scoring	Availability	Comments	Notes
2. Stanford Hypnotic Clinical Scale for Children, Form A (SHCS: Child, Standard Form)	Standard range of hypnotic tasks for children aged 6-16. Items more similar to SHSS:C than to SHSS:A and held to be especially useful in clinical practice.	Relaxation/eye closure induction. Used also with alternative "imagination" induction, giving permission to keep eyes open.	1. Hand lowering, right 2. Arm rigidity, left 3. Visual hallucination (television) 4. Auditory hallucination (television) 5. Dream 6. Age regression 7. Posthypnotic response (rehypnosis)	Items scored pass or fail. Maximum score = 7. Scoring based on assessment of both behavior and experience (via verbal report).	Available; see Morgan & Hilgard, (1978-1979b).	Tasks designed to be particularly natural for children and mechanical practice avoided. Brief test to administer (20 minutes).	Scale developed in context of studying the control of pain in children; see Hilgard & Hilgard (1975).
3. Stanford Hypnotic Clinical Scale for Children, Form B, Modified Form. (SHCS: Child, Modified Form.	Modified form similar to standard form except that child is permitted to keep eyes open throughout test. Test constructed to measure responsiveness in children aged 4-8.	Imagination instructions to experience what is suggested.	1. Hand lowering, left 2. Arm rigidity, right 3. Visual hallucination (television) 4. Auditory hallucination (television) 5. Dream 6. Age regression	Scored as above. Maximum score = 6	As for SHCS: Child.	Substitutes active fantasy induction for standard relaxation instructions. Better suited to younger child. Brief test to administer (20 minutes).	As for SHCS: Child.

SHSS:A test being adapted slightly for use with children. The test, however, is a shortened scale and is subject to the same difficulties that have been discussed for the Stanford Hypnotic Clinical Scale for Adults. But the shortened length of the test is more appropriate with children than with adults because of childrens more limited attention span.

So far, this review has focused on tests of hypnotizability (and suggestibility) and has dealt for the most part with tests measuring aspects of hypnotic behavior and its associated experience. We now consider experienced-based scales of assessment, tests that place primary emphasis directly on the measurement of the subjective components of hypnotic response and look at hypnotic depth in particular.

Experience-Based Scales of Assessment: Self-Report Depth Scales

A number of self-report depth scales exist in the hypnotic literature. The more widely cited ones include the LeCron Scale, the North Carolina Scale, the Brief Stanford Scale, the Long Stanford Scale, the Harvard Discrete Scale, the Harvard Continuous Scale, and Field's Inventory Scale of Hypnotic Depth. The details for these scales together with their sources and relevant references are listed in Table 2.6. The collective assumption of these scales is that hypnosis is not an all-or-none state but a discrete state of consciousness, different in kind from waking consciousness, and one in which the state of awareness that is current is subject, or may be subject, to rapid variations in intensity. The scales are tuned to the vagaries of hypnotic reaction and attempt to recognize the essential variability underlying hypnotic response. They are sensitive, for instance, to the fact that some phenomena may increase in intensity, whereas others may decrease. Standard scales of the type listed in Tables 2.2–2.5 (especially those in Tables 2.2 and 2.3) tend to ignore temporal changes in hypnotic consciousness; for the most part, they provide a total index of response that omits important and relevant information about shifts in subjects' depth of hypnotic reaction. The goal for the approach promulgated by self-report scales is well stated by Tart (1978–1979) who notes that the main objective of the approach is to: "carry out very wide-scale assessment of experiential and behavioral aspects of hypnosis over many and varied time periods, interrelate these phenomena to each other, and come up with a comprehensive experiential/behavioral relationship map, illustrating the kind of variations that were obtained [p. 188]."

Self-report scales provide useful data to help answer a variety of questions that are not readily addressed by the standard type of assessment scale. They recognize explicitly, for instance, that relevant experiences in hypnosis may not always result in behavior of the kind measured on standard scales, and they acknowledge overtly that subjective appreciation of altered perceptions is a primary characteristic of hypnotic consciousness. Depth reports measure something

TABLE 2.6
Experience Based Scales of Depth

Scale	Description	Categories for Rating		Special Features	Relevant References
1. Le Cron Scale	Self report scale of depth where subjects told their "subconscious" will register their depth. Rating given immediately (without deliberation).	0 1-20 20-40 40-60 60-80 80+	= awake = light trance = medium trance = deep, or somnambulistic trance = a still deeper trance = a deep stuporous state	Note that scale for rating ranges from 0-100, and ratings said to come automatically.	LeCron (1953). For statement on test's validity, see Hatfield (1961).
2. North Carolina Scale	Self report scale of depth where subjects are asked to provide an immediate rating after each phenomenon as suggested. Extended version available where there is no ceiling defined for the scale.	0 1-20 20 25 30 40 50+	= waking = relaxed, ideomotor movement = analgesia = dreams = amnesia, very high suggestibility = all effects experienced as real = mind sluggish	Extended version of scale claimed by Tart (1979) to be the most useful measure of hypnotic depth.	Tart (1963, 1967, 1970, 1972b, 1978-1979, 1979); see also Perry & Laurence (1980).
3. Brief Stanford Scale	Self report scale of depth where subject reports estimate of depth frequently under instructions that rating will come to mind immediately.	0 1 2 3 4	= wide awake = borderline = light = medium = deep	Correlations between average self-report scores and SHSS:C scores are high and appreciable. Level of reliability found to be comparable with SHSS:C.	Hilgard & Tart (1966); Tart (1966) and Tart & Hilgard (1966).
4. Long Stanford Scale	Self report scale of depth where subject reports rating frequently under instructions that rating will come to mind immediately. Used also under set for "deliberate" rating.	0 1 2 5 10	= wide awake = borderline = light = deep = very deep, very high suggestibility	Research has shown (see Tart, 1970) that scale measures significant variation in responsiveness in course of hypnotic session over short time periods.	Larsen (1965); see also, Tart (1966, 1972b, 1979).

(continued)

TABLE 2.6 (*Continued*)

Scale	Description	Categories for Rating	Special Features	Relevant References
5. Harvard Discrete Scale	Self report scale of depth administered after hypnosis. Specific criteria of depth not given.	1 = awake 10 = as deeply as possible	Depth dimensions not well defined for subject, but scale discussed in literature (e.g., Tart, 1979). Scale given after hypnosis because specifically argued that testing would influence ratings of items in hypnosis.	O'Connell (1964).
6. Harvard Continuous Scale	Self report scale of depth employing "circular" depth induction (HDI). HDI is adaptation of Cheek's (1959) finger-signaling method to provide continuous numerical ratings of subjective changes in trance depth.	1-10 = awake to deep as possible (as reported by Tart, 1970).	Research shows scale detects unexpected fluctuation in hypnotic depth associated with termination of trance.	Cheek (1959), Field (1966), and Orne & Evans (1966).
7. Field's Inventory of Hypnotic Depth	Comprehensive self report questionnaire pertaining to subjective experiences. Taken following hypnosis. Subset of 38 items selected as specific scale of hypnotic depth.	Original test of 300 inventory items assesses dimensions of hypnotic experience selected for face validity. These include: sleep vs. awake; movements; attention-concentration; the E and his/her voice; transcendence; lethargic vs. carefree; dreaming and hard to remember; awareness and orientation; bodily sensations; role-play and simulation; hallucina-	Aims to differentiate hypnotic depth in subjects with identical objective performances, to compare hypnotic depth in subjects who have been given different suggestions, and to detect inadvertent hypnosis. Distinct from other inventories measuring trance-like experiences in everyday life (e.g., Shor, 1960; As, 1963). Scale of hypnotic	Field (1965). For study of trance-like behaviors relevant to waking life, see As (1963) and Shor (1960).

		tions; visual sensations; trance depth estimates; resistance-cooperation; friendly-controlled; previous experience; and miscellaneous.	depth discriminates well with wide range of hypnotizability. Items related to specific depth scale tap absorption, unawareness, automaticity and compulsion, and distractivity from normal waking experience. Items on scale rated true or false.	
8. Shor's Phenomenological Method	Method consists of multiple rating scales applied retrospectively to subjective descriptions of what experience of hypnosis was like for experiencing subject. Method to be used only under conditions where it can be assumed that subject will report honestly about his or her experiences.	Method evaluates responsivity on three major dimensions of hypnotic depth: (a) trance; (b) nonconscious involvement; and (c) archaic involvement Ratings conducted additionally on five variables: (a) drowsiness; (b) relaxation; (c) vividness of imagery; (d) absorption; and (e) access to the unconscious. Each of above 8 dimensions rated on 6-pt. scale. Unit of evaluation may be single phenomenon, larger segment of session, or session as a whole.	Test is discriminated from standard self report scales of depth (see above) in that assessment is not conducted by subject. Subject's experience rated by person other than subject, and ratings also conducted on more than one dimension of hypnotic depth. Multidimensional analysis is key feature of method. Relationships between examiner and subject defined in terms of free and open interchange where both persons share in the inquiry into the subject's experience. Amount of experience held to be far less important than its "profundity" (Shor, 1979, p. 131). Method not concerned with difficulty level of hypnotic tasks, but rather, with underlying psychological process.	Shor (1979).

more general than simply how a subject judges he or she has responded to specific suggestions; for example, application of the scales has shown that waking from hypnosis does not always proceed directly and monotonically in a regular fashion (Field, 1966). Stated more generally, the major goal of the self-report scales listed in Table 2.6 is the measurement of momentary or temporary changes in reported state or observed performance, or other changes as they are correlated at one point in time or at different points in time. Their special value is that they can be used to monitor momentary conditions of consciousness when the subject is not specifically responding behaviorally to a suggestion. In addition, they are sensitive to the measurement of such change among persons or within the same person from one point in time to another.

The scales listed in Table 2.6 vary on a number of different dimensions with respect to their administration and internal structure. For some tests, definition is provided of what the scales aim to achieve, whereas on others it is not; some also require subjects to make a conscious effort to judge how deeply they feel hypnotized; and the scales also differ in how frequently they require the subject to make a rating. The evidence that is available on their use (see Tart, 1970, 1972a, 1978–1979, 1979) would seem to suggest that judgments should be taken frequently so that depth reports remain maximally sensitive to shifts in hypnotic consciousness. Further, subjects should not be asked to estimate their depth deliberately; rather, the reports that are given should be offered spontaneously.

Despite the many positive claims that are made for the utility of depth scales, a number of assertions are made about them that require careful justification. For example, Tart (1979) argues that they are basically nonreactive in character; the mere fact of making the report is not regarded as interfering at all with the accuracy of the judgment of depth that the subject is making. There are a number of caveats, however, concerning their indiscriminate use. Self-rating tests are prone to influence by response sets; attitudes of the subjects making the ratings come to distort subjects' judgments. Field (1966) also asserts that complications can result from subjects stating that they feel the very act of indicating depth lightens depth of trance; if this is a result that is generalizable at all across subjects, then the technique is not unreactive at all. Self-ratings are also likely to be the result of complex judgmental processes at work—processes that involve the operation or influence of demand characteristics and good or bad scale-using habits. Perry and Laurence (1980) demonstrated this point forcefully in a study aimed at replicating Tart's findings on subjective depth with a larger sample of subjects. Testing independent samples of subjects in two successive years, Perry and Laurence found that passing or failing an item was the main factor determining the degree of hypnotic depth; importantly, however, there was a parallel fluctuation of reported depth for low as well as for highly susceptible subjects. This suggests that the correspondence between behavioral performance and subjective depth is not necessarily a close one and that subjective depth reports may be mediated by particular internal processes at work.

These and other factors, if present, mitigate against considering self-report scales as providing simple, uncomplicated indices of trance experience. Despite the caveats that we have discussed, the data on the validity of the scales are encouraging. Self-report judgments of depth correlate .73 with total scores on SHSS:C, although 100-point graded scale depth ratings correlated only .32 with SHSS:B (E. R. Hilgard, 1979b).

The Phenomenological Method.   This method was recently proposed by Shor (1979) and represents a novel technique of assessment, which is predominantly experience-based and oriented to the measurement of depth of hypnotic experience. The method is essentially diagnostic in nature and involves an interpretive judgment made by a skilled examiner who applies specific rating scales to retrospective subjective descriptions of what the experience of hypnosis was like to the subject. Traditionally, depth scales measure depth of trance in a way that assumes depth is univariate rather than multidimensional in character. Shor's phenomenological method, on the other hand, involves assessment on eight distinct dimensions of trance experience (see Table 2.6 for full listing), with judgments made strictly in terms of the quality of the subject's experience. The criterion of successful accomplishment for the method is the degree of subjective convincingness of the experience for the subject at the time of hypnosis.

Shor argues that the examiner who rates the subject's experience must as far as possible adopt the role of a coinvestigator who works with the subject in the spirit of open conversational (or informal) interchange. The context of testing to be created should facilitate positive rapport between examiner and subject and foster immediacy of response from both participants in the interaction. Despite the spontaneous nature of the interchange, the examiner's role is nevertheless a relatively directive one in which he or she asks the subject questions and judges the adequacy of response on the basis of the information that the subject provides. The unit of evaluation for the method can vary; for instance, it may be a single hypnotic event or phenomenon, a larger segment of the hypnotic session incorporating a number of phenomena, or even the entire hypnotic session itself. Working with this unit of evaluation, the examiner makes separate diagnostic ratings for the eight different dimensions and inquires about the relationship of the different variables being rated.

To date, there has been relatively little evidence gathered on this scale, and research needs to establish the precise reliablity and validity of the separate rating scales that are recommended for application. The technique, however, does derive considerable theoretical support from Shor's (1962) own three-factor theory of hypnosis, which points to the complexity of hypnotic depth better perhaps than any other existing theory. The theory recognizes, for instance, the relevance of depth defined in terms of the loss of generalized reality orientation; depth defined in terms of the unconscious involvement of the hypnotic subject in the world created by the suggestions of the hypnotist; and depth defined in terms of the closeness of relationship existing between subject and hypnotist, which may be strongly influenced by transference-based motivations to cooperate and please the hypnotist in a manner that signifies the hypnotist as a person who is especially important to the subject. The value of Shor's scheme lies precisely in the variability of consciousness that combinations of these three factors can imply. For instance, the theory (Shor, 1979) recognizes that at a deeper level of consciousness the hypnotized subject may be actively keeping his elbow stiff while: "simultaneously orchestrating for himself the illusion that he is really trying his best to bend it [p. 124]."

Finally, a major concern facing the clinician or researcher when selecting an assessment scale is to know what the test in question actually measures. The factorial validity of a hypnotic test, then, is an issue of primary importance and one that is independent of the orientation of those who wish to use the test. We now consider this question of the scales' validities in some detail. Emphasis is placed on the structure of the Stanford scales because these are the tests that have been researched most comprehensively to date.

THE FACTORIAL STRUCTURE
OF HYPNOTIC SCALES

There is considerable debate in the hypnotic literature regarding whether hypnotic test scales measure a general factor or dimension. The unity of hypnotic phenomena is an attractive hypothesis, and perhaps the strongest support for this contention comes from the evidence showing that when varied tests are gathered together and multiple aspects of the hypnotic domain are tapped by different measuring instruments, then a pattern of high positive intercorrelation among the tests appears to hold. Certainly, with relatively few exceptions, the tests of hypnotic susceptibility reviewed in this chapter do appear to intercorrelate highly together. Following E. R. Hilgard (1965), arm catalepsy seems to be the only hypnoticlike behavior that does not correlate positively with other hypnotic test tasks. On the other hand, the rich diversity of behavior and experience that exists among susceptible individuals implies that more than one dimension should really characterize their hypnotic performance.

The studies of the factorial composition of hypnotic test scales are many and varied with respect to the techniques of analysis that researchers have employed. One of the earlier comprehensive studies on test structure was the analysis conducted by Hammer, Evans, and Bartlett (1963) of batteries of waking suggestion and hypnotic test tasks. Their data indicated three factors that accounted for the majority of test variance: an ideomotor factor, an imagery factor, and a factor the authors labeled "dissociation." E. R. Hilgard (1965) criticized the study, however, and argued that the factorial structure of the hypnotic tasks was changed considerably by including a number of tests that bore no significant relationship to hypnosis. Hilgard (1965) himself reports extensive analyses of the SHSS:A, B, and C and the SPS:I and II, and further discusses these data in later references to the validity of the Stanford scales (see Hilgard, 1978–1979). For instance, three factors appear to characterize the two standard individual scales, SHSS:A and SHSS:C. Based on the study of data for 307 subjects, analysis of the SHSS:C showed that 10 of the 12 items on the test loaded on the first factor that was extracted, ideomotor items and the dream and age regression items loaded on the second factor, and the hallucination task loaded highest on the third factor. The three factors were identified as ideomotor inhibition (affecting both the control of voluntary muscles and inhibition of sensory impressions and recall), a difficulty factor, and a positive hallucination factor, respectively.

The pattern of results from analysis of data collected on 402 subjects given the SHSS:A was somewhat similar. Here again, three factors emerged that were identified as representing loss of voluntary control, direct suggestion (or difficulty), and cognitive function, respectively. Summarizing the results for the different factorial studies, E. R. Hilgard (1965) concluded that some eight or nine factors accounted best for the hypnotic domain. The first factor extracted in the analyses was defined as a general factor, the data indicating that this factor accounted for approximately ⅓ to ½ of the variance for items typically regarded as related to hypnosis. The second factor was defined in terms of response to suggestions of a motor kind and was labeled as ideomotor in nature; this factor, however, broke down into more specific dimensions relevant to easy, direct suggestions and motor-inhibition items as tapped by standard challenge suggestions. Related to the motor-inhibition factors was a fourth factor labeled as cognitive and sensory inhibition, including hallucination and amnesia test tasks. Positive hallucinations formed a fifth discernible specific factor, which was relevant to tasks that facilitated fantasy involvement as distinct from inhibiting it. The production of fantasies from memory or imagination represented a sixth factor; persistence of both positive and negative effects and affective distortion represented the seventh and eighth factors, respectively.

In an aggregate look at the data, particular factors emerged as being specific to particular test scales. The ideomotor factor was differentiated into its two components in the SHSS:A and SHSS:C, for example, whereas the positive hallucination factor was most evident in the analysis of the two profile scales. Although the complexity of hypnotic consciousness is represented clearly in the multifactorial structure represented by this pattern of factors, E. R. Hilgard (1965) nevertheless makes the point that hypnosis is: "sufficiently *one thing* to permit the high common or general factor to emerge [p. 281]." However, this conclusion is debatable.

The vicissitudes of the factor analytic work with hypnotic test scales can be best illustrated through detailed comparison of two scales differing in their structure, form of administration, and assumptions underlying their development as tests. The two chosen for comparison and contrast are the Harvard Group Scale of Hypnotic Susceptibility, Form A (HGSHS:A) and the Creative Imagination Scale (CIS) (see Tables 2.2 and 2.3 respectively, for a summary of test characteristics).

Comparison of HGSHS:A and CIS

In the majority of the studies that have investigated the factorial structure of hypnotic test scales, the technique that has largely been adopted is the principal components method of analysis. This technique, however, can be criticized on several counts, even though it is both relevant and useful in its application. For instance, the method makes no special assumptions about how a test is structured. The HGSHS:A (like most of the standard tests of hypnosis that are reviewed in Table 2.2) is a scale that was designed to measure a single aspect of behavior (viz., hypnotic susceptibility, or hypnotizability). But it can be argued that the most suitable technique for analysis is one that examines what is common among the various test items that a scale uses. In attempting to analyze the underlying structure of any test of hypnosis, it is also relevant to ask whether the differences that appear to exist in the content of the items reflect natural groupings that define different or distinct dimensions or whether the variation in level of subjects' performance reflects the shifting difficulty level of the items in the test. For instance, Coe and Sarbin (1971; see also Sarbin & Coe, 1972) assert that the different dimensions one finds on standard hypnotic test scales can be identified in terms of how easy or how difficult it is to pass the test's items. Their argument is that hypnotic tests interrelate as positively as they do precisely because they lie at comparable levels of difficulty and that hypnotic test performance can be identified solely in terms of the aptitude required to pass the tasks, rather than the particular content or psychological character of the tasks involved.

Clearly a method of statistical analysis is required that will take account of the influence of item-difficulty level when drawing inferences about the underlying factorial structure of a hypnotic scale. This is provided by the Rasch (1960) model of analysis, which basically determines whether a set of variables tapped by a test can be interpreted in unidimensional space by taking direct account of any difficulty parameter that may exist. Thus, if the factorial structure of the HGSHS:A is determined by the clustering of items of similar or comparable difficulty, and not by the nature of subjects' responses to those tasks, the unidimensional character of the test will be highlighted explicitly by the model. A study conducted by McConkey, Sheehan, and Law (1980) tested this hypothesis. Data from administration of the HGSHS:A to different samples comprising a total of 1944 subjects were analyzed first by a technique that was most compatible with the assumptions underlying the test's construction (i.e., that items measure something in common) and by a model of analysis (the Rasch method) that explicitly examined the influence of item difficulty in accounting for the factorial structure of the test. For purposes of comparison, data were also analyzed by the method of principal components.

Results for the analysis by the principal components method were consistent across all of the samples studied and were in agreement with the findings of Peters, Dhanens, Lundy, and Landy (1974) in their analysis of the HGSHS:A. A three-factor solution emerged, and these factors were labeled challenge, ideomotor, and cognitive, respectively. The items loading on the challenge factor were arm immobilization, finger lock, arm rigidity, and communication inhibition; the items loading on the ideomotor factor were head falling, eye closure, hand lowering, and hands moving; the items loading on the cognitive factor were hallucination, posthypnotic suggestion, and amnesia. Alpha factor analysis (Kaiser & Caffrey, 1965) was then applied to the test items to determine the factors defining the common variance among them. Data from this analysis indicated that the principal components analysis overestimated the amount of common variance shared by the items on the HGSHS:A. The common factor model of analysis indicated that Factors 1 and 2 represented comparable dimensions to those highlighted by the principal components model.

The analysis by the alpha factor technique, however, called into question whether the hallucination, posthypnotic suggestion, and amnesia items really shared common variance with the remainder of the items on the scale. One needs to note that the alpha factor model, like the principal components technique, assumes that the tasks on the scale are of equal difficulty. Application of the Rasch model investigated the changes in the factor structure that result when the differential difficulty of the 12 test items on the HGSHS:A are taken into account. Normative data on the HGSHS:A (Sheehan & McConkey, 1979) demonstrated that items do clearly differ in the level of their difficulty, and application of the Rasch technique was thus considered appropriate.

Analysis of the data by the Rasch method for three distinct samples indicated that the HGSHS:A scale was not unidimensional. Also, in contrast to the assertions of Coe and Sarbin (1971), data demonstrated that when item difficulty was taken into account it was not possible to represent the pattern of responses to the scale as tapping a single general factor.

The results just discussed elaborate importantly on previous findings concerning the factorial structure of standard hypnotic test scales and the structure of the HGSHS:A in particular. The principal components analysis yielded findings comparable to other studies using the same technique (e.g., E. R. Hilgard, 1965; Peters et al., 1974). Concentrating on the dimensions revealed by the principal components and alpha factoring models, data indicated a marked degree of consistency for two factors (ideomotor and challenge) only. These two factors—the sole factors reported by Tellegen and Atkinson (1976) and Coe and Sarbin (1971) and the first two reported by Hilgard (1965) and Peters et al. (1974)—would appear to represent the basic dimensionality of the HGSHS:A. The third (cognitive) factor appeared inconsistently across samples and the different methods of analysis that were used.

Inasmuch as the data indicate that hallucination, posthypnotic suggestion, and amnesia tasks don't have a lot in common with other tasks on the scale, a number of different alternatives for the assessment of hypnotizability by scales illustrated in Table 2.2 present themselves. Either research can proceed by locating cognitive dimensions that share common vector space with ideomotor and challenge items, or special subscales can be constructed that specifically recognize the special contribution that the tasks loading on the third factor make to the measurement of hypnotizability. Cognitive items of these kinds may be sufficiently distinct from ideomotor and challenge items that the essence of hypnosis can perhaps best be captured by attempting to recognize the character of these tasks more overtly in the measurement process. One could do this, for instance, by adopting measurement procedures better suited to tapping the various cognitive processes that may underlie a given person's particular hypnotic reaction. The utility of this way of proceeding is reinforced by the data that we present in the chapter to follow and by the clinical observations reported in the literature that the cognitive-delusory types of items appear to be the very tasks that characterize the deepest levels of hypnotic involvement.

Comparison with the CIS.   We saw in our review of the tests listed in Table 2.3 that the CIS was a useful test for assessing subjects' internal cognitive processing as it relates to responsiveness to test suggestions, and it obviously taps skills that are relevant to the measurement of hypnotizability. Therefore, it seems relevant to examine the extent to which the CIS relates to traditional measures of hypnotizability such as the HGSHS:A. McConkey et al. (1979) examined this relationship for a sample of 237 subjects who participated in two independent programs of research. All subjects were tested on the CIS and on the HGSHS:A, the order of testing being random. The administration of both scales was in group format and by tape recording. Think-with instructions (especially designed for the CIS by the scale's constructors) were used with the CIS. In order to clarify the nature of the cognitive abilities that might be associated with the two scales, subjects also received a battery of imagery-related tasks. The results of the study were in essential agreement with the item-response features reported in the literature for the CIS (Wilson & Barber, 1978) and the HGSHS:A (Sheehan & McConkey, 1979). The correlations between each of the individual items of the two scales are illustrated in Table 2.7, which shows that the relationship between the total scores for the two scales was significant but low in order of magnitude ($r = .28, p < .01$). Alpha factoring was again employed to examine the dimensions of the total set of 22 items (10 CIS and 12 HGSHS:A tasks) so as to isolate the common factors that were present. Data from this analysis indicated a six-factor solution; the loadings of the items on the two scales are illustrated in Table 2.8.

Observation of the results for the first three factors in Table 2.8 indicates that

TABLE 2.7
Intercorrelation Matrix of Items on the CIS and the HGSHS:A

	CIS										HGSHS:A											
---	1	2	3	4	5	6	7	8	9	10	1	2	3	4	5	6	7	8	9	10	11	12
CIS																						
1. Arm heaviness		.51	.35	.30	.34	.18	.39	.38	.24	.36	.25	.00	.01	.21	.20	.17	.12	.14	.25	.16	.08	.09
2. Hand levitation			.32	.28	.26	.13	.25	.19	.17	.23	.19	.07	.08	.14	.08	.17	.14	.26	.19	.10	.10	.10
3. Finger anesthesia				.27	.24	.19	.28	.21	.30	.25	.10	-.02	-.04	.03	.01	.06	-.05	.05	.08	.01	.08	.09
4. Water "hallucination"					.52	.27	.33	.21	.27	.42	.03	.15	.03	-.03	.07	.11	.09	.13	.10	.06	-.02	.02
5. Olfactory-gustatory "hallucination"						.21	.28	.21	.33	.29	.09	.09	-.05	.05	.10	.11	.06	.11	.15	.14	-.09	.03
6. Music "hallucination"							.24	.25	.41	.40	-.02	.03	-.01	.04	.06	.06	.00	.14	-.02	.06	.05	-.01
7. Temperature "hallucination"								.24	.14	.26	.17	.11	.12	.13	.28	.22	.16	.19	.25	.12	.12	.16
8. Time distortion									.27	.34	.12	-.05	-.03	.16	.14	.11	.05	.16	.11	.08	.05	.03
9. Age regression										.47	.01	.06	-.01	.08	.14	.13	.09	.14	.11	.12	.14	.00
10. Mind-body relaxation											.17	.08	.14	.04	.16	.13	.11	.14	.12	.18	.01	-.03
HGSHS:A																						
1. Head falling												.27	.28	.06	.29	.22	.27	.22	.17	.27	.04	.19
2. Eye closure													.23	.15	.28	.20	.15	.21	.11	.29	.08	.12
3. Hand lowering														-.07	.21	.08	.28	.15	.17	.22	-.07	.07
4. Arm immobilization															.29	.33	.14	.26	.18	.23	.17	.14
5. Finger lock																.36	.33	.39	.25	.47	.06	.23
6. Arm rigidity																	.19	.39	.21	.34	.09	.11
7. Hands moving																		.29	.20	.34	.10	.13
8. Communication inhibition																			.19	.41	.09	.17
9. Hallucination																				.38	.09	.13
10. Eye catalepsy																					.08	.24
11. Posthypnotic suggestion																						.05
12. Amnesia																						

Note. Table adapted from McConkey, Sheehan, & White (1979). Reprinted from the July 1979 *International Journal of Clinical and Experimental Hypnosis.* Copyrighted by the Society for Clinical and Experimental Hypnosis, July 1979. Reprinted by permission.

TABLE 2.8
Loadings of Items on the CIS and the HGSHS:A
for the Varimax-Rotated Factor Solution Indicated
by Alpha Factor Analysis

		Factors					
Item		1	2	3	4	5	6
CIS							
1.	Arm heaviness	.18	.19	.75	.03	-.06	-.25
2.	Hand levitation	.16	.12	.53	.06	.04	.01
3.	Finger anesthesia	-.07	.23	.52	-.03	.11	.10
4.	Water "hallucination"	.04	.41	.39	-.01	-.31	.36
5.	Olfactory-gustatory "hallucination"	.13	.31	.40	-.11	-.43	.24
6.	Music "hallucination"	.02	.58	.12	-.05	.03	.05
7.	Temperature "hallucination"	.24	.19	.46	.08	.02	.11
8.	Time distortion	.14	.35	.32	-.05	-.03	-.22
9.	Age regression	.10	.65	.16	-.04	.12	.04
10.	Mind-body relaxation	.08	.69	.23	.20	-.13	-.07
HGSHS:A							
1.	Head falling	.31	-.03	.22	.40	.02	.05
2.	Eye closure	.35	.03	-.03	.21	.04	.34
3.	Hand lowering	.16	.01	-.02	.64	-.08	.05
4.	Arm immobilization	.52	.02	.11	-.24	.17	-.08
5.	Finger lock	.66	.08	.06	.19	-.02	.02
6.	Arm rigidity	.55	.10	.10	-.02	.02	.03
7.	Hands moving	.40	.04	.06	.31	.05	-.01
8.	Communication inhibition	.56	.14	.10	.09	.04	.04
9.	Hallucination	.35	.01	.24	.14	.01	-.03
10.	Eye catalepsy	.66	.06	.03	.24	-.02	.05
11.	Posthypnotic suggestion	.14	.07	.09	-.06	.40	.03
12.	Amnesia	.26	-.09	.15	.10	.08	.09
Percentage of Total Variance		20.9	11.6	6.4	5.9	4.9	4.6

Note. Table adapted from McConkey, Sheehan, & White (1979). Reprinted from the July 1979. *International Journal of Clinical and Experimental Hypnosis.* Copyrighted by the Society for Clinical and Experimental Hypnosis, July 1979. Reprinted by permission.

the initial dimension of the entire item set was predominantly represented by items on the HGSHS:A, but the next two factors were predominantly represented by items on the CIS. Results would appear to suggest that the two scales sample the hypnotic domain differently, and the evidence taken collectively suggests that the two scales are not measuring responsiveness in the same way.

Table 2.9 sets out the intercorrelations of total scores on the CIS and HGSHS:A and the battery of imagery-related tests including Tellegen and Atkinson's (1974) absorption questionnaire, the Betts QMI test of imagery (Sheehan,

1967), and Gordon's (1949) test of imagery control. Correlations are reported for male and female subjects separately. Data indicated that the CIS relates more obviously to imagery-related tests than does the HGSHS:A and that this relationship is especially strong for females; for example, CIS performance relates positively to the variables of absorption and imagery. Results are indeterminate, however, with respect to how one might maximize imagery performance to enhance test scores. Imagery control, for example, appears to be less relevant than imagery vividness. Further research needs to establish more definitely how optimal enhancement can specifically be achieved on the CIS and what kinds of preliminary instructions might best achieve that goal.

If the CIS taps subjects' imagery skills and capacities and if these can be utilized effectively so as to facilitate subjects' experience with effects that are suggested, it remains to be said what special capabilities are relevant to the HGSHS:A and other standard scales like it. The data do not bear exactly on the nature of those capacities, but dissociation seems particularly relevant to performance on the cognitive-delusory items, which play a special part in contributing to the factorial complexity of the scale (as shown by the research of McConkey et al., 1979).

When making comparisons with the CIS and HGSHS:A, conclusions must be tempered by recognition that the procedures for the two scales differ in many significant ways. The scales vary in the way they are meant to be administered, the nature of the wording that is used, and the scoring emphasis of each test. Further, the CIS focuses on the experience of subjects with respect to the vividness of the effect (see Table 2.3), whereas the HGSHS:A stresses the behavior arising from the effect as rated by the subject retrospectively (see Table 2.2). Such differences aside, however, it would be difficult to argue from the data that

TABLE 2.9
Correlation of Susceptibility and Cognitive Measures for
Male and Female Subjects Taking both CIS and HGSHS:A

	CIS	HGSHS:A	TAS	Betts QMI	Gordon's
CIS		.26*	.15	.28**	.10
HGSHS:A	.27**		.24*	.17	.04
TAS	.43**	.21*		.38**	.26**
Betts QMI	.47**	.18*	.45**		.48**
Gordon's	.26**	.07	.26**	.34**	

Note. Coefficients for males and for females appear above and below the diagonal, respectively. Minus signs associated with the Betts QMI have been omitted where they simply reflect an artifact of that scale's scoring procedure. Table adapted from Sheehan, McConkey, & Law (1978). Reprinted from the Fall 1978 *Journal of Mental Imagery.* Copyright 1978 by Brandon House Inc. Reprinted by permission.
  * $p < .05$
  ** $p < .01$

have been collected that the tests can be regarded as parallel forms, measuring the same dimensions in a comparable manner.

Conclusions: Hypnotic Test Scales

A substantial body of data has now accumulated to indicate that several different dimensions underlie performance on hypnotic test scales (As & Lauer, 1962; Coe & Sarbin, 1971; Curran & Gibson, 1974; Hammer et al., 1963; E. R. Hilgard, 1965; McConkey et al., 1979; McConkey, Sheehan, & Law, 1980; Monteiro et al., 1980; Peters et al., 1974; Tellegen & Atkinson, 1976), and data have generally demonstrated that three major types of items are included in standard tests of hypnotic responsivity. These involve ideomotor response (e.g., arm levitation), challenge reaction (e.g., clasping hands together), and cognitive-delusory performance (e.g., hallucination). The techniques of analysis that have been used, however, have at times been inappropriate to the assumptions that appear to underlie the tests' construction. When one considers the collective body of data that is available, there is relatively little support for the notion that tests of hypnotic susceptibility measure a general factor. Nor does there appear to be support for the contention that the structure of standard test scales can be accounted for in terms of item difficulty as opposed to item content. The different tests that are available clearly need to be considered in relation to particular purposes of testing. For example, the HGSHS:A and CIS are not interchangeable even though they share features in common (Hilgard et al., 1981), and the use of both tests for the same purpose is contraindicated.

Strong argument about the variable nature of factor analytic work has been made by Curran and Gibson (1974), who found that when changes in procedure were made in order to make Stanford test items easier to administer, variation in factor structure was revealed in the data. Curran and Gibson varied the time taken for test of amnesia (among other seemingly minor changes) on Stanford hypnotizability scale items (based on SHSS:A and SHSS:B). Data for a sample of 43 subjects showed that amnesia loaded on a different factor than reported earlier by E. R. Hilgard (1965). Four factors emerged in their analysis rather than the original three, and Curran and Gibson expressed some difficulty with Hilgard's original interpretation of the factors that were found in the Stanford work. The authors' first factor represented loss of voluntary control over musculature, but amnesia loaded here more highly than before; the second factor was labeled hallucination, and the third and fourth factors were labeled active motor compliance in and out of hypnosis, respectively. Inasmuch as amnesia is usually reported in the literature as a significant item for defining hypnosis, it is important to note that the item varies in its factorial loading quite appreciably when seemingly minor alterations in procedure are adopted.

Even considering the paucity of their sample size, the special difficulty posed by Curran and Gibson's data is that for two items, amnesia and hallucination—

which, combined with posthypnotic suggestion, made up Hilgard's third factor—the loadings were actually lower on Hilgard's third factor than their loadings on Curran and Gibson's first factor. One interpretation that fits the data collectively is that the factor represented by these three items (amnesia, hallucination, and posthypnotic suggestion) is distinctive and needs to be considered separately in relation to the other kinds of items on standard hypnotic test scales. Arguments about hypnotic scales measuring a single factor or dimension clearly need to be tempered by the fact that it is possible to create factors in statistical analyses of hypnotic (and other) test scales by particular selection of test tasks and by making changes or modifications in test procedures.

The data would appear to indicate that the search for a limited number of dimensions may be as frustrating as the search for a well-defined set of major correlates of hypnosis. The complexity of hypnotic consciousness and of hypnotizability itself suggests the necessity of considering multiple dimensions of hypnotic performance that will account for the essential variability of hypnotic reaction. It is perhaps not too unfair to state that the major thrust of factorial work on hypnotic test scales challenges our traditional assumptions about the meaning of the behavior tapped by these scales more than it clarifies our understanding of the precise nature of hypnotic process and experience.

SUMMARY DISCUSSION

In Chapter 1 we conceptualized hypnosis as a relatively discrete state of consciousness that can involve shifts in quality of mentation over time. By implication, the major goal of all assessment instruments should be to measure the manifestations of that consciousness in as accurate and sensitive a manner as possible. Tests approach that goal in different ways, and some are more successful in achieving it than others.

Behavioral scales attempt to index hypnotic consciousness in an objective and quantifiable fashion, relying on observations of actual behavior to produce subjects' test scores. But close analysis of the tests of hypnotizability that exist in the literature indicates that relatively few scales satisfy this goal. A large number of so-called "objective" tests, for example, actually employ inferences made by the hypnotist about the respondent's experience as part of the process of arriving at scores on the scales. Consider the SHSS:C scale: Three items on this test obviously use the reported experience of the subject to determine a success or failure response. For instance, a subject does not pass the taste-hallucination item unless he or she reports experiencing sweet and sour tastes in the mouth, and dream performance is assessed entirely in terms of the subject's report. In fact, among the individual scales for assessing hypnotizability, only the SHSS:A and B and the BSS rely exclusively on judgments about actual behavior when arriving at objective test scores. Hence, the distinction between subjective and objective response blurs somewhat when one carefully examines the nature of the scoring procedures that exist. Regardless of the specific format of the test, authors of available tests obviously consider the subjective report of the hypnotized subject to be necessary datum when forming a judgment about the meaning of some of the behaviors that are demonstrated on their scales.

Behavioral tests of hypnosis have the advantages of a standard format and relatively precise scoring criteria. They have been constructed so as to communicate their instructions uniformly in a way that is understood by the majority of subjects who take them; however, this assumption is not always justifiable, especially if the experience of subjects is recognized as primary data. Standard laboratory scales also lack the flexibility of the clinical scales (see Tables 2.4 and 2.5), which are geared far more to assessment of subjects' idiosyncrasies. Behavioral scales also frequently consider hypnotic performance across a range of different kinds of tasks that attempt to tap something of the complexity of hypnotic responsiveness. For the most part, however, the assumption of many of the behavioral tests is that a general characteristic is being measured by the scale, and this assumption perhaps puts the scales most at risk with respect to the valid measurement of hypnotic phenomena and process.

Self-report depth scales, more than behavioral scales, are constructed on the assumption that hypnosis is not an all-or-none state but a relatively discrete state of awareness, and they are more sensitively geared to detecting changes in the quality of experience throughout the hypnotic session. They better recognize and attempt to index the discrepancies that can result between reported experience and its accompanying pattern of behavior, and so highlight the multifaceted nature of hypnotic reaction. Their disadvantage, however, is that they involve the subject in making judgments about his or her hypnotic experience while in trance, thus raising the question of whether the process of making the judgment in hypnosis interferes with the quality of consciousness that is being assessed.

As discussed in Chapter 1, some verbal report data are likely to be more veridical than others, depending on the conditions under which they were collected. Traditional self-report scales (see Table 2.6) have focused on only limited aspects of hypnotic involvement and review only a portion of the relevant experiences of the hypnotized subject. One method that overcomes this last difficulty and attempts to avoid some of the limitations that may result from measuring the experience of trance is Shor's (1979) phenomenological method (see Table 2.6 for its summary description). The scales used with this method are broad ranging in the aspects of the hypnotized subject's experience that they address, and the evaluations of the subject's involvement in the events of hypnosis are made by an examiner on the basis of the subject's descriptions of the quality of his or her experience offered retrospectively after hypnosis has terminated.

The data are not yet in hand to document the reliability and validity of the phenomenological method, as we indicated earlier in this chapter. It offers us a promising means of assessment to detect not just the presence of a response and its accompanying experience, but also the kinds of processes that may underlie that response. Different types of response to hallucination suggestion may occur; for instance, a subject may know that there is no fly buzzing around his face, but nevertheless feel compelled to brush it away and does so. Such a subject would pass the hallucination item on an objective test, but would fail to be distinguished on the same test from subjects who are convinced that a fly is present and make an attempt to brush it away because they are sure that if they do so it will go away soon.

Likewise, with respect to amnesia, subjects who maintain they really cannot remember anything that happened in the last session need to be differentiated from those who say they can probably remember if they want to, but cannot be bothered to try because they know the hypnotist would prefer them not to. This variability may reflect differing processes at work in determining outcome or express an aspect of the different ways in which subjects may have perceived the suggestions that they received in the first instance.

Despite the arguments that we have offered in support of adopting a phenomenological approach to analysis of the complexity of hypnotic conscious-ness, there are a number of assumptions made by specific methods using this framework that may be difficult to justify and point to the necessity of locating alternative methodologies that are phenomenologically oriented and that attempt to overcome the particular artifacts that may be associated with the procedures defining existing techniques. Shor's (1979) technique, for instance, makes the assumption that hypnotic subjects can describe their hypnotic experiences accu-rately after hypnosis has concluded. Although such an assumption avoids the problem that reporting in trance can interfere with experience at the time, it may well be unreasonable to conclude that accurate retrospective recall is possible while subjects are completely unaided in their efforts to remember, especially considering that verbal reports about cognitive processes may not be accurate when they are based only on incidental memory (Ericsson & Simon, 1980).

Conscious events in hypnosis are subtle and complex, and that complexity may well be difficult, if not impossible, to retrieve if the subject is not in some way assisted in retrieving the events that happened in exactly the way that they occurred. Shor (1979) refers to the necessity for assuming the presence of "con-ditions of presumptive accuracy [p. 109]" and argues that the data from the phenomenological interview should not be used unless accurate recall has been established and is likely to remain. However, it is not clear how such accuracy can be guaranteed in the absence of special procedures to facilitate memory.

Another possible weakness of Shor's (1979) method is that the hypnotist and the examiner who collects and assesses the subject's retrospective observations is most commonly one and the same person. Clinically speaking, this procedure has considerable validity. For instance, it is very practical to employ the same person to hypnotize a subject and to inquire into the nature of his or her experiences. But the point should be made that someone who has no knowledge of what happened in the hypnotic session is more likely to gather an unbiased record of the subjects' recall of trance experiences. The advantage of using the same person is clearly that the hypnotist knows exactly what did occur (though he or she may interpret events in a particular way), whereas an independent inquirer is solely reliant on the report of the subject. It is always relevant to ask, however, how an independent inquirer using this or some alternative methodology that is phenomenologically oriented can guarantee that accurate memories are being reported. Of course, this raises the need to distinguish between the kinds of verbal report data that are significant and those that are not.

The final point about the phenomenological method is that the role of the examiner is seen as establishing a methodological partnership with the hypnotized subject in which, according to Shor (1979), both subject and examiner work together "for getting at the truth [p. 111]." The climate of trust and cooperation that is to be engendered is important, but one may raise the question that the examiner's role places too little initiative with the subject. It is the subject's experience that is paramount in determining the nature of hypnotic consciousness, and examiners who adopt too judgmental a role can seriously interfere with the validity of the inquiry. Any labeling from the interviewer or any attempt at too rigid an interpretation can begin to structure the nature of the verbal report that the subject is making and will continue to make. Thus, phenomenological modes of assessment should take special steps to render the inquiry subject oriented rather than experimenter oriented.

With respect to hypnotic phenomena, hypnotized subjects reliably report that their response to hypnotic suggestions is different from ordinary subjective experience (Sheehan, 1979c). The nature of the regularity of individual differences in susceptibility also leads us to have some degree of confidence in the assertion that it is meaningful to talk of a trait of hypnotizability and to assume that it has some degree of stability over time. As Perry (1977a) has pointed out there is no evidence that low susceptible subjects can be transformed into high susceptible persons as the modification position of Diamond (1974, 1977) would seem to imply. The conceptualization of hypnosis in terms of a single trait or dimension has lead to a lengthy and frustrating search for the correlates of the hypnotizable person, with work focusing on the imaginative abilities of the susceptible subject (Sheehan, 1979b; Spanos & Barber, 1974). But just as one can emphasize the trait attributes or person characteristics of the hypnotizable subject, one also needs to take careful account of the influence of the hypnotic test situation and the influence of task parameters; imagination plays a role, but only in part.

The question of what influence situational variables actually have on hypnotizable subjects performing in the hypnotic setting has not been adequately clarified by research. A trait account of hypnosis tends to emphasize that skills and abilities for hypnosis are the prime determinants of hypnotic responsiveness and that situational influences have relatively little effect on the behavior and experience of those being hypnotized. But detailed analysis of the concept of trait and its interaction with situation as determinant assists us in placing the two sources of influence in relevant perspective (Sheehan, 1979c).

The trait position does not assert that behavior is stable in any absolute sense. The influences of such social factors as prior expectancies and attitudes obviously shape and modify subjects' responsiveness (Sarbin & Coe, 1972), and few of us would assert otherwise. Rather, the trait position actually holds that behavior will be relatively stable across different situations. This position argues that although situations will influence subjects to perhaps modify their response, their behavior will still be consistent in the sense that two subjects differing in hallucinatory or age-regression ability (for example) across two situations of testing will be differentiated comparably in each setting even though the contexts themselves may have an appreciable effect on both subjects' hypnotic performance.

The correct meaning of "relatively stable" is not fully recognized in the hypnotic literature, and argument about the influence of trait is frequently based on the invalid assumption that hypnotic behavior will be consistent in an absolute sense across contexts that differ in the degree of their social complexity. In areas other than hypnosis, the importance of recognizing trait and person characteristics operating in interaction with situational influences is acknowledged far more fully. It is person-in-context that will shape hypnotic behavior and experience and, if individual differences in hypnotizability do exist, their importance is not at all reduced by our acknowledging that the social features of the hypnotic context will interact in an active manner with these characteristics to structure the detail of subjects' final hypnotic response. As Ekehammer (1974) argues, the interaction between the two sets of factors (trait and situational influence) should be viewed as one that involves mutual, bidirectional causality. Hypnotic responsiveness should be regarded as a function of both level of hypnotizability and the social-influence character of the specific hypnotic setting; each may interact with the other to determine actual response. For example, in investigating trance logic Sheehan (1977) reported that the nature of an object to be hallucinated determined whether the object would be seen in transparent fashion; only susceptible subjects, however, took the opportunity to respond in that fashion.

One is frequently asked whether hypnotic responsiveness is more a matter of the trait characteristics of the hypnotizable person than either setting characteristics or some altered state of awareness produced by trance induction. It is misleading to take sides on this question or to polarize the issue by emphasizing one facet to the exclusion of another.

Assuming that a relatively discrete state of consciousness does exist in hypnosis, then it seems plausible to argue that some persons may attain that state more easily than others by virtue of their particular person or traitlike characteristics. It is not inconsistent with the concept of state of consciousness (see Chapter 1), for instance, to assert that if imagery is facilitated in hypnosis or if there is a discernible shift in perceived reality achieved through hallucination, then the subject responded in that fashion for reasons attributable in part to the fact he or she had the relevant aptitudes or skills to do so in the first place. It is important to be able to discriminate the consequences of each of the separate components in the interaction: trait, situation, and awareness.

In our view, the variability that exists with respect to hypnotic performance highlights the basic relevance of both trait and situational influence to an understanding of the processes responsible for hypnosis. For instance, the data from investigations of the dimensional structure of test scales indicate considerable diversity in the factors that appear to underlie the tests. Hence, one might reasonably expect that task specificity on the various scale items will interact with subjects' specific aptitude for hypnosis and their particular style or mode of cognitive response to the items in question. The nature of that interaction is not readily observed through the application of standard routine forms of assessment.

Undoubtedly, there are more questions raised by our review of assessment scales than answers we have provided. Perhaps the most pressing issue for future work is the exploration of the relationships that exist among the various methods of assessment outlined in Tables 2.2–2.6. The behavioral, clinical, and experience-based modes of assessment all make different assumptions about hypnotic phenomena and their measurement and, for the most part, imply different theoretical leanings concerning what processes best explain hypnotic phenomena. Many of the existing scales assume that they tap the primary dimensions of hypnotic experience and responsiveness, but it is not until we know much more about the specific cognitive capacities of subjects that we can design any test that will fully achieve this objective.

We now consider the development of an assessment method for the study of hypnotic phenomena. The technique is phenomenologically oriented and has been developed by us as an extension of existing measurement procedures. It aims to be sensitively attuned to nuances of the individual subject's responsiveness to hypnotic suggestion and to examine in some detail the complexity of cognitive processes that are likely to be involved. In applying the technique to study the phenomena, however, we need to be alert to the specific interaction that may exist among trait, task situation, and the subject's state of awareness.

3 The Experiential Analysis Technique

Chapters 1 and 2 have placed a good deal of emphasis on the experience of individuals during hypnosis and the fact that theoretical frameworks for explaining subjects' involvement in hypnosis are converging upon internal processes at work within the hypnotic setting (E. R. Hilgard, 1975; Spanos & Barber, 1974). Among theorists who consider hypnosis to be an altered state of consciousness (e.g., E. R. Hilgard, 1965, 1974; Orne, 1972, 1974; Orne & Hammer, 1974; Shor, 1970, 1979), the principal reason for holding that view stems almost exclusively from subjects' reports that, while hypnotized, they experience their environment in a particularly distinctive fashion, different from that of their normal waking state. For instance, Orne (1972) clearly reflects the state theorist's appeal to phenomenal events when he comments: "The hallmark of the hypnotic phenomena . . . is the nature and quality of the concomitant subjective events [p. 421]." Theorists who reject the notion of hypnosis as an altered state of consciousness (e.g., Barber, 1972; Sarbin & Coe, 1972; Spanos & Barber, 1974) also highlight the experience of subjects within their own particular theorizing (see Chapter 1 for further discussion); for these theorists, however, the altered experience of subjects is not considered in any way to reflect the influence of a particular hypnotic state. For instance, Spanos and Barber (1974) consider that: "hypnotic phenomena involve genuine changes in the subject's experience that cannot be explained away in terms of faking or sham behavior [p. 508]."

Looking across current theorizing about hypnosis, it appears that in order to account for hypnotic phenomena most theorists make a substantial appeal to the internal processes and subjective events experienced by individuals during hypnosis. This appeal is reflected directly in assessment procedures that focus on scales of hypnotic depth (e.g., O'Connell, 1964) as well as on phenomenologically oriented interviewing techniques such as Shor's (1979) method of assessment (see Table 2.6). The importance of the experiential correlates of hypnotic-like phenomena is also recognized explicitly in scales such as Wilson and Barber's (1978) CIS and more implicitly in scoring procedures for most so-called "objective" scales of hypnosis where the subject's report of his or her experience frequently enters into the assessor's judgment of pass or fail response (see Chapter 2). On major standardized scales such as those reviewed in Chapter 2, the emphasis has primarily been placed on assessment of the behavioral components of hypnotic response. In the move toward psychometric definitiveness, there has been a relative paucity of attempts by research investigators to inquire directly into the subjective mechanisms and impact of hypnosis. Where attempts have been made to inquire overtly into the phenomenal events of hypnosis, researchers have frequently used the routine method of postexperimental inquiry.

Following hypnotic testing, the method of postexperimental inquiry is normally conducted by either the hypnotist or an independent experimenter. Subjects are generally asked to comment on their hypnotic testing, and particular test items may be investigated in detail. Subjects, for instance, may be asked the extent to which they felt hypnotized on an age-regression item or hallucination task during testing. They may be asked to indicate the vividness with which they experienced particular effects suggested to them by the hypnotist. Further, they may be asked to comment on their perceptions of the particular hypothesis under test during hypnosis. That is, during the postexperimental inquiry subjects are typically requested to reflect upon their hypnotic performance and experiences of testing in order to try to assist the investigators in defining and determining the mechanisms underlying their behavioral performance. Although researchers generally consider the qualitative information provided by the postexperimental inquiry data as an aid in interpreting the behavioral performance of subjects, such an approach does not put primary emphasis on the qualitative evidence itself. Whereas contemporary theorizing in hypnosis has swung toward a greater emphasis on cognitive process and subjective reaction, current assessment procedures, for the most part, still accentuate the behavioral aspects of subjects' performance; in this sense, we would argue that there is a theory-assessment mismatch.

Although data gathered by a routine postexperimental inquiry are generally regarded by researchers as providing secondary information, the evidence gathered from the technique needs to be considered closely in terms of its validity and the existence of possible biasing factors present in the standard inquiry situation. In the context of the postexperimental inquiry, subjects typically provide verbal responses to questions from the experimenter and, quite possibly, subtle factors are at work to shape the particular responses given by subjects. For instance, subjects could be motivated to give the verbal report of an experience that they consider appropriate to and consistent with the behavior they demonstrated during hypnosis. Further, the experimenter may unintentionally cue subjects in such a way that their comments reflect the form and structure of the questions themselves rather than the nature of their actual trance experiences. Problems relating to the influence of demand characteristic and experimenter-bias factors during the postexperimental inquiry can be handled to some extent by having subjects answer open-ended questions. Such a procedure, however, does not necessarily overcome the potential problem of the structural nature of the inquiry, highlighting those aspects of the hypnotic test setting that the investigator considers to be important and thereby shaping subjects' reports about the hypnotic events.

In summary, the routine postexperimental inquiry is limited in the amount and type of information that can be elicited from subjects; responses may be shaped, modified, or altered by the inquiry method itself. It could also be argued that this method of investigation may result in the loss of subtle and complex information of potential importance to our understanding of hypnotic effects as individually experienced by subjects during hypnosis. Given that the method is directive in nature, structured in its orientation, limited in both the amount and quality of information that it collects, and given that subjects' responses may well be tied to the way in which the questions are phrased by the investigator in the first instance, new techniques of inquiry clearly need to be developed. Argument is made not for discarding the postexperimental inquiry (see Sheehan & Perry, 1976, for a detailed discussion of its advantages) but, rather, for the development of new techniques of assessment geared more obviously to tapping the idiosyncrasy of subjects' hypnotic reactions so that different modes of assessment that are available can converge on the same phenomena.

We now consider the development of a new method of assessment labeled the *Experiential Analysis Technique* (EAT), which has been reported only briefly elsewhere (Sheehan, McConkey, & Cross, 1978). The technique is primarily oriented to the assessment of the individuality and distinctiveness of individuals' responses to hypnosis. It seeks to examine the ways in which individual hypnotic subjects pattern their personal meanings of and responses to the suggestions that they receive and purports to focus on the interactions between persons and context by examining those interactions in specific detail. As Mischel (1979) argues, the thrust of the traditional trait approach to assessment in general is to stimulate the search for the central tendencies in subjects; but, this loses sight of the within-person variances. Techniques of assessment are required that will not discount what Mischel (1979) calls "molecular inconsistencies" and will not gloss over invariances to build meaningful coherences about individuals' distinguishing characteristics. This focus on the individuality and patterning of subjects' reactions to hypnotic suggestion picks up the trend in the hypnotic literature toward greater emphasis on measuring variable reactions to suggestion (e.g., as assessed through clinical scales of hypnosis; see Tables 2.4 and 2.5) and the analysis of personal reactions to hypnosis (e.g., as measured by experience-oriented scales; see Table 2.6).

The EAT is most akin in its assumptions to Shor's (1979) phenomenological method of trance inquiry. Both the EAT and Shor's method focus primarily on the experience of the subject and aim distinctively to sample multiple dimensions of trance experience. But whereas Shor's method does not attempt to aid retrospective recall of hypnotic events, the EAT is built around explicitly assisting subjects to recall the hypnotic testing through video-tape playback. The EAT also emphasizes the importance of an independent assessor to collect and observe subjects' experience reports and focuses more directly than does Shor's phenomenological method on the initiative of the subject in commenting on the events of the hypnotic session. More than any technique of assessment developed to date, the EAT aims to study what is idiosyncratic or unique about the subject's experience of trance.

THE INQUIRY TECHNIQUE

In essence, the EAT is a technique of inquiry that has been specifically designed to elicit information about the experiences of subjects in a way that is sensitively attuned to the complexity of these phenomenal events. It is an attempt to develop a strategy of assessment that is equipped to study the subjective events underlying hypnotic behavior in a fashion detailed enough to tap the subtleties of hypnotic phenomena. In doing so, the technique also attempts to yield the type of data that is relevant to the emphasis of current theoretical frameworks on cognitive process. In its application, for instance, the method attempts to gather information on the subjective experiences of hypnotic subjects in a way that acknowledges the totality of functioning of the hypnotized person and, in so doing, takes into account the possible interactions between motives, expectancies, and cognitions that may occur for individuals during hypnosis. Procedurally, the technique is based on the use of the video-tape playback of the hypnotic test session in the presence of an independent person (referred to as the inquirer) who inquires into subjects' hypnotic experiences as these experiences are stimulated and recalled while viewing the video-tape playback of the hypnotic testing.

This chapter describes the background, development, and procedures for the application of the EAT and focuses on the assessment of the phenomenological experiences of hypnotic subjects that may be tailored to the measurement of hypnotic responsivity in either the laboratory or clinical setting. In the chapters to follow, we review and analyze a range of hypnotic phenomena, using data from application of the technique as a way of exploring the nature of the various hypnotic experiences.

The Complexity of the Hypnotic Setting

In researching and theorizing about the nature of hypnotic response, one needs to focus on the ways in which subjects perceive, think about, and respond to the situation in which they are placed. Reality always exists for the hypnotic subject, but we know relatively little about how hypnotizable subjects perceive it and how they process reality information. E. R. Hilgard (1977) and Tellegen (1978–1979) argue that hypnotic subjects process real and suggested information either in parallel or in series, but other possibilities exist for processing as well.

Hypnotic response in a sense can be viewed as a compromise reaction—a resolution of the processing of the information that is suggested by the hypnotist and reality events as they impinge on the susceptible subject in the trance situation. Viewed in this way, the complexity of the hypnotic situation becomes clearly evident. The hypnotist who tells a subject to "fall deeply asleep now" can safely assume that the subject knows really not to do that; the expectation of both hypnotist and subject alike is that the subject should be able to hear what the hypnotist is saying at all times.

Consider further a subject who experiences a positive visual hallucination (a phenomenon that we examine in some detail in Chapter 6). He or she can respond appropriately, but yet be aware that the object being hallucinated is not actually present, attempt to ignore that fact, or attempt to incorporate information regarding its absence into the hypnotic experience itself. Subjects in the age-regressed situation (see Chapter 5) must also at some level be aware that they are not actually regressed to an earlier period, and their awareness of this may be expressed in a number of ways. They may, for instance, correctly spell words that they could not possibly spell at the age-regressed period; further, the person age-regressed to an embryonic stage can obviously still hear and respond to the hypnotist's instructions. The diversity of reaction evident in this brief description of a few phenomena illustrates the effectiveness of suggestion, but more important, the variability in question essentially argues for the need to assess the specificity of susceptible persons' reactions to the communications they receive.

The fact that reality and suggestion are frequently opposed, but coexist in the trance situation, highlights the potential discrepancy between cognitions as suggested by the hypnotist and cognitions generated by the realistic aspects of the trance situation; Tellegen (1978–1979) terms this discrepancy *incongruence*. If suggestion and reality are congruent or compatible in the information that is conveyed, there still remains the problem of whether the suggested experience is available or not. If the suggested experience is available, then the subject can generate it by drawing on stored and accessible images; but if it is not available, then the experience needs to be attained in some problem-solving fashion by arousing the kind of cognizing that will facilitate the response. The arousal of images and the nature of the problem-solving process that is activated will change the nature of the experiencing subject's cognitions about hypnosis and the trance situation (Tellegen, 1978–1979).

The same complexity that is evident in the subject's attempts to process suggested and reality events simultaneously is illustrated in the nature of the communications that are given hypnotic subjects by the hypnotist instructing them. A hypnotist routinely communicates with subjects so as to initiate a pattern of behavior that is based on fantasy or imaginative involvement. Usually the hypnotist's communications are oriented completely toward fantasy involvement and make no special comment regarding the objective reality features or demands of the situation. For instance, Field (1979) examined hypnotic communications empirically and reported that the language employed by the hypnotist is typically characterized by redundancy and simplicity. The communications generally attempt to withdraw the subject's attention from the external environment to his or her inner experience in ways that minimize critical, logical evaluation of either the suggestion or the setting itself, but the success of that attempt can be considered only partial; otherwise, the hypnotist cannot be assured that contact with the subject will never be lost completely.

The essential conflict between the hypnotist's message about a hallucinated object (which indicates that the object should be seen) and the message provided by the objective stimulus information (that the object doesn't really exist) is resolved by subjects in terms of their specific experience of the events as they are suggested. The resolution of that incompatibility, particularly as it is posed by the more difficult (i.e., cognitive delusory) items of hypnotic tests (e.g., amnesia, hallucination, and posthypnotic behavior) illustrates the idiosyncratic nature of susceptible subjects' experience of hypnosis. This complexity poses a major challenge to researchers and clinicians alike. Instruments for assessing hypnotizability clearly need to tap the specificity of susceptible subjects' reactions to hypnotic suggestions.

Types of Hypnotic Scales

There is a rich variety of scales for measuring hypnotizability. Generally speaking, they emphasize behavior or experience and may be clinical in character or rely predominantly on the subjective report of the subject. Behavioral scales aim to achieve the goal of psychometric definitiveness (Shor, 1979)—the measurement of precisely quantifiable response—and in so doing often lose the feature of flexibility that characterizes the clinical scale. The essential characteristic of the behavioral scale is that it presents a range of hypnotic test tasks to the subject, which are typically ordered according to item difficulty. Usually the tasks range across a number of abilities said to characterize hypnotic performance. These include: the capacity to experience motor response consequent on imagining movement taking place; the ability to resist or challenge the suggestions of the hypnotist when told it is permissible to do so; and the capacity to experience gross distortions of reality as evidenced by forgetting the events of the session that have just taken place, seeing or hearing events that are not (actually) occurring, and acting according to suggestion even after awakened from hypnosis.

Behavioral performance tasks are also typically scored according to detailed and objective criteria. A subject who passes all such items on a scale is said to be deeply susceptible to hypnosis and capable of experiencing hypnosis to an extensive degree. The issue of hypnotic depth and susceptibility as assessed on the scale needs to be distinguished, however, at least in theory if not in fact. Hypnotic depth depicts the extent of involvement in the events of trance at any given point of time, whereas susceptibility depicts the trait or set of abilities and capacities that illustrate the hypnotic persons' propensity to respond successfully to the tasks that are administered. How deeply involved a person is in hypnosis at any particular time is only partly a function of that person's level of skill or talent; depth depends on the time taken to induce hypnosis, the match between the suggestions used and the person's skills, the level of motivation, the degree of rapport with the hypnotist, as well as other social aspects of the test setting (E. R. Hilgard, 1981).

E. R. Hilgard (1979b) draws the relevant distinction between potential hypnotizability and depth of hypnosis when he argues that they are not the same. Explicit measurement of hypnotic depth is usually reserved for the scales that overtly emphasize the subject's experience of hypnosis. Scales that measure the behavioral or enactive (motor) aspects of hypnotic response normally do not tap the experiential components of depth of hypnosis in any comprehensive way. These experiential components pose problems for assessment. The experience of subjects that fail a response defined in a specific objective way is frequently ignored with respect to the potential relevance of that experience to the subject's susceptibility. Further, when an item is passed objectively, experience that is incompatible with the behavior may be judged as relevant as experience, which is consistent with the suggestion that is given. Again, the agreement and discrepancies between behavior and experience are more relevant to the subjective or clinical test of hypnosis. However, such tests lack the definitiveness or precision of the behavioral scales and frequently fall far short of the level of agreement that the more standardized scales engender about what exactly is meant by a positive (successful) response. On the other hand, in defining scoring criteria as they do, objective scales fail to tap relevant information concerning the processes underlying the responses that are given; this is an issue that we address frequently in this book.

Scales for measuring hypnotizability obviously should be complementary; one needs the assessment of both experience and behavior. Well-defined criteria for successful response are important; interpretative judgments of the hypnotist about the subject's response, as employed with clinical scales, can quite usefully extend our understanding of hypnotic process; and subjects' own diagnoses regarding their hypnotic performance, as typically offered in subjective scales of hypnosis, are also relevant to our understanding of the trait dimension. Objective and subjective indices of response also need to be viewed in combination even on the one scale, if possible. As discussed in Chapter 1, the evidence (e.g., Ruch et al., 1974) shows that subjective scores on some tests (e.g., Barber Suggestibility Scale; see Barber, 1969) are curiously lower than objective scores on other tests (e.g., Stanford Hypnotic Susceptibility Scale, Form A; see Weitzenhoffer & Hilgard, 1959). When corresponding corrections are made on the scales, there is less of a reduction in score on the latter than on the former, the data implying that subjective correction of objective scores on the former test is not as desirable as on the latter.

Ultimately, the aim of any particular test of hypnotizability should be to select an appropriate scale for the purpose the investigator has in mind. The scale need not necessarily tap the complete domain of hypnosis or all hypnotic phenomena, but if it aims to be representative it should cover as large a variety of hypnotic tasks as possible. The range that is tapped should include tasks such as motor response to suggestion, motor inhibition, positive and negative hallucination, age regression, posthypnotic amnesia, and affective distortions. The scores should discriminate between persons who have little aptitude for hypnosis and those who have some (and a great deal); measurement should be reliable and valid to the extent that scores on the test can be expected to correlate positively with other scales of hypnosis. Preferably, also, the tests should have norms associated with them and be equipped to detect and measure the individual's particular abilities for specific hypnotic response. Finally, tests should be sensitive to assessment of the individual nature of susceptible persons' attempts to integrate both reality and suggested information.

No existing scale satisfies all of these criteria for assessment of hypnotizability; perhaps one never will. Two major reasons for this are: (1) the variety of purposes for which assessment of hypnosis is used; (2) the multiplicity of factors that may affect the level or type of hypnotic response. Special responsiveness, for example, needs to be examined in the clinical setting but may be regarded as having little relevance in the laboratory context. Further, hypnotic response can be affected easily by the way in which the situation of testing is defined, misconceptions the hypnotic subject may have about testing, the difficulty of obtaining cooperation and rapport, and the extent to which the hypnotist facilitates, or permits, the initiative of the subject in "working through" suggestions. What the subject thinks the hypnotist wants has also been long regarded as a contaminating factor in obtaining valid assessment of hypnotizability. Finally, the purpose for which the clinician intends assessment may result in bias emanating from his or her interpretive judgment, just as the purpose for which the laboratory worker intends assessment can result in the type of controlled inquiry that misses the real essence of hypnotic phenomena.

This question of bias requires further comment because assessment of whatever kind in the hypnotic situation is prone to reflect the assessor's theoretical leanings. This is especially true in the assessment of hypnosis, which involves the measurement of an inferred condition. The compatibility of an instrument with the user's own conceptual leanings will exert a major influence on how well the test in question operates in practice. As discussed in Chapter 1, the link between assessment and how we theorize about hypnosis is a strong one, but no stronger in principle than the same link viewed in relation to other areas of psychological inquiry. The conceptualization of hypnosis in terms of a single trait, for example, has led most investigators in the field to consider the existence of a "hypnotizable personality." One of the special advantages of looking for such a person is that we become alert to particular personality characteristics about which we can then theorize predictively.

However, the search for the hypnotizable personality has been long and frustrating (see, e.g., Deckert & West, 1963; Sheehan, 1979b), and work has come to focus most recently on the imaginative capacities or skills of the susceptible person. With all of the data in hand to demonstrate the relative stability of individual differences in susceptibility (Perry, 1977a), it is somewhat surprising that evidence supports so particularly the relevance of imaginative capacity and related skills such as the capacity for absorption (Tellegen & Atkinson, 1974). The correlation of waking and hypnotic suggestibility among susceptible subjects is high enough (E. R. Hilgard, 1973) that we know hypnosis is clearly a function, at least in part, of the person. Situations, however, also have a decided impact on hypnotic response and traitlike measures appear relatively ill-equipped to detect that influence. Barber (1969, 1972) and others (Sarbin & Coe, 1972) have drawn attention to the powerful influence of subjects' motivations, expectancies, and attitudes on the level of their hypnotic response. Hypnosis can, for instance, be usefully viewed as an attitude-change situation where the hypnotist is an agent of influence working through the social communications that he or she gives to the subject. The evidence tells us that if subjects believe they will experience catalepsy of the dominant hand—even when there is no compelling reason why this should be the case—they will, in fact, demonstrate that response (Orne, 1969; Sheehan, 1971a, 1980).

The problem of assessing the interaction between trait and other determinants of hypnotic response looms large in assessment, and the relative influence of trait and situation, in particular, is a question that remains unanswered in any precise fashion. No one working in the field assumes that hypnosis reflects a durable trait in any absolute sense. When claims are made for the modification of susceptibility, for example, few would argue that one can modify the absence of a skill to the point where the person becomes highly responsive to hypnosis. There is a strong tendency for final scores to correlate with original scores on hypnotic tests (Perry, 1977a), but levels of hypnotic response can be modified to some degree by conditions of sensory deprivation (Sanders & Reyher, 1969) and drug-induced alterations in cognition and thinking (Levine & Ludwig, 1965; see also, Bowers, 1976).

The exact nature of the relative stability of hypnosis is unclear. Situational influences such as the interpersonal climate established by the hypnotist do have a definite effect on hypnotic response (Perry & Sheehan, 1978; Sheehan, 1980), but the extent to which susceptible subjects will maintain their relative ranking in terms of their aptitude for trance (as compared with other persons when the same pressures for change are present) is altogether uncertain. A variety of issues is raised by this uncertainty. What, for example, distinguishes the trait of susceptibility in operation from the depth of trance that is achieved through the performance on different items on standardized hypnotic test scales? What is the relationship in different test situations between hypnotic susceptibility and other conceptually distinct cognitive aspects of functioning such as the capacity to attend selectively to communications of a particular kind or to tolerate seemingly inconsistent aspects of communications? And do these same relationships exist in the waking state? Finally, what relationships exist between the various cognitive skills relevant to hypnotic performance and what do these variables tell us about hypnotic experience per se?

We now consider in some detail the scales that currently exist in the hypnotic literature. Consideration of the scales, however, necessitates first some comment on their historical development.

HYPNOTIC TEST SCALES
AND MEASURING INSTRUMENTS

Traditionally speaking, measurement in hypnosis has been largely dependent on assessment of hypnosis in relation to some (rather than all) of the dimensions of hypnotic experience (Shor, 1979). For example, scales appearing in the early literature probed in relevant fashion for the experience of hypnotic response as involuntary in character or the degree to which what the hypnotist had suggested was established in the forefront of the subject's consciousness. Rarely, however, did these scales explore the affective or rapport aspects of the interaction between hypnotist and subject, nor did they define hypnotic response in a very precise way. Emphasis on the internal aspects of hypnotic reaction meant that in the initial stages assessment was necessarily subjective in character; but the impression was established early that the items of greatest relevance to the understanding of hypnosis were those that were the most difficult to respond to successfully, and these obviously lay within the deep hypnosis category of the trait continuum.

Table 2.1 sets out the scales that were the precursors to contemporary standardized forms of assessment. Predominantly tapping depth of hypnosis, these scales presented a range of items to subjects, including those that were both easy and difficult to pass. The earliest scale of some influence in the history of the assessment of hypnosis was Davis and Husband's (1931) depth scale, which ranged from low to high susceptibility to hypnosis and involved the rating of

The Method of Interpersonal Process Recall

The EAT itself is an adaptation of the method of Interpersonal Process Recall (IPR) (Kagan, Krathwohl, & Miller, 1963), which has been developed for use in the counseling context. Following the observation that lecturers who viewed a video-tape playback of their lecture presentation often spontaneously reported many of their previous thoughts and concern during that playback, the IPR was developed as a method by which therapists could view and react to immediately preceding contact with their clients through the technology of video-tape playback (Kagan, 1975b). There are a number of variations of the method in the counseling setting (e.g., Archer & Kagan, 1973; Bradley, 1974; Kagan & Schauble, 1969; Van Noord & Kagan, 1976). But basically, IPR uses the video-tape playback of the counseling situation in the presence of an independent person who inquires into and stimulates recall of the underlying dynamics involved in the interaction between counselor and client. The method was first constructed as a means of educating counselors in their interactions in the therapeutic setting (Kagan, 1975b), and it has been widely used for that purpose (e.g., Archer & Kagan, 1973; Bradley, 1974; Grzegorek & Kagan, 1974; Hartson & Kunce, 1973; Jason, Kagan, Werner, Elstein, & Thomas, 1971).

Although the use of video-tape playback was assumed initially to provide a potent situation for the development of counseling skills, substantial research has indicated that use of video-tape playback alone does not yield significant improvement over more traditional methods of counseling training (Kagan, 1973, 1975a, 1975b; Kingdon, 1975; Ward, Kagan, & Krathwohl, 1972). The basic method of IPR was developed further into a general method of teaching, which involved the didactic presentation of material, simulation exercises concerning interpersonal effectiveness, video-tape and physiological feedback, the study of oneself in action, feedback from clients, and complex interactions with others (see Kagan, 1973, 1975a, 1975b, for a description of the training procedures).

The use of video-tape playback itself, however, has been used to develop a scale of affect sensitivity (Campbell, Kagan, & Krathwohl, 1971; Danish & Kagan, 1971; Greenberg, Kagan, & Bowes, 1969) and has been combined with affect simulation (Kagan et al., 1969) and empathy training (Carkhuff & Berenson, 1967) to modify interpersonal skills and interactions across populations ranging from medical students (Werner & Schneider, 1974) to police officers (Danish & Brodsky, 1970).

Although the method was first constructed to educate counselors in their interactions with clients, clients also demonstrated insight into their experiences through application of the technique and showed an increased ability to identify, label, and discuss the meaning of both their overt and covert behavior (Kagan et al., 1963). The method has further been used as a means of uncovering the covert processes used by experienced medical practitioners in their examination and diagnosis of the conditions of patients with complex symptomatology (Elstein, Kagan, Shulman, Jason, & Loupe, 1972).

Only two published studies appear to have acknowledged the relevance of the method of IPR to hypnosis in particular. Woody, Krathwohl, Kagan, and Farquhar (1965) reported that hypnosis facilitated the use of the IPR method in the uncovering of subjective material in therapy; Hammer, Walker, and Diment (1978) have used the method of IPR to explore some of the nonsuggested effects of hypnosis. The study by Hammer et al. (1978; see also Diment, 1974; Hammer, 1976) was a specific application of IPR strategies to explore the nature of hypnotic experience and supports the importance of using appropriate techniques of assessment to focus on the nature of the phenomenal experiences of hypnotic subjects.

In testing the hypothesis that hypnotized subjects engage in primary process thinking more than nonhypnotized subjects, Hammer et al. (1978) used an IPR format of audio-tape playback to analyze the subjective reactions of hypnotized and nonhypnotized subjects to an audio-tape recording of a poem. Comparison groups of subjects were matched on age, prior studies and interest in poetry, and level of susceptibility (a score of 10–12 on the HGSHS:A). One group of subjects was administered a hypnotic induction and then played the poem; the other group of subjects was not given a hypnotic induction prior to listening to the poem. Following this, Hammer et al. (1978) report that the hypnotist/experimenter informed subjects:

> Now I can reveal the true purpose of this experiment. I want to find out in as much detail as possible any thoughts or feelings or any reactions at all you may have had while the poem was being played. To help you recall these thoughts and feelings, I shall shortly replay the poem and if at any time during the replay you can recall what you were thinking or anything at all while it was playing the first time just let me know and I will stop the tape and you can tell me about them [p. 95].

The poem was then replayed and the hypnotist/experimenter adopted the role of an inquirer into subjects' experiences in their initial listening of the poem as experiences were recalled. The comments subjects made about their experiences were recorded and later transcribed for analysis. A sophisticated rater, blind to the identity of those subjects who had received a hypnotic induction, was asked to classify subjects on the basis of their reported experiences as to whether they were hypnotized while listening to the poem. The rater was able to classify 80% of the subjects correctly on the basis of their comments made during the inquiry into their subjective reactions to the poem. A more systematic analysis of the contents of the transcripts was then conducted by an investigator who was unaware of the source of the transcripts or the hypothesis under test. This investigator rated the transcripts on scales relevant to primary process mentation. Results from this analysis indicated appreciably more evidence of primary process thinking in the reports of those subjects who had received a hypnotic induction as compared with those who had not. Hammer et al. (1978) concluded that hypnotic induction leads to a different state of cognitive arousal than the normal waking state and that one of the effects of hypnotic induction is an increase in primary process thinking.

Importantly, this study points to the subtleties of hypnotic experience manifest in subjects' reactions during hypnosis and highlights the need for methods of assessment tailored to tap the individual complexities of phenomenal events. This application of the method of IPR also highlights the potential applicability of phenomenologically oriented modes of assessment to the study of hypnotic responsiveness in general. Such methods not only may be used to gain new insights into hypnotic phenomena themselves, but they also may be brought to bear on predictive tests of theoretical viewpoints (e.g., hypnotic induction leads to increased primary process mentation) that place a specific interpretation on the meaning of subjects' trance experiences.

The Experiential Analysis Technique: A Description

In using the technology of video-tape playback and the role of an inquirer (as developed by the method of IPR), the EAT offers a very potent method for eliciting comment on those processes involved in the experiencing of hypnotic phenomena. Methodologically speaking, the technique attempts to gather data on hypnotic events as they are experienced by subjects and encourages subjects to direct and explain personally their own hypnotic involvement.

With the EAT, the standard procedure is that the hypnotist leaves the test setting after hypnosis and has the subject then interact with an independent experimenter (the inquirer). This second person in the assessment process functions to stimulate subjects to relate new and additional thoughts and feelings that are activated by viewing the video tape of the hypnotic session. The videotape playback of the hypnotic session offers subjects an immediate and literal record of the events of the hypnotic session. This record, as viewed by subject and inquirer alike, serves explicitly to aid subjects' recall, to elicit spontaneous comment by subjects, and to provide the inquirer with an accurate record of what happened in the hypnotic session. By means of this procedure, the inquirer is kept fully informed of the events of the session yet is able to remain independent from the possible contaminating biases resulting from actual involvement in the hypnotic testing (e.g., where particular impressions can be formed about the responsiveness of the subject by the hypnotist who conducts the session).

Importantly, in this method the initiative for response is placed with the subject rather than with the person who is conducting the assessment. A critical feature of the method is that subjects are asked specifically to stop the playback as often as they wish to discuss the hypnotic events or to elaborate on their experiences. It is relevant to note in this regard that the standard scales of hypnotizability reviewed in Chapter 2 place little emphasis on the degree to which subjects either initiate their experience with the hypnotist's suggestion or cumulatively shape or reconstruct their experience as the items on the test evolve. The absence of such a focus forces us to rely heavily in our interpretation of hypnotic test data on the categories used by those who have constructed the tests rather than on the phenomena pertinent to the subjects who are taking them. The advantage of this is that the goal of psychometric definitiveness may be well served, but the disadvantage is that such quantification of performance may not accurately reflect the processes that truly operate. The EAT aims to investigate carefully the qualitative events underlying hypnotic subjects' interpretations of the complex communications that emanate from the hypnotist, and the technique attempts specifically to provide minimal cues to subjects as to the particular type of experience that they should report. Subjects, themselves, direct the discussion of their hypnotic experiences. Placing this initiative on subjects has clear advantages over having an experimenter direct the questioning as in the routine postexperimental inquiry. Subjects, for instance, are able to comment freely on those particular events that they found personally important and meaningful in their hypnosis session.

We now consider the basic format of EAT procedures as developed by us for application in the assessment of hypnotic phenomena. The example we take is the application of the method to the laboratory context of testing. The use of the video-tape playback, the role of the inquirer, and the nature of the inquiry are elaborated and discussed in order to concretize the method and its potential impact.

Video-Tape Playback. A video-tape recording is first made of the hypnotic test session (or the particular hypnotic items under scrutiny), and the playback of this record forms the basis of the inquiry session. The playback and its accompanying proceedings constitute the formal application of the EAT. Subjects are informed prior to hypnotic testing that their hypnotic performance will be video-tape recorded but are not informed that this recording will form the basis of their discussions with another experimenter following the hypnotic testing. If interest is on a particular part of the session or individual items of hypnotic testing, then subjects should not be informed that only part of the testing will be recorded. We would, in fact, recommend that the entire session be recorded and that only a selected portion of it be replayed and inquired into during the application of the EAT. For the EAT inquiry session itself, a video monitor should be placed at a comfortable distance from subjects so that they can view their hypnotic session easily and maintain positive rapport with the inquirer.

The video-tape playback unit should be placed close to the subject, and it should be preset for simple stop–start operation; either a remote switch or a manual switch on the unit itself should be available so that subjects can stop and start the video-tape playback whenever they wish during the inquiry session. The inquirer should be seated to one side of the subject where he or she can focus on the subject and the reactions to the material being viewed. It is more important that the inquirer focus on the subject than on the video-tape playback of hypnotic events so that spontaneous reaction by the subject is not inhibited by thinking the inquirer is not interested in his or her other response. The inquiry session itself is also video-tape recorded so that the information gathered from the application of the EAT can be analyzed fully.

The Role of the Inquirer.   The role adopted by the inquirer is important in determining the success of the EAT application. Adequate training and practice in the skills of listening and paraphrasing nonevaluatively are generally necessary prior to the formal application of the technique; it is recommended that inquirers be trained carefully to accentuate personal skills in communicating empathy and positive rapport. The basic role of the inquirer is that of a nonevaluative, noninterpretative collaborator or coparticipant in determining the nature of the events as experienced by subjects during the actual hypnotic testing. The inquirer encourages subjects to adopt an active and involved commitment to report on and personally interpret their hypnotic experiences. We view an uncritical approach by the inquirer, a positive relationship of the inquirer to the subjects, and a noninterpretative attitude adopted by the inquirer toward the information provided by the subject as important to the standard application of the EAT. The inquirer should minimize the possibility of subjects' keeping secrets (Sarbin & Coe, 1979) by providing a situation of open honesty and self-disclosure.

The essence of the inquirer's personal approach lies in adopting a collaborative, nonauthoritative, and supportive style of interaction that explicitly aims to assist and encourage subjects to discover and report on the phenomenal aspects of their own hypnotic experience. Generally, the EAT is conducted in a more personalized and nonevaluative test situation than is normally associated with a routine postexperimental inquiry session, the assumption being that the fostering of a relatively close positive involvement between subjects and the inquirer during the application of the EAT will lead to the gathering of important information bearing on the nature of the subject's private hypnotic experiences.

The collaborative stance adopted by the inquirer has a number of implications in terms of the relationships of the inquirer to the subject. The subject is an active, rather than passive, participant in the task of discovering and commenting on aspects of his or her hypnotic experience. In this sense, the EAT procedures aim to maximize the subject's freedom of participation, which fosters control on the part of the subject more than on the part of the inquirer but explicitly recognizes that the period of assessment is one that involves bilateral investigation. A spontaneous interaction between the subject and the inquirer is promoted by allowing the inquirer a high degree of flexibility to explore the nature of the spontaneous comments offered by the subject. In this respect, the approach of the inquirer to the material offered by subjects is important. The inquirer gently probes the comments of subjects in order to establish firmly the nature of the subjective experience. The role of the inquirer is to listen and gather data on the comments made by subjects rather than to elicit subjects' explanations or interpretative comments. Further, the inquirer's task is to attempt to maintain the subjects' attention upon the particular events being discussed. Subjects, for instance, are generally encouraged by the inquirer to restrict their comments to the immediately relevant events; similarly, the comments made by the inquirer should not sidetrack the subject from the relevant experience that the subject has indicated he or she wishes to describe.

The Nature of Inquiry.   The inquirer introduces the subject to the EAT session in a way designed to maximize the impact of the cues to recall. The instructions given by the inquirer at the beginning of the EAT session are prescribed as follows:

> In hypnosis research generally there is still wide interest in what actually does occur during hypnosis. In order to clarify what happened in your particular session, I am going to ask you to help us both by watching a video tape of things that happened during your hypnosis session.
>
> As (the hypnotist) told you at the beginning of the session, the hypnosis session has been video taped, and we are going to play back that video tape now. Playing the video tape will provide for you a precise, detailed record of what happened and, therefore, you will probably find it easier to recall how you felt and what you thought, for instance, than you would if there were no playback of the video tape.
>
> Now, during your hypnotic session you probably felt and thought a lot of things that you didn't or weren't able to say aloud. Generally the mind works faster than the voice, for instance, and so there were probably times when you didn't have the time to say all you wanted. Perhaps also, you didn't want to tell some of the things to the hypnotist or else you might have just had some vague impressions or reactions or ideas that you weren't able to verbalize at the time. As you watch the video tape now, you'll find that these sorts of thoughts and feelings will come back to you. I want you to feel completely free to stop the video tape at any point and tell me about whatever it is that you are recalling. Anything at all that you recall, just stop the video tape right then and there and tell me about it, anything at all. It may be a little point that you remember or a bigger point that you wish to make. No matter how important you consider it to be, anytime you want to stop the video tape and comment is fine. All of your comments are important and valuable.
>
> It is important, though, that you stop the tape as soon as you want to comment on something. Don't wait till later but stop the video tape immediately. It's a good idea to keep hold of this (stop–start switch) so that you can easily stop the playback. Okay, do you have any questions? Fine, if you're ready you can start the playback anytime you want.

Subjects then personally operate the playing of the video tape of their hypnotic testing. The decision about when to stop the video tape can be left to subjects who are instructed simply to stop the playback whenever they recall something about their hypnotic experience. Whenever subjects stop the video tape and report on their hypnotic experiences, the inquirer can explore the nature of those experiences by asking questions that focus on clarifying the descriptions subjects give.

The exact questions employed by the inquirer following a comment by a subject about his or her hypnotic experience depend on the nature of that comment. For instance, the questions or probes should be appropriate to the content of the comment rather than appropriate to the theoretical viewpoint of the investigator. In this sense, the EAT is designed to provide subjects with minimal cues as to the nature of the information that they should give about their experiences. To meet this end, the probes employed generally focus on the specific aspects of subjects' recall and are open ended, brief, and tentative; further, the inquirer probes those aspects of the hypnotic experience on which subjects comment. If, for instance, subjects do not comment on a hypnotic event that the inquirer judges to be important, then the inquirer generally does not draw that to the subjects' attention. For, in doing so, the subject may well be cued as to what the investigator considers important and hence respond in a way that tries to satisfy the possible biases or opinions of the inquirer.

In classifying the comments made by subjects, the inquirer may use a number of different categories of inquiry, each focusing on potentially relevant aspects of the subject's experience. Also, the inquirer has available a number of questions, each focusing on related aspects of experience, which allow for some considerable degree of spontaneity on the part of the inquirer in terms of the probes employed. One may structure the probes more directively, of course, but this would be only to reflect specific goals or purposes of testing. Areas of inquiry include cognitions, images, expectations, perceptions, image presentation, interpersonal relationship, associations, and sundry feelings. Also, at the end of the session, the inquirer can probe the recall of subjects with respect to a number of relevant experiences of the overall session; these questions have been adapted from those recommended by Kagan (1975b). It is important to keep in mind that probing by the inquirer is intended to encourage subjects to describe and interpret their own hypnotic experiences. The questions themselves are thus designed to minimize the cues available to subjects as to what would be the most appropriate experiences to report. Table 3.1 sets out each of the major areas of inquiry with four questions that illustrate the nature of each category.

In this chapter, we have thus far set out the procedures that are designed to present the EAT as a technique for assessing the individuality of subjects' responsiveness to hypnosis. We now discuss some data that have come from the application of these procedures. Our data highlight a number of relevant processes and response dimensions that the technique can be used to tap.

TABLE 3.1

Summary Table of EAT Inquiry Categories and Sample Questions

Inquiry Categories	Sample Questions
Cognitive	What were you thinking at the time? What thoughts were you having about the situation at that time? Were you consciously thinking about what was happening then? What was going on in your mind then?
Images	Were you having any fantasies at that moment? Were any pictures or images in your mind then? What was going on in your mind at that time? Did you imagine what the outcome might be?
Expectancies	What did you want to hear from the hypnotist? Were you expecting anything of the hypnotist at that point? What did you want to happen next? What were you expecting to happen next?
Image Presentation	How do you think you were coming across to the hypnotist? How did you want the hypnotist to see you at that point? What kind of image were you wanting to project? What message did you want to give the hypnotist?
Perceptions	How do you think the hypnotist was seeing you at that point? What did you think the hypnotist wanted at that point? How do you think the hypnotist felt about giving you this? Do you think your description of what took place would coincide with the hypnotist's?
Associations	What meaning did that have for you? Did this remind you of anything else you have experienced? Was this familiar to you? Did you connect that experience with anything in particular?
Sundry Feelings	How were you feeling about your involvement in the session at that point? What did you feel like doing? How were you feeling about your role as a subject at this point? What would you like to have said or done to the hypnotist at that point?
End of Session	What things did you learn from this recall session with the videotape? Did you like the "you" you saw on the screen? In retrospect, how do you think you felt about the hypnotist throughout the session? Were you satisfied with your behavior? Are there any parts you would like to see again? Did you enjoy talking about what you did in this way?

DATA YIELDED BY APPLICATION OF THE EAT

In order to provide an illustration of a general use of the EAT to investigate the qualitative events underlying subjects' hypnotic performance, we consider a study that focused on a select group of highly hypnotizable subjects. In this study (McConkey, 1979), the EAT was employed to investigate the individual reactions of a small, highly selected group of hypnotic subjects on cognitive-delusory hypnotic task items. Focus was on the close analysis of the reactions of 10 highly susceptible hypnotic subjects in order to determine in a comprehensive fashion the nature of their individual reactions to the hypnotic situations. A high degree of selection was used to insure that subjects were quite familiar with hypnosis and could reasonably be said to have obtained their plateau level of hypnotizability (Shor et al., 1966). The data tentatively provided the basis for the classification of a sample of the dimensions that we suggest are relevant to the analysis of hypnotic consciousness.

Following the standard procedure described earlier in this chapter, subjects were informed by the hypnotist that they would be administered a number of hypnotic tasks, and then they would discuss their experiences with another person. Subjects were informed that the hypnotic testing would be video-tape recorded but were not informed that this recording would form the basis of their discussions with the inquirer. Subjects were then hypnotized and administered the following eight hypnotic items (the source of items is listed in parentheses): hand lowering (Weitzenhoffer & Hilgard, 1962), arm immobilization (Weitzenhoffer & Hilgard, 1962), age regression (adapted from Weitzenhoffer & Hilgard, 1962), glove analgesia (Perry, 1977c), missing number (Obstoj & Sheehan, 1977), hallucination (especially constructed), missing watch hand (E. R. Hilgard, 1965; see also Obstoj & Sheehan, 1977), and posthypnotic amnesia (Weitzenhoffer & Hilgard, 1962).

Laying aside the initial ideomotor (i.e., hand lowering) and challenge (i.e., arm immobilization) items, the items were especially selected in order to test subjects on aspects of hypnosis of a cognitive-delusory nature said to index deep levels of hypnotic involvement. Following current theorizing (e.g., Orne & Hammer, 1974), the items were presumed to tap aspects of dissociation (e.g., age regression and posthypnotic amnesia), tolerance of logical incongruity (e.g., missing number and missing watch hand), and ideationally based distortions of reality (e.g., glove analgesia and hallucination). The hypnotic session was video-tape recorded from the beginning of the age-regression item until the end of the posthypnotic amnesia test. The cognitive-delusory items were recorded in order to form the basis of the inquiry session using the EAT. Following hypnotic testing, an independent inquirer employed the EAT to conduct an intensive investigation into subjects' experiences during testing. Data indicated that the EAT was perceived positively by subjects. Ninety percent of the subjects considered the review of their hypnotic involvement provided by their viewing of the video tape was a valuable stimulant to their remembering of experiences. Subjects also indicated that the EAT session led them to have insights of a personally meaningful kind about their hypnotic behavior. The technique was considered to have immediacy and was enjoyed by at least 80% of the subjects who felt that it gave them the opportunity to relive events in a lively and concrete way. One subject, for instance, commented: "Here, where I can see it, I can get into it more." The one subject who did not react favorably to the session reported that she was embarrassed by viewing her hypnotic performance, during which she thought she looked "silly"; notably, this subject commented less and stopped the playback less than any other subject.

In summary, the EAT was seen to provide a context for a high degree of comment by subjects and elicited a large amount of material concerning subjects' experiences. This is consistent with other data that have shown that the EAT yields more information than does routine questioning (Bell, 1978). We now examine in some detail the material that was provided by subjects during the EAT session, which suggests the relevance of process and response dimensions that we discuss further in the chapters to follow.

The qualitative data yielded by the EAT were analyzed for information concerning subjects' experiences associated with the range of selected items. In particular, two raters inspected the material for the information it contained with respect to: (1) subjects' perceptions of the hypnotist's communications; (2) the styles or modes of cognizing that the subjects employed. One of the main inferences that can be drawn from the data is that there was marked variation in the way in which events were processed during trance. One major factor that appeared to be involved was that subjects idiosyncratically interpreted the hypnotist's messages. We now consider this characteristic more closely and attempt to clarify some of the styles of cognition that may be evident in subjects' EAT reports.

Individuation

Subjects demonstrated reliable evidence that they accepted or interpreted the communications of the hypnotist in an individual or personal way; we have labeled this process *individuation* (Sheehan, McConkey, & Cross, 1978). The same term was used by Jung (1923) to express the development of the individual personality and the "building up of the particular [p. 562]" but in essence we use it simply to express the individuality or personal idiosyncrasy of response. The incidence of individuation in subjects' comments across the hypnotic tasks is set out in Table 3.2. Some subjects demonstrated this characteristic more obviously than others. For instance, one subject almost always reinterpreted the hypnotist's communications in order to accomodate her personal views and experiences. Two other subjects also displayed a relatively high degree of individuation,

TABLE 3.2
Incidence of Individuation Evident in Subjects' EAT Comments
on a Sample of Cognitive-Delusory Items

Subject number	Age regression	Glove analgesia	Missing number	Hallucination	Missing watch hand	Post-hypnotic amnesia
				Items		
1		+(+)				
2	+(+)					
3						
4			(+)		+(+)	
5						
6	+(+)	+(+)	(+)	+(+)	+(+)	+(+)
7					(+)	
8			+(+)	+(+)		
9				(+)		
10			+(+)			

Note. + = comments indicated idiosyncratic interpretation of hypnotist's communication. Ratings of second rater appear in parentheses. Raters agreed in 73.33% of cases.

whereas others displayed this characteristic only during certain hypnotic tasks. It appears to be that for at least some subjects the complexity of the task interacts with subjects' idiosyncratic perceptions of the hypnotist's messages.

The process of individuation clearly needs to be considered in relation to the issue of subjects' aptitude for hypnotic events. For example, data suggested that it may be erroneous to infer that differences in aptitude are necessarily implicated when hypnotic tasks are not passed in an objective fashion. There is considerable argument in the literature, for instance, concerning the level of hypnotizability of subjects who imagine rather than hallucinate when asked to perceive events not physically present (Sheehan, 1972, 1979b). The testimony of one subject who imagined rather than hallucinated the effect suggested by the hypnotist during the hallucination task illustrates this point. This subject's rationale for her response indicated that imagination was an entirely legitimate response in terms of her evaluation of the reality and fantasy demands of the setting: ''The television screen is not switched on [which it wasn't], and then I thought that he must want you to imagine it, you know, you need not necessarily see it. So, he might want you either to pretend to see it or to imagine it.'' The process of individuation can also be seen in another subject's comment on the glove-analgesia task:

I have been in an operation and the anesthesia went in my left hand and I felt the needle [suggested by the hypnotist] go into my left hand [in fact, the suggestion was for the right hand], and I had a tremendous pain in my right foot, and yet he was talking about my right hand. The pain in the foot was killing me and my left hand was going numb, and then after a while my right hand went numb.

The uncertainty that subjects expressed about their behavior and whether it was appropriate to the suggestion further highlighted the conflict that they were experiencing. In commenting on the missing watch-hand item, for instance, one subject indicated:

> First time I saw it, it had two hands and I was shocked. It's got two hands, and it's only supposed to have one. Then I tended to put my finger over that hand and I kept stroking the minute hand. He asked me what the time was and I kept stroking. Well, to tell the time you've got to have a minute and an hour hand and I answered "one," because it was on the one. I was hoping he wouldn't say "one what?"

This subject was responsive to the requirements of the suggestion as well as the reality demands of the situation; in addition, she appreciated the limitations of her own response. This example also reflects a particular style or mode of thinking about the reality and fantasy demands of the hypnotic situation. We now examine in more detail some of these individual differences in styles of cognizing that were evident in subjects' reports about their experiences.

Modes of Cognition

Three modes of cognitive response were observed and abstracted from the data. These modes reflect particular ways in which subjects cognitively evaluated the situation and processed incoming stimuli information in order to respond. The modes have been labeled *concentrative, independent,* and *constructive* (Sheehan, McConkey, & Cross, 1978). These categories are not necessarily exhaustive or independent, but the data suggest that they reflect discrete styles of cognitive processing in hypnosis. No support is claimed for personality types, but rather for the operation of relatively distinct modes of cognition that may well interact with task complexity as well as the nature of the conflict existing in the setting. Table 3.3 sets out the incidence of the various modes of cognitions across the hypnotic tasks. Subjects were generally seen to prefer a particular mode of cognition, although interactions were also evident between style of cognizing and type of item.

Concentrative Mode. The concentrative mode of cognizing was characterized by subjects concentrating on the communications of the hypnotist and thinking along in literal fashion with the messages contained in these communications. In this mode, subjects typically did not allow irrelevant thoughts to be considered but attempted to focus their attention on the suggestion. One subject who consistently manifested this type of thinking commented with respect to the missing-number item: "I am not supposed to be thinking about [the missing number], and when I put my mind to it I didn't. You realize it's wrong, and you just ignore it and concentrate on doing something better." Failure to resolve the

TABLE 3.3
Modes of Cognitions Evident in Subjects' EAT Comments
on a Sample of Cognitive-Delusory Items

Subject number	Age regression	Glove analgesia	Missing number	Hallucination	Missing watch hand	Post-hypnotic amnesia
1	CC(CC)	CC(CC)	CC(CC)			
2	ID(ID)		ID(ID)			
3			CC(CC)			
4					CS(CS)	
5	CS(CS)		CS(CS)			
6	CS(CS)	CS(CS)	CS(CS)	CS(CS)	CS(CS)	CS(CS)
7	(CS)				CC(CC)	
8		ID(ID)	CS(CS)	CS(CS)	CS(CS)	
9					CS(CS)	
10	CC(CC)		CS(CS)			

Note. CC = concentrative, ID = independent, and CS = constructive style of cognizing. Ratings of second rater appear in parentheses. Raters agreed in 95.83% of cases.

conflict engendered by thinking of the missing number was directly attributed by this subject to reduced concentration. The style of response expressed by this subject fits very well the mode of cognition argued by those who consider the concept of hypnosis expendable (e.g., Barber, 1972; Spanos & Barber, 1974). According to this view, suggestions simply evoke a well-motivated desire for subjects to cooperate fully and to think along with what is happening. A number of subjects, however, were quite different in their cognitive style, and data indicated that this mode was not characteristic of all subjects.

Independent Mode. The independent mode of cognizing was characterized by subjects assessing the experience suggested by the hypnotist in terms of its personal meaningfulness. Subjects who demonstrated this mode did not simply concentrate on the literal messages of the hypnotist but chose, as it were, those aspects of the experience that they themselves considered appropriate to their situation and responded in quite independent fashion. Subjects in this category displayed individuation of response more than those in the previous category, more often responding in an idiosyncratic manner. For instance, one subject in this category stated in commenting on the age-regression item: "I think in varying shades of grey all the time. It doesn't worry me what [the hypnotist] really wanted me to do. I was doing what I was able to do. I don't know whether I was in grade 1, I don't really think the writing was a kid's writing, but it was what I was doing and I felt happy about it. Whether it fits or not, what [the hypnotist] wanted, I don't know."

It is important to note that this subject was the only one to consider that the words should be spelled correctly in the age-regressed situation. Also notable for this type of subject, failure was not at all an event to be explained (e.g., "I just do what I do"), whereas for other subjects failure was attributed to lack of susceptibility or conflict in the situation. The naturalness of one's own responsiveness to the situation appeared to be the most important facet of response for the type of subject who displayed independent processing. For example, there was little evidence of any compulsion to concentrate on and adhere to what the hypnotist was literally suggesting.

Constructive Mode. The constructive mode of cognizing was characterized by subjects considering the communications of the hypnotist from a position of preparedness to process incoming stimulus information in a schematic way so as to structure events in accord with what the hypnotist was suggesting. Subjects who demonstrated this mode did not simply concentrate on the literal messages of the hypnotist and did not necessarily interpret them personally, but rather they cognitively responded by actively seeking out ways to construct or synthesize the experience that was being suggested. Some subjects consistently reacted with much more effort than others. For instance, one subject handled the reality and fantasy demands of the missing-number item by substituting a letter of the alphabet for the missing number. The experience she constructed was within the bounds of the hypnotist's suggestion and offered a unique solution to the conflict contained in the task: "There were some [missing numbers] in those sums and they didn't sort of register. They looked like letters or something, you know, say you had *3, 2, 5,* and *L* written down and you added them up. *L* just wouldn't go with the others." Also, on the missing watch-hand item, this subject reported that she "thought [the hypnotist] just meant to say 'what number is it on?' not 'what's the time?'" That is, by reconstructing or purposively misperceiving the hypnotist's request to tell the time, the subject was able to respond positively and experience minimal conflict.

The solutions and responses offered by subjects who displayed cognitive processing in the form of constructions resolved the various demands so that substantial opportunity was available to minimize any conflict present and to respond positively. It appeared that these types of subjects made an effort and planned cognitively to interpret the reality and suggestion demands present so that they could respond appropriately to the suggestions that were given. Across the types of cognizing evident in subjects' reports, it was apparent that subjects handled the interface of reality and suggestion that necessarily presents itself to all hypnotic subjects in quite different ways. Concentrative subjects tended simply to try to ignore the reality information; independent subjects assessed the overall situation in terms of personal meaningfulness; and constructive subjects tended to process the total nexus of information schematically in order to build a solution that they thought was appropriate in terms of the hypnotist's suggestion.

Subjects observing video-tape records of their own hypnotic performance revealed subtle meanings of their behavior and experience that help to define the nature of hypnotic phenomena. Results demonstrated substantial inter- and intraindividual variability in subjects' experience with and response to the hypnotist's suggestions. There were marked differences, for instance, in subjects' interpretations of the hypnotist's messages and in the modes of cognizing they employed. We return to these themes of individuality of response and essential variability of hypnotic reaction when we come to analyze particular hypnotic phenomena in Chapters 4–8.

Another salient inference that we draw from the data we have collected, and a major theme that we wish to emphasize, is that hypnotic subjects should not be conceptualized as passive recipients of hypnotic instructions. Subjects not only interpret the instructions they receive and embed them into their preferred fantasies, but they also often demonstrate simultaneous awareness of suggestions and the reality demands of their environment. At one level, subjects appear to receive the communications and respond to them in quite passive fashion, whereas at another level they often examine the communications from their particular cognitive position regarding the most appropriate response to make in order to resolve the incongruities of the situation. Data cited in the chapters to follow highlight the fact that subjects are frequently aware of apparent inconsistencies in their behavior, but at the same time they may privately debate the interaction of reality and suggestion demands. To capture something of the complexity of this response, psychoanalytic theory appeals to partial regression of the ego (e.g., Gill, 1972; Gill & Brenman, 1961), neodissociation theory invokes the notion of shifting hierarchies of cognitive control (e.g., E. R. Hilgard, 1977), and other theorists talk about registration without perception (e.g., Bowers, 1976). Whatever theorizing is adopted, however, the evidence appears to illustrate dramatically the fluid operation of multiple streams of awareness in hypnotic subjects.

In summary, subjects vary substantially in the nature of the hypnotic response that they demonstrate, and responsiveness in many instances is highly individual or idiosyncratic in character. For many subjects, hypnosis is best viewed as a problem-solving situation in which active cognizing requiring effort frequently occurs to produce the kind of response that reflects the subject's personal understanding of what the hypnotist's suggestion means. Marked individual differences are obviously present in the ways in which susceptible subjects cognize about hypnotic events. We now consider data relating to the consistency with which the particular styles of cognizing that we have outlined may be utilized, as well as the interaction of these styles with the specific hypnotic tasks presented to subjects.

Consistency of Cognitive Style

The data we have considered suggest that the EAT is a very useful method for investigating the subjective events that underlie the performance of hypnotic subjects. The evidence implies that a major issue relates to the style or mode of cognizing that subjects may adopt in the hypnotic setting. In the application of the EAT just discussed, for instance, the data from the sample of highly susceptible subjects that was studied indicated concentrative, independent, and constructive cognitive styles. The data presented in Table 3.3 indicate that for some subjects a particular cognitive style was evident across the majority of hypnotic test items, whereas for others a particular cognitive style appeared to be more evident on specific hypnotic items rather than as a general strategy for processing the communications of the hypnotist. Bell (1978) specifically investigated the consistency of subjects' cognitive approaches to hypnotic test tasks.

Bell (1978) applied the EAT as a means of inquiry into the hypnotic experiences of separate groups of high and low susceptible subjects and examined the data with respect to the cognitive styles that were evident on four separate hypnotic test items: hand lowering, mosquito hallucination, dream, and hallucination. The cognitive processes reported by the 12 high and 12 low susceptible subjects were classified in relation to criteria for the operation of concentrative, independent, or constructive modes of cognition by two independent raters. The categorization of subjects' cognitive styles across the four hypnotic items are set out in Table 3.4; the criteria selected for rating were those discussed earlier in the subsections dealing with these three modes of cognition.

Inspection of the data indicates variability in cognitive approach across the four hypnotic items for a number of the highly susceptible subjects. Low susceptibility subjects, on the other hand, demonstrated a similar style of cognizing regardless of the type of hypnotic task being presented to them. These data suggest that susceptible subjects may be more willing and more able to adapt their cognizing to the task presented by the hypnotist in order to experience the suggested effect. The degree of cognitive flexibility on the part of susceptible subjects appears to be complicated, however. The concentrative style was predominant among both high and low susceptible subjects, but highly responsive subjects were more likely to display independent or constructive styles of cognizing than low susceptible subjects.

The concentrative style of cognizing was evident in comments such as: "I was really concentrating on seeing [the suggested hallucination], just thinking about seeing it"; or "I was really trying to see it, to see what [the hypnotist] had said"; or (with respect to the hand lowering suggestion) "I was just thinking you've got to let your arm down." The independent style of cognizing was evident in comments such as: "I couldn't do anything I didn't want to"; "I'd start to do the right thing, then I'd just forget about it and do what I wanted to do"; and (with respect to the hallucination suggestion) "I thought blue would be easier to see [than the orange suggested by the hypnotist]." The constructive mode was evident from subjects employing particular embellishing strategies to experience the suggested effect. For instance, one subject, instead of seeing the hallucinated event as suggested, constructed an entirely imaginary object: "I could see an

TABLE 3.4
Style of Cognitions Evident in Subjects' EAT Comments
on Four Hypnotic Test Items

Subject Grouping and Number	Hand lowering	Mosquito hallucination	Dream	Hallucination
High Susceptibility				
1*	CC(CC)	CS(CS)	ID(CC)	CS(CS)
2	CC	CC	CC	CC(CC)
3	CC(CC)	CC(CC)	(CC)	CC(CC)
4		CC(ID)	CC(ID)	CC(CC)
5*	CC(CC)	CC(CC)	CC(ID)	ID(CC)
6	CC(CC)	CC(CC)	CC(ID)	CC(ID)
7	CC(CC)	CC(CC)	CC(CC)	CC(CC)
8	ID(ID)	ID(ID)	ID(ID)	ID(ID)
9	(CC)	CC(ID)	CC(CC)	CS(CS)
10*	ID(ID)	CS	(ID)	CC(ID)
11*	CS(CS)	CS(CS)	ID(ID)	ID(ID)
12*	CC(CC)	CS(CS)	CS(CS)	CC(CC)
Low Susceptibility				
1	(ID)	CC(CC)	(ID)	CC(CC)
2				CC(CC)
3	CC(CC)	CC(CC)	CC(CC)	CC(CC)
4	CC	CC(CC)	CC(CC)	CC(CC)
5	CC	CC(CC)	CC(CC)	CC(CC)
6	CC(CC)	CC(CC)	CC(CC)	CC(CC)
7	CC(CC)	CC(CC)	CC(CC)	CC(CC)
8	CC(CC)	CC(CC)	CC(CC)	CC(CC)
9	CC(CC)	CC(CC)	CC(CC)	CC(CC)
10	CC(CC)	CC(CC)	CC(CC)	CC(CC)
11		CC(CC)		CC(CC)
12	ID(ID)	ID(ID)	ID	

Note. CC = concentrative, ID = independent, and CS = constructive style of cognizing.
Ratings of second rater appear in parentheses. Raters agreed in 85.90% of cases.
*Variability in style of cognition evident across items.

orange chair right beside the white chair [which the hypnotist had said to see as orange]." Another subject who displayed constructive cognizing initially visualized the suggested hallucination on her hand prior to transferring it to the appropriate place: "I started to visualize it on my hand and then moved it across [to the chair]."

Subjects who displayed a concentrative mode of cognizing sometimes reported a degree of nonconscious involvement or involuntariness in their experience; the experience of involuntariness was not at all specific to a particular cognitive mode. For instance such subjects reported: "It felt like I had no control, I just had to wait to see what my hand would do''; ''As soon as he said that, my fingers started twitching''; and ''I knew my hand shouldn't be going down, but it just kept pulling and pulling, and I couldn't do anything, I didn't have the power to stop it.'' Similarly, on the mosquito-hallucination item one subject commented: ''When he said that it was on my hand, all of a sudden it was down there''; and on the dream item: ''I felt vaguely helpless, I didn't want to dream, and [the hypnotist] seemed to be making me.''

Across these comments it appears that some subjects obviously feel that they are not in control of their experiences; notably, this type of response was associated with different modes of cognizing. But individuation, rather than involuntariness, appears to be tied to the constructive and independent modes of thinking; there was substantial evidence of individuation among high, rather than low, subjects tested in the study. One subject, for instance, in commenting on the dream said: ''I wanted not to wake up yet, because it was just getting interesting, so I sort of stretched and yawned. I wanted to tell (the hypnotist) to wait, that I hadn't finished.'' On the mosquito-hallucination item, another subject displayed a high degree of initiative in order to experience the effect: ''I had a twitch in my left arm so I transferred it to my right arm and then moved it down to my right hand [to experience the suggested mosquito].'' Clearly, the experience of this subject is vivid, but it differed in an important qualitative way from the response of other subjects, which was based in an apparent involuntary occurrence of the suggested effect.

With respect to the hallucination for an orange chair (which was actually white), another subject indicated: ''I psyched myself into thinking I'd see what I wanted to see [a blue chair] and not what [the hypnotist] wanted me to see.'' Another subject reported: ''I could picture an orange chair right beside [the white one] and I could see that that chair wasn't orange; I was comparing mine and that [white] one.'' This subject clearly incorporated reality and suggested aspects into her experience as well as responded to the hypnotist's hallucination instruction in quite individual fashion. The degree to which subjects constructively cognize about suggested hypnotic effects and the way in which they then attribute responsibility for their experience is clearly an important area for research.

Reliability of Ratings of EAT Data

Up to this point, we have considered the procedures for the standard application of the EAT in the laboratory setting as well as some of the substantive data yielded by the method that illustrate the essential variability of hypnotic subjects' reactions. Findings have indicated that application of the EAT can provide novel information on dimensions that appear relevant to our understanding of the hypnotic experiences of susceptible subjects. In this section, we consider data relating to the reliability of ratings that can be made on the data gathered by application of the EAT. Here, we specifically examined ratings made on the EAT data from 44 highly susceptible subjects on the hypnotic items of dream, finger lock, and hallucination. Two independent raters scored the data in terms of the dimensions of concentrative cognitive style, independent cognitive style, constructive cognitive style, individuation, imagery vividness, absorption, involuntariness, awareness of reality information, physical sensation, and rapport. Each of these dimensions was rated on a 5-point scale (0 = not present; 1 = slightly present; 2 = moderately present; 3 = substantially present; 4 = extremely present). The two raters scored all subjects on each of the test items for these dimensions, and one rater also rescored the records of 10 subjects in order to index intrarater reliability. Table 3.5 presents the inter- and intrarater reliability coefficients for the dimensions that were studied on the three items. Inspection of these data clearly indicated a high degree of reliability on the various dimensions that were considered.

Data on the reliability of ratings of EAT data were also provided by Bell (1978) who examined the performance of high and low susceptible subjects on the dimensions of trance, nonconscious involvement, rapport, and individuation. These dimensions were rated independently by two experimenters on a 5-point scale (1 = no amount; 2 = less than slight amount; 3 = slight amount; 4 = moderate amount; 5 = extensive amount of dimension). Ratings in this instance were conducted across four hypnotic items (hand lowering, mosquito hallucination, dream, and hallucination). In order to get session scores for each subject, the individual item scores for each of the dimensions were summed to provide a

TABLE 3.5

Inter- and Intra-Rater Reliability Coefficients for a Range of
Cognitive, Physical, and Interpersonal Dimensions on the
Dream, Finger Lock and Hallucination Items Using EAT Data

| | Reliability Coefficients | | | | | |
| | Inter-rater | | | Intra-rater | | |
Dimensions	Dream	Finger lock	Hallucination	Dream	Finger lock	Hallucination
Concentrative style	.12	.00	.79	.00	00	.94**
Independent style	.67**	.00	.95**	1.00**	.00	.00
Constructive style	.01	.73**	.83**	.00	.80**	.64*
Individuation	.88**	.68**	.71**	.96**	.97**	.95**
Imagery	.92**	.85**	.84**	1.00**	.87**	.95**
Absorption	.83**	.69**	.61**	.90**	.85**	.95**
Involuntariness	.81**	.44**	.70**	1.00**	.85**	.93**
Reality awareness	.86**	.44**	.76**	.77**	.00	.46
Physical sensation	.46**	.70**	.00	.67**	.74**	.00
Rapport	.81**	.96**	.80**	.93**	.00	1.00**

*p < .05
**p < .01

total. Table 3.6 sets out the interrater reliability coefficients for the total scores on each of the dimensions for high and low susceptible subjects. Data demonstrated an appreciable level of agreement between the two raters on the three dimensions.

Overall, these data indicate that the material gathered through the application of the EAT can be reliably scored in terms of dimensions relevant to hypnosis. We now consider data relating to the validity of the technique. Specifically, we contrast information yielded by application of the EAT with that yielded through a routine inquiry.

TABLE 3.6
Inter-Rater Reliability Coefficients for the Trance,
Nonconscious Involvement, Rapport, and Individuation
Dimensions for High and Low Susceptible Subjects on
Data Gathered by EAT

Subject Grouping and Dimension	Reliability Coefficient
High Susceptible	
Trance	.85**
Nonconscious involvement	.89**
Rapport	.95**
Individuation	.62**
Low Susceptible	
Trance	.70**
Nonconscious involvement	.80**
Rapport	.94**
Individuation	.35*

$*p < .05$
$**p < .01$

EAT Versus Postexperimental Inquiry Information

We have argued that inquiry into the hypnotic experiences of subjects is of critical importance for an accurate and meaningful assessment of hypnotic phenomena and process. The validity of any method of inquiry, however, is central to the question of the nature and the degree of information that may be obtained from its use. Bell (1978) constructed a postexperimental inquiry (PEI) that was designed to parallel the type of questioning used in the EAT as far as possible without violating the usual format of a routine postexperimental inquiry. Four dimensions were considered (trance, nonconscious involvement, rapport, and individuation) across four hypnotic items (hand lowering, mosquito hallucination, dream, and hallucination), and this produced a possible set of 16 ratable responses for each subject. The question was whether the EAT (or the PEI)

TABLE 3.7
Mean Number of Rateable Responses on Data Gathered by
Application of the EAT or PEI with High and Low
Susceptible Subjects

Subject Grouping and Inquiry Method	Ratable Responses
High Susceptible	
EAT	9.67
PEI	5.75
Low Susceptible	
EAT	9.83
PEI	5.42

Note. Maximum number of ratable responses = 16.

would provide more data for consideration (i.e., more ratable responses). Table 3.7 presents the mean number of ratable responses for the high and low susceptible subjects given in relation to the inquiry methods. Analysis indicated that the EAT provided appreciably more ratable information. But whereas high and low susceptible subjects provided similar amounts of ratable information on the EAT, there was a substantial difference in the type of information provided. Significantly more ratings could be made on the data gathered by the EAT. Thus, the findings indicated that the EAT is substantially superior to the PEI in terms of providing information about the subjective events of hypnosis. Evidence also shows that the PEI is not an altogether reliable technique for eliciting detailed information about hypnotic experience.

Table 3.8 illustrates this point by presenting the interrater reliability coefficients for data gathered by the PEI. Collectively, the evidence demonstrates that the EAT provides a more satisfactory data base for the reliable rating (see Table 3.6) of dimensions relevant to a fuller understanding of hypnotic process and function. This is not to negate the value of the PEI for what it was best designed to do, but we suggest that the EAT is a more sensitive and stable assessment procedure for isolating detailed and idiosyncratic aspects of hypnotic subjects' trance experiences.

This question of the idiosyncrasy of the subject is important because it expresses the distinctiveness of subjects' experience in suggested events. Hypnotic subjects clearly manifest their responsiveness in diverse and qualitatively different ways that frequently interact with the nature of the task that is attempted. The EAT presents itself as a reliably scored technique of inquiry that explores in depth the task-aptitude specificity of susceptible subjects' hypnotic responsiveness. In so doing, it reveals some of the hitherto undetected subtleties of hypnotic phenomena and the complexity of the consciousness that those phenomena reflect.

We now consider a range of phenomena illustrated by the EAT. As in the

TABLE 3.8
Inter-Rater Reliability Coefficients for the Trance, Nonconscious
Involvement, Rapport, and Individuation Dimensions for High
and Low Susceptible Subjects on Data Gathered by PEI

Subject Grouping and Dimension	Reliability Coefficient
High Susceptible	
Trance	.28
Nonconscious involvement	.53*
Rapport	.30
Individuation	.32
Low Susceptible	
Trance	.34
Nonconscious involvement	.31
Rapport	.32
Individuation	-.19

*$p < .05$
Note. For corresponding analysis of EAT data, see Table 3.6.

present chapter, emphasis is placed on aspects of hypnotic consciousness that reveal process as well as function. We consider five sets of phenomena in turn. The first four (see Chapters 4, 5, 6, and 7) are phenomena that are placed at different points in scales of hypnotic responsiveness (see Chapter 2). The other set discusses a phenomenon (see Chapter 8) not normally categorized in terms of standard measures of responsiveness, but one that illustrates the need to evaluate the effects of suggestion in terms of the perceived meaning of the suggestions that are administered.

4 Ideomotor Response in Hypnosis

INTRODUCTION

The notion that thinking about a movement tends to produce that movement forms the explanatory basis for much of the behavior that is observed in response to hypnotic suggestions. This general notion has a long history in psychology that is best characterized by James' (1890) classic statement that: "every representation of a movement awakens in some degree the actual movement which is its object [p. 526]." This principle of ideomotor action is clearly relevant to many suggested events of hypnosis such as eye closure, arm levitation, and arm lowering, which are among the most widely known, easily experienced, and frequently demonstrated hypnotic phenomena. In fact, most individuals can experience the hypnotic phenomena that are based on ideomotor responding.

The majority of hypnotic induction procedures (see Weitzenhoffer, 1957, for a review) are based on ideomotor suggestions, hence consideration of this type of response is central to our understanding of hypnosis. In research inductions, for example, closing of the eyes following the suggestion that they are getting heavy forms the basis of many of the measures of susceptibility that we considered in Chapter 2 and is commonly taken as a sign that the subject is entering hypnosis. Similarly, in clinical inductions, ideomotor suggestions such as arm levitation are often employed because it is relatively easy for the client to experience the suggestion. In addition, the type of response that is made can frequently give the hypnotist information about the nature of the responses to be expected when more difficult hypnotic instructions are administered. Following the hypnotic induction procedure, the first items that are commonly administered to subjects or clients involve ideomotor responding. Virtually all of the scales that we considered in Chapter 2, for example, initially ask subjects to display some motor movement of their hands and arms and score hypnotic response in terms of the degree of movement that is observed. In fact, some scales focus just on ideomotor responding to obtain an assessment of hypnotizability (e.g., HIP, SHALIT, see Chapter 2).

It is important to note that when discussing ideomotor response, the cues of the hypnotic context clearly require the subjects to experience their motor response without any conscious effort on their part. For example, when given a suggestion for arm levitation, those subjects who purposefully lift their arms are not considered to have displayed a genuine hypnotic response; only those persons who feel that their arm rose as if by itself are considered to have shown true hypnotic responsiveness. This feeling of nonvolitional responding is regarded as a central aspect of the classic suggestion effect of hypnosis, and data have indicated that most subjects who pass the test items of standard measures of hypnotic susceptibility do report that those experiences seemed to occur with very little effort on their part (see Bowers, 1981).

Although much of the theoretical discussion concerning the meaning of hypnosis has focused on the complex hypnotic phenomena of amnesia and analgesia (these phenomena are correctly considered to be indicative of deep hypnosis), it needs to be acknowledged that many of the processes underlying these and other hypnotic phenomena, such as age regression (see Chapter 5) and dreams and hallucinations (see Chapter 6), may be better understood if we can identify and understand the internal processes that affect the simpler ideomotor responses. Our argument here is that important and meaningful information about process can be obtained through a careful analysis of even simple hypnotic phenomena, and to that end this chapter presents a brief analysis of induction procedures and simple motor effects in hypnosis. Specifically, we consider some of the processes that may underlie ideomotor (as well as the more complex cognitive) phenomena that occur in hypnosis and examine data yielded by the application of the EAT to investigate hypnotic induction and ideomotor response.

INDUCTION AND IDEOMOTOR RESPONSE: A CASE ILLUSTRATION

In order to capture more fully the flavor of the procedures routinely associated with a hypnotic induction and the testing of a simple ideomotor suggestion, we first present the transcript of a brief hypnotic test. In this test, the hypnotist (PWS) administered a routine hypnotic induction to a highly responsive female subject, then presented her with a standard hypnotic suggestion for the ideomotor response of hand lowering, and finally awakened her. The transcript illustrates the quite routine procedures that facilitate the phenomena of induction and ideomotor response. The case we present, however, also provides the necessary background for our consideration of the evidence that is available on ideomotor response and the processes that are implicated by the phenomenon.

Hypnotic Induction

H: I want you to relax comfortably in the chair there and to try and put outside your mind anything other than what I say and what I draw your attention to. I want you to concentrate on the feelings of relaxation you have in your body. Try to relax and experience just the things I ask you to experience and just the things I tell you to notice.

I want you to look at these keys, you've seen them before. I want you to look closely at them and I'm going to count from 1 to 10. You've seen these keys before and as I count just keep looking intently at them and your eyes will become tireder. Looking intently now and concentrating just on what I tell you and what I draw your attention to, 1, 2, more and more relaxed now. As you go on looking at these keys, 3, you've seen them before, 4, more and more relaxed, concentrating on what I draw your attention to, relaxing more now, 5, more and more relaxed as you sink into these feelings of relaxation. Your eyes becoming so tired, they'll close of themselves, 6, 7, 8, your eyes are becoming heavier now as the feelings of relaxation increase, just let them close when they're ready. Eyes closed now, eyes closed, more and more relaxed, slipping deeper and deeper now into this comfortable, pleasant state of relaxation. When I reach 10 you'll be completely hypnotized, 9, 10, deeper and deeper now, concentrating on all the feelings of relaxation. But you can become even more hypnotized than you are now.

I want you to imagine yourself on a ladder, stepping down the ladder, and as you step down the ladder, you'll step deeper and deeper, into this state of deep relaxation and deep hypnosis, 1, stepping down now, deeper and deeper, 2, deeper and deeper now, more and more relaxed, further and further relaxed, you're stepping down. As you listen to me and what I say, and you notice the things I draw your attention to, 3, 4, stepping down now, 5. You've reached the bottom now, deeply relaxed, deeply hypnotized.

Testing of Ideomotor Response

H: I want you to hold your right arm and hand up. Just keep it there and notice all the sensations that are going on in your right arm and hand. I want you to think of yourself holding something heavy in your hand and once you think about it, your hand becomes heavier and heavier, heavier, heavier, and heavier. As you think about that heavy object, it begins to pull your arm down, down, heavier and heavier, getting quite heavy now. Your whole arm heavier and heavier. The object is pulling it down, further and further down, moving down now, heavier and heavier, heavier and heavier. That's fine now, just rest your arm comfortably back on your lap. Your arm and hand are no longer heavy, no longer holding that heavy object. Your arm and hand, right back to normal, restful and relaxed.

Awakening

H: I am going to wake you up now and take you right back up the ladder and when you get to the top of the ladder, you'll be wide awake, refreshed, and alert. But before I do I want you to have a look at these keys. Do you see them? Whenever you see those keys you'll fall very quickly and easily into the state of hypnosis that you're in now. Waking up now. Stepping up the ladder, 1, waking up, 2, 3, almost to the top, 4, 5. Wide awake now, alert and refreshed. Wide awake now. How do you feel?

S: Okay.

Comment on the Session

In this hypnotic testing, the subject responded behaviorally as expected. In line with her high level of hypnotic ability, she responded quickly to the induction procedure by rapidly closing her eyes and becoming comfortably settled in the chair. In response to the ideomotor suggestion, she held her right arm and hand out and lowered them following the hypnotist's instructions regarding arm heaviness. Finally, during the awakening procedure, the subject easily opened her eyes and after the count of 5 indicated that she felt fine. Behaviorally, the session progressed in quite standard fashion. Application of the EAT to this session, though, revealed subtle shades and movements in the experience of the subject that were not apparent at all from observation of the subject's hypnotic behavior. But before examining the data yielded by this application of the EAT, we consider some of the evidence that bears on the phenomenon of ideomotor response that the foregoing set of procedures illustrates and the processes that may underlie it.

IDEOMOTOR RESPONSE:
PHENOMENON AND PROCESS

Normative and factorial analyses of standard scales of hypnotic susceptibility (e.g., E. R. Hilgard, 1965; McConkey, Sheehan, & Law, 1980; Sheehan & McConkey, 1979) have indicated that ideomotor suggestions are the easiest items to experience and also form the most stable factorial dimension of hypnotic performance. This central role of ideomotor response in hypnotic testing has led theorists such as Barber (1972) to argue essentially that all hypnotic events, whether or not they involve motor action, are based on the notion that thinking with suggestions and imagining things to be happening lead to the behavior and reported experience that is traditionally labled as hypnosis.

Interestingly, this argument is perhaps most obviously demonstrated with a suggested event that is nonhypnotic in character. This nonhypnotic ideomotor reaction is the Chevreul pendulum illusion (see Easton & Shor, 1975, 1976 for an experimental analysis of this phenomenon), which is a kinesthetic illusion whereby a subject suspends a pendulum from his or her finger tips and concentrates on it moving in a suggested direction. The subject's imaginings of movement cause minute movement in the finger tips, and these movements are amplified by the pendulum thereby causing a substantial amount of movement in the pendulum itself. The general ideomotor principle is powerfully illustrated in this example and translates to more hypnoticlike phenomena (e.g., arm levitation). In the situation of suggested arm levitation, the subject concentrates on the idea of his or her arm rising and floating in the air. This imagining generally leads to the arm rising in the air without the subject experiencing upward movement that requires any deliberate lifting effort. This principle of ideomotor action applies to a range of induction procedures and simple tests of hypnotic responsiveness.

In order to define more fully the nature of the phenomenon of ideomotor response and to pave the way for our discussion of phenomena more indicative of deep hypnosis (see Chapters 5–7), we turn now to discuss some of the internal variables that may mediate the behavioral response and reported experience of the hypnotized individual. Specification of process in this way not only helps to define more clearly what really happens in ideomotor response but also makes us aware of the range of processes that can underlie both simple and complex hypnotic performance.

Internal Mediating Processes

A wide range of internal processes has been implicated in the literature as being highly relevant to understanding both the nature of hypnotic response and the variables that affect it. Although we present our discussion of these processes in the context of ideomotor response in hypnosis, it is important to appreciate that the processes can be easily generalized to the other phenomena considered in this book (see Chapters 5–8 for their relevance). Specifically, the variables that we outline here concern the relevance of imagination processes, the use of imaginative strategies such as goal-directed fantasy, the role of absorption and imaginative involvement, and the attribution by subjects of involuntariness or effortlessness underlying their hypnotic behavior. There are others, but these reflect the major patterns of consistency in the data that are reported in the literature.

Imagination.   Particular appeal has been placed on the processes of imagination ever since the Benjamin Franklin Commission of 1784 decided that the apparent impact of animal magnetism could be explained in terms of the influence of imagination. This emphasis on imagination can be seen in a wide range of present-day formulations of hypnosis (e.g., Arnold, 1946; Barber, 1972; J. R. Hilgard, 1970, 1974a; Sutcliffe, Perry, & Sheehan, 1970). Modern investigators routinely assert the relevance of imagination to the manifestations of hypnotic phenomena and generally agree that imagination is one of the most important ongoing internal processes of the hypnotized individual (see E. R. Hilgard, 1975; Sheehan & Perry, 1976; Spanos & Barber, 1974 for a discussion of the convergence of current research on the role of imagination in hypnosis). Across a range of measures of imagination performance it seems apparent that response to hypnotic test tasks is positively related to subjects' capacities to employ imagery and involve themselves in the imagined events, although the theoretical relevance of this observation may be difficult to specify with any high degree of precision (Sheehan, 1979b), and the relationship is only moderate in strength.

Some theorists (e.g., Barber, 1972; J. R. Hilgard, 1970, 1974a) have focused on the contribution of imagination to hypnotic performance more explicitly than others. In emphasizing imagination as an internal process that is central to the hypnotic experience, Barber (1972) characterized a subject's hypnotic experience in much the same way as one might characterize the experience of a member of an audience who is responding to the communications of an actor in a movie or play. From a quite different theoretical perspective, Shor (1970) also emphasized the relevance of imagination processes by drawing an association between engagement in hypnotic involvement and book-reading fantasy—as some individuals come to experience the emotions of a character in a book, so do they come to experience the events communicated to them by the hypnotist.

Theoretically speaking, Barber is most explicit about the role imagination processes have to play. For example, Barber (1972; Barber, Spanos, & Chaves, 1974) cites thinking and imagining with the suggestions or involvement in suggestion-related imaginings as the principal mediating construct for explaining responsiveness to suggestions given in the test situation and has developed an imagination scale as a major means of measuring susceptibility (see Chapter 2 for comment on the development of the CIS). It is argued that subjects experience test suggestion by actively elaborating their imaginings so as to be consistent with suggestions while simultaneously failing to attend to contradictory information (see Chapter 6, though, for a discussion of the degree to which contradictory information impinges on subjects). Overall, then, imagination is regarded as a basic process for understanding hypnotic response. Broad review of the empirical findings that justify this association is provided elsewhere (Sheehan, 1979b), but a number of imagination-related processes deserve specific mention. Examples of these are goal-directed fantasy and experienced absorption because they represent the foci of extensive research programs.

Goal-Directed Fantasy. Empirical work by Spanos (1971; Spanos & Barber, 1972; Spanos & McPeake, 1974; Spanos, Rivers, & Ross, 1977; Spanos, Spillane, & McPeake, 1976) has demonstrated that a particular kind of directed imagining is relevant to some hypnotic experiences, most obviously those involving motor responses. This directed imagining or goal-directed fantasy involves imagining a situation that, if it occurred in reality, would tend to produce the suggested behavior. The relevance of this type of process is most easily seen in ideomotor responsiveness where, for instance, subjects can be considered to employ a goal-directed fantasy if they report such events as imagining a heavy object in their hand as a way of facilitating the experience of arm heaviness. Although it is an interesting construct, analysis of directed imaginings has failed to find any consistent relationship between goal-directed fantasy and positive reaction to hypnotic test suggestions (Spanos et al., 1977). Nevertheless, it has been correctly noted that differential responsiveness to some hypnotic items may be based on the fact that the wording of hypnotic suggestions differs widely in the extent to which it provides subjects with specific strategies for imagining (Barber et al., 1974; Spanos & Barber, 1974). Most of the ideomotor instructions in the standard test scales considered in Chapter 2, for example, explicitly ask subjects to employ directed imaginings; however, many cognitive items such as age regression (see Chapter 5), hallucination (see Chapter 6), and amnesia (see Chapter 7) frequently do not. Further, comparisons of the efficacy of similar suggestions when they either do or do not ask subjects to employ goal-directed imaginings have not indicated any enhancement of response when goal-directed imaginings are requested (Spanos et al., 1976). This finding provocatively points to the fact that some subjects will construct their own imaginative strategies rather than simply adopt those provided by the hypnotist. It also reinforces the general point we would wish to make (see also Spanos & McPeake, 1977) that what people do and the instructions you give them can be quite distinct.

It is important to note that goal-directed fantasy is both similar to and different from the style of cognizing that we have labeled constructive (see Chapter 3 for a fuller discussion of this mode of cognition). Similarities lie in the subjects' structured use of their imaginative capacity, and important differences can be seen in the degree to which the directed imaginings are initiated by the subjects themselves. Goal-directed fantasy, on the one hand, essentially stems from the specific instructions of the test suggestion and is mainly confined to simple motor suggestions of the sort that we have discussed and illustrated in this chapter. Constructive cognizing, on the other hand, stems from the subject's motivated cognitive involvement in the events of testing and may involve quite idiosyncratic strategies for responding that are not obviously tied to the instructions given by the hypnotist. Further, the use of constructive strategies is probably most evident in response to demanding cognitive suggestions such as hypnotic dreams and hallucinations (see Chapter 6) rather than in response to other types of hypnotic test items such as those that we review in this chapter, which are relatively easy to perform. Our data would suggest that the subject employing a constructive mode of cognitive response is also highly involved in the experience. One possible dimension of that involvement is the degree to which the subject is imaginatively absorbed in the experience, and we now consider the relevance of this type of involvement in more detail.

Absorption.   Intrinsic to the cognitive orientation that we adopt throughout this book is an emphasis on the particular skills that subjects may bring to the hypnotic test situation, and one of these skills that has been consistently associated with hypnotic response is the capacity for absorption. Tellegen and Atkinson (1974) initially delineated absorption as a significant (but less than perfect) correlate of hypnotic ability and specified the essential components of the capacity in terms of internal processes in interaction (for further discussion of this point see Chapter 10). In particular, the trait of absorption explicitly recognizes both cognitive and motivational components that appear to define an ability on the part of the subject that is consistent with the skills needed to interpret and construct actively in imagination the experiences that are suggested by the hypnotist. Tellegen and Atkinson (1974) interpret the cognitive aspect of their absorption variable as one of total attention involving a: "full commitment of available perceptual, motoric, imaginative, and ideational resources to a unified representation of the attentional object [so that it] is experienced as present and real [p. 274]." The motivational component of the trait is considered to be one of devotion-trust, which Tellegen and Atkinson (1974) define as: "a desire and readiness for object relationships temporary or lasting, that permit experiences of deep involvement [p. 275]." The emphasis is clearly on spontaneously generated imaginative experience rather than on compliance with instruction to generate specific imagery. In this sense, the trait of absorption seems more closely allied to the constructive or independent modes of cognition rather than to the concentrative-cooperative style of cognition that we reviewed in the previous chapter.

The work of J. R. Hilgard (1970, 1974a, 1979) has highlighted, in particular, the role that imaginative and sensory-affective involvements may play in both the hypnotic performance and the everyday life of individuals who have a high level of hypnotic ability. In fact, she uses the processes of absorption to explain individual differences in hypnotic responsiveness in terms of subject differences in capacity for imaginative involvement. From structured interviews conducted outside hypnosis, she found (J. R. Hilgard, 1970, 1974a) that responsive individuals are especially capable of carrying out a pattern of fantasy that is initiated by some external source (e.g., the words of a book) and can become totally immersed in their imaginative productions to the extent that reality is temporarily set aside. Just as these patterns of fantasy appear to occur without any conscious effort during the person's everyday life, their occurrence during hypnosis is also linked with a quality of nonvolition. We now briefly consider the relevance of this particular process to understanding hypnotic events.

Experienced Involuntariness.   When reporting on their hypnotic experiences, subjects often report that the suggested events occurred in seemingly automatic, involuntary fashion and that they, themselves, had little to do with initiating or controlling the experience. This apparent effortlessness or involuntariness has been traditionally associated with hypnotic response and is a highly relevant variable to explore in relation to the phenomena and processes of deep hypnosis (see K. S. Bowers, 1981; P. Bowers, 1978; Spanos et al., 1977 for recent work on this topic). Relevant to this exploration are the recent analyses by Spanos and his associates of the cognitive strategies that are employed by subjects when they are faced with difficult hypnotic tasks such as analgesia (see Spanos, 1981; Spanos, Radtke-Bodorik, Ferguson, & Jones, 1979). As Spanos (1981) points out, hypnotic subjects typically define an experience such as arm lowering not as something they did but rather as something that happened to them, and in this regard a clear distinction needs to be made between the processes underlying a subject's response to a hypnotic suggestion and the factors that determine how that subject accounts for his or her behavior; that is, the processes of response need to be conceptually and empirically separated from the attributions of the behavior that is being demonstrated.

In this regard, empirical analysis to date has indicated that subjects who employ directed imaginings are more likely to report their hypnotic experience as occurring involuntarily than are subjects who do not employ such imaginings (Spanos et al., 1976; Spanos et al., 1977). In addition, the degree of absorption that subjects report having in a hypnotic experience is positively related to the degree to which subjects attribute their behavior as occurring without effort (Spanos & McPeake, 1974). However, much more work is needed before it becomes clear how we can separate the differences between actual process variables and attributional variables in accounting for the apparent effortless way that hypnotic subjects respond. We would argue that the EAT procedure is a useful method to adopt for conducting investigations into the processes that underlie hypnotic response. Specifically, our analyses to date have highlighted the role of active and appropriate cognizing rather than automaticity in forming the basis of hypnotic responding (see Chapters 5–8 for the presentation of data and Chapter 10 for a fuller discussion of this point).

In summary, we have seen that the ideomotor response is a central component of many of the routine scales of hypnotic responsiveness, and a variety of the internal processes traditionally associated with hypnosis (e.g., imaginative involvement and experienced involuntariness) are easily identified when considering ideomotor responsiveness. Subjects involve themselves in some form of imaginative strategy or ideation in order to promote a motor response and, although the literature assumes that there is a high level of similarity across individuals in terms of the processes that are responsible for such reactions, there are few data on this issue. Research is clearly needed to scrutinize closely the cognitive processes that are associated with ideomotor responding, and it is impossible to account for them without some appeal to the influence of internal, subjective processes of the hypnotized person. The EAT elicits in-depth comments from subjects about their experiences of hypnotic phenomena, and we now consider its specific application to analysis of the induction and ideomotor response that occurred in the hypnotic session presented earlier in this chapter.

EVIDENCE FROM EAT ANALYSIS

As we detailed in Chapter 3, the EAT is a method of inquiry that is attuned to the subtleties and complexities of subjects' experiences. It is based firmly on the theoretical assumption that the subjective events of hypnosis are the hallmark of the hypnotic experience. In its application, the technique acknowledges the interaction among motives, expectancies, cognitions, and need states, which occurs for persons in the hypnotic context. The EAT aims to place minimal constraints on subjects by virtue of task demands and direct cueing as to what they should report about their personal experience.

We consider the use of the EAT in its usual format of video-tape playback following a hypnotic session in the experimental setting (see Chapter 9 for other modifications of the technique), and we present the EAT transcript of the subject whose hypnotic session was discussed earlier in our case analysis. The subject interacts with an inquirer while watching her induction and ideomotor performance on a video-tape playback of the hypnotic test session. The inquirer (I) initially presents routine instructions for the use of the EAT and then discusses with the subject (S) her experiences of the hypnotic induction and testing of the ideomotor response as she recalls them via the video-tape playback. The interaction between the inquirer and the subject is crucial to the application of the technique, and it is important to note that the inquirer probes the subject's comments in a relatively unstructured fashion that minimally cues as well as encourages her to comment further about her experiences in hypnosis.

Introduction

I: As [the hypnotist] told you at the beginning of the session, the hypnosis testing you have just completed has been video-tape recorded. We've kept that video tape, and what we want to do now is play it back for you and gather feedback on how you see it, your perceptions about it all, and what you think is happening and going on. One of the reasons for providing the video is that initially, when you were going through the hypnosis session, you probably had lots of thoughts and feelings about what was going on, but you didn't get a chance to talk about them. Also, there may have been some vague feelings that you had; you will have a chance to talk about them. When you see the video, these thoughts, feelings, and impressions, whatever they may be, will come back to you again because you are looking at a mirror image of what went on—an exact replica of what happened before.

I want you to feel completely free to stop the video at any point where you are recalling something. Talk to me about it, no matter how big or how small the matter may be. Whether you think the matter is important or not, feel completely free just to stop the tape at any time and comment. I may ask you some questions, and we might discuss it, or whatever. Does that make sense to you?

S: Yes, that sounds fine.

Playback of Hypnotic Induction

Stop 1

S: [Stops tape where hypnotist attempts to induce hypnosis by showing the subject his keys.] When he showed me those keys there, I thought, "No, this isn't possible; I couldn't possibly be hypnotized today, not with the lights on and looking at those keys." It just didn't mean anything. I thought, "No, this isn't going to work."

I: So initially, your impression was this just isn't going to be a goer here.

S: That's right.

I: Is there something you would have liked to have said to the hypnotist at that point?

S: Probably not. I just felt like laughing inside; I thought the whole thing was rather funny. I just thought, "This isn't going to work with all these lights and stuff, you know."

I: Yes. It did work though.

S: Yes, in the end it did, I think. [Starts tape.]

I: Okay! Fine! Perhaps we can pick up from that point.

Stop 2

S: [Stops tape where hypnotist is nearing the end of counting from 1 to 10.] It was only at this point around 9, that I was, in fact, starting to feel relaxed. I couldn't before. Everything still felt kind of strange, you know.

I: Right! Is it usual for you to take that long?

S: No, I don't think so. I usually begin to feel some sort of relaxation, but I didn't this time. You know something happened about 9, though; I was surprised that my eyes did get heavy and they did close, and I felt I was relaxing, but it was coming rather slow, and it was only about 9 or 10 when it happened.

I: How did the fact that it was coming slow for you affect you?

S: It didn't! It didn't make any difference.

I: It didn't: Were you happy with that?

S: Yes.

I: Is there anything you would have liked to have said to the hypnotist [at that time]?

S: Just that I'm not really relaxed.

I: I'm not really relaxed.

S: Not yet.

I: "Not yet," "give me time," something like that.

S: Something like that.

I: Okay!

S: I felt that the test was coming up and I wasn't really as relaxed as I would have liked to have been, at that stage; but there was a feeling that it was coming.

I: Was the hypnotist aware of your thoughts and your feelings at this point?

S: I very much doubt it.

I: You very much doubt it. How do you think, then, you were coming across as a subject?

S: Maybe he thought I was relaxed, when in fact I wasn't.

I: So his impression of you was that you were quite relaxed and you were up with him, but what you're telling me is "no," you weren't. You would have liked more time.

S: Yes.

I: Did you expect that you would become more relaxed?

S: I could feel it. I could feel myself becoming more and more relaxed, and the 10 just seemed to come up rather quickly and I wasn't really there yet. [Starts tape.]

Stop 3

S: [Stops tape where the hypnotist attempted to deepen trance by taking the subject down a ladder.] This was terrible. This was dreadful, you know. I hate ladders, and I was terrified even to go on a ladder, and he said I was on a ladder stepping down. He had never done this before and I could feel myself tensing up with every step that he said I'd become more relaxed. I could feel myself getting tense.

I: You say you could see yourself very clearly on the ladder.

S: I was on the ladder. He put me there and I was there, and I couldn't. I really didn't want to be because I can't stand going up on ladders.

I: What could you have said to him?

S: "Don't! You know, I don't want to be; take me off. I don't want to be on the ladder."

I: What stopped you from saying that?

S: I don't know, I just, he put me there you know. He said you're going down and that's what I did.

I: Okay, just let me see if I've got this. He put you on the ladder. That was a very terrifying experience, extremely terrifying, and yet you never said anything to him because he wanted you to be there.

S: I wanted to say it, I think, but I, I didn't. I don't know why I didn't. I felt like making a movement or saying stop. I don't know whether I actually did, but as he took me down the ladder I felt myself getting very tense.

I: Getting tense as you went down.

S: Yes.

I: What happened when you hit the bottom?

S: I was so relieved. [Starts tape.]

Playback of Testing of Ideomotor Response

Stop 4

S: [Stops tape where the hypnotist told the subject that she was holding something heavy.] There was really no object in my hand. I couldn't imagine one and I couldn't feel one. My arm simply felt very heavy; every time he said it was heavy, it felt extremely heavy and stiff, stiff and heavy. But I wasn't holding an object.

I: How did that affect you? The fact that it was indicated that there ought to be some sort of object there and yet, you didn't have one?

S: I didn't have one.

I: It didn't, didn't affect you.

S: No.

I: I suppose in this instance I'm looking for something that is interesting for me. In this instance I hear the hypnotist saying look, some object and you don't take one. Yet, previously he says get on the ladder and you do.

S: That's right.

I: Have you any explanation for that?

S: My arm just felt heavy, so I suppose I just didn't need an object.

I: I see. Okay.

S: It was so heavy and stiff that I don't think I could have held an object even in my imagination. I think my arm would have needed to be somehow more flexible to have held an object.

I: All right. So, you were doing so well that you just didn't need that extra something.

S: Yes; maybe that was it.

I: Is that what you're saying?

S: Probably. It just felt very heavy and stiff and when he said, "Hold the object," I just thought, "Well, I don't think I can hold anything; my arm's just too heavy for that."

I: I see. So, it's not necessarily that you're doing really well; it's just that physically you just couldn't picture yourself holding an object because your arm was in such a state.

S: Yes. It was so stiff and heavy I couldn't hold anything.

I: Aha. Do you think the hypnotist was aware of your thoughts and feelings?

S: I don't think so.

I: Well, how do you think you were coming across to him: Have you any ideas?

S: No.

I: None. whatsoever? If you had to take a guess, how do you think you were doing?

S: He may have thought, "Well, my arm was obviously going down; I couldn't hold it up." So, he may have thought that my arm was heavy.

I: Aha. Good.

S: Okay? [Starts tape.]

Playback of Awakening

Stop 5

S: [Stops tape where the hypnotist begins to waken the subject by taking her up the ladder she initially came down.] See my breathing; I was all tensing up. It's terrible! I'm getting, I can even feel my heartbeat now. It, it was terrifying, and I didn't realize he was going to do the same thing and put me back on the ladder this time, going up, which is even worse.

I: Than coming down?

S: Than coming down. Oh, this terrified me. My heart was pounding.

I: It affects you physiologically just to see it.

S: I saw it there, and my heart started pounding because going up ladders is just something I just don't do.

I: But you did it. How come?

S: Yes, I know. It was terrifying. I thought I'd slip off.

I: How come?

S: I thought to myself, "Don't. Don't do it, don't put me on the ladder, don't, don't." He made me go up higher and higher and with every step. I could hear this voice crying out inside, "Don't, don't."

I: I'm fascinated by the fact that it was such a terrifying incident to put you through and yet you did it for him.

S: Well, he's, he's doing it. He's putting me there.

I: Okay. We can just perhaps end off with me just looking globally at what we've done. Were you satisfied with your behavior as you saw it on the video?

S: It amazed me a little, because all these emotions going on, and me crying out, "Don't do this. Don't do it." Yet I see myself sitting there calm, as if nothing was happening. I sort of, can't understand that in a way.

I: Okay. Because there is so much happening inside of you. And yet, what you get is to look at visually is . . .

S: Nothing! Just a blank; and I just sit there as if everything was fine and dandy, and it wasn't.

I: Okay, right. I stopped the tape there because we were just about at the end and I thought it might be interesting to ask you those few global questions. So perhaps we can leave it there.

Comment on the EAT Session

Our major aim has been to illustrate the rich phenomena that may be associated with even simple ideomotor reactions in the hypnotic setting and to highlight the complexity of consciousness that accompanies hypnotic behavior across the full range of phenomena that can be seen to occur in hypnosis. The use of the EAT for subjective inquiry in this case suggests the relevance of a number of important process features.

Although it would be misleading to imply that all behavioral indices of hypnosis oversimplify the reactions of hypnotic subjects, application of the EAT in this instance highlights the fact that the observation of behavioral response does not, in itself, fully reveal the complexity of hypnotic performance. As we argued in Chapter 2, a common aspect of traditional hypnotic assessment and research is a lack of interest or regard for the importance of examining the ways in which individual hypnotic subjects pattern their personal meanings of the suggestions that they are given. However, this orientation severely limits our understanding of underlying psychological processes. With the present case, for example, although the subject's behavioral performance was quite routine, application of the EAT illustrated highly personal reactions to the hypnotist and his communications.

In terms of the subject's reactions to the hypnotic induction procedure, the hypnotist utilized an induction technique that had the subject descend an imaginary ladder in order to achieve a deeper trance state. During this procedure, the subject neither reported nor displayed any overt signs of fear, but in the EAT session she related how her experience of this suggestion was quite anxiety arousing. In her conversation with the inquirer, when the video-tape playback came to where the hypnotist suggested the ladder, the subject reported that the experience was distinctly unpleasant, that she hated ladders, and that she was actually terrified. This idiosyncratic response of the subject highlights the fact that researchers need to recognize that active cognitive processing of induction suggestions readily occurs and that induction is not necessarily associated with passivity on the part of highly susceptible subjects. Consistent with this notion is the work of Banyai and Hilgard (1976) who found that an active and alert induction procedure (having subjects pedal a stationary bicycle) had an impact comparable to that achieved by routine hypnotic induction. In this instance, our subject reported in quite active fashion the use of constructive strategies in formulating the image of the ladder and also displayed a high degree of motivated cognitive commitment to the hypnotist and his communications. Specifically, the level of rapport that was engendered between the hypnotist and subject appeared sufficiently intense to enable the subject to lay aside her personal apprehension of ladders in order to meet the hypnotist's instructions to use an imaginary ladder as part of the induction.

In contrast to this, the subject did not employ an imaginary heavy object in order to facilitate the experience of arm lowering, even though the hypnotist suggested this directed imagining. In commenting on this apparent anomaly, the subject reported that her arm was simply too heavy for her to hold even an imaginary object in her hand. This idiosyncratic response indicates that in terms of the suggestion that was given the subject responded in quite literal fashion to the communication she received about heaviness and no direct imagining was employed to achieve the effect of holding the object in her hand. Looking across the subject's reports concerning her response to the induction and the ideomotor suggestion, it is apparent that there was a change in the type of cognitive style employed, which supports data presented elsewhere in this book (see especially Chapters 3 and 6) that the nature of hypnotic tasks interacts with the type of cognizing that subjects bring to bear on their solution.

In summary, these EAT-elicited data highlight the idiosyncrasy of response by subjects, the relevance of the level of rapport between hypnotist and subject, and the interaction of cognitive styles and hypnotic test tasks. Although none of these process features are normally associated with the simple phenomena of induction and ideomotor response, current data suggest that these important aspects of trance experiences can be isolated through a close analysis of subjects' experiences of ideomotor and induction phenomena.

The question arises, of course, as to whether comparable information about phenomena and process can be obtained from observation and analysis of the hypnotic behavior itself or whether further inquiry into subjects' experiences of the kind provided by the EAT is required. This question is one that directly addresses the utility of the EAT as a technique suited to gathering more information than can be gathered through direct observation of hypnotic testing. We now look at data collected on this issue before moving to consider the more cognitively demanding hypnotic phenomena such as age regression, hallucination, and amnesia in the chapters to follow.

Utility of the EAT

Throughout this book, we argue that there are many meaningful aspects of the hypnotic experience that neither researchers nor clinicians can know about through simply observing the behavior of their subjects or clients. In order to investigate the degree to which the EAT provided meaningful information about the subject we have been discussing—beyond what was yielded through inspection of her hypnotic behavior—Crebolder (1980) compared the information supplied by viewing the hypnotic session with the information supplied by viewing both the hypnotic session and the EAT session that followed it (the transcripts of both these sessions appear earlier in the chapter). Three groups of subjects were used as raters in the study. They consisted of a group of physicians and psychologists who were skilled in the clinical use of hypnosis, a group of advanced psychology students familiar with the concepts (but not the clinical use) of hypnosis, and a group of students who were unfamiliar with hypnosis. In the study, half of the raters viewed the video tape of the hypnotic testing, and the other half viewed the video tapes of the hypnotic testing and the EAT session. All raters were initially alerted to look for any peculiarities or signs of difficulty during hypnosis, and the instructions were specifically designed to motivate them to gather as much information concerning the hypnotized subject's behavior and experience as their skills and level of clinical knowledge would permit.

Following their instructions, the raters viewed the appropriate video tape and then completed a questionnaire that was constructed for the purpose of determining whether the application of the EAT provided accurate and clinically relevant information about the hypnotic events, was useful in terms of providing information about relevant process dimensions, or facilitated understanding of the overt hypnotic responses and their underlying covert determinants.

The findings of the study indicated that raters who viewed both the hypnotic and EAT sessions were markedly more efficient in identifying the difficulties related to the hypnotic testing, as well as the underlying psychological events that were involved, in comparison with those who saw only the hypnotic session. This was the case irrespective of the raters' level of knowledge about hypnosis or their clinical skills. Raters who viewed only the hypnotic session were unable to identify any signs of the fear experienced by the subject; in this regard, it is important to note that there was no restraint placed on the subject by the hypnotist to refrain from verbalizing her concerns or indicating in any way her feelings during hypnosis, and raters were alerted to look for "problems" in the session. The fact that a viewing of the hypnotic session yielded minimal clinical information about the experiences of the subject points to the potential diagnostic value of the EAT in terms of yielding relevant information about clinical problems or difficulties (see Chapter 9 for data relating to this issue and further discussion of this point).

In terms of the observers' ratings of the level of the subject's involvement, findings indicated that simple observation of the subject's hypnotic behavior suggested that she was not in a deep trance; however, the information provided by viewing the EAT session indicated in contrary fashion a high level of trance involvement. That is, for the case that we have analyzed, the information gathered from application of the EAT led to a quite different diagnosis of hypnotic involvement from the diagnosis that was based solely on observation of the events that occurred during the hypnotic session.

Overall, subjects who viewed both sessions were more aware of the subject's involvement and emotional state during hypnosis than those who viewed only the hypnotic session. The hypnotist's awareness of a hypnotized individual's emotional state is a particularly important factor when hypnosis is used clinically, and these results suggest that the EAT may be usefully adopted for clinical analysis (see Chapter 9 for some suggested modifications and adaptations of the technique for clinical purposes). In summary of Crebolder's (1980) data, then, the responses of raters shown the hypnotic and EAT displays were found to be more accurate than those shown only the hypnotic session. However, it needs to be acknowledged that because this study focused on only one case example, further research that incorporates similar procedures, but analyzes different hypnotic sessions, varying problems as experienced by subjects, and tests larger numbers of subjects is needed. Depending on the data that such research provides, researchers and clinicians may need to develop new techniques of inquiry in order to define hypnotic phenomena accurately in terms of the actual, rather than supposed, experiences of hypnotized individuals.

CONCLUSION

In this chapter, we have looked at some of the relevant evidence bearing on the nature and processes of ideomotor response in hypnosis. Behaviorally speaking, we saw that this type of hypnotic response forms the core dimension of many of the routine scales of hypnotic ability that we reviewed in Chapter 2. Importantly, however, our application of the EAT to a simple induction and ideomotor test session illustrated that the observation of behavior alone does not fully reveal the complexity of the phenomena that occur. Rather, it can be argued that observation of behavior often fails to detect the richness and variety of effects that characterize the performance of the hypnotized individual. We presented data showing that even clinicians with knowledge and experience in the use of hypnosis were no better than untrained students at specifying the problems experienced by the subject when observation was based simply on hypnotic behavior. But, application of the EAT allowed them to specify in far greater detail the level of involvement of the subject, as well as the particular problem that she had experienced during hypnosis.

We would argue, then, that the phenomenon of ideomotor response is not as easily defined or delineated as the literature would imply. Both interindividual and intraindividual differences occur in subjects' reactions to ideomotor suggestions, and investigators need to look more carefully at the multifaceted involvement of subjects in these type of hypnotic events. Processes of imagination, goal-directed fantasy, and absorption are clearly involved in ideomotor hypnotic phenomena. Processes of rapport are also associated with ideomotor responses, and not just with hypnotic responses such as age regression (see Chapter 5) and others that involve comparable reality distortion. The case illustration that we presented in this chapter highlighted the role of rapport features in determining the type of response that was shown. The level of involvement experienced by the subject obviously tended to override the problems associated with the hypnotist asking her to imaginatively experience an event that would normally be highly aversive to her and which she would not normally do. The role of rapport that we witnessed here strongly suggests that ideomotor responses do not necessarily involve a restricted range of underlying processes. Although the behavior itself is apparently quite simple, it is clincially inappropriate to assume that the processes influencing that behavior are necessarily limited.

Individuality of response at an experiential level is associated with the full range of hypnotic phenomena (see also Chapters 5–8), and we argue that the essential variability and complexity of hypnotic experience needs to be more obviously recognized in the assessment procedures that researchers and clinicians bring to bear in order to index the phenomena in which they are interested. It can be argued that both researchers and clinicians see in their empirical or clinical data what their biases dictate. By being highly selective about the data that they allow the hypnotized subject to provide, this state of affairs is likely to continue. On the other hand, although we recognize the need for directed inquiry (see Chapter 9 for a discussion and illustration), much of the approach that we present in this book is based on the notion that allowing subjects to speak for themselves in a relatively unstructured fashion will reveal much that is important about hypnotic phenomena and process.

By gathering more data on phenomena in this way, issues are raised that do not fit easily into preconceived notions about the meaning of hypnosis. These issues pose formidable challenges for further inquiry. In the present case, for instance, many more complexities in ideomotor responding were observed through the use of the EAT than could be classified on the basis of the subject's behavioral performance. Although some of these complexities may be difficult to accomodate into traditional views, their presence poses a potentially fruitful area for future investigation.

5 Age Regression and Tolerance of Incongruity in Hypnosis

INTRODUCTION

Age regression is typically regarded as a hypnotic task that is highly demanding of susceptible persons in terms of their skills, capacities, and involvement. The subject is routinely instructed by the hypnotist to return to some earlier age and is usually coaxed by the hypnotist, who creates an appropriate situation for the subject to display his or her imaginative talents. In the sense that the hypnotist returns the subject to the past, the phenomenon can be viewed as a special case of memory distortion (Orne & Hammer, 1974), although argument exists in the literature as to how much memory is, in fact, distorted and how much memories and past experiences are revived just as they actually occurred. To classify age regression simply in terms of memory, however, does little justice to the richness of ideation and experience that accompanies the phenomenon. Age regression is often associated with strong affect, especially as it occurs in the therapeutic setting, and may involve the subject or client in a wide range of hypnotic experiences (e.g., incorporating positive or negative hallucinations that are compatible with the suggested regression). LeCron (1948) argues that there may be temporary amnesia for present events, hypermnesia for past events, and possibly physiological changes as well.

Many different theories about the processes responsible for hypnotic age regression have been proposed. It has been viewed as a procedure for reinstating developmentally earlier modes of thinking or cognitive functioning (Reiff & Scheerer, 1959), as producing a partial revivification of past experience (Nash, Johnson, & Tipton, 1979), as a form of elaborate imaginative involvement (Barber et al., 1974), or as instancing a state of delusion in which the hypnotic subject comes to be convinced of the truth of what the hypnotist is asserting (Orne, 1974). Regardless of what theory one adopts (we examine these in more detail later), it is clear that age regression involves a substantial alteration of perceived reality and facilitates a profound subjective involvement on the subject's part in what is being suggested. It is misleading, as Barber (1962a) states, to ask whether hypnotic age regression is real or role-playing.

As we see when we examine the evidence relating to age regression, the phenomenon is not real in the sense that regressed behavior matches behavior at the age to which the subject is regressed, nor is it role-playing if that term in any way implies deception or sham performance. What the layperson means by "Is the individual really age regressed?" is "Does the individual think (or believe, as Orne, 1974, would claim) that he or she is actually 6-years old?" In an important sense, argument is not about the genuineness of age regression and the phenomena that define it, but about the most appropriate way of accounting for the distortions of memory and perception that the phenomenon illustrates, regardless of the accuracies or inaccuracies of the regressed subject's performance.

One of the most compelling reasons for arguing that age-regressed behavior is a genuine phenomenon comes from examining the incongruities or illogicalities of performance that occur when people are regressed to an age where the events and experiences that they are reporting could not possibly take place. Instances abound in the literature to illustrate this point. For instance, subjects are able to spell complicated words when hypnotically regressed to a time when such behavior would be impossible (Orne, 1951). Paradoxes of this kind illustrate the phenomenon of *trance logic* (Orne, 1959), which specifies a characteristic of hypnotic performance that is claimed to be an essential feature of hypnosis (E. R. Hilgard, 1965; Orne, 1959). Subjects whose behavior expresses this phenomenon appear capable of combining perceptions that stem from reality with logically contradictory ones that derive from the hypnotist's suggestions or instructions.

There is a variety of test situations that delineate trance logic; for example, hypnotic subjects may see two images of the same people—one real and one suggested—or may spontaneously report transparency of perception of a hallucinated stimulus. Its occurrence is actually pervasive throughout the domain of hypnosis. Binet (1905) captures the phenomenon in relation to suggested anesthesia, for instance, when he gives the example: "Let us put a key, a piece of coin, a needle, a watch into the anaesthetic hand, and let us ask the subject to think of any object whatsoever; it will happen . . . that the subject is thinking of the precise object that has been put into his insensible hand [p. 28]." It is age regression that provides the most dramatic citing of subjects' tolerance of incongruity, the regression context highlighting in a particularly vivid way the apparent paradox of subjects not recognizing the inconsistencies one may infer from their adult attempts to involve themselves imaginatively in past events.

We now offer three case illustrations of age-regressed behavior. In each case there is either evidence of trance logic or recognition by the subject of a reality that is quite different from what is being suggested. Case 1 is an extract from a hypnotic session with a very susceptible and experienced subject. Case 2 is an extract from a session with a naive subject who evidenced the same phenomenon, though in a different way. And Case 3 is an especially vivid illustration of the complexity of consciousness that may result in susceptible subjects' response to age-regression instructions. Collectively, the illustrations also serve to tap a range of ways in which hypnotic age regression may be induced and encouraged. Testing in each case was conducted by one of the authors.

CASE ILLUSTRATIONS OF AGE REGRESSION

Case 1

The very highly susceptible subject (somnambule) in this case illustration is capable of passing all of the items on standard tests of hypnotic susceptibility and had experienced hypnosis several times previously. In the session discussed, the hypnotist (H) administered a standard induction based on eye closure, counted the subject (S) into deep hypnosis, and subsequently tested her on an ideomotor task as well as age regression. The instructions for age regression were as follows:

H: Now I'm going to take you back through time. I want to take you back through time, to when you were a small girl sitting in a classroom at school, 7 years of age, many years ago. As I count, you'll slip back through time, right back to the time when you were a small girl, 7 years of age sitting in a classroom. I'm going to count from 1 to 5, and at the count of 5, you're right back there, right back there sitting in class with your teacher and your classmates, 1. It's no longer 1979, 1978, moving back now through time, 2, 3, younger and younger, almost back there, small girl, 7 years of age sitting in class, 4, further and further, almost back there, 7 years of age, 5, right back there now, 7 years of age, sitting in class with your friends and a teacher, 7 years of age.

I want you to tell me what it's like. Can you describe the scene to me, what's happening now? Can you tell me, tell me now what's happening?

S: Helga mag mich nicht. [Helga doesn't like me.]

H: Who is your teacher?

S: Frau Hammer. [Mrs. Hammer.]

H: Do you like your teacher?

S: Nein. [No.]

H: Why not?

S: Ich mag sie nicht. [I don't like her.]

H: What about your school friends?

S: Gerda.

H: Who is sitting around you?

S: Gerda.

H: Do you like her?

S: Mmm.

H: What are you doing?

S: Heather schreibt. Ich kann dode nicht singen. Die dumme Gans, die spielt immer die, die, das kann ich nicht. Ich kann doch nicht singen, die mag mich nicht ich mag sie auch nicht. Gerda hat ne gute stimme sie singt sehr schon. [Heather is writing. I cannot sing, the silly goose, she always plays the, I cannot do it, I cannot sing, and she doesn't like me, but I don't like her either. Gerda has a good voice, she sings beautifully.]

H: That's fine, just sit there and relax, now restful. I'm going to count from 1 to 5 and you're going to come back through time, no longer a little girl of 7, right back through time, deeply hypnotized, sitting in the chair at the University of Queensland.

S: Es schneit, es schneit! [It's snowing, it's snowing!]

H: Just relax. Why don't you count yourself back through time? Just lift your hand, 1, count with me, 2, lift your hand when you are back, restful and re-laxed, 3, coming back now through time, 1978, 4, lift your hand when you get back to 1979, to the University of Queensland. Just lift your hand to let me know you're right back, right back here, coming back now, that's fine, to the University of Queensland. Sitting in the chair, deeply hypnotized, right back to normal now.

At this point in the session, the hypnotist (PWS) woke the subject up and checked that everything was back to normal.

Case 2

The second case is that of a 21-year-old male university student who was tested first on the HGSHS:A and passed 9 of the 12 items on the scale. In the next session, he passed a battery of test tasks that included suggestions for hand levitation, temperature distortion, eye catalepsy, amnesia, hallucinated move-ment, and hand lowering. Age-regression instructions were given midway through the session, and the subject was regressed to 7 years of age. The instruc-tions for regression were as follows:

H: You are 7 years old. You and your friends are playing at a neighbor's house after school. Everyone has brought along toys to play with and it's fun to play different games with them. In one of the games that you thought up, one of your friends takes your favorite toy and won't give it back to you, even though you ask him for it. He takes your toy and won't give it back to you. So you go up to him and hit him quite hard. You hit him hard and knock out his front tooth. You meant to hit him because he wouldn't give you back the toy. You asked him for it but he held onto it even more tightly and wouldn't give it back. Now when you go home you hear a neighbor calling and she wants to speak to your mother. It is your friend's mother and she seems quite upset. Your mother wonders why the neighbor has called and if you've done anything wrong. You know that the neighbor is calling about your knocking out your friend's tooth. You would like to deny it, even though it is actually true that you started the fight and knocked out his tooth. But you'd prefer not to say anything.

Following these instructions, the hypnotist (KMMcC) explored the subject's reaction in a standard, open-ended fashion, inquiring broadly into the subject's feelings and behavior in the conflict situation. In his response to the age-regression suggestions the subject spoke fluent French spontaneously in reply to the hypnotist's questions. The verbatim text of that part of the record in relation to the questions that were asked was as follows:

H: What was the toy that your friend took?
S: Un ballon. [A ball.]
H: And what was your friend's name?
S: Marc Lucien.
H: Why wouldn't he give it back to you?
S: Il veut me taquiner. [He wants to tease me.]
H: What does your mum say to you about it?
S: Qu'il ne faut pas frapper mes amis. [That one should not hit my friends.]
H: How do you feel about that?
S: Ne voulait pas me donner mon ballon. [Didn't want to give me my ball.]
H: What does your dad say when he finds out about it?
S: Il ne dit pas beaucoup. [He doesn't say much.]
H: What do you think your dad would have done in that situation?
S: Je ne sais pas. [I don't know.]
H: If tomorrow your friend takes your toy again, what would you do?
S: Je le frapperais. [I would hit him.]
H: What would your mother think about that?
S: Elle me frapperait probablement [She would probably give me a smack.]
H: Okay.

Case 3

The final case concerns a 29-year-old graduate student working in the field of hypnosis who is also highly responsive to hypnosis and is fluent in both French and English. The subject was given a standard hypnotic induction and was counted into a relaxed state; trance was deepened through arm levitation and suggestions given to the subject that he was on a magic carpet drifting him further and further into hypnosis. Suggestions of heaviness were also given for the right arm and hand while he was on the carpet, prior to administration of age-regression instructions. In age regression, the subject was regressed to the age of 5 and tested by the hypnotist on routine questions to determine the extent of his involvement in the past situation. After regression had been established by the hypnotist (PWS), hidden observer instructions (see E. R. Hilgard, 1977, for a discussion) were then given to clarify the nature of age-regressed consciousness. Following these instructions, the subject was awakened. All items tested in the session were passed successfully by the subject.

Age-Regression Instructions

H: This is a very special sort of carpet and it is beginning to drift you back through time. It is drifting you back through time now. Back through high school, back further and further, right back to the time you were 5 years of age, right back to the time you are 5 years of age. Back at school, sitting in a classroom listening to your teacher. Right back now. Back at 5. Sitting in a classroom listening to your teacher.

H: Who is your teacher? Can you tell me her name?

S: Madame Pilon.

H: How do you spell her name?

S: P I L O N.

H: That's fine. That's good. What day of the week is it?

S: Le dernier jour d'ecole. [The last day of school.]

H: What month is it?

S: Janvier. [January.]

H: Who is your friend, your best friend in class?

S: Racine.

H: Can you describe him to me? Tell me a little bit about him. Tell me why he is your friend.

S: Il est gros, il est gentil, on joue souvent ensemble. [He is big, and nice, and we often play together.]

H: Does he like you?

S: Oui. [Yes.]

H: Is there anything else you would like to tell me about your friend? Something else?

S: Non. [No.]

H: That's fine. In a little while I am going to ask you to open your eyes and there is a question written on a piece of paper and I want you to answer the question by writing down the answer, as best you can. When you open your eyes you will still remain just as deeply relaxed and deeply hypnotized as you are now. I am going to place the pad on your lap and the pencil in your hand so that you are comfortable. Just open your eyes and read what's on the paper. Can you read it out loud for me?

S: [Subject reads falteringly in English.] "Can you spell the name of the school you are at, at this period of time?"

H: Can you answer that question for me?

S: Oui. [Yes.]

H: Would you write down the answer for me?

S: Je peux le dire. [I can say it.]

H: Sorry?

S: St. Jean Vianney. [Subject speaks it.]

H: That's fine. Thank you. Just close your eyes now while I take the pad and pencil away from you. Just keep your eyes closed now. That's fine. You're 5 years of age, sitting in a classroom and you've just answered some questions for me. That's good. I want you to remain deeply hypnotized, deeply relaxed. You're 5 years of age and sitting in the classroom, very relaxed, deeply hypnotized, right back at 5 years of age.

Hidden Observer Instructions

H: Now, often it's possible for people who are hypnotized to comment in some way on their experiences, what they are feeling at the time, the various sensations and experiences they feel while they are hypnotized. You're back in the classroom at 5 now, and you're deeply hypnotized. In a little while I am going to tap you on the shoulder. When I do that, I want that other part of you that can comment on these experiences to tell me what you are feeling at the time, just simply tell me what's happening. When I tap you on the shoulder again, the other part of you will go and you will be right back to where you are now, 5 years of age. So, when I tap you the first time, the other part of you can tell me what you are feeling and thinking and when I tap you again you will be back, 5 years of age. I'll tap you the first time now. Describe to me the feelings and thoughts at the moment.

S: It was exactly like if I was in that class. I can really remember, relive the emotion I had with my friend there, Racine.

H: Can you tell me a little more about that? What's it like?

S: It seems very vivid. I should have gone back there. It's better there.

H: Do you want to?

S: Yes.

H: Do you want me to tap you on the shoulder again?

S: Yes.

H: Can you describe what's happening now?

S: On bâtit avec du papier, de la colle. On fait des maisons [We're building with some papers, with glue. Making houses.]

H: That's fine. Just stay there completely relaxed, deeply hypnotized now. Drifting backwards and forwards on that carpet. Back on the carpet, drifting backwards and forward. The carpet begins to drift you back through time. It has been a pleasant and enjoyable experience. You've thought and lived through a time that you've enjoyed with your friend, your close friend, and the carpet is drifting you on now back through time, growing up. Soon you will be back at [your] university sitting in a chair deeply hypnotized; sitting in a chair in the laboratory, listening to me, deeply hypnotized. Back now. Right back now. No longer 5 years of age, sitting in a chair deeply hypnotized. What year is it?

S: 1978.

H: That's fine. Everything back to normal now.

Comment on Cases

The meaning of these phenomena is explored later in the chapter, but some comment can be passed at the outset on the behavior that occurred. The three cases illustrate both the subjective reality of age regression for the subjects who were studied and the distortions of perception that age-regression suggestions may elicit. Each illustration demonstrates strong imaginative involvement of a highly susceptible subject in the events of the hypnosis. When regressed to school age, Case 1 spontaneously supplied the imagery of winter and snow and obviously created a situation that was both pleasurable and absorbing for her—one the hypnotist could not share because it was described in a language (German) that he did not understand. All three subjects also evidenced trance logic response. This is not meant to imply that trance logic behavior is a routine response to age-regression instructions. Rather, it is an idiosyncratic response that some susceptible subjects may demonstrate in hypnosis, whereas others may not (Sheehan, 1977). Each of the subjects combined perceptions gathered from reality with others that were compatible with the suggestions of the hypnotist and, despite the apparent incongruity, processed them simultaneously.

Each subject displayed a seemingly incongruous response by answering in another language the hypnotist's questions, which were phrased in English. If the subjects had been behaving consistently, they would have chosen either to understand the hypnotist's questions in English and reply to him in the same language, or not to understand the hypnotist's questions and fail to communicate with him because he could not speak French or German, which was appropriate to the age to which they were regressed. The exact meaning of incongruity aside (and this is an important issue that we consider later), the subjects clearly found it more enjoyable to speak in the language familiar to them at the age that was suggested.

The extent to which reality information was processed by the subjects is evidenced particularly in the response of Case 3 to the hidden observer instructions. While the subject was still age regressed, the hypnotist was able to move the subject from responding in French to responding in English. It was as if the hidden observer instructions focused on the "analyzing part" of the subject by allowing him to comment on reality now that the situation had been defined as appropriate for him to do so. In a sense, the hypnotist was permitting the experiencing subject to say his piece, and the subject took the opportunity. However, these case illustrations raise interesting questions that cannot be answered easily on the basis of the data that have been gathered thus far. For instance, each subject was bilingual, and the evidence does not say anything about the likelihood of such trance logic behavior occurring in subjects who are not facile in more than one language, or who have never actually been in a country at an early age where the language the hypnotist was using was not actually spoken. But there seems little doubt that the behavior illustrated by these cases is more than role-playing or purely voluntary behavior. As Orne (1974) suggests, play actors would not be so stupid as to respond in such an apparently inconsistent way.

The reactions of these three cases were explored by applying the EAT (outlined and discussed in Chapter 3). This was done to assess in more detail the nature of the phenomena and processes implicated by the case abstracts that we have presented. But before turning to discuss these, it seems instructive to review the evidence concerning age regression in order to highlight more analytically the issues to which we should attend when the EAT data come to be examined. Not only was the EAT applied to the three cases presented, but it was also used in an independent research study that examined a number of specific issues raised by our review of the evidence dealing with the phenomenon of age regression.

REVIEW OF THE PHENOMENON

Although there is consensus that the phenomenon of age regression cannot be explained away as faking (Bowers, 1976), research has focused mostly around the theoretical explanation of age regression rather than around the conditions that affect its occurrence. There is little evidence, for instance, to tell us how different capacities for imaginative involvement among susceptible persons relate to type of response in the age-regressed situation, or what the influence of subjects' expectations and attitudes is on their age-regression performance. In the search for explanations, research has tended to focus on whether past memories or perceptions are accurately recalled or whether the performance under age regression matches what one might expect if the person were really back at the age that was being suggested.

Researchers appeal to physiological criteria, perceptual criteria, or behavioral criteria to assert the genuineness of the phenomenon, and there are a number of adequate reviews of the literature (e.g., Barber, 1962a; Gebhard, 1961; Nash et al., 1979; Yates, 1961), which comprehensively list the relevant studies in the field. One may generally conclude from these reviews that there is little evidence for true neurophysiological or physiological regression. It is possible, for instance, to demonstrate plantar reflexes in hypnosis when subjects are regressed to early infancy (see Gidro-Frank & Bowersbuch, 1948), and the result has been confirmed (True & Stephenson, 1951). But it is also possible to elicit a Babinski response in normal adults under conditions that involve depressed muscle tone (e.g., in sleep, fatigue, and drowsiness). The Babinski response in the experiments cited may well have been due to diminution of tonicity following relaxation in the hypnotic setting (Barber, 1962a) or to the influence of demand characteristics arising from the fact that the subjects being tested had knowledge of the medical field, thus resulting in an artifactual response.

Perhaps the most dramatic evidence of physiological regression comes from case histories where regression is to a particular age when the subject has undergone some physiological trauma or distinctive episode—one that has well-defined physiological accompaniments. Such an instance was cited by Kupper (1945), who found that EEG patterns of response changed radically under conditions of hypnotic age regression. The subject was an adult who had had convulsive seizures since the age of 18, these seizures being associated with emotional difficulties experienced by the subject in relation to his father. When the subject was tested under hypnotic age regression, abnormalities in the EEG record were observed at the critical age of 18, not before.

In another study, Erickson (1937) tested a 19-year-old subject who had been earlier assaulted and beaten and was unconscious for more than 24 hours. When regressed to the day on which the assault occurred, the subject lost consciousness, and it was argued that the subject was reliving events as they had actually taken place. As Barber (1962a) states, however, fainting may occur for many reasons, and it seems clear from the evidence that emotions play a dominant role in shaping physiological reactions—at least to the extent that it is difficult to argue that true regression is actually at issue.

The evidence for age regression creating an earlier level of cognitive function is rather more sharply debated in the areas of perceptual and behavioral functioning. In the field of perceptual function, studies for the most part have concentrated on the question of whether perceptual illusions characteristic of particular ages will reappear and whether eidetic imagery (known to characterize the cognitive function of children more than adults) will be more obviously evidenced in hypnosis when regression is to childhood. For example, Parrish, Lundy, and Leibowitz (1969) studied the occurrence of response to the Ponzo and Poggendorff perceptual illusions in subjects who were: (1) tested in hypnosis and out of hypnosis; (2) given no age-regression instructions; and (3) motivated for the task. Using experimental subjects as their own controls, they showed that hypnotic induction facilitated retrieval of the age-appropriate perceptual response, whereas task motivational instructions did not. The differences that occurred, however, were more apparent for the Ponzo illusion than for the Poggendorff illusion.

Perry and Chisholm (1973) later addressed the issue of whether the Parrish et al. data demonstrated that hypnotic age regression really involved a literal reversion to childhood modes of cognition and perception. They argued that control subjects in the earlier study were not treated in the same way as experimental subjects (e.g., with respect to how they were instructed, the presence or absence of the hypnotist, and the experimenter's awareness of the subjects' status). Employing real and simulating subjects (as a quasi-control group), Perry and Chisholm tested high, medium, and low susceptible subjects on the same perceptual tasks employed by Parrish and his associates. Results failed to replicate the previous findings, and this failure to replicate was confirmed by an independent study conducted by Ascher, Barber, and Spanos (1972). As far as perceptual illusions are concerned, then, it appears that procedural factors are more likely than hypnosis to account for the presence of group differences.

More recent research has examined the incidence of eidetic imagery among adults who are regressed to a time where that form of cognitive functioning is more salient. For instance, Walker, Garrett, and Wallace (1976) used the differential frequency of eidetic imagery between children and adults as a basis for testing the validity of hypnotic age regression, their argument being that eidetic imagery is so distinctive (e.g., the image is projected externally, it persists, and it can be scanned) that its occurrence confirms the reality of the regression. If the incidence of the phenomenon as it is reported for normal populations of children is correct, one would expect it to occur approximately 8–20% of the time. Each subject in the study was tested during waking, neutral hypnosis, and hypnosis with age regression, and the order of conditions was randomized. Subjects were regressed to age 7, and the technique for measuring eidetic imagery was the random dot stereogram technique developed by Julesz (1971), the subjects being asked to indicate the picture that emerges when one pattern of apparently meaningless dots is superimposed upon another. In this instance, the first pattern is the eidetic image of what was shown to subjects previously.

Results for these conditions of testing showed that two subjects correctly identified the composite image when regressed, but not awake, and postexperimental inquiry showed that these same subjects remembered having distinctive imagery experiences as children. The study used no independent control group (task-motivated or role-playing) and did not employ children as subjects so as to contrast real and regressed performance directly.

To some extent, some of these deficiencies in the Walker et al. (1976) study were rectified in an experiment by Wallace (1978), which employed both hypnotically instructed and task-motivated subjects, half the subjects in each group having had prior experience with eidetic imagery and the other half not. In this experiment, the experimenter did not know the identity of the group of subjects being tested, and three composite stimuli were used, again employing the random dot stereogram technique. Results indicated no eidetic imagery among task-motivated subjects, whereas in the hypnosis group, 2 of the 24 subjects correctly identified all three forms in the stereograms and were able to do so only in the hypnotically regressed state. However, both of these subjects were childhood eidetikers, and the history of subjects' imagery experiences clearly emerged as a relevant factor in the prediction of their experimental imagery response. For the reasons that these subjects obviously were aware of the significance of the phenomenon at issue, it would have been useful to use role-playing subjects so as to detect what demand characteristics may have been apparent to subjects during testing. But, no study examining eidetic imagery in the regression context has used such a comparison group. Finally, it should be noted that an attempt to replicate Wallace's findings has been made (see Spanos, Ansari, & Stam, 1979), but it was unsuccessful. Results, then, have been inconsistent.

Behavioral studies for the most part have concentrated on increased recall of remote events and the reinstatement of cognitive processes (Nash et al., 1979). Hypnotic age regression, for instance, has been studied using intelligence tests (e.g., Spiegel, Shor, & Fishman, 1945; Young, 1940), projective tests (e.g., Orne, 1951; Taylor, 1950), specific tests of memory such as recall of birthday dates (e.g., True, 1949), the occurrence of early emotional attachments (Nash et al., 1979), and specific cognitive tests (e.g., O'Connell, Shor, & Orne, 1970; Reiff & Scheerer, 1959). Generally, the results show that age regression is not a unique reinstatement of past memory or cognitive processes and that hypnotically regressed subjects distinctively overplay in their response (i.e., they show behavior and reported experience that exceeds the norm and is not in character with the regressed age that is under consideration).

This overplay that age-regressed subjects demonstrate appears to be a general characteristic of the performance of hypnotically regressed subjects. Sarbin (1950), for instance, found a sample of adults who had taken the Stanford–Binet test of intelligence at age 8 or 9, regressed them to the day that they completed the test, and compared their performance with actual test records. Evidence showed that the scores of the regressed subjects were higher on suggested testing than on the original tests. Likewise, Spiegel et al. (1945) regressed subjects to the original date of testing (18 months earlier) and found superior performance for the age-regressed group. Fellows and Creamer (1978) also found that their regressed subjects (performing on the Goodenough–Harris Drawing Test) responded at a level of 9 years instead of 7, the age to which subjects were regressed; in this study, the data differed from both published norms and the actual drawings of 7-year-old children. Studies using projective tests have revealed the same trend toward superior hypnotic performance. For example, Orne (1951) found aspects of Rorschach drawings made under hypnotic age regression (to age 6) that were out of phase with the record made at that age by the same subject. Crasilneck and Michael (1957), working with the Bender-Gestalt test, also concluded from their data that age-regressed subjects perform at a level that exceeds the level of performance characterizing actual norms for the ages being suggested.

One of the most comprehensive studies in the area of age regression was conducted by O'Connell et al. (1970), in which a battery of test tasks was given to real and simulating subjects who were tested at three distinct age levels; real children aged 10, 7, and 4 were tested as validation groups. Data replicated many of the major findings of Reiff and Scheerer (1959), who argued for a reinstatement of early experience. The study found that regressed subjects were more childlike than real children on some measures, but they scored more highly on other measures. Regressed subjects, for instance, took twice as long as real children on their Arithmetic Test (at age 10), but they performed at a higher level on spelling *Pledge of Allegiance* (at age 4) and on their Hollow Tube Test. This same superiority has been evident for tests of perceptual functioning as well. For example, Parrish et al. (1969) found that the mean illusion response on the Poggendorff test for subjects who were regressed hypnotically to age 5 exceeded the norms for 5-year-old children.

It is also important to note when reviewing the literature in the field that the evidence indicates that the performance of hypnotic subjects in age-regressed situations duplicates, for the most part, the performance shown by nonhypnotic subjects. In the O'Connell et al. (1970) study, for instance, there were no appreciable differences between the hypnotically age-regressed subjects and simulating (insusceptible) subjects who were tested, and Fellows and Creamer (1978) showed that mean drawing scores on the Goodenough–Harris Drawing Test indicated significantly more decrement from base rate to regression for susceptible subjects in both the task-motivated and hypnotic induction conditions, as compared with low susceptible subjects.

Although in some instances the superior performance of hypnotic subjects (in terms of perceptual or behavioral criteria for regression) may be attributed to the inequality of control conditions, hypnotic subjects have been shown to reveal effects that are not duplicated by nonhypnotic subjects who are motivated for the task at hand. One such set of evidence is provided in a study by Nash et al. (1979), who based their criteria of regression on emotional components of the situations to which their subjects were regressed. These researchers studied the characteristic ways in which young children utilize objects such as teddy bears and blankets, which serve as important play objects (called transitional objects) with which children form deep emotional attachments. The subjects in their study were regressed to age 3, placed in emotional situations, and the real-simulating model of hypnosis was applied to test the reactions of highly susceptible (real) subjects and simulating (insusceptible) subjects in the age-regressed context.

Results showed appreciable group differences in response. Hypnotized age-regressed subjects conformed more closely than simulating subjects to the prediction that 3-year-olds want transitional objects during periods of anxiety or stress;

for example, 11 of the 16 real subjects spontaneously produced transitional objects, whereas only 4 of the 15 simulators acted in the same fashion. Nash et al. interpreted their findings in terms of age regression reinstituting affective processes that could not be explained in terms of the demand characteristics for appropriate response that existed in the total test situation. This study actually represents a rare instance of differences between real and simulating subjects in the age-regression test situation.

We now discuss some of the processes that are claimed to explain regression and examine the evidence used to support them. The two explanatory frameworks that we consider either purport to explain age regression in terms of a revivification of experience or attempt to explain the phenomenon in terms of the hypnotically regressed subject being deluded about what is really the case.

Some Processes Attempting to Explain Age Regression

Revivification.   Revivification can be defined as the regressed subject living through previous experiences in a compelling and literal way. Clearly, the evidence just reviewed that exists with respect to age regression lends little credence to the notion that memories are functionally ablated in hypnotically induced age regression, or that subjects literally return in full to earlier modes of cognitive functioning. Claims made previously about the total reinstitution of childlike mental processes and associated memories (cf. Reiff & Scheerer, 1959) are not supported by the evidence when appropriate controls are introduced into the experimental setting. The study by Nash et al. (1979), however, suggests that affective rather than cognitive and memory components may be fruitfully studied and that the most meaningful hypnotic age regressions to examine are those that relate to affect-arousing stimulus situations. They claim, for instance, that: "Real subjects exposed to meaningful and stressful material appear to evidence a more complete and accurate reinstatement of earlier emotional processes [p. 554]." Their study makes a distinction between affective and cognitive components of memory and provides partial support for the revivification hypothesis. While generally accepting the validity of their findings, however, one should be careful before assuming that the subjects in their experiment duplicated earlier emotional experiences in a way that reflected the age to which they were regressed. There were indications, for instance, that subjects tested in the study overplayed (as we have observed elsewhere in age-regression studies)—69% of the real group spontaneously reported the presence of transitional objects, whereas the norms for children showed a lower (though not appreciably so) rate of 60%.

The fact that this trend replicates the lack of matching demonstrated in so many other studies of age regression suggests the need for further research to determine whether the discrepancy observed here was, in fact, a chance occurrence. Laying aside the possible equivocality of the data in this respect, their results do appear to highlight the special relevance of studying age regression in relation to emotionally arousing stimulus situations. It is in such situations, it seems, that the quality and magnitude of age-regression response will be most apparent. The study also reflects a useful shift away from experiments that depend on precise behavioral norms to studies that tap subjective processes relating to specific age periods and developmental sequences.

The importance of this shift in emphasis is reinforced by arguments proposed by Brenneman (1978) that regressed subjects may be cognitively constrained by certain cognitive tests that they are given because—as she states—new schemata have swallowed old ones. Preoperational schemata as measured by Piagetian-type tests are known to be replaced by those of later cognitive operations (Piaget, 1970), and it may be totally unreasonable to expect that regressed adults can genuinely lose the new operations that have come to replace the old. Alternative schemata—ones that have a better chance of being recaptured—may be better candidates for analysis, and Brenneman argues that the most likely candidates are cognitive structures related to a person's social and emotional life.

Following this account, it is not surprising that performance on formal cognitive tasks has generally failed to match the performance typical of the ages to which hypnotic subjects have been regressed. Measures that tap emotional elements of the regressed situation may show a more obvious parallel between age-true and suggested behavior and experience. In her data collection, Brenneman used peer descriptions in the age-regressed context to study the response of eight highly susceptible subjects. Subjects were regressed to Grade 1 or kindergarten and were asked to describe two schoolmates. The data showed some degree of correlation between hypnotic performance and data for actual kindergarten (vs. college students), but the results for hypnotized nonregressed subjects also differed from norm data (that were available) in a way that paralleled, in part, the trends observed for the age-regressed subjects. It is possible, however, that the measures taken in terms of peer descriptions would have been far more discriminating if the age-regressed situation were defined as stressful or emotionally arousing, as was done in the study conducted by Nash et al. (1979).

Delusion.   In their age-regression study, O'Connell et al. (1970) argued that a view of hypnotic age regression more parsimonious than the literal reinstatement hypothesis was an account that describes age-regressed behavior in terms of the hypnotic subject being temporarily deluded. This argument is reinforced especially by the research that appeals to the data available on trance logic, where the subject performs inconsistently in terms of the suggestions being administered by the hypnotist. The glaring nature of the errors illustrated by trance logic behavior (see Cases 1, 2, and 3 for illustrations of the phenomenon) leads theorists (see Orne, 1959, 1974) to conclude that hypnosis is real for the age-regressed subject in the sense that the hypnotized individual is subjectively convinced that what is suggested is, in fact, true.

This subjective conviction, defined as a transient delusion, is argued to be a defining characteristic of hypnosis. The process of trance logic that illustrates the delusion is akin to other processes as well, however. For example, the process can be linked with autistic thinking or primary process mentation (E. R. Hilgard, 1965; Orne, 1959) and illustrates partially regressive features of cognitive organization in hypnosis (Gill, 1972; E. R. Hilgard, 1965). The processes that are labeled by "tolerance of incongruity" clearly embody the notion that a person can register information at one level of cognitive functioning, and argument must be made for the existence of multiple, quasi-independent levels of information processing (Sheehan, 1977).

In all but one of the major studies of trance logic (e.g., Johnson, Maher, & Barber, 1972; McDonald & Smith, 1975; Obstoj & Sheehan, 1977; Orne, 1959; Peters, 1973; Sheehan et al., 1976) employing the measure of double hallucination, the incongruous behavior being examined (double hallucination) has been cued or suggested by the procedures that have been adopted. Detailed analysis of studies shows that the test procedures have usually conveyed the expected response to subjects in a clear and obvious fashion. This challenges contemporary theorizing that asserts that subjects' tolerance of incongruity demonstrates a nonsuggested attribute of hypnotic behavior, a quality of consciousness that is not related either to the characteristics of the test setting nor to the cues that exist to index appropriate response. Sheehan et al. (1976) tested the effect of cue structure by examining the occurrence of logically incongruous behavior in contexts that varied appreciably in the degree to which they cued subjects about appropriate responses. Data from the application of the real-simulating model of hypnosis showed that double hallucination response was evidenced by simulating subjects as by real subjects, and simulating response was most evident when the cues for the appropriate response were highlighted in the test situation. A further study analyzed whether tolerance of incongruity was manifest among nonfaking subjects who were motivated to respond in the normal waking state (Obstoj & Sheehan, 1977). Data showed that some subjects in the waking imagination group also displayed tolerance of incongruity. Although the data argue strongly against the view that tolerance of incongruity is a unique attribute of hypnosis, they do not detract from the genuineness of the phenomenon.

The evidence suggests that it is more legitimate to view incongruous behavior as an outcome of the cognitive processing that subjects employ in hypnotic test situations (Sheehan, 1977) than as a spontaneously occurring, unsuggested attribute of hypnosis. The subtle communication features of the test situation appear to determine the pattern of the incongruous response that is shown, and the data indicate that we should study more thoroughly the motivated cognitive planning functions of hypnotic subjects than subjects' prior attitudes of acceptance about what they believe might be correct (Sheehan, 1977). There is evidence that inconsistent behavior is favored as a distinctive (though not unique) mode of response by hypnotic subjects, even when they are initially led to believe otherwise. For example, in a study of the effect of messages communicated directly to subjects about what could be expected, it was hypnotic subjects who, overall, behaved appreciably more illogically than simulating subjects when the appropriateness of logical behavior was stressed to them beforehand (McConkey & Sheehan, 1980).

Careful analysis of the evidence relating to the occurrence of inconsistent behavior in the age-regression context indicates that the data can be only fully explained by drawing distinctions about the kinds of responses that different hypnotic subjects may demonstrate. Such an approach again recognizes the individuality of the susceptible subject and the strong differences that exist among hypnotic subjects themselves. Lack of literalness (e.g., at the age of 6, the subject looks at a hallucinated watch, which could not exist), presence of dualistic thinking (e.g., the subject answers affirmatively to the question "Are you as good as you are now?"), gross anomalies (an answer is given at age 4 to the question "Who is the Prime Minister of Canada?"), and internal inconsistencies (e.g., denying being able to write or add in answer to a question but proceeding to do so at another time) have been analyzed in a detailed study by Perry and Walsh (1978) of the different types of incongruous response that may occur in the age-regression context.

Regressing subjects who differed in their aptitude for trance, Perry and Walsh studied the patterns of incongruous response in both real and simulating subjects. Their results failed to substantiate Orne's (1974) emphasis on gross anomalies as characteristic of hypnotized subjects' behavior, but there were clear indications of inconsistent response and dualistic thinking among highly susceptible subjects. Highly susceptible subjects showed significantly greater inconsistency in their response than did simulating subjects, although there was no evidence of appreciably more gross anomalies in their performance. But perhaps the major conclusion of the study was that qualitative differences in cognitive function and subjective experience differentiated separate groups of hypnotic and nonhypnotic subjects.

Drawing the evidence relating to the processes of revivification and delusion (as inferred from the presence of trance logic behavior) together, it seems that the study of age regression can be best pursued through the application of techniques of assessment that are oriented to the more qualitative features of subjects' performance and, in particular, to the subjective reality of subjects' age-regressed experience. Accordingly, we now consider the results of the application of the EAT to the study of age regression and trance logic behavior in order to explore more fully the phenomena that are being debated. Two studies reporting unpublished data are discussed, which are based on detailed analysis of the behavior of separate samples of hypnotically regressed subjects. However, future research must determine how well the patterns of response that are indicated stand up against comparison with the performance of motivated waking groups of subjects.

The first study follows up some of the issues raised by our review of the literature. In particular, we look at some of the implications of the Nash et al. (1979) experiment that analyzed the behavior of highly susceptible subjects in an age-regressed situation where attempt was made to facilitate the arousal of strong emotions about the events that subjects were asked to experience. Here, the EAT was used to analyze age-regression response in an emotionally arousing context. The second study outlines the results of the application of the EAT technique that was used to assess the meaning of the response presented for the three cases that were reported earlier in this chapter. Here, the EAT attempted to measure the meaning of trance logic as evidenced by all three of the subjects in the age-regression context. Specifically, it was considered that the pattern of differences and similarities in the reported experience of the subjects would help clarify the nature of the processes underlying their behavior.

AGE REGRESSION UNDER EMOTIONAL AROUSAL

Fifteen susceptible male undergraduate students at the University of Queensland participated voluntarily in testing. The mean age of subjects was 22 years ($SD = 7.55$), and the mean score of subjects on the HGSHS:A was 9.80 ($SD = .94$). Subjects were tested hypnotically by one of the authors on eight hypnotic test tasks, including two age-regression items. Regression was to both 7 and 17 years of age. Subjects were regressed first to age 7 and then to age 17, and in each case they were presented with an emotional situation involving the arousal of aggression. Instructions emphasized either physical aggression (e.g., hitting someone else when angry) or acquisitive aggression (e.g., stealing money from someone else's handbag). A subject was tested with the same type of aggression (physical or acquisitive) instruction at both age levels; the type of aggression to be administered was determined randomly with respect to subjects. The full text of the physical aggression instructions at age 7 is reported for Case 2 at the beginning of the chapter (the subject reported in this case took part in the present study). After each suggestion relating to aggressive behavior, the hypnotist explored subjects' reactions in a standard, open-ended fashion.

Following hypnotic testing, the EAT was employed to investigate closely subjects' reactions to the age-regression situations and their aggression components. Subjects were initially informed that the video-tape record of their hypnotic performance during the two age-regression items would be played and that their viewing of it would most likely assist recall of their experience during hypnosis. Subjects were told that during these items they probably thought many things that they either did not or were not able to say at the time, that there were most likely things that they did not have time to say, or else that there were only vague impressions and reactions that were not verbalized during hypnotic testing. The inquirer told subjects that as they viewed the record these sorts of thoughts and feelings would probably return to them and that whenever they recalled something about their experience during hypnosis they should stop the video-tape recorder and describe their experience. The recorder unit was within easy reach of subjects who then personally operated the playing of the video-tape record. The decision as to when to stop the record was left entirely to subjects who were instructed simply to stop the recorder whenever they recalled something about their hypnotic experience, whether or not they considered it important; cues were maximized for subjects to relive their earlier experiences as vividly and concretely as possible.

Whenever subjects stopped the video-tape record and commented on their behavior during hypnosis, the inquirer explored the exact nature of their experience by employing probes designed to encourage subjects to describe and personally interpret their feelings and experiences. Areas of questioning used by the inquirer related to subjects' cognitive activity, imagery and imagination, expectancy and perception of events, and associations of events. The inquirer probed as many of these areas as was considered necessary to establish the nature of subjects' behavior and experience.

The EAT session was video-tape recorded, and the records of the EAT inquiries into subjects' experiences were analyzed by two independent raters at the end of testing. These raters scored the records in terms of the incidence of a range of cognitive styles (independent, concentrative, constructive, and individuation) and process dimensions (absorption, imagery vividness, involuntariness, reality awareness, body sensations, positive rapport, negative rapport, and nonconscious involvement) that were evident in the age-regression data yielded by the EAT. If raters decided that sufficient information was not available, then no rating was made.

Results. Table 5.1 sets out the data for subjects' passing and failing on the different types of aggression tasks that were tested. The main data of the study, however, were derived from analyses of the records of recall of those individual subjects who had responded positively to age-regression suggestions (for 7 to 17 years of age) and had been administered aggression instructions (either physical or acquisitive). Table 5.2 summarizes the data for the various dimensions rated for each of the two raters who judged the test protocols. Results show high reliability for the dimensions that were considered. But most importantly, data illustrate evidence of styles of cognition that reflect idiosyncratic features of subjects' processing of suggestions, paralleling effects observed in Chapters 3 and 4, and which we report in Chapters 6, 7, and 8. There was also evidence that regression to times more distant (i.e., to age 7 vs. age 17) was more directly characterized by an independent style of cognition, highlighting again the in-

TABLE 5.1
Hypnotic Scores and Responses to Age Regression and
Aggression Suggestions

Aggression Suggestion and Subject Number	Hypnotic Score	Age Regression to 7 Years	Aggression	Age Regression to 17 Years	Aggression
Physical Aggression					
1.	6	+	+	+	+
2.	6	+	+	+	+
3.	6	+	+	+	+
4.	5	−		+	+
5.	5	+	+	+	+
6.	4	−		+	+
7.	6	+	+	+	+
Acquisitive Aggression					
8.	6	+	+	+	+
9.	6	+	+	+	+
10.	6	+	−	+	−
11.	6	+	+	+	+
12.	4	−		−	
13.	6	+	+	+	+
14.	5	+	−	+	+
15.	6	+	−	+	−

Note. + = positive response and - = negative response to suggestion. Criterion for positive response was verbal report of suggested age. Maximum score on battery of hypnotic tasks (excluding age regression) is 6.

teraction that exists between qualitative features of subjects' cognitive processing of suggestions and the type of hypnotic test task that they are administered. One notes also the high level of reality awareness that characterized regressions to both ages (see Chapter 6 for further discussion of this aspect of response) despite the strong degree of absorption with which subjects were immersed in the experience.

The styles of cognitive response that most often characterized age regression were the independent and constructive modes. These categories are not necessarily independent of each other (see Chapter 3 for definitions and discussion), but data exist to suggest that they reflect relatively discrete styles of cognitive reaction. The independent mode of cognition seems most dominant as far as the age-regression situation we studied is concerned, and subjects' comments help to illustrate the modes of cognizing that were apparent.

The independent style of cognitive response was seen to be tied to individua-

TABLE 5.2

Incidence of a Range of Cognitive Styles and Process Dimensions
in Age Regression Data Using the EAT

Styles and Processes	Regression	
	Age 7 (n = 11)	Age 17 (n = 13)
Styles		
Independent	7 (6)	2 (2)
Concentrative	1 (1)	0 (0)
Constructive	2 (2)	1 (1)
Processes		
Individuation	9 (9)	9 (7)
Absorption	10 (10)	10 (9)
Imagery Vividness	5 (5)	2 (1)
Involuntary	1 (1)	3 (2)
Reality Awareness	6 (6)	8 (7)
Body Sensations	4 (3)	1 (1)
Positive Rapport	1 (1)	2 (2)
Negative Rapport	2 (2)	2 (2)
Nonconscious Involvement	7 (6)	6 (5)

Note. Entries in parentheses reflect data for the second rater; agreement occurred in 52 of 55 cases (95%).

tion (see Chapter 3 for definition and discussion) in subjects' responses to the communications of the hypnotist. In commenting on the 7-year-old physical aggression item, for instance, Subject 2 commented that the "suggestion given by [the hypnotist] was close to a real fight I had over a toy about that time." As did others, this subject cognized about an actual event during the age-regressed period in order to facilitate the experiences of the suggested event. For these sorts of subjects, interpreting the communications of the hypnotist so as to support the experiences they were having was important; here subjects refrained from attempting simply to concentrate on and adhere to the direct messages as provided by the hypnotist.

For constructive subjects, generally, individuation was also apparent, and subjects expended cognitive effort to construct the particular response that they considered appropriate. For instance, Subject 14 reported that in order to try and experience the 7-year-old acquisitive aggression situation (i.e., stealing money from a teacher's purse) he "clicked back to something else, a similar sort of experience, but then somebody else did it." That is, this subject attempted to employ, actively and effortfully, an experience similar to the one being suggested, but one which he only witnessed, so as to construct his participation in the suggested event. This subject prepared himself cognitively, as it were, for the item in a quite idiosyncratic way.

Subject 8 was faced with a problem in the suggestion for 7-year-old acquisitive aggression and had to employ a constructive solution. He commented that: "when [the hypnotist] gave me this situation, I had a sort of problem, really, because when I was in Grade 2 the teacher I had was a nun, because I went to a convent, and consequently she didn't bring her purse and her bag over, so I had to sort of make up the thing." To complete the details of the suggestion, which were not immediately available to him, this subject appropriately constructed cognitive features of the situation so as to attempt to coincide with the communications he had received from the hypnotist.

In an important sense, these data highlight the individual differences that exist in responsiveness among highly susceptible hypnotic subjects. Styles of processing clearly differed across subjects and interacted with the kind of hypnotic test task that was administered (see also Chapters 3 and 6 for similar findings). We now consider the application of the same technique of inquiry to analysis of the trance logic behavior illustrated in the three case descriptions presented at the beginning of this chapter. The case histories presented earlier highlighted for us several puzzling features of response that are pertinent to major issues in the field, and further data are needed to help meet challenges that they present.

EAT DATA ON TRANCE LOGIC RESPONSE

We have extracted the part of each EAT session that comments on the spontaneous occurrence of trance logic behavior that was reported earlier (see case descriptions). In each case, the EAT was used to explore the meaning of the subject's behavior during the hypnotic session, and an attempt was made to follow the rules for the inquiry procedure as set out in Chapter 3. For Cases 1 and 2, the person conducting the EAT session was not involved in hypnotic testing in any way, but the hypnotist and the inquirer for Case 3 were the same person (PWS). Each of the cases is illustrated in turn.

Case 1

This extract begins midway through the EAT session at a point where the subject (S) stopped the tape on her own initiative to comment to the inquirer (I) on her smiling during the session. Her comment begins as an explanation of why she was smiling.

S: Because of the way I spoke in German there. It didn't, it seems a bit funny now, but not really. I don't know, but at the time it didn't, you know, seeing myself and hearing myself speak like that, and I called the teacher a silly goose or something like that, you know, sort of coming out that I didn't like her.

I: [Subject moves to turn tape back on.] Just before you go on, you said that was sort of funny.

S: Now [it is].

I: How was it funny now?

S: Now it seems, you know, how can I say that, now even.

I: I'm not just sure if I've got that, it sounds interesting. What's the funny part?

S: Well, to hear myself say in German, "silly goose." I don't like her and being all sort of upset about it, seems funny to me now, you know.

I: For what reason might it be funny?

S: Well, you know, I just, seeing myself and saying those things. I wouldn't normally say them and I haven't thought of this for many, many years. In fact, I'd forgotten all about it.

I: Okay. Fine. You'd forgotten it.

S: Yes.

I: You used the word "normally"; you normally wouldn't do that. I suppose I was getting the picture that you were saying that the person on the screen was different.

S: Yes. Yes. Yes.

I: Almost different. Divorced from you.

S: I could see myself and I acknowledge that that's me. And I said that but, I didn't, I can't sort of see myself saying much, you know?

I: It's like you're not really involved in it.

S: No, not now. I was then.

I: You were then. How do you know you were then?

S: That's a funny way, I can almost, the feelings I had, you know, sort of, not really hostile, but a bit angry because I didn't like that teacher. I can sort of remember the feeling but it doesn't really, you know, it was so long ago. It's there, it wasn't long ago, it was happening there and then.

I: Right. It was very real, very real.

S: Yes. Yes.

I: I noticed that you spoke in German to the hypnotist who was speaking in English. Do you have any explanation as to how that came about?

S: I could understand him all right. That was very natural.

I: It was natural for what [reason]?

S: That I could understand him. Like it's part, I don't know.

I: It is hard, I know. I can appreciate that. I suppose I'm just wondering whether you've got any thoughts on it at all.

S: No. I didn't think about it much. Put it that way.

I: Okay. You used the word "naturally." Are you able to say that it might have been natural that he would speak English and you would naturally understand [him]?

S: I think part of me was with him.

I: Okay. Can we just follow that for a little while? How was it that part of you was with him? In what sense was that?

S: The little girl who was there, who didn't like the teacher. It's very hard to explain. It was me and yet it was separate.

I: Right. And what's the part that was with the hypnotist?

S: Me.

I: What you're saying is that you could communicate with the hypnotist because part of you was with him.

S: It was really the hypnotist, who was sort of, well, really guiding. He was in control of this whole thing.

I: It seems to be a very difficult area for you.

S: Very difficult.

I: Yes.

S: It's very difficult to explain. It's almost as if I, well, part of me is there listening to him, but part of me is away from here. It was actually there all happening.

I: I find that really fascinating. Admittedly, we can't find explanations for all of it, but it happened.

S: Yes. Yes. [Starts tape.]

I: Good!

S: [Stops tape when hypnotist begins to count subject out of age-regressed situation. At this point, subject spontaneously interrupted the hypnotist.] I said it was snowing. I was still in the classroom while he was talking and I looked out of the window and snow was falling. And I thought it was such a pretty sight. And he said "you're going back," and I saw the snow and I thought "how beautiful it was" and I felt like saying, "Well, wait a minute. I just want to see the snow for a moment."

I: Just wait on because it's such a nice scene.

S: Mmm. I just wanted to watch that for a moment, and he was calling me back and I felt like saying, "Well, just a moment, you know!"

I: Just hang on a moment.

S: Yes. Yes.

I: Well, how come you didn't say that to him?

S: I was telling him that it was snowing.

I: Okay, but he didn't understand you.

S: Well, I guess at the time I thought he might.

I: How come he didn't pick up the fact that you were telling him that it was snowing?

S: Well, he didn't listen.

I: I mean if he's a sensitive sort of hypnotist he ought to have recognized that you said it was snowing and you'd like to stay there.

S: Well, maybe he was in a hurry. He tried to sort of, you know, rush things a little.

I: Yes. So, the fact you said to him, did he understand that?

S: Well, looking at it now, he probably didn't even understand what I was saying. But at the time, I certainly assumed that he'd understand what I'm saying.

I: Okay. So, at the time it seemed very correct that you should speak in the way that you did and that he ought to understand you.

S: Yes. Yes.

I: Okay. Looking back on it now, do you realize there's an explanation for what you've done?

S: Yes. It makes sense, now, but it didn't at the time.

I: Is that in perspective for you? Is there any conflict there?

S: No, not now.

I: Can you explain that for me?

S: At the time there was, you know, I was desperately trying to tell him that it was snowing and I'd just like to watch the snow for a moment. And he wouldn't listen to that, and he kept going, and eventually I thought, "let it go," but now it makes sense. Obviously he couldn't understand what I was saying.

I: How did that affect you when you were actually saying to the hypnotist "it's snowing, it's snowing," and he didn't take any notice, or seem to take any notice?

S: You know, I just got a little bit tense because he didn't take notice of me.

I: Did you have any feelings about the fact that he didn't take notice of you?

S: Apart from feeling a little bit tense, and perhaps a little bit sad because I thought it was so beautiful. I hadn't seen snow for such a long time, you know, it was quite a novelty.

I: But you decided in the end to go with him?

S: I had no choice.

I: You had no choice. What makes you say that?

S: I guess he was, well, he was controlling the whole thing. He was telling me to, I don't know, he took me there and then he took me away from there. [Starts tape.]

I: Okay, good, fine.

Case 2

This case begins with the subject spontaneously stopping the tape in the EAT session and commenting on the way he has written his name after having been regressed to age 7.

S: (Stops tape.) That's probably where I've just written my name in French—Jean Paul.

I: Were you having any particular thoughts or images going through your mind at that point?

S: No, just writing my name. [Starts tape.]

The session at this point proceeded with the subject commenting on his family and where he lived as a child. After some time, he stopped the tape again and made the following comment:

S: An interesting thing about that was, now seeing this again, I remember I had difficulty—not difficulty reading English, but I found that I was thinking in two languages.

I: What were you actually doing when you said that you were thinking in two languages?

S: I looked at it in English, I knew what the English was, and I think I was thinking in French, and some indecision as to just what to put down. I suppose it's funny, but perhaps, oh, I don't know, perhaps I shouldn't have been able to read English at all. I just don't know.

I: You were aware of the two languages when you were filling out the questionnaire?

S: Aware of difficulty. The English was common, but I was thinking about something else. I don't know whether or not you've had that feeling, or where you more or less can't recall a word. It was just that feeling. [Starts tape again.]

Case 3

This case begins during the EAT session shortly after the tape reached the age-regression test. The subject stopped the tape at this point and made the following comment:

S: I had very ambiguous feelings, because of the friend there, who was named Racine. Like I was really happy to be there and to see him, but at the same time I was sad that he wasn't there anymore, on my adult side. What went on in my head at this time is a new thing, the first time it ever happened. When you asked me if I wanted to spell the name, what I was saying before, I kind of drifted back to answer in English and then I said to myself, ''No way, it is fun there. I am going to speak French and that's it.'' And I just went back into the classroom, in French.

I: You were speaking in French then, were you?

S: Yes. Does that bother you? [Subject laughs.] I didn't question myself. If I had to answer in French or English, it just went naturally into French.

I: In a sense, that was a decision point for you.

S: Yes.

I: And you decided because it was fun, you'd like to stay in French?

S: Yes.

Later, the subject stopped the tape and made the following comment:

S: As soon as you said, "I want you to write something" I began to ask myself, "Oh, oh. I suppose they didn't think to write it in French; they didn't think to write it in French." It's funny, because it is like a series of reflections I had which is: "Oh well, anyway, if they write it in English, I can always translate them." Why did you place the pencil in my left hand? As soon as you put the pencil in my left hand I said, "Why is he doing that? He knows that I write with my right hand."

I: I didn't know that.

S: Yes I know, I just moved the pen across. After I asked this question and these reflections, I opened my eyes and I just transferred automatically the pen to my right hand.

At a later point in the EAT session, the subject reported that he thought the hypnotist had intruded into the age regression because of all the questions he was asking. The subject's comments on the tape about this were as follows:

S: Why don't you let me just do my thing? Why do you have to ask these questions?

I: That bothered you?

S: Yes, it was taking me out of the situation.

I: What did you want me to do at the time?

S: [Subject laughs.] Stop asking questions, or ask them in French.

I: Did you want me to ask them in French or did you think I shouldn't?

S: Well, I probably wouldn't have to do this shifting each time and maybe I could stay in the situation and just integrate you into the situation.

I: You understood my questions in English. At no time you indicated you didn't. Why did you do that?

S: Why did I understand the questions?

I: Why did you? You accepted my asking everything in English; you communicated with me at all times. Did you ever feel you'd prefer not to?

S: Not really. See, the questions were like, when you were asking questions, I was saying the questions myself and saying it to myself in French and then answering it.

I: Whatever I said you'd translate?

S: Yes. But at the same time, it was really at the end of those questions that it started to bother me, to go bang, bang, bang.

The hidden observer instructions were used to explore the nature of hypnotic consciousness more closely. The subject stopped the tape in the EAT session and commented as follows on these instructions:

S: The shift that goes on when you touch the shoulder is like a zoom back. Like going back to a part that has a clearer understanding of the situation, a kind of holistic view of the situation.

I: Going back with a view, was it? You were going back with a whole view of the situation?

S: Yes. Where I can kind of dissociate "me playing there" from "me seeing and experiencing what I'm doing here."

I: In a way that you couldn't before, or not as well, or what? How does that going back, or being back, compare with what was happening before? If you could say a bit more about that part.

S: When you started, I was there playing and you started saying various things. When you touched the finger, the shoulder, the moment you touched the shoulder it was like suddenly the rest of me was intruding into the situation and showing me now that in the situation you've been living in, there is something else you can comment on this. That is what I call by zooming back and seeing the old situation, the old being me at 5 in the classroom but also me at 29 looking at it and being aware of what's going on.

I: You talked a little earlier about the ambivalence—the joy of seeing Racine and the sadness which is a little like being back, but you're there also. What were you thinking at the time that that happened? What were the kinds of thoughts and feelings and images that came through your mind?

S: I suddenly saw myself more as an analyzer, stopping enjoying the emotion that was going through and just going back and saying, "Okay, now I analyze these things," and I was just commenting on the scene that was there, there it was more like me looking at a TV show when I am not involved into it, but at the same time, also knowing that it is a part of me.

I: This is all on the first tap?

S: Yes.

I: What happened on the second tap?

S: On the second tap it was like if you were giving me the permission to continue living this experience, so I could forget about this analyzing part and just go back into the play.

I: And you wanted to do that?

S: I wanted to do that.

I: Why did you want to do that?

S: That is another ambivalent thing. Both, because actually, it was enjoyable to do it, and moreover because I was conscious that I was playing it, and it was enjoyable to enjoy this. I don't know if you can again, it is like different parts looking at different parts.

I: You were enjoying it but at the same time you knew you were playing it and liked it.

S: Yes. Right.

I: And that was different from the other part of you that had been analyzing it and looking at it.

S: Yes, right. Different and not that much different, except that for . . . No, it is different. Yes, I guess it is, but it is the same kind of real.

I: Can you tell me a little bit more about the playing part?

S: It is like a kind of retrospection. I'm in it, I'm playing it, then all of a sudden something passing through my mind which says, "isn't it fun to be able to play like this?" And I know that the one who says that is not the one who is in the play; it is someone else. Well, someone else which is me also, but it is another part of me.

I: You were thinking these things at the same time?

S: Yes.

I: What did you think I wanted you to do?

S: The whole thing is pleasurable. First, experiencing the playing itself, which is enjoyable, and then being conscious of this enjoyable thing, so it is a double pleasurable experience.

Comment on Cases

Collectively, these cases assert the individual ways in which hypnotic subjects process suggestions that they are given—ways not readily detectable from their behavior and reported experience that they gave during hypnosis. (See extracts from the hypnotic sessions.) The distinctive feature of the case records considered together is the light the EAT data shed on the nature of trance logic response as it occurs in the age-regression context. All three subjects displayed behavior defined in the literature as characterizing paradoxical or incongruous response. When the EAT data are examined, however, the incongruous character of the subjects' behavior is not actually reflected in subjects' waking reflections about what they did. Subjects 2 and 3 involved themselves in a complicated translation process in order to process the questions that were asked by the hypnotist. The decision to respond in another language was quite consistent in nature with the way they processed the suggestions and the type of involvement in the events of hypnosis that they manifested.

Subjects did not simply experience the hypnotist's questions in English and respond in another language without thinking about the consequences of what they were doing. Rather, they attempted to make their behavior consistent, in terms of their experience, by translating the hypnotist's comments into the language they preferred to use. We would ask why such translation was necessary if hypnotic subjects accept—altogether uncritically—reality and suggested information that are contrary or incompatible.

What characterized each subject's experience during the hypnotic session (as revealed by the EAT) was that reality was registered at the same time that suggestions were being processed and performed successfully. For example, while intensely involved in the age-regressed experience, Case 3 was asking himself why the hypnotist put the pencil into his left hand rather than his right; this same subject also reflected on whether the hypnotist would be sensible enough to write the questions in French because that was the language he preferred to speak. Rational thinking occurred contemporaneously with intense imaginative involvement. The occurrence of this kind of information processing was also reported by Laurence (1980; see also Laurence & Perry, 1981) who studied the hidden observer effect using the EAT as the method of inquiry. In this study, 9 of 23 subjects reported the hidden observer effect. When questioned postexperimentally through the EAT, subjects were asked if they really felt that they were 5 years of age during the age-regression test. The 9 subjects who reported the hidden observer effect also gave duality reports (see Laurence & Perry, 1981; Perry, 1980; Perry & Walsh, 1978). Each of these highly susceptible subjects indicated that he or she alternated between being an adult and a child, felt being an adult or a child simultaneously, or felt that he or she was a child in an adult's body. The processing of reality information in our study emerged most strongly in Subject 3's response to the hidden observer instructions.

It seems important to note that the EAT testing yielded the kind of data on the "analyzing part" of the subject that was detectable elsewhere in the session when hidden observer instructions were not employed. It also indicated aspects of the subject's performance that revealed clinically important features of the subject's hypnotic involvement. It was as if the hidden observer instructions focused on the component of cognitive functioning that allowed the subject to comment on reality now that the situation had been defined as appropriate to do so. The EAT data suggest that reality-based functions were always present. The hidden observer instructions simply permitted that part of the experiencing subject to say his piece in a more overt and clearly permissible way.

The complexity of hypnotic consciousness that is apparent from the data clearly demonstrates a subtle mix of reality and suggestion—a mix that is illustrated forcibly by the ambivalent feelings reported by Subject 3 concerning his friend, Racine. Here the subject felt both joy and sadness—joy because the friend was there, but sadness because he knew he was not really there. It is important to note that the subject's feelings were not resolved in favor of either reality (expressed by sadness) or suggestion (expressed by joy). The presence of both reality and suggestion was captured in a distinctive experience of "ambivalence" that reflected the impact of both affective states.

There are also lessons to learn from these case illustrations about the difficulty of using the EAT inquiry in a nondirective manner. In Case 1, for instance, the inquirer was fascinated by the fact that the subject was not speaking in his own language. The incongruity of that behavior was evident to him, if not to the subject (who when awake described the reason the hypnotist did not know it was snowing as "well, he didn't listen"), and he probed directively in order to clarify the confusion in his own mind about the complexity of consciousness that was apparent. The directiveness that was evident here, as well as in the other case records that we presented, raises the possibility that the subjects' reports of their experiences may have been shaped or modified by the inquirers who were involved in the testing. At the same time, however, the opportunity to probe directively can pose relevant questions for the subject, which when answered may very usefully help to clarify the processes that are likely to be involved. The ways in which the EAT may be used toward such specific ends and objectives are explored in some detail in Chapter 9.

SUMMARY DISCUSSION

We find that the evidence relating to the occurrence of age regression in general can be summarized in terms of four basic conclusions drawn from the available data:

1. Hypnotically regressed subjects experience effects that do not parallel exactly events that have happened in the past.
2. The subjects usually indicate superior rather than matching performance with age-relevant norms or actual child response.
3. They perform in a way that is noticeably distinct from adult levels of behavior.
4. But they also behave in a manner that can be duplicated by nonhypnotic subjects working under a variety of sets of motivated instructions.

This chapter began with a descriptive account of three cases of age-regression behavior centering around the demonstration of trance logic, a phenomenon defined in terms of behavior that appears logically inconsistent or incongruous to those who observe it. However, our case descriptions of age regression indicate little about the nature of the cognitive processing that actually accompanied the subjects' response and highlighted the need for further assessment to clarify in an in-depth way the nature of the processes at work. Interpretation of the meaning of their behavior was clearly aided by sensitive inquiry into the phenomenology of their experience.

Data from the EAT inquiry are consistent with the position that subjective events reveal the ultimate essence of hypnosis and that the experience of the susceptible subject needs to be assessed closely in order to understand the meaning of the behavior that occurs. The interpretation offered in the literature for the basic incongruity of trance logic behavior is out of phase, as it were, with the actual experience of the hypnotized subject who, when we look closely at the data, appears to be processing the hypnotist's communications in a problem-solving fashion. This suggests that the diagnosis of incongruity is an inference of the fascinated observer more than a characteristic of the experiencing subject. In order to comprehend the degree of inconsistency or lack of congruity in the behavior of hypnotic subjects, appeal must be made ultimately to the features of the age-regressed experience, the nature of the subjects' cognitive abilities and controls, and the communications of the hypnotist. Data suggest that all of these factors interact to define the full complexity of consciousness that is distinctive to the deeply hypnotized subject.

Results in Table 5.2 tell us that subjects were highly individual in the nature of their cognitive processing of suggestions and that the way in which they cognized about the suggestions they received was a critical factor in determining the kind of age-regressed response that was elicited. It seems that regression is more an active construction process than a cooperative attempt by the hypnotic subject to do what is requested, and hypotheses built around the concepts of revivification and delusion fail to recognize this fact sufficiently. Evidence from the studies reported here and from the work of Nash et al. (1979) suggests that it is under emotional test conditions that the appropriate schemata or organized memories may best be tapped, and further research under affect-laden conditions is needed to indicate the degree to which past memories are revived in detail in hypnosis. Many of the cognitive tests adopted in the studies that have been conducted on age regression would appear to be inappropriate for assessment and have given too little emphasis to the importance of the qualitative or style features of hypnotic subjects' reactions, such as those that we have discussed in this book.

At times, qualitative differences have emerged in the experiments on age regression conducted to date, but few studies have pursued their relevance. O'Connell et al. (1970), for instance, observed differences that were difficult to quantify. Children tested in their study substituted inappropriate words (that they understood) for similar-sounding phrases that they couldn't comprehend and also indicated nonverbal responses that adult subjects did not give; in response to the stimulus *red,* for instance, children handed a red toy to the experimenter, acting out in a way that was not apparent for the adults. Data clearly suggest the need to analyze carefully the type of hypnotic response given by susceptible subjects. Perry and Walsh (1978) found that gross anomalies were not as discriminating as internal inconsistencies in their analysis of age-regressed behavior, but our analysis of the qualitative features of subjects' processing of suggestions indicates that the term "inconsistency" is perhaps not an appropriate concept for reflecting the active way in which some (but not all) subjects structure their involvement to experience what the hypnotist is suggesting.

Discussion of the data from age-regression studies, and particularly data from application of the EAT that we have gathered in the age-regression context, argues forcefully for recognizing the relevance of individual differences in response among hypnotic subjects themselves. Level of aptitude alone is clearly insufficient to account for the essential variability of the data. The three case studies reported here were based upon the responses reported by three very susceptible subjects who all passed age-regression suggestions in a positive way; yet they showed definite differences in the nature of their imaginative involvement, the degree of reality awareness, and the extent to which they complied in a literal fashion with what the hypnotist was suggesting. The individuation that characterized much of their age-regression behavior is consistent with the data from recent research (see McConkey & Sheehan, 1980), which indicates that highly susceptible subjects may lay aside strong cues to behave in a particular way and perform in a manner that nonhypnotic (e.g., simulating) subjects do not. This pattern of response has also been observed in other contexts of testing that have pitted preconceptions about hypnosis against the intent of the hypnotist as communicated in hypnosis (Sheehan, 1971a, 1980).

The process that appears to incorporate best the strong individual differences in response style that may operate in the age-regression context is the motivated cognitive commitment (Dolby & Sheehan, 1977) of susceptible subjects, a process that reflects the active cognitive effort on the susceptible subject's part to process suggestions in terms of his or her preferred experience. The way in which this process manifests itself is no doubt related to the level of the subject's imaginative involvement and the extent to which the subject is influenced by the cue demands for appropriate behavior that are conveyed explicitly or implicitly in the hypnotic setting. Data from several sources now confirm that there are different types of susceptible subjects, and their performance in the hypnotic setting appears to illustrate quite contrasting cognitive and motivational orientations to their tasks.

Future research needs to isolate the sources of this variability in the data and the factors responsible for its occurrence. In that pursuit, attention may very usefully focus on the relationship between particular styles of cognition as shown by hypnotic subjects, the extent to which awareness of reality may structure the form of hypnotic (e.g., age-regressed) behavior, and the impact of the task the subject is completing on the mode of cognition that is being displayed. These and other questions await detailed analysis of the richness of experience of individual susceptible subjects that has yet remained relatively untapped.

6

Hypnotic Dreams and Hallucinations

INTRODUCTION

Central among the wide range of hypnotic phenomena that are fascinating to both the researcher and the clinician are hypnotic dreams and hypnotic hallucinations. In fact, for many they are the most intriguing of the various experiential events that occur during hypnosis. The two hypnotic phenomena overlap in the kinds of underlying processes that they imply, are peculiarly cognitive in nature, and also relate meaningfully to other hypnotic phenomena considered in this book in terms of the quality of the experiences that are associated with them. Both have been described as constructions of imagination that may be transiently confused with reality (E. R. Hilgard, 1977) such that the hypnotized individual may come to believe that his or her dream or hallucination is actually occurring. Both phenomena also involve processes such as absorption and imagery (see Chapter 4) and implicate different modes of cognizing (see Chapter 3) that are employed by susceptible subjects to facilitate their experience.

In our discussion of these phenomena and the processes that underlie them, we review relevant background literature concerning hypnotic dreams and hallucinations and then turn to consider, in some detail, findings arising from our investigation of these phenomena through application of the EAT. We then turn to focus specifically on the notion of reality awareness and present data highlighting its relevance to the understanding of subjects' reactions to hypnotic phenomena. Finally, we look closely at a case study of a highly susceptible subject who experienced a suggested hallucination and was deluded about the reality of what was suggested. Specifically, we examine the subject's reactions when she is confronted by the hypnotist with the reality that contradicts her hallucinatory experience. From these different perspectives and sets of data, we attempt overall to come to a fuller understanding of the processes underlying the phenomena.

Hypnotic Dreams

Hypnotic dreams generally refer to the reported experience of hypnotized subjects in response to a suggestion to dream (Tart, 1965) and, if hypnotized individuals are instructed by a hypnotist to dream about some particular topic, approximately 40% of these persons will subsequently report that they vividly experienced a dream following the suggestion (E. R. Hilgard, 1965). However, the majority of these reports often seem to consist of relatively brief products that could be regarded as simple verbal associations to the topic. Only detailed questioning can determine whether the dreams reported by the individuals are based on delusional, imaginal, or even nonimaginal ideation. Apart from their intrinsic interest as a phenomenon, however, in the clinical context hypnotic dreams can serve as valuable diagnostic and therapeutic tools, and in the experimental context they can provide evidence on the nature of imaginative cognizing.

The literature on hypnotic dreams has been subjected to a number of reviews and critiques (see, e.g., Barber, 1962b; Moss, 1967; Stross & Shevrin, 1967; Tart, 1965), and these reviews have highlighted both the methodological shortcomings of much of the work on hypnotic dreams that has been published as well as the overdependence of investigators on comparisons of hypnotic and nocturnal dreams as a means of investigating the nature of hypnotic dreaming itself.

E. R. Hilgard (1965) has pointed out that there a number of reasons why hypnotic dreams should not be compared too closely with night dreams. Hypnosis, for example, is not the same as sleep, the time and topic of the hypnotic dream is generally specified by the hypnotist, and the subjects know that they are to report their hypnotic dream. Yet, research continues to focus on the comparison, and this focus has largely been on the circumstances of the occurrence, content, accompanying physiological state, and personal experience of the subjects (Levitt & Chapman, 1979). Across each of these comparative points, the data indicate that the circumstances (E. R. Hilgard, 1965), content (Barber, 1962b), psychophysiology (Domhoff, 1964), and subjects' own experience (Tart, 1966) of hypnotic and nocturnal dreaming are quite distinct.

Given the differences in the situational demands that surround hypnotic and sleep dreams, it is somewhat surprising that a number of investigators consider natural and hypnotic dreams to be very similar (e.g., Sacerdote, 1967; Schneck, 1963). For instance, the two types of dreams are quite different psychophysiologically largely because the hypnotic and sleep states differ in terms of their physiological bases (Levitt & Chapman, 1979); interestingly, however, there is some evidence that rapid eye movements, which normally accompany night dreams, may also accompany some hypnotic dreams (e.g., Brady & Rosner, 1966). Nevertheless, as Sacerdote (1967) has argued, although there may not be psychophysiological equivalence between hypnotic and sleep dreams, there may be some psychological equivalence, and a recent study by Barrett (1979) provides some support for this view.

Barrett (1979) related the content of hypnotic dreams to that of nocturnal and waking dreams collected from the same subjects. Her study also investigated the importance of hypnotic ability in determining the type of content across the different dreams. Specifically, those individuals who were capable of deep trance displayed consistencies in the content of hypnotic and nocturnal (but not waking) dreams in terms of characteristics such as length, emotional themes, characters, settings and confabulation. Her study highlighted the fact that hypnotic ability may interact with type of dream and produce different findings; for medium susceptible subjects, for instance, the hypnotic dreams were unlike both nocturnal and waking dreams on the majority of content characteristics that were analyzed (Barrett, 1979).

Dreaming within hypnosis can have therapeutic relevance, and one of the implications of Barrett's (1979) findings is that, in the therapeutic setting, hypnotic dreams should be used differentially with clients of different hypnotic ability. Dreams, for instance, may indicate the nature of the therapeutic relationship. In this regard, Sheehan and Dolby (1979) experimentally illustrated the nature of clinical rapport through a content analysis of hypnotic dreams. Specifically, the dream reports of hypnotic, task-motivated, and imagination subjects were judged by independent raters in terms of subjects' responses to a suggestion to dream about hypnosis. Their findings indicated that hypnotic subjects were much more positive, perceived the hypnotist in a more authoritative manner, and displayed greater rapport evidenced by either protection, care, or guidance than did nonhypnotic subjects. That is, the type of involvement hypnotic subjects displayed in their dreams was appropriately seen as bearing significantly on the nature of hypnotic subjects' interactions with the hypnotist. Dreams, then, can index in clinical fashion the positive cognitive commitment that subjects often make to the hypnotist and his or her communications.

This type of motivated commitment by highly responsive subjects to involve themselves personally in the events of testing was also seen in the data presented in Chapter 5; there, the personal affect and cognitions of subjects were seen to influence the types of age-regressed reactions that the subjects experienced. Dreams and age regression during hypnosis both require some degree of personal input by the hypnotized individual and it seems that input of this type may radically change the way in which subjects process and respond to the communications they receive. The theme of hypnotized subjects' individual reactions to hypnotic instructions is one that we return to frequently throughout this book; it seems that the influence of individuation (see Chapter 3) is most evident in those hypnotic situations where subjects are minimally constrained by the instructions from the hypnotist. In this respect, the commitment of subjects to hypnotic responding is not operationalized through goal-directed fantasy (see Chapter 4), which essentially stems from the cues of the hypnotist, but rather through constructive or independent cognizing (see Chapters 3, 4, and 5), which essentially stems from the personal initiative of the hypnotized subject. Hypnotic hallucinations can also be highly influenced by a subject's personal cognitions and motivations, and we now consider relevant literature dealing with this phenomenon.

Hypnotic Hallucinations

Binet and Fere (1886/1888) originally pointed out that the germ of a hallucination is in every mental image and argued that the development of one to the other is most likely to occur in hypnosis. Hallucinations essentially occur when an event that has no objective basis in external sensory stimuli is accepted as real and externally present by the individual. In fact, the potential for confusing mental events with the perception of events occurring outside of the organism exists in most normal individuals (Orne, 1962). Hypnosis is a condition in which radical distortions of perception occur (Bowers, 1976; E. R. Hilgard, 1965; Orne, 1977) and, consequently, to hallucinate in response to an appropriate suggestion during hypnosis is widely considered to be one of the basic phenomena of hypnosis. In fact, one of the most interesting demonstrations of the validity of hypnotic effects is to see a hypnotized individual exercise his or her imagination following a suggestion by the hypnotist where the experience is vivid enough that the absent object or person is perceived and interacted with as if actually present (the phenomenon in this instance is a case of positive visual hallucination). A range of positive and negative (i.e., responding to an object or person that is present as if it was not) hallucinations can occur across the entire range of sensory modalities. In this chapter we focus on positive visual hallucinations, and the reader is referred elsewhere for a review of other types of hallucinatory experiences (see, e.g., Bowers, 1976; E. R. Hilgard, 1965).

A typical hypnotic hallucinatory experience is illustrated by the test item on the Stanford scales (see Chapter 2 for description), where instruction is given for the hallucination of a fly or mosquito. This item involves distortions of visual, auditory, and tactile perception and, although it is considered to be an item that requires cognitive skills such as imagination, it is scored in terms of the subject's motor response (see Chapter 2 for further details). E. R. Hilgard (1965) correctly reports that not all of those subjects who pass the item on the basis of a motor response necessarily experience it as hallucination; in fact, subjects who respond positively to the suggestion often report a great variety of underlying sensory experiences. This finding is consistent with our concern throughout this book with the essential variability of experience underlying apparently similar hypnotic behavior by responsive individuals.

Another test of positive hallucination that has provided important data on the nature and reality value of the experience of hallucination is that of a hallucinated second light (see E. R. Hilgard, 1965; Hilgard, Lauer, & Morgan, 1963), which is an item from the SPS:I and II (see Chapter 2 for a discussion of these valuable, though little used, scales). In this test, subjects are informed that they will see two lights on a box, which actually has only one light on it. Analysis of the subjects' descriptions of the experience suggests that there is a wide range of reality awareness or monitoring by subjects who are experiencing a hypnotic hallucination. E. R. Hilgard (1965) reports that about half of the subjects considered they knew which light was real (although at least one of these subjects was wrong). In determining which light was real, most subjects reported that it was the brighter one. The intensity of the experience of the light was generally greater for the externally present (i.e., real) rather than the internally generated (i.e., hallucinated) event; nevertheless, some subjects were quite deluded about the nature of their suggested experience. For some, but not all, hypnotic subjects, then, hallucinations seem to have a high level of equivalence with perceived events, and the degree of reality awareness obviously varies among susceptible subjects who indicate that they are experiencing hallucinatory effects by passing hallucination items on test scales.

The concept of hypnotic hallucination is difficult to define, and the major problem in attempting to define the construct appears to lie with classifying the relative importance of the imaginal and delusional components of the hallucinatory experience (Sheehan, 1979b). The issue is complicated by the fact that these components may be cued by the hypnotist. Instructions to subjects to hallucinate in the hypnotic context frequently convey explicit cues that may form the basis for the way in which the experience is reported. The cues that are present, for instance, may lead subjects to report their experience of events as either imaginal or externally real and delusional. Evidence has accumulated to indicate that the processes of imagination play a central role in hypnotic hallucinations (e.g., J. R. Hilgard, 1970; Sheehan, 1979b), but debate continues about the involvement of perceptual processes in the phenomenon.

There has been considerable research on whether hypnotic hallucinations result in an activation of actual perceptual processes. There is some evidence, for instance, of transfer effects of perceptual processing during hypnosis (e.g., Dolby & Sheehan, 1977; Graham & Leibowitz, 1972; Sheehan & Dolby, 1975). Reports of afterimages to hallucinated colors (e.g., Barber, 1959; Sutcliffe, 1960, 1961) have also been presented, although much of this evidence can be viewed in terms of the influence of demand characteristics of the hypnotic situation, rather than the impact of hypnosis. In summary of the evidence to date, just as there is little ground to support the notion of reinstatement of particular effects during age regression (see Chapter 5), no study yet unequivocally supports the notion that hypnotic hallucinations reinstate the processes of actual perception.

The close inspection of the phenomenon and processes of age regression that we undertook in Chapter 5 assisted in clarifying its nature and effects. We turn therefore to look in detail at data on hypnotic dreams and hallucinations that were yielded through application of the EAT as a technique of inquiry into subjects' experiences of the two phenomena.

EAT EVIDENCE ON DREAMS AND HALLUCINATIONS

In this section, we first consider the procedures we used in analyzing subjects' responsiveness in a hypnotic test session in which they were asked to dream and to hallucinate prior to the application of the EAT, which followed the standard guidelines for the technique that we set out in Chapter 3. We then consider the data obtained from judges' ratings of subjects' EAT comments concerning their dream and hallucination experiences and present relevant case extracts from their reports.

Hypnotic and EAT Testing

Initially, in our study, 44 highly responsive subjects who had received a mean score of 10.14 (SD = .84) on prior testing on the 12-item HGSHS:A were individually tested on seven routine hypnotic items as well as on hypnotic dream and hypnotic hallucination items. The dream suggestion was adapted from Weitzenhoffer and Hilgard's (1962) SHSS:C and was as follows:

> We are very much interested in finding out what hypnosis and being hypnotized means to people. One of the best ways of finding out is through the dreams people have while they are hypnotized. Now neither you nor I know what sort of dream you are going to have, but I am going to allow you to rest for a little while and you are going to have a dream, a real dream, just the kind you have when you are asleep at night. When I stop talking to you very shortly, you will begin to dream. You will have a dream about hypnosis. You will dream about what hypnosis means. Now you are falling asleep, deeper and deeper asleep, very much like when you fall asleep at night. You will begin to dream.

The hypnotic hallucination item involved a suggestion for the positive visual hallucination of a person with whom the subjects had spoken prior to meeting the hypnotist; the hallucination of this person was chosen in order to provide a controlled stimulus that was equally familiar to all subjects and one with which they could interact in a personal way. The instructions for the hallucination suggestion were as follows:

> In a moment I am going to get you to open your eyes, remaining deeply relaxed and deeply hypnotized. When you open your eyes, you will see somebody sitting in the chair over to your left. You remember [the person] with whom you met and spoke

at the beginning of the session. When you open your eyes she will be sitting in the chair over to your left, just where she was sitting at the beginning of the session when she met you. [The person] will be sitting in the chair to your left. You remember her with the long brown hair and wearing [the hypnotist here describes a salient item of her clothing]. The person who was sitting and talking with you here at the beginning of the session, sitting in the chair over to your left. In a moment I will get you to open your eyes slowly and gently and to look over to the chair on your left. She will be there; you will see her sitting there. Now open your eyes and tell me what you see.

Following hypnotic testing, another experimenter (the inquirer) conducted an intensive investigation of subjects' experiences of the dream and hallucination items through application of the EAT. Subjects were initially given the routine EAT instructions to encourage their involvement in the recall and discussion of their hypnotic experiences, and then shown the video-tape playback of their hypnotic performance on the dream and hallucination items. In accordance with the procedures that we have developed for nondirective inquiry using the video-tape method of the EAT (see Chapter 3 for a full discussion), the inquirer explored the nature of subjects' recall of their hypnotic experiences whenever they spontaneously stopped the video-tape playback. Specifically, the inquirer attempted to question subjects in a way that elicited and clarified the nature of their cognitive processes and phenomenal awareness during the hypnotic dream and the hypnotic hallucination.

Judges' Ratings of the Data

The EAT session itself was video-tape recorded, and the segments relating to the dream and the hallucination were both rated by two independent judges who were trained and experienced in the rating of subjective dimensions relevant to gaining an understanding of the nature of hypnosis. For both the dream and hallucination items, the raters scored the material elicited by the EAT in terms of the information that it revealed concerning each of 10 dimensions; these dimensions were rated on a 5-point scale in terms of the degree to which subjects' comments indicated that the dimension was present in their hypnotic experience (0 = not present; 1 = slightly present; 2 = moderately present; 3 = substantially present; and 4 = extremely present). The 10 dimensions and brief descriptions of them are as follows.

Concentrative Cognizing.   The concentrative mode of cognizing is characterized by subjects concentrating on the communications of the hypnotist and thinking along in literal fashion with the messages contained in those communications (see Chapter 3 for a full description). In this mode, subjects typically do not allow irrelevant thoughts to be considered but appear to focus their attention on the text of the suggestion.

Independent Cognizing.   The independent mode of cognizing is characterized by subjects processing the experience suggested by the hypnotist in terms of its personal meaningfulness (see Chapter 3 for a full description). Subjects who demonstrate this mode of thinking do not simply concentrate on the literal messages of the hypnotist but choose, as it were, those aspects of the experience that they themselves consider appropriate to their situation and respond in quite independent fashion. The naturalness of one's own responsiveness to the situation appears to be the most important facet of response for the type of subject who displays independent processing, and there is generally little evidence of any compulsion to concentrate on and adhere to what the hypnotist is literally suggesting.

Constructive Cognizing.   The constructive mode of cognizing is characterized by subjects considering the communications of the hypnotist from a position of preparedness to process the incoming stimulus information in a schematic way so as to structure events in accordance with what the hypnotist is suggesting (see Chapter 3 for a full description). Subjects who demonstrate this mode do not simply concentrate on the literal messages of the hypnotist, nor do they necessarily interpret them personally. Rather, they cognitively respond by actively seeking out ways to construct or synthesize the experience that is being suggested. It appears that this type of subject plans cognitively in a specifically effortful fashion in order to respond in a way that he or she considers appropriate to what is being suggested.

Individuation.   Subjects demonstrate individuation when they indicate that they accept or interpret the communications of the hypnotist in a particularly individual or personally meaningful manner (see Chapter 3 for a full description). The degree to which subjects idiosyncratically perceive and interpret the hypnotist's messages in order to accomodate their personal views and experiences indexes this dimension, which appears related to independent and constructive, rather than concentrative, cognizing (see Chapters 3 and 4).

Imagery.   Subjects demonstrate imagery to the extent to which they indicate that mental events occurring during hypnosis function at a level of vividness somewhat akin to that of actual percepts (see Sheehan, 1979b; Shor, 1979; Chapter 4 for a full description). The degree to which subjects employ imaginal strategies in their experiences indexes this dimension.

Absorption.   Subjects demonstrate absorption to the extent that they indicate they are attentively engrossed in the hypnotic experience suggested by the hypnotist (see J. R. Hilgard, 1970; Shor, 1979; Tellegen & Atkinson, 1974; Chapter 4 for a full description). The degree to which subjects report being imaginatively involved in their experiences in this way indexes this dimension.

Involuntariness.   This dimension is evidenced by subjects indicating that the hypnotic experience has a quality of occurring without any conscious effort or control on their part (see Bowers, 1978; Spanos, 1981; Chapter 4 for a full description). The degree to which the hypnotic event is experienced as occurring nonvolitionally indexes this dimension.

Reality Awareness.   This dimension is evidenced by subjects indicating that they are aware of the reality of the situation in which they are placed. The reporting of that reality occurs in association with an experience of the hypnotic event that is often inconsistent with that reality (see McConkey, 1979; see also this chapter and Chapter 10 for further discussion). The dimension is indexed by the degree to which subjects monitor and process reality (together with suggested) information.

Physical Sensation.   This dimension is evidenced by subjects indicating that they experience distinctive physical feelings of one sort or another when they are experiencing the hypnotically suggested event. Changes in physical sensation were not a suggested aspect of either item; hence, this dimension indexes a nonsuggested attribute of the experience.

Rapport.   The degree of positive interpersonal reactions between subject and hypnotist are specifically tapped by this dimension. The extent to which subjects indicate that they feel a positive and trusting relationship with the hypnotist during their hypnotic experiences indexes this dimension (see Sheehan, 1980; Shor, 1979; Chapter 5 for a full description).

The raters independently scored both the hypnotic dream and the hypnotic hallucination on each of these dimensions for the 44 subjects, and one rater rescored 10 randomly selected subjects so that we might measure intrarater reliability. Table 3.5 (see Chapter 3) includes the correlation coefficients that index inter- and intrarater reliability on each of these dimensions for the two items; the majority of these correlations are significant and indicate a high degree of agreement between the raters for the various subjective dimensions that were assessed. This reliability of ratings of EAT data is consistent with what we observed and reported in Chapters 3, 4, and 5.

Rating of Hypnotic Dream

Table 6.1 sets out the mean ratings on each of the dimensions we are considering for those subjects who responded positively and negatively to the dream suggestion. On the 7-item hypnotic scale that we employed, those subjects who responded positively to the dream suggestion ($M = 6.14$, $SD = .77$) received scores similar to those subjects who responded negatively ($M = 5.77$, SD

TABLE 6.1
Mean Ratings on Each of Ten Dimensions for Subjects Who
Responded Positively and Negatively to the Dream Suggestion

	Response	
Dimension	Positive (n = 35)	Negative (n = 9)
Concentrative cognizing	.14 (.42)	.00 (.00)
Independent cognizing	.63 (1.12)	.00 (.00)
Constructive cognizing	.14 (.54)	.00 (.00)
Individuation	1.06 (1.29)	.11 (.31)*
Imagery	1.49 (1.27)	.33 (.47)*
Absorption	1.60 (1.13)	.67 (.47)*
Involuntariness	.80 (1.12)	.00 (.00)*
Reality awareness	.31 (.71)	.78 (.92)
Physical sensation	.26 (.50)	.22 (.42)
Rapport	.97 (1.16)	1.44 (.83)

Note. For ratings on each dimension, 0 = not present and 4 = extremely present.
*$p < .05$

= .44); that is, differences among subjects can not be explained on the basis of their different degrees of hypnotic responsiveness. This finding is consistent with others presented in this book, which highlight the variability in experience underlying objectively similar hypnotic response.

Comparisons of the mean ratings on each of the dimensions obtained by positive and negative responders indicated that these two groups of subjects differed significantly on the dimensions of individuation, $t(42) = 2.14$, $p < .05$; imagery, $t(42) = 2.60$, $p < .05$; absorption, $t(42) = 2.39$, $p < .05$; and involuntariness, $t(42) = 2.10$, $p < .05$. That is, those subjects who experienced the hypnotic dreams were more obviously characterized by the individual quality of their dream experiences, the vivid nature of their dream imagery, the degree to which they were attentively engrossed in their dream experience, and the nonvolitional quality of the dream experience itself. The characteristics of imagery, absorption, and involuntariness are consistent with the processes we saw to be associated with ideomotor response in Chapter 4, and the data help us to understand some of the relevant process features of susceptible subjects' involvement in hypnotic dreaming.

In order to explore more fully the pattern of relationships among these response features, the data were intercorrelated, and the resulting matrix for subjects who responded positively to the dream suggestion is presented in Table 6.2. Data indicate that independent cognizing is appreciably related to individuation, imagery, absorption, and physical sensation; individuation, in turn, is related to imagery, absorption, and physical sensation; imagery is appreciably related to absorption and involuntariness but negatively related to reality awareness or monitoring; and absorption is positively related to involuntariness and rapport but negatively related to reality awareness. This pattern of relationships, especially that of independent cognizing, individuation, and absorption highlight the degree to which some highly responsive subjects become imaginatively involved in personally meaningful hypnotic dreams. In Chapter 3, we discussed the relevance of hypnotic task to the type of cognitive processes brought to bear by subjects, and these data indicate that particular patterns of cognitive responding are meaningfully associated with hypnotic dreaming. But data from our study suggest that the dimensions we analyzed tapped the style of independent cognizing much more than the style of concentrative cognizing.

The independent cognizing by subjects during the dream suggestion was reported clearly in a number of cases. For instance, one subject reported: "When [the hypnotist] asked me to dream about hypnosis, it wasn't so much what it meant to me, but how I felt, and so I had a relaxed sort of dream of sitting by a tree patting a dog''; this subject went on further to point out that she "wasn't really thinking of the hypnotist and what he wanted at all,'' and only when he moved did she become aware of him (but then she did so). Another subject who displayed independent cognizing employed the dream experience in a personally meaningful fashion to fantasize about a desired event. This subject reported dreaming that she "was with a friend who is skeptical about hypnosis and was tripping around Europe and people were trying to hypnotize her friend.'' The subject explained that she was planning a trip to Europe with this friend and often daydreamed about the planned adventure. The majority of subjects personalized

TABLE 6.2
Intercorrelation Matrix for Ten Dimensions for Subjects Who
Responded Positively to the Dream Suggestion

Dimensions					Dimensions					
	1	2	3	4	5	6	7	8	9	10
1. Concentrative		-.19	-.09	-.28	-.02	.06	.24	.23	-.17	.24
2. Independent			-.15	.77*	.55*	.54*	-.01	-.14	.43*	.12
3. Constructive				.15	.23	.14	-.19	-.04	-.14	-.08
4. Individuation					.86*	.77*	.29	-.30	.42*	.21
5. Imagery						.89*	.51*	-.33*	.21	.24
6. Absorption							.57*	-.31*	.29	.39*
7. Involuntariness								-.17	-.16	.30
8. Reality awareness									-.15	.08
9. Physical sensation										.11
10. Rapport										

*$p < .05$

their dream experience to some degree, and this is reportedly consistent with their experiences of both nocturnal and waking dreams.

Individuation was also evident in the dream reports of a number of subjects. The subject who took the dream opportunity to fantasize about her planned trip to Europe, for instance, offers an example of the process at work. Another subject who experienced a dream in personally meaningful fashion reported that thoughts of ''a desert island and playing in a football cup final'' were both going through his mind even though the hypnotist had asked him to dream about hypnosis; he went on to explain that both of these fantasized events were things that he very much wanted to do and he found himself ''just sort of becoming involved in them'' when asked to dream about hypnosis.

In all of these dream reports that we have selected, the degree of imagery reported by subjects as part of the dream experience was quite vivid and compelling. One subject, for instance, reported that she was wondering what she could dream about when ''all of a sudden a picture of a brain in color came to mind and the dream sort of backtracked from there with a person being wheeled into an operating theater and their brain was laid bare''; this subject's further descriptions of the ''bits of tinsel that flowed out of the brain like a fountain and lit up the patient's veins'' dramatically highlighted the compelling and vivid nature of her imaginal ideations during the dream experience. Another subject, who had a somewhat more conventional dream of watching a demonstration of stage hypnosis reported that her ''imagery was intense, I could see exactly where I was sitting, who I was with, and even what I ate during the interval.'' Overall, vivid images played a major role in the experience of the hypnotic dream for the majority of subjects.

Most subjects displayed a high level of absorption in their dream experiences, even if the dream experienced was somewhat unpleasant. This situation was illustrated by the subject who reported that for the dream ''an image of a hospital seemed to come from nowhere, and I seemed to have the exact state of mind like when you are drifting off to sleep.'' The same subject also reported that she was ''upset about the hospital scenes and would have liked to have had a rest at one point during the dream, but the scenes just seemed to keep going on.''

This nonvolitional quality of subjects' dreams was observed in a number of instances. For instance, one other subject reported: ''I tried to set my mind to dreaming about hypnosis but I couldn't because all I could see was a red color that turned into flames with a house burning and I couldn't get off the fire to dream about hypnosis.'' Another subject reported that she felt as if she was very deeply hypnotized and that she could not focus her mind to think about hypnosis but nevertheless ''all the hypnosis sessions I've seen and all that I've experienced about hypnosis came to me in a very jumbled up fashion, all sort of out of focus.'' In a sense, mixtures of active cognizing and involuntariness were evident in the subject's experience of the dream item suggesting that a number of hypnotic experiences may evidence both cognitive effort and nonvolitional experiencing, albeit at different levels of awareness. This state of affairs can perhaps be understood if one considers the experiences of normal nocturnal or waking dreaming. In both of these cases, particular cognitions may facilitate the focus and content of the dream, but the experience itself can seem involuntary. Still, many questions remain unanswered concerning this type of event, and there is obviously need for close analysis of the way in which subjects attribute their experiences.

Rating of Hypnotic Hallucination

Subjects' EAT-elicited descriptions of their experience of the hypnotic hallucination were also rated on the 10 dimensions that we have outlined. Table 6.3 sets out the mean ratings on each of the dimensions for those subjects who responded positively and negatively to the hallucination suggestion. On the 7-item hypnotic scale that we employed, subjects who responded positively to the hypnotic hallucination suggestion ($M = 6.47$, $SD = .51$) received scores similar to those subjects who responded negatively ($M = 5.76$, $SD = .73$). As with the dream item, then, differences among subjects in terms of their experience cannot be explained on the basis of their different levels of hypnotic responsiveness. Comparisons of the mean ratings on each of the dimensions obtained by positive and negative responders indicated that these two groups of subjects differed signifi-

TABLE 6.3

Mean Ratings on Each of Ten Dimensions for Subjects Who Responded
Positively and Negatively to the Hallucination Suggestion

| | Response | |
| | Positive | Negative |
Dimension	(n = 19)	(n = 25)
Concentrative cognizing	.68 (.86)	.12 (.43)*
Independent cognizing	.16 (.67)	.00 (.00)
Constructive cognizing	.42 (.94)	.16 (.37)
Individuation	.74 (1.16)	.12 (.33)*
Imagery	2.05 (1.10)	.44 (.57)**
Absorption	1.79 (.89)	.40 (.49)**
Involuntariness	.68 (1.17)	.04 (.20)
Reality awareness	.89 (1.25)	1.80 (1.36)*
Physical sensation	.05 (.22)	.00 (.00)
Rapport	.84 (1.09)	.72 (.96)

Note. For ratings on each dimension, 0 = not present and 4 = extremely present.
*$p < .05$
**$p < .01$

cantly on the dimensions of concentrative cognizing, $t(42) = 2.77$, $p < .05$; individuation, $t(42) = 2.47$, $p < .05$; imagery $t(42) = 6.16$, $p < .01$; absorption, $t(42) = 6.43$, $p < .01$; and reality awareness, $t(42) = 2.21$, $p < .05$. Those subjects who experienced the hallucination displayed more concentrative cognizing, idiosyncratic experiences, vivid mental images, engrossing attention, feelings of nonvolition, and less awareness of the reality of the situation than those who did not experience the hallucination.

These findings indicate that, for the suggestions which we used, concentrative cognizing and individuation were more closely associated with subjects' experience of the hallucination response than they were with their experience of the dream. In this instance, hallucinations seemed to be characterized more by subjects focusing their attention on the communications of the hypnotist in concentrative fashion than by their attempting to construct a response to the hypnotist in terms of their involvement in the suggested events. It is also important to note that, although there was appreciably less reality awareness for subjects who passed as compared with those who failed the hallucination suggestion, the EAT data show that reality information was processed by subjects, even though they were also experiencing the hallucination.

To explore further the pattern of relationships among these data, ratings were intercorrelated and the resulting matrix for those subjects who responded positively to the hallucination suggestion is presented in Table 6.4. The data indicate that for the experience of hypnotic hallucination, independent cognizing was positively related to individuation and reality awareness; constructive cognizing was positively related to individuation, which in turn was related to imagery and absorption; imagery was positively related to absorption, involuntariness, and rapport; and absorption was related to involuntariness, which was also related to

TABLE 6.4
Intercorrelation Matrix for Ten Dimensions for Subjects Who
Responded Positively to the Hallucination Suggestion

Dimensions		1	2	3	4	5	6	7	8	9	10
1.	Concentrative		-.19	-.36	-.35	-.32	-.09	-.31	-.18	-.19	-.11
2.	Independent			-.11	.46*	.20	.32	-.14	.58*	-.01	-.18
3.	Constructive				.59*	.23	.42	.07	-.01	-.11	-.19
4.	Individuation					.67*	.76*	.36	.24	.05	.13
5.	Imagery						.82*	.71*	.20	.42	.45*
6.	Absorption							.54*	.22	.32	.24
7.	Involuntariness								.01	.67*	.66*
8.	Reality awareness									.00	.32
9.	Physical sensation										.69*
10.	Rapport										

*$p < .05$

physical sensation and rapport, both of which themselves correlated appreciably together. Those subjects who cognized in independent fashion were quite likely to interpret the situation in a personally meaningful fashion as well as being aware of the reality aspects of the situation while experiencing the hallucinated person. Constructive cognizers, on the other hand, also became highly involved with the hallucinated event but showed less evidence of being aware of what was really occurring.

The relationship between independent cognizing and individuation that we observed here was not as strong as what we observed in the data concerning subjects' dream experience (although the association was appreciable for both items). Arguably, hallucination, more than the dream situation, placed constraints on subjects in terms of the degree to which they could involve themselves personally in the hypnotic events. In this regard, also, the finding that independent cognizing was related to reality awareness by subjects was distinctive to the hallucination experience; such a relationship was not observed in the data concerning the dream experience and suggests that reality events play a much greater role in delimiting some hypnotic responses rather than others.

Looking across the dream and hallucination tasks, there are obvious differences as well as similarities in the patterns of correlations that we observed. Constructive cognizing, for instance, was more related to individuation in the hallucination than in the dream data, and this again suggests the relevance of considering task-style interactions when investigating the processes that underlie the hypnotic phenomena (a theme we discuss further in Chapters 3 and 10). In terms of similarities, the relationships among the dimensions of individuation, imagery, and absorption formed a strong and clear pattern, as did the association between absorption and involuntariness across both tasks. These data support the observations made in Chapter 4 and elsewhere in the hypnotic literature (e.g., Spanos, 1981; Tellegen & Atkinson, 1974) concerning the importance of subjects' attentive involvement in their tasks and the fact that they often attribute their experience as occurring effortlessly.

Consistent with our theme of interindividual differences in hypnotic performance, the cognizing of susceptible subjects in response to the hallucination suggestion was quite diverse. The majority of subjects attempted to focus their thinking and imagination on the suggested event. One subject, for instance, reported that when the hypnotist gave the hallucination suggestion, she thought "that [the suggested person] must have quietly entered the room and I just started thinking of [that person] and thinking that I must see her." Most other subjects displayed a similar positive expectancy to see the suggested hallucination and, as one subject put it, they "really expected to see her there." Independent cognizing was clearly evidenced by some subjects in their reports of the hallucinatory experience. For instance, one subject reported that she was "thinking about her thoughts rather than thinking about what the hypnotist was saying"; this subject nevertheless experienced the hallucination because she "personally identified with [the hallucination]." This particular subject also reported a transparent quality to the hallucination in commenting that "[the hallucination] was not solid enough to touch, but was sort of there even though I knew it wasn't really there." Another subject clearly used strategies to construct the hallucination by reporting that she "thought [she] heard someone come into the room and so it was quite easy to see [the hallucinated person] there. I just thought of her coming in and heard the door open and was thinking of her when I opened my eyes and saw [the hallucination] sitting there."

Individuation was also evident to varying degrees in the reports of subjects. One subject, for instance, reported in quite independent fashion that she saw the hallucination because she wanted to; that is, she "had the power of mind to see anything then, because I was feeling really comfortable in the session and had a very trusting sort of feeling toward the hypnotist." This particular subject also considered that during hypnosis her feelings of total honesty and imaginative capacity were easily brought to the fore, and it was personally important for her to have the hypnotist see this deeper, more meaningful part of her.

The vividness of the imagery involved in the positive experience of the hallucination was especially evident in one subject's report that "I could clearly see [the hallucinated person] sitting there wearing a blue shirt and jeans and a leather belt." In fact, the person that was being hallucinated actually wore an orange shirt and black slacks, so this response again highlights the confabulation that can occur in the private experiences of hypnotically responsive subjects during hypnosis. As indicated in the data, subjects who vividly experienced the hallucination were also clearly absorbed in their experience. The subject who reported that she heard the hallucinated person walk into the room, for instance, was attentively engrossed in her ongoing experience as was the subject who reported that she could see the hallucinated person "taking notes about what was happening."

As with the dream experience, there was some evidence of cognitive effort initiating the hallucinatory event, with the event itself apparently being experienced in a somewhat involuntary fashion. However, some subjects reported no conscious cognitive effort and were clearly surprised by their perception of the hallucination, reporting for instance, "that I'd just wait for things to happen and was amused to find that they did." But overall, there was an intermixing of effort and involuntariness, albeit at apparently different levels of cognizing about the suggested event.

Collectively, these data relating to subjects' experiences of hypnotic dreams and hallucinations highlight the individual differences that exist in subjects' cognitive modes of responding. The processes of individuation, imagery vividness, absorption, and experienced involuntariness emerge as highly relevant dimensions for coming to an understanding of the nature of phenomenal awareness and cognizing during hypnosis. The data tell us in a rather intriguing way, however, that subjects' reality awareness or monitoring of hypnotic events has a meaningful influence on their experience of hypnotic suggestions. We now consider this issue in more detail.

REALITY AWARENESS IN HYPNOSIS

Consistent with the data presented here, a previous program of research by McConkey (1979) has indicated that subjects are frequently aware of incompatible reality information even when the hypnotist does not explicitly supply the information. Analysis indicated that awareness of events discordant with those being suggested by the hypnotist may interfere with the hypnotic responding of some subjects but not others. Similar to the findings of Zamansky (1977), McConkey (1979) reported that some, but not all, susceptible subjects employed their knowledge of how the hypnotist wanted them to respond in order to structure their handling of reality information; other subjects, however, engaged in cognitive activity in order to resolve the situation in terms of their own experience.

The communications of the hypnotist are an important determinant of response, but they are not the only one. As we have seen, subjects interpret the hypnotist's communications often in quite idiosyncratic fashion. In this respect, McConkey (1979) found that subjects sometimes make a large effort to respond within a framework of suggestion so as to prevent the reality information from interfering with their performance. For these types of subjects, it appears that their response is constructed on the basis of their desired experience rather than on the environmental input. This comment that the constructive act of responding is controlled by subjects' experience rather than reality constraints is compatible with theorizing of others about the processes of visual imagination (Neisser, 1967, 1976) and effortless experiencing (Bowers & Bowers, 1979).

The interaction of reality and suggestion in hypnosis indicates that some hypnotic subjects, when faced with reality constraints, attempt to incorporate that knowledge within a framework consistent with their preparedness for positive response. That is, reality as it impinges on hypnotic subjects may be processed cognitively by some subjects to match the suggestions that are given. White (1941) emphasized this cognitive effort of hypnotic subjects when he cogently argued that subjects respond to suggestions in ways that are consonant with their strivings. The data presented in this book are collectively consistent with the general theorizing of White (1941) and highlight the importance of recognizing hypnotic subjects' cognitive readiness to process incoming environmental inputs idiosyncratically in order to respond to the suggestions given by the hypnotist in ways perceived as appropriate.

However, the hypnotic situation is complex and, given such complexity, it becomes especially relevant to try and determine the degree to which subjects are aware of the reality of their situation or the event that has been suggested to them, and whether the processing of reality and suggested information occurs contemporaneously in hypnotic consciousness. In order to investigate this, 10 highly susceptible subjects were shown video-tape versions of their previous hypnotic sessions in the presence of an independent inquirer who fostered subjects' personal comments about their experiences. Following this application of the standard version of the EAT (see Chapter 3 for procedural details), the information provided by subjects was scored by two independent judges in terms of the degree to which subjects' EAT comments indicated that they had an awareness of both reality and suggested events during the various hypnotic items that they were administered. The hypnotic items on which subjects were tested included age regression, glove analgesia, missing number, hallucination, missing watch hand, and posthypnotic amnesia. In objective terms, most subjects responded positively to each of the suggestions.

The incidence of reality awareness reported by subjects in terms of each of the hypnotic test items is set out in Table 6.5. Overall, the data indicated that subjects perceived and experienced both reality and suggestion demands. Subjects commented on reality aspects of their orientation when asked to spell difficult words while age regressed, on the glove analgesia item, when asked to do arithmetic during the missing number item, during the hallucination item, and when asked to tell time under the suggestion of a missing watch hand. Clearly, most subjects were aware of reality demands across a range of hypnotic tasks and frequently processed features of their environment from outside the framework of suggestion that was established by the hypnotist while still responding success-

TABLE 6.5

Incidence of Reality Awareness Evident in Subjects' EAT
Comments Across a Range of Hypnotic Items

				Items		
Subject number	Age regression	Glove analgesia	Missing number	Hallucination	Missing watch hand	Post-hypnotic amnesia
1	+(+)	+(+)	(+)			
2	+(+)		(+)			
3	+(+)					
4	+(+)		+(+)		+(+)	
5	+(+)					
6	+(+)		+(+)	+(+)	+(+)	
7	+(+)		+(+)		+	(+)
8	+(+)		+(+)	+(+)	+(+)	
9	+(+)	(+)	+(+)		(+)	
10	+(+)		+(+)		+(+)	

Note. + = comments indicated awareness of the demands of both reality and suggestion.
Ratings of second rater appear in parentheses. Raters agreed in 79.31% of cases.

fully to the item. The following examples illustrate the point at a more clinical level.

A major factor underlying subjects' attempts at processing reality information was their apparent preparedness or readiness to respond positively to suggestions. The set to respond in positive fashion was seen to create different effects in the way subjects processed suggestions. One subject, for instance, gave a particularly vivid account of her motivated cognitive commitment to respond, despite being aware of the conflicting features of the situation in which she was placed. The way in which this subject resolved her awareness of reality demands points to an important issue in understanding some of the salient features of hypnotic subjects' consciousness. In commenting on her experience of the hallucination item, for instance, this subject said: "I feel such a hypocrite when he says things like that. It's not really there, and everything like that, but once he says something, it stacks a lot of thought, and you think, it's there, it's positive." In commenting further about reality intruding into her experiences, this subject added: "He tells me to visualize something, and here I am trying hard to visualize something, and then I visualize it. In all common sense you have to say 'no, it's not there,' but that's where the hypocrisy comes in, you know, I can still see it, because it's in my line of thought." Reality information had a definite impact on the experience of this subject, but conflict was resolved through a strong cognitive set to respond positively to the hypnotist's suggestion.

Data are also available that index the varying types and degrees of awareness experienced across different hypnotic test tasks. For instance, in commenting on the age-regression item, one subject said: "When we were going right back and I was one, he was asking me my name. Well I couldn't really respond to that. I didn't have that much verbal command, speech or anything. I felt like saying 'I can't think of my name.'" This example illustrates how the subject perceived and responded to the conflict in the situation by acknowledging the difficulties that were involved. Another subject experienced both reality and suggested features of his environment in the following way on the missing number item: "I did the rest of the sums, but it kept worrying me [that I had used the missing number 6] and so I went back and changed it to a 7, because I thought it should be 1 more"; this subject differed by taking definite action to resolve the conflict that was experienced. Other subjects not only acknowledged the difficulties but were critical of the hypnotist because of them. In commenting on being asked to spell while age regressed, one subject indicated: "How the hell do I spell something like *journal?* Obviously, I wouldn't have the ability at that age. It seemed to me a little unfair of [the hypnotist] to give a spelling test to a 5-year-old kid."

One of the major inferences that can be drawn from these data is that reality is often experienced, but there is marked variation in the way in which it is processed, and we return to discuss some specific theoretical implications of this inference for understanding process in Chapter 10. Obviously, the processes of cognition, motivation, and situation influences operate together to determine the behavior and experience of hypnotic subjects. The ways in which subjects perceive and operate on the reality demands of the situation clearly vary across items, however, despite the fact that there is a general orientation among hypnotic subjects to respond behaviorally in positive fashion. These subjects' positive set to respond has clear motivational implications and, although they have not been studied intensively in the research reported here, data from elsewhere point to the special willingness on the part of some highly susceptible subjects to please hypnotists by structuring incoming reality information in accordance with their suggestions (Dolby & Sheehan, 1977; Ryan & Sheehan, 1977).

Given the complexities of the various dimensions and their interactions discussed in this chapter, it is important for contemporary hypnosis theorizing to come to grips with the experience of the person in context rather than to try to focus specifically on either person or situation accounts of hypnotic phenomena. Laying aside our specific concern with hypnotic phenomena for the moment, much of the data in this book can be said to support the interactional model of behavior, which argues that person-mediating variables, person-reaction variables, and situation variables are all important in determining how individual behavior develops and maintains itself (Bowers, 1973; Cantor & Kihlstrom, 1981; Endler & Magnusson, 1976).

HALLUCINATION AND REALITY AWARENESS: A CASE ANALYSIS

Valuable information can be obtained about the phenomena and processes of hypnosis through a close and detailed analysis of the experience of individual hypnotic subjects. Consistent with this theme and in order to better understand some of the issues raised by the data reported earlier in this chapter, we intensively explored the reactions of a highly susceptible hypnotic subject to a hallucination suggestion. Our intent was to examine the degree to which an individual's motivated cognitive commitment to a positive response together with a high level of hypnotic ability might work to maintain the hallucination in the face of conflicting information that was provided through the hypnotist confronting the subject with the actual nature of the hallucinated event. In order to explore this subject's experience of events and the way in which the conflict engendered was resolved, we employed a modified version of the EAT (for its rationale and development, see Chapter 9) as a means of immediately inquiring into the subject's phenomenal awareness of the various real and suggested events associated with her experience of hallucination.

Specifically, the subject that we employed was highly responsive and had displayed a variety of difficult hypnotic phenomena on previous testing occasions. In the session presented here, the subject was hypnotized by the first author (PWS) and, following induction, given a hallucination suggestion for a double hallucination.

Procedurally, two other people were in the testing room. One (Kevin) was operating a video camera situated directly in front of the subject, and the other (Ken) was seated in a chair in front of and to the right of the subject. It is important to note at the outset that the subject was personally familiar with Kevin (who had worked with her in other hypnotic sessions), but she had first met Ken immediately prior to the hypnotic session and had agreed to allow him to observe her hypnotic testing. The specific hallucination suggestion was that when she opened her eyes she would see Ken operating the video camera and Kevin seated in the chair. Subsequent to the subject's positive response to this suggestion and without canceling it, the hypnotist (H) informed her that this was not the way things actually were and again asked her to indicate which person was Kevin and which was Ken. The details of the hypnotic induction and hallucination testing are conveyed in the transcript that follows.

Hypnotic Induction

H: Look at those keys, you've seen them before. I want you just to look at them and concentrate on them carefully, keep watching them, just keep looking at them. As you keep looking at them your eyes are going to feel tireder, they'll become tired and fall, just as they get tired, as relaxation spreads through your body. Eyes becoming tired as I begin to count; your eyes becoming tired, so tired they'll just drop closed. Keep looking at the keys, just let your eyes close when you want to; 1, 2, tireder and tireder now, 3, tireder and tireder now. All the tiredness and relaxation spreading through your body as you drift into a pleasant state of relaxation; 4, 5, that's fine now, just resting there comfortably now. I want you to think of yourself on a carpet, just drifting backwards and forwards, it's a pleasurable experience. It's an enjoyable experience, you're back on it again, just drifting backwards and forwards, as I count from 1 to 10 you'll go deeper and deeper into a state of relaxation, just drifting backwards and forwards, pleasantly, comfortably relaxed, drifting to and fro, backwards and forwards, all the time more and more relaxed, as the relaxation spreads through your hands, to your legs, and your body, more and more relaxed. More and more relaxed. Six, drifting to and fro, more and more relaxed now, 7, 8, almost there now. Soon you'll be deeply hypnotized. On the count of 10 deeply hypnotized, 9, 10, deeply hypnotized now. Just listening carefully to what I say and what I draw your attention to and noticing the things I ask you to think about. You'll be able to experience many things, and to open your eyes if I ask you to.

You'll be able to see, hear, tell, and experience the things I tell you to experience, in a state of deep, complete relaxation.

Hallucination Testing

H: In a little while I'm going to ask you to open your eyes, and I want you to look across to the camera. You'll see someone standing there and that person will be Ken, whom you've just met. The person on the left, working the camera is Ken; you've just met him. Sitting to the right is another person in a chair, and that's Kevin. You know Kevin well. Ken is working the camera, on the left; and Kevin is sitting on the chair, to the right. When I ask you to open your eyes, you'll be able to see Ken working the camera and Kevin sitting on the chair. Now I want you to tell me what you see and what you experience, when you see them. Just open your eyes and look over to the front now. [Subject opens her eyes and looks forward to camera.] Who's working the camera?

S: Hello, Ken.

H: And who's that sitting in the chair? [Subject moves her eyes right to chair.]

S: Kevin.

H: That's Kevin. Do you want to ask him any questions? Do you want to say anything to him at all, or relax again?

S: Just not to forget the watch.

H: Not to forget the watch? What should he not forget about the watch?

S: Ah, well, he'll know. It's just the watch that I'll need soon.

H: You asked Kevin for the watch before?

S: Hhmm. [Subject assents.]

H: And you want him to remember it?

S: Hhmm. [Subject assents.]

H: That's fine. Just close your eyes now, close your eyes and relax. In a moment, I'm going to ask you to open them again. When you do, I want you to look over to the people in front of you, the person on the left and the person on the right. I'm going to ask you to look over to Kevin on the right and Ken on the left. You saw them before, and they'll still be sitting there. You know, however, that Kevin is really on the left and Ken is on the right. You don't normally see them the other way around. Let's see whether or not you see Kevin on the right, and Ken on the left just like before, now that you know they are really the other way around. Let's see now, just open your eyes now, and tell me what you see. [Subject opens eyes and moves eyes right to chair.]

S: Hhmm, Kevin.

H: Kevin, where? [Subject points right to chair.] What about Ken? [Subject moves

eyes forward to camera and nods.] Is that the way they normally are? [Subject
shakes head "no".]

S: No. [Subject laughs.]

H: No? Can you tell me a little more about that?

S: Well, just that, Ken's there [Subject points to camera], but Kevin's there too.
[Subject continues to look at camera.]

H: What do you think is happening?

S: [Subject moves eyes to chair.] No, that's Kevin.

Following the testing of the hallucination suggestion in the context of alerting
the subject to reality, a modified version of the EAT was employed to explore her
experience of the events. The version of the EAT that was employed capitalized
on this subject's high level of imaginative skill and required her to hallucinate in
her mind's eye the events of testing. The hallucinatory playback version of the
EAT (see Chapter 9 for a full description and data relating to its application in
both the research and clinical settings) served to facilitate the subject's recall of
relevant and personally meaningful events during the hypnotic testing. The details of the EAT procedure as well as the report of the subject are conveyed in the
following transcript.

Hallucinatory EAT

H: Okay, just close your eyes now. Slipping further and further now, into a state
of deep hypnosis. Hypnotized now. I want you now to do something for me.
I want you now to think about all that we've done, from the moment I came
into this room and asked you to look at my keys, till now. I want you to think
vividly, in your mind's eye, to see the whole session, right from the beginning
to the end. Let it roll through like a film. Just exactly as a film unwinding.
But I want you to stop the film whenever you want to comment on any of
your experiences, anything at all. To stop it just lift your finger, or hand, to
let me know that you want to comment, and then we can talk about it. Do you
understand now? When I say "start," let the film roll, exactly as it happened,
from the start right to the end. Just lift your finger or hand when you want to
say something about your experience. Let's start now, just let the film roll on.
[Subject lifts finger.] Just comment now, what's happening?

S: Well, Ken looked so much different from what I imagined him to be.

H: What were you thinking at the time?

S: I was thinking that that was a pleasant surprise. He was much nicer than I
thought he would be.

H: Anything else you were thinking?

S: Only that it's very nice that I don't have to be worried.

H: That's fine. Do you want to let the film roll on now? [Subject nods.]

S: [Subject lifts finger.] It is just that you counted so fast and I thought I wouldn't be able to drift away on the carpet, but I did.

H: You did. No trouble?

S: No trouble.

H: What were you thinking about when you were drifting away?

S: [Giggles.]

H: Were you expecting anything to happen?

S: No. I was wondering what you would say to me. I wondered about what we were going to do, and then I just drifted away. I just drifted away on the carpet. I lost your voice for a while, and I didn't know what you were saying.

H: How did you feel at that time?

S: I don't remember.

H: That's fine. Do you want to let the film roll on? [Subject nods.]

S: [Subject lifts finger.] I was a bit confused.

H: Why was it confusing?

S: Well then he was on the left, then he was on the right, then he wasn't really there, when he wasn't on that side. I didn't know what you said in the end. I was all confused.

H: Well, what were you thinking at that time?

S: I thought, "Oh my goodness, I don't know, who's supposed to be on the right and who's supposed to be on the left."

H: What did you think I wanted?

S: Well, I didn't know what you were saying. It was all left and right, somebody's there, and I was too confused. I didn't know what I'd see when I opened my eyes.

H: What did you see?

S: I saw Ken on the right, and then I saw Kevin, Kevin was there, and that was alright. But, what was odd, was that Ken was really on the camera, but Kevin was behind him. There were two. But the one sitting on the chair, that was Kevin alright. I could just see Kevin.

H: What did you think about seeing the two?

S: It was funny.

H: That struck you as unusual?

S: No, no. I just thought it was funny to have two there. There were two there.

H: What do you mean funny?

S: [Giggles.] Funny, funny.

H: What else were you thinking?

S: Nothing. I want to tell Kevin not to forget the watch. I forgot it before and I might forget it again. So when you asked me to talk to him, that's the first thing that came to my mind..

H: He won't forget it. Were you having any thoughts about me at the time?

S: No. I forgot about you.

H: Do you want to let the film roll on? [Subject nods.] Okay, just let it roll now.

S: [Subject lifts finger.] I was very uneasy, very uneasy.

H: You want to tell me about it?

S: You didn't put things back.

H: What do you mean, didn't put things back? What should I have put back?

S: Two people, two people. You should have put them right. I said all the time, put them back, put them back, but you didn't listen to me. It was terrible.

H: Did you think I was forgetful?

S: Why don't you listen to me? It's wrong.

H: Were you angry with me at the time?

S: No, just felt terrible.

H: What else were you thinking about at the time?

S: The carpet was coming back too quickly, and I didn't like that either. I would have liked it to have come down slowly, and it was coming down too fast. I didn't like that. I had to jump off.

H: You had to jump off the carpet, and that worried you?

S: No, I just didn't like it. But I kept saying all the time, to put it back, and you didn't. You didn't listen.

H: Did it surprise you?

S: No.

H: Do you want the film to roll on? Or do you want to tell me something more about that experience?

S: No, I just wanted you to listen. I still feel uneasy.

H: Do you want to let the film roll on now? [Subject nods.] Okay fine, just let it roll.

S: [Subject lifts finger.] I feel better now, I feel better now, my heart is not beating so fast. I feel better.

H: You feel better now? Is there anything else you'd like to tell me?

S: After I got off the carpet, things still weren't right either.

H: Would you like me to put them right?

S: Things are still funny.

H: Things are still a little funny, are they? [Subject nods.] Would you like me to put them right? [Subject nods.] That's fine. Stop the film rolling, stop the film now. Let me put things right. You're back on the carpet. Jump back on the carpet. Just drifting backwards and forwards now. Just comfortably relaxed now. I'm going to bring that carpet back down to the ground and you can hop off, naturally, quietly, comfortably, and no need to rush. Just drifting backwards and forwards. Now when I ask you to open your eyes, I want you to see Kevin back at the camera. That really is Kevin at the camera and Ken is sitting over on the right-hand side. Now they're really and truly back to normal. No longer any confusion, right back to normal. Kevin is at the camera and Ken is on the chair to the right. Just open your eyes now. Kevin [Subject looks straight ahead to camera and smiles.] and Ken [Subject looks right to chair and smiles.] are there. Close your eyes now. Before I'm going to wake you up, I'm going to count from 10 to 1, and I want the carpet to just drift down now. Drifting down now. 10, 9, drifting down now, everything will be back to normal when the carpet is back down on the ground, 8, 7, 6, 5, 4, drifting down now, almost there, 3, 2, 1. Open your eyes now, wide awake, alert and fresh. How do you feel?

S:　Good.

H:　Do you feel unsettled at all?

S:　No.

H:　Is there anything you'd like to say, or comment about what we've done today?

S:　Uhm, no.

H:　No?

S:　No.

H:　That's a hesitant no. [Subject giggles.]

S:　It's just that I don't know. [Subject looks backwards and forwards from left to right.] At some stage, things looked quite different, but they look alright now. [Subject giggles.]

H:　Everything okay now?

S:　Yes. [Subject giggles.] At some stage I saw Ken there as well [points to camera]. I suppose you could, ah, call it sort of transparent. I saw Ken there, but I saw Kevin there as well, at the same time.

H:　Any reason you saw two of them?

S:　And yet I saw, I saw, them both there. And I saw Kevin there [points to chair]. I thought, well, "I don't know."

H:　Everything is okay now?

S:　Yes.

H:　Is there anything else you'd like to comment on?

S:　Uhm, at some stage, I don't know when that was, I felt my heart beat, like mad. I don't know when, at some stage.

H:　Is it okay now?

S:　Yes.

H:　That's fine.

Comment on Case Analysis

This application of the hallucinatory EAT inquired intensively into a subject's reaction to a difficult hallucination suggestion. During testing, the hypnotist facilitated the subject's awareness of the reality of the situation, and data highlight the extremely individual nature of the subject's experiences. For this subject, her level of motivated involvement in the suggested events was apparently such that, although the reality information shaped and modified the nature of her experience, it did not overly interfere with positive response. After being alerted to the reality of the situation, for instance, the subject saw one of the hallucinated people in a transparent fashion with the real and suggested persons occurring in the same place at the same time. In this way, the subject incorporated the reality information into the overall stimulus nexus impinging on her and cognitively processed events in such a fashion as to maintain successful hypnotic response.

These data essentially support those presented elsewhere (see especially Chapters 5 and 8) that indicate the variations in hypnotic consciousness and shifts in cognizing that can occur within an individual during a particular hypnotic session. The analysis and assessment of such cognitive shifts are obviously complex matters, but by focusing on cognitive process variables so as to highlight the individual character of response we feel that meaningful information can be obtained about both phenomena and process. The data on the subject's level of reality testing and monitoring raise important, intriguing questions about the nature of hypnotic consciousness, and some attempt to answer them is made in Chapter 10.

SUMMARY DISCUSSION

In this chapter, we have considered data relating to the hypnotic phenomena of dreams and hallucinations, looked at the degree to which subjects are aware of reality that may conflict with the suggestions given by the hypnotist, and presented a detailed case analysis of the reactions of one highly responsive subject to a specific hallucination suggestion. Across these different sets of data, a number of findings have emerged that bear usefully upon the nature of the hypnotic phenomena themselves and the processes that are involved in subjects' experiencing of them.

In our EAT analysis of hypnotic dreams and hallucinations, the data revealed subtle but meaningful patterns of differences and similarities concerning the process features of subjects' experience of the two phenomena. The differences that occurred in subjects' experience of these events could not be explained simply on the basis of variations in level of susceptibility; for both tasks, no appreciable difference in level of susceptibility was observed between those persons who passed and those who failed the suggestion. This finding suggests that for explanation of the variation in objective behavior and subjective experience that occurs among susceptible individuals appeal is most appropriately made to the various cognitive skills, strategies, and processsing styles that subjects bring to bear on their response to suggestions. For those subjects who responded positively, the pattern of interrelationships among the process dimensions of imagery, absorption, and feeling of involuntariness was what the literature would generally lead us to expect; all were closely related, and the same pattern of relationship was evident across both tasks. However, in terms of the cognitive styles that subjects employed across the two related, though different, hypnotic tasks, important differences emerged that point to the relevance of task constraints for defining the type of cognitive style that subjects will employ. For instance, data suggest that constructive cognizing was differentially relevant to the two tasks, and results demonstrated that a concentrative style characterized successful response on the hallucination but not the dream item. In these instances, it may be that the specification of the limits of the suggestion by the hypnotist partially determined the style of cognizing that subjects employed. Arguably, cognitive styles such as the independent and constructive modes of cognition may arise or generate in situations that do not simply elicit a narrowly defined response but rather require the subject to produce a response somehow through his or her own cognitive manipulations of real and suggested events. The task specificity of cognitive styles observed in this chapter is consistent with that seen in Chapter 3. It also supports the arguments presented in Chapters 4 and 8 for the need to acknowledge shifts in particular hypnotic subject's cognitive strategies that can occur throughout hypnotic testing as subjects come to be faced with different task demands.

One aspect of the situation that may also influence the type of cognitive style employed is the degree of subjects' reality awareness. The data in this chapter indicated that reality awareness was negatively related to imagery and absorption on the dream task but positively related to independent cognizing on the hallucination item. The case study we presented indicates that awareness of reality bears a complex relationship to positive response to hallucination suggestion, and data challenge somewhat the assumptions that are made in the literature about the extent to which subjects refrain from actively processing reality information while positively responding to hypnotic instructions. Such assumptions may apply more correctly to those subjects who employ concentrative cognizing, which is more heavily reliant on the text of the communications of the hypnotist. For those subjects who can employ their cognitive skills and strategies more independently in order to integrate appropriately or not attend to conflicting information, reality processing may play a greater part.

Our analysis of reality awareness clearly showed that, despite the influence of any processing of reality information, the majority of highly susceptible subjects are motivated and oriented positively to working toward hypnotic response, as they perceive it to be appropriate. This willingness by hypnotic subjects to lay aside the reality constraints of the situation is an important component of their approach to hypnotic responding, and it raises issues relating to the abilities that subjects display, which enable them to demonstrate multiple streams of awareness or adopt different cognitive perspectives in fluid enough fashion so as to mesh the various personal and situational demands that impinge on them in their attempts to produce hypnotic behavior that they perceive as suitable. Positive response is the essential goal of their interaction with the hypnotist, and it seems clear that subjects may actively orient their cognizing toward such response, even though they attribute the experience associated with that response as involuntary.

This interactive mix of motivated effort and attributed involuntariness was strongly evident in the case analysis that we presented in this chapter. Given the various demands of the situation, the subject was obviously highly motivated to maintain a positive response but also acknowledged in perceptive fashion the actual reality of the situation. Information yielded by the hallucinatory EAT suggested, however, that the subject was not consciously aware of any specific activity on her part to formulate her compromise response and essentially saw the majority of her reactions as occurring involuntarily. Nevertheless, the motivated commitment of this subject is consistent with the types of process features under-lying responses that we have seen in other chapters (see Chapters 4, 5, and 8, in particular), which highlight the active and constructive role that subjects may play in initiating and maintaining their hypnotic experience.

Given that individual differences obviously occur in the way that subjects of similar susceptibility go about experiencing various hypnotic effects and that subjects do vary in terms of the cognitive strategies that they employ when faced with different hypnotic tasks, the need exists to isolate the patterns of similarities and differences in subjects' cognitive approaches on a wider variety of hypnotic phenomena than those we have considered in this chapter. But overall, this chapter (like those before it) has highlighted the need for a close inspection of the experiential reactions of subjects in order to understand correctly the nature of hypnotic response in the first instance. The analysis of subjects' experiences of hypnosis through phenomenologically based assessment can be important to help us not only index the nature of hypnotic events in novel and process-oriented ways, but ultimately to assist in developing a sophisticated conceptual model of hypnosis.

7 Posthypnotic Amnesia

INTRODUCTION

The occurrence of amnesia in the hypnotic setting is one of the more intriguing phenomena that characterize the domain of hypnosis. Historically speaking, hypnotic amnesia has provided the impetus for substantial empirical investigation and theoretical speculation about hypnosis; it is also a phenomenon that has direct implications for other areas of psychological inquiry. For instance, observations made about the nature of amnesia in the hypnotic context are generally considered to have the potential for bridging a variety of important topics in contemporary psychology. The processes of posthypnotic amnesia, for example, can be associated with the study of both normal and pathological functioning of memory and psychopathology in general (Kihlstrom, 1977; Kihlstrom & Evans, 1979; Sarbin & Coe, 1979).

The phenomenon of posthypnotic amnesia generally refers to the temporary inability of hypnotic subjects to remember, after hypnosis, the events of hypnosis for which they have received a suggestion to forget (for recent reviews see Coe, 1978; Cooper, 1979; Evans, 1980; Kihlstrom, 1978b; Kihlstrom & Evans, 1979). Posthypnotic amnesia appears to relate to other sorts of functional amnesias that can be observed in research and therapeutic settings as well as in everyday life situations (Bowers, 1976; E. R. Hilgard, 1977; Kihlstrom & Evans, 1979). For instance, forgetting a friend's name or forgetting whether or not one has seen a particular movie until a certain scene occurs appears similar in kind to some of the experiences associated with posthypnotic amnesia (see Reed, 1979, for a review of everyday anomalies of memory). In the laboratory setting also, definite similarities can be observed between the phenomena of state-dependent learning (Overton, 1973) and posthypnotic amnesia as well as between clinical syndromes such as hysteria, fugues, dissociative states, and multiple personalities (Evans, 1980; E. R. Hilgard, 1977; see also Nemiah, 1979). E. R. Hilgard (1977), for instance, considers amnesia, in the sense of transiently unavailable memories, to be the key to understanding dissociation as it is observed in a variety of everyday situations.

Posthypnotic amnesia is only one type of amnesia that can occur in the hypnotic setting. E. R. Hilgard (1965, 1977) has listed a number of suggested hypnotic amnesias such as posthypnotic recall amnesia, amnesia for the events of hypnosis, posthypnotic recall amnesia for learned material during hypnosis, posthypnotic source amnesia or the retention of learned material but forgetting of the context of learning, posthypnotic partial amnesia or the forgetting of only some of the hypnotic events, and amnesia for in-trance events while the subject is still hypnotized. Of these, the contemporary hypnosis literature has focused largely on posthypnotic amnesia.

Because of the special significance of this phenomenon for inquiry into hypnotic responsiveness, some historical comment on amnesia appears appropriate at the outset. History seems to have played a more significant role in relation to current thinking about amnesia than about many of the other phenomena that we have considered elsewhere in this book (see especially Chapters 4, 5, and 6). Historically, the most common behavioral and subjective phenomena of hypnosis, as they were induced by the magnetic procedures of the Mesmeric period, were vomiting, expectoration, evacuation, various convulsive behaviors (crises), warmth, tickling, and pain. But, in the general emotional climate that existed in relation to these phenomena, others were overlooked (Sheehan & Perry, 1976). For instance, the Societe Royale de Medecine Commission of 1784 (quoted in Podmore, 1909/1964) reported on a case of spontaneous posthypnotic amnesia in the following way:

> A young man who was frequently in a state of crisis became in that state quite silent, and would go quickly through the hall, often touching the patients. These regular touches of his often brought about a crisis, of which he would take control without allowing anyone to interfere. When he returned to his normal condition he would talk again, but he did not remember anything that had taken place, and no longer knew how to magnetize [p. 70].

The particular relevance of posthypnotic amnesia to hypnosis also came to the notice of Braid, who actually coined the term *hypnosis*. Braid's (1855/1970) views are particularly relevant because of the fact that he confined his use of the word hypnosis to those individuals who displayed amnesia for the hypnotic events; he (1855/1970) considered that: ''all short of this is mere reverie, or dreaming, however provoked [p. 370].'' That is, Braid considered that only response to the more difficult hypnotic tests qualified as hypnosis, a view that is reflected widely in contemporary notions of hypnosis. Of those subjects who displayed posthypnotic amnesia, Braid made a further distinction between subjects whose memories could be retrieved by a subsequent hypnotic induction (such subjects were said to be in hypnosis) and subjects whose amnesia could not be broken down in a subsequent induction (such subjects were considered to be in a hypnotic coma) (Braid, 1855/1970).

The presence of (spontaneous) posthypnotic amnesia, then, was observed by a number of people during the Mesmeric period, but it was brought to special prominence a few decades later. The phenomenon was then regarded as a central characteristic of hypnosis. However, today, spontaneous posthypnotic amnesia is considered a relatively rare occurrence. In an analysis of the frequency of spontaneous versus suggested amnesia, Hilgard and Cooper (1965) reported that 7% of subjects displayed spontaneous amnesia, whereas 35% displayed amnesia following suggestion. Of those subjects who reported spontaneous amnesia, it is unclear, of course, how many persons did so on the basis of the implicit cues for forgetting inherent in the assessment situation. For instance, the sleep metaphor that characterizes many of the scales reviewed in Chapter 2 subtly reinforces amnesia as a possible expected response, and most likely the majority of cases of spontaneous amnesia—either in Braid's time or today—can be explained in terms of subjects' beliefs, motivations, and expectancies about appropriate response.

Today, focus is largely on the outcome of specific suggestions for posthypnotic amnesia. As E. R. Hilgard (1977) points out, when one specifically suggests amnesia, then the variables that potentially affect the outcome of that suggestion can be more easily defined and manipulated. The suggestion that certain events will be unable to be remembered, for instance, defines the source of the amnesia as well as its content, and because this suggestion can be easily cancelled, the amnesia is reversible. Consequently, a distinction can be readily made between the effects of normal forgetting and the effects of specific suggestion. The phenomenon's acceptance as a major part of the domain of hypnosis is almost universal, and almost all of the standard scales reviewed in Chapter 2 include a test of amnesia.

In testing posthypnotic amnesia on standardized scales such as the HGSHS: A or SHSS:C just prior to the termination of hypnosis, the hypnotist normally instructs subjects to forget everything that happened during hypnosis, until they are told that they can remember. After termination of hypnosis, subjects are asked to recount their experience with testing, and the hypnotic test items mentioned are then recorded by the hypnotist. Following this, the amnesia suggestion is typically cancelled by means of a prearranged reversal cue, and subjects are then asked to report any additional memories that they may have of the testing session.

Posthypnotic amnesia is routinely assessed in terms of the number of items that the subject remembers after hypnosis but before the administration of the reversibility cue. On the SHSS:C, for example, the response is scored as positive if subjects recall three or fewer items before being told: "Now you can remember everything." Operationally, then, posthypnotic amnesia refers to subjects reporting relatively few events following the termination of hypnosis. Despite agreement that reversibility is a conceptually important component (e.g., Cooper, 1979; E. R. Hilgard, 1965; Orne, 1966), the reversibility is not generally scored in any of the standard hypnotic scales listed in Chapter 2, and only a handful of investigators have employed it as part of an objective criterion of responsiveness to amnesia suggestions.

Taking such a measure into account, however, helps separate the effects of normal forgetting from the impact of instructions for suggested forgetting. Also, studies of populations such as schizophrenics indicate that subjects may display posthypnotic amnesia not because of the impact of the suggestion but because of their failure to attend to and process the hypnotic events in the first place (Lavoie, Sabourin, & Langlois, 1973). Furthermore, the use of reversibility of amnesia as an index has helped define conceptual differences by distinguishing between amnesia (i.e., full amnesia and full reversibility), pseudo amnesia (i.e., full amnesia but no reversibility), partial amnesia (i.e., some amnesia and some reversibility), and nonamnesia (i.e., no amnesia and no reversibility). Clearly, a better measure of posthypnotic amnesia would rely not only on the items forgotten, but also on items recovered; in this way, the difference between ordinary forgetting and the impact of the suggestion could more easily be observed (Kihlstrom & Evans, 1976; Nace, Orne, & Hammer, 1974). Routinely, however, the criterion for posthypnotic amnesia is the number of items that subjects remember prior to the administration of the reversibility cue.

Kihlstrom and Evans (1976, 1977, 1979) have reported data relating to the number of items recalled by 691 subjects tested on the HGSHS:A and 391 subjects tested on the SHSS:C. Those subjects who recalled three or fewer items were considered to pass the amnesia item, and this criterion was met by 31% of subjects on the HGSHS:A and 32% of subjects on the SHSS:C. These pass rates are consistent with normative data (e.g., Sheehan & McConkey, 1979; Shor & Orne, 1962; Weitzenhoffer & Hilgard, 1962), which indicate that relatively few subjects respond positively to the amnesia suggestions of the HGSHS:A and the SHSS:C. Studies with quite different populations, however, have indicated a somewhat higher percentage. Analyses of the hypnotic susceptibility of schizophrenics, for instance, have indicated between 78% and 100% positive response to the amnesia suggestion (Lavoie et al., 1973; Lieberman, Lavoie, & Brisson, 1978), although there is a relatively low incidence of reversibility of schizophrenic subjects' amnesia. This suggests that factors not associated with the specific suggestion for the amnesia may appreciably determine these subjects' responses.

THE NATURE OF POSTHYPNOTIC AMNESIA

Conceptually speaking, four broad models have defined the theoretical and empirical work about the nature of posthypnotic amnesia (Kihlstrom, 1977), and these have been labeled: (1) amnesia as forgetting; (2) amnesia as the keeping of secrets; (3) amnesia as repression; (4) amnesia as memory "on the tip of the tongue." In summary of the evidence regarding each of these models, we know quite definitely that posthypnotic amnesia cannot be explained in terms of functional ablation or repressionlike processes (e.g., Coe, Basden, Basden, & Graham, 1976; Coe, Baugher, Krimm & Smith, 1976; Hilgard & Hommel, 1961; O'Connell, 1966; Pettinati & Evans, 1978); the forgetting and repression models are not generally supported by empirical analysis. Rather, data have more clearly indicated that the nature of posthypnotic amnesia is far more likely to be revealed through the problems subjects have in retrieving the information from their memory store.

The contextual (e.g., Coe, 1978) and cognitive (e.g., Kihlstrom, 1978b) models of posthypnotic amnesia are quite distinct in their foci. Cognitively, work investigating the order of recall of events by partially amnesic subjects has indicated that posthypnotic amnesia involves the loss of strategies normally employed in the retrieval of information from memory. Kihlstrom and Evans (1979) report that amnesic subjects tend not to structure their recall in temporal fashion, and this deficit in temporal organization appears to be functionally tied to the amnesia. In summary of this cognitive approach, Kihlstrom and Evans (1979) consider that data confirm the notion of: "the disruption of retrieval processes in posthypnotic amnesia—that the subject's inability to capitalize on appropriate organizational cues and strategies renders the act of remembering difficult, inefficient, and unproductive [p. 213]." Although related work (e.g., Radtke-Bodorik, Planar, & Spanos, 1980; Spanos, Radtke-Bodorik, & Stam, 1980) has shown similar disorganization in word recall as a result of suggested amnesia, recent evidence by St. Jean and Coe (1981) questions the reliability of temporal disorganization as a characteristic of posthypnotic amnesia. The finding that relatively few amnesic subjects showed disorganized recognition memory questions the relevance of cognitive disorganization and led St. Jean and Coe (1981) to argue for an explanatory model that examines the phenomena and processes of posthypnotic amnesia from a contextual viewpoint.

The contextual approach (Coe, 1978; Sarbin & Coe, 1979) holds that amnesic subjects begin with the notion that it is "as if" they cannot remember, and when their involvement in this "as if" process heightens, then they consider that something is happening to them (e.g., that it is an involuntary response). Under these conditions, subjects are likely to drop the "as if" metaphor and report their experience as literal in the sense that they cannot, in fact, remember (Coe, 1978; Sarbin & Coe, 1979). Following this approach further, Sarbin and Coe (1979) have reported that there are essentially two types of amnesia: (1) subjects who know the events but do not report them (these subjects are said to keep secrets); (2) subjects who know the events but do not know that they know (these subjects are said to engage in self-deception). The essential difference between the contextual and cognitive approaches is the variation in emphasis these two theories place on the situation in which posthypnotic amnesia takes place and the cognitive processes by which the amnesia occurs.

Although there is general agreement that amnesia is a genuine experience for subjects, its manifestations are clearly variable and its explanation remains incomplete. Full account of the processes responsible for amnesia is as yet undetermined. If the mechanisms of amnesia were better understood, then many of the puzzles associated with the phenomenon would be resolved. From a cognitive viewpoint, for instance, it is considered (see E. R. Hilgard, 1977) that central control processes are implicated in the production and maintenance of posthypnotic amnesia, together with such factors as direct suggestions, voluntary selective inattention to the material to be forgotten, the use of imagery strategies to facilitate the amnesia, and repression. In the literature, all of these factors are said to play their respective roles in the experience of amnesia, but the nature of their separate contributions is not entirely clear. Further data are needed to illustrate the processes at work.

The essential paradox of posthypnotic amnesia is that subjects report that they cannot remember, yet all of the objective indicators suggest that the nonreported memories are active and retrievable. Barber (1969) notes that the existence of such a paradox has led some investigators to conclude that: ''practically all instances of suggested amnesia may be characterized by a motivated unwillingness to verbalize the events to the experimenter or hypnotist [p. 215].'' As Bowers (1976) points out, however, the fact that indirect measures indicate that hypnotic memories are available is not at all surprising, because all of us know more than we can consciously remember and this knowledge in some way must surely affect our behavior. Nevertheless, Kihlstrom (1977) states that investigators need to come to grips with the fact that during this period of amnesia: ''the extent of amnesia appears to vary appreciably, depending on the type of memory test that is employed [p. 287].'' Recognition memory, for instance, is generally less impaired than is recall memory (Kihlstrom & Shor, 1978; Williamsen, Johnson, & Eriksen, 1965). Also, research employing tasks that involve retroactive inhibition (e.g., Coe, Basden, Basden, & Graham, 1976; Graham & Patton, 1968) or word associations (e.g., Kihlstrom, 1978a; Stewart & Dunlap, 1976; Thorne & Hall, 1974) indicates that the hypnotic memories are available for certain uses as illustrated by physiological indices of memory (e.g., Bitterman & Marcuse, 1945). Such findings have given rise to strong debate concerning the credibility of subjects' claims that they cannot remember the events of hypnosis (see Coe, 1978; Kihlstrom, 1978b, for coverage of the arguments).

Up to this point in the book, we have discussed the application of the EAT as a means of in-depth exploration of the nature of hypnotic phenomena and processes at work. The data presented have served in an intrinsic way to bear meaningfully on the reliability and validity of the EAT itself as a technique of inquiry that recognizes the primacy of experience. In this chapter, we use the EAT instrumentally not as a technique producing data on itself, but as a means of facilitating the systematic manipulation of environmental conditions for testing amnesia as a genuine phenomenon. The focus here is clearly on the technique as an experimentally useful rather than clinically relevant procedure. However, the data we cite in this chapter, as in the preceding chapters, still bear on the definition of hypnotic phenomena and the processes that underlie them. The issue that we take up here is the breaching of amnesia, and we argue for the utility of the EAT as a means of testing the durability of the phenomenon.

AMNESIA AS A DURABLE PHENOMENON

Research that aims to provide important evidence concerning the credibility of posthypnotic amnesia comes from attempts to break down, or breach, amnesia prior to the presentation of the reversibility cue. The findings of studies that have adopted this particular methodological approach (e.g., Bowers, 1966; Howard & Coe, 1980; Kihlstrom, Evans, Orne, & Orne, 1980; McConkey & Sheehan, 1981; McConkey, Sheehan, & Cross, 1980; Schuyler & Coe, 1981) can be summarized by commenting that under a variety of different demands it appears that amnesia can be broken down for some, but not all, hypnotic subjects. However, these studies have varied substantially in the degree of stringency of the attempts at breakdown that they have used.

Bowers (1966) employed an independent experimenter and demands for honesty to test the amnesia response of hypnotic and role-playing subjects; his findings indicated that all of the role-playing and approximately half of the hypnotic subjects breached their amnesia. Howard and Coe (1980; see also Schuyler & Coe, 1981) tested subjects who had all displayed amnesia in a previous testing under conditions of high (connected to a polygraph), medium (demands for honesty), and low (standard test procedures) cues for amnesia breakdown; their results showed that it was those subjects who had reported feeling in control of the previous amnesia who breached, whereas subjects who had not felt in control in the previous testing did not breach their amnesia. Kihlstrom et al. (1980) employed various instructions prior to a second test of the amnesia item of the HGSHS:A; subjects were told either to recall again routinely, to list the items temporally, to exert more effort in their recall of the items, or to report honestly all that they could remember. The findings indicated that approximately half of the subjects in each group breached their amnesia on the second testing, no matter what instructions they received.

The most stringent demands for breakdown have been employed by McConkey and Sheehan (1981) and McConkey, Sheehan, and Cross (1980). These two studies are detailed here because they illustrate the in-depth assessment of amnesic response and provide important evidence on the processes that may be said to underlie it. The EAT was applied in both of these investigations. Prior to the administration of the reversibility cue that cancelled the suggestion for posthypnotic amnesia, subjects were shown a video-tape playback of their hypnotic test session in strict application of the procedures of the technique as set out in Chapter 3.

The data from these studies illustrate the relevance of the EAT procedures as a test of the durability of hypnotic amnesia as it occurs in the experimental laboratory setting. Specifically, the use of the EAT under conditions of posthypnotic amnesia provided the means by which it could be unambiguously communicated to subjects that hypnotic memories were available to them for retrieval. In essence, the use of the EAT with amnesic subjects made it possible to impress upon subjects that they really did know the source and content of their memories even though they may be temporarily convinced otherwise.

Applications of the EAT reported in Chapters 3, 4, 5, and 6 have focused primarily on the gathering of relevant information concerning the experience of hypnotic phenomena. As mentioned earlier, the application of the EAT with amnesic subjects illustrates in a somewhat different way the investigative use of EAT assessment. Instrumentally, the method was adopted as a means of attempting to break down the amnesic experience of subjects in novel fashion. No previous studies, for instance, have presented subjects with a visual representation of the content of their hypnotic memories and asked them to comment openly and freely about their recall of the events being depicted. This served to intrude, as it were, the reality of subjects' memory into their amnesia experience while at the same time allowing the investigator to focus on some of the processes associated with the experience of being amnesic. By focusing in process fashion on the ways in which subjects handle the experience of amnesia when the situational demands are clearly for them to recall and report on the amnesic events, relevant insights should be gained into the nature of the events underlying hypnotic responsiveness.

An important way of viewing the application of the EAT (described earlier) is in its providing a context of maximal cueing for the recall of the subjects' experiences with hypnosis. By confronting subjects with the actual hypnotic events and the inquirer asking them to comment directly on their experiences with those events, subjects are required to process a highly explicit, temporally organized account of the events of their memories. The test that is thus afforded of whether amnesia can be broken down seems an especially stringent one. If amnesia can be sustained even when the events that happened are observed directly, then the phenomenon of amnesia can be said to be durable and resistant to optimal cueing for retrieval. It is also important to note that the social context of the relationship of the inquirer to subject in the EAT is one of collaboration and trust (see Chapter 3 for a full description and comment on the nature of this relationship), and this interpersonal environment is essentially one that is antithetical to the keeping of secrets by subjects (Sarbin & Coe, 1979). Because the personal context accompanying the application of EAT encourages subjects to honestly self-disclose about the nature of their experiences as they perceive them, EAT procedures offer an especially stringent test of the genuineness of posthypnotic amnesia. In the two investigations, McConkey, Sheehan, and Cross (1980) employed a group of highly susceptible subjects, and McConkey and Sheehan (1981) employed both hypnotic and simulating, insusceptible subjects; the design of the studies is illustrated in Table 7.1. Although the two studies differed in the degree to which the suggestion for posthypnotic amnesia specified the precise time period of the amnesia, findings across the studies were similar and can be reported together.

Review of the Evidence

Both behavioral and experiential data relating to the breakdown of and processes involved in amnesia were provided by the two investigations under discussion. The behavioral data were provided by subjects' performance on three tests of recall conducted by the hypnotist as well as performance during the application of the EAT. With respect to the tests of recall, the initial test was taken immediately following the termination of hypnosis (and served to classify subjects as amnesic or nonamnesic), the second test was taken when the hypnotist re-

TABLE 7.1
Design of Studies

McConkey, Sheehan, & Cross *(1980)*	*McConkey & Sheehan* *(1981)*
	Pre-experimental instructions given to hypnotic and simulating subjects.
Subjects tested by hypnotist on routine scale and their hypnotic performance videotape-recorded. The final test item is a suggestion for posthypnotic amnesia. Following hypnosis, subjects' recall is tested but the amnesia suggestion is not cancelled.	
An independent experimenter conducts an inquiry into subjects' hypnotic experiences through the application of the EAT.	
Following EAT session the hypnotist conducts a second recall test, then cancels the amnesia, and conducts a reversibility test.	
	Postexperimental inquiry, finally conducted to determine the reasons underlying subjects' performance.

Note. McConkey, Sheehan, & Cross (1980) employed hypnotic subjects only.

TABLE 7.2
Incidence of Response to Amnesia Suggestion
in Each of the Studies

Study and Subject Grouping	Amnesia Status	
	Amnesic	Nonamnesic
McConkey, Sheehan, & Cross (1980)		
Hypnotic	14	9
McConkey & Sheehan (1981)		
Hypnotic	16	8
Simulating	24	0

turned following the EAT session, and the third test was taken following the reversal of the amnesia. The major data that relate to the possible breakdown of amnesia are based on subjects' performance on the second recall test (i.e., following the EAT). Table 7.2 sets out the number of subjects who passed the criteria for amnesia in each of the studies. With respect to subjects' performance while viewing the video-tape playback of their hypnotic session with the inquirer, data are available to index the number of hypnotic events they commented on, the number of times they stopped the playback in order to comment on their hypnotic experience, and the number of words that they spoke in making such comments. The experiential data relate to subjects' reports about the nature of their recall during the EAT, with special reference to the extent to which the viewing of the video tape and the questioning of the inquirer broke down subjects' amnesia.

The behavioral performance of subjects on the three measures taken during the EAT is set out in Table 7.3. Data indicate that hypnotic amnesic subjects commented on appreciably fewer events, stopped the video tape less, and spoke appreciably fewer words than did hypnotic nonamnesic subjects in the study reported by McConkey, Sheehan, and Cross (1980) but not in the study by McConkey and Sheehan (1981); simulating subjects commented on fewer items and stopped the tape less than hypnotic subjects. This finding of the differences in behavioral response of subjects across the studies again underscores the essential variability of individual subjects' reactions and highlights the importance of focusing closely on more individualized measures of assessment. Qualitatively, hypnotic amnesic, nonamnesic, and simulating subjects differed substantially in their comments during the EAT. Amnesic subjects, for instance, reported not remembering (or simulated not remembering) the hypnotic events being depicted on the video tape, whereas nonamnesic subjects commented openly and freely on their experiences and for the most part did not comment directly on their recall until viewing the posthypnotic amnesia item itself.

The performance of subjects on the three tests of recall is set out in Table 7.4.

TABLE 7.3
Mean Number of Events Commented on, Stops Made, and
Words Spoken by Hypnotic Amnesic, Hypnotic Nonamnesic,
and Simulating Amnesic Subjects During the EAT

Subject Grouping and Amnesia Status	Events Commented On	Measures Stops Made	Words Spoken
McConkey, Sheehan & Cross (1980)			
Hypnotic			
Amnesic	3.07 (2.12)	3.93 (3.32)	530.11 (551.03)
Nonamnesic	6.78 (2.91)	11.00 (6.60)	2021.00 (1597.26)
McConkey & Sheehan (1981)			
Hypnotic			
Amnesic	5.88 (3.05)	9.56 (6.74)	1672.88 (1327.83)
Nonamnesic	7.63 (1.51)	14.00 (7.76)	2186.13 (1393.34)
Simulating			
Amnesic	3.54 (2.26)	4.74 (3.98)	657.38 (633.79)

Note. Standard deviations appear in parentheses. Maximum number of events = 9. Top section of table adapted from McConkey, Sheehan & Cross (1980). Reprinted from the February 1980 *British Journal of Social and Clinical Psychology.* Copyright 1980 by the British Psychological Society. Reprinted by permission. Bottom section of table presents previously unreported data of McConkey and Sheehan (1981).

Subjects' performance on the initial test served to classify them as amnesic or nonamnesic. Across the initial and second recall tests, amnesic subjects recalled appreciably fewer items than did nonamnesic subjects, but both groups of subjects recalled appreciably more events following, rather than preceding, their participation in the EAT. Close inspection of the data relating to the second test of recall, however, indicated that 50% of the amnesic subjects in the study by McConkey, Sheehan, and Cross (1980) and 37.50% of the amnesic subjects in the study of McConkey and Sheehan (1981) maintained their complete amnesia even after viewing the video-tape playback of their hypnotic testing during the application of the EAT when they were supposed to be amnesic. That is, the intrusion of the reality through subjects' memories being made available via the EAT led to the breakdown of amnesia for some, but not all, susceptible subjects. The amnesia that was intact was also reversible on cue.

In summary, these two studies demonstrated that after the intrusion of reality via the application of the EAT recall was greater for both amnesic and nonamnesic subjects. The results clearly indicate, however, that amnesia was not broken down for all amnesic subjects. Even under conditions of high stringency for breaching, amnesia for some subjects remained intact and, despite the fact that subjects viewed the hypnotic events that actually did occur, total recall was not evidenced for any amnesic subject in either study.

Other independent evidence (Murphy, 1980) has indicated that even when a segment of events that did not actually happen during hypnosis is incorporated into the EAT video-tape playback, some subjects still maintain their amnesia. The fact that in all of these studies amnesia was not broken down for all subjects when reality was intruded into their suggested experience is an important finding, which suggests once more the particular relevance of interpreting hypnotic reactions in terms of subjects' experiences with events. In particular, the data we present in Chapters 4–8 argue forcibly for the need to recognize the relevance of hypnotic subjects' phenomenal awareness in determining the reasons underlying trance behavior.

We now consider the EAT data on subjects' experiences in some detail. Analysis of subjects' reports during the EAT session provided evidence that

TABLE 7.4

Mean Number of Total and/or Additional Events Recalled by Hypnotic Amnesic, Hypnotic Nonamnesic, and Simulating Amnesic Subjects on the Initial, Second, and Reversibility Tests

Subject Grouping and Amnesia Status	Tests			
	Initial	Second		Reversibility
	Total Events	Total Events	Additional Events	Additional Events
McConkey, Sheehan & Cross (1980)				
Hypnotic				
Amnesic	.79 (.89)	2.64 (2.21)	2.00 (1.75)	3.57 (1.60)
Nonamnesic	4.56 (1.88)	6.56 (1.59)	2.67 (1.22)	.33 (.71)
McConkey & Sheehan (1981)				
Hypnotic				
Amnesic	.69 (.95)	3.63 (2.75)	3.06 (2.41)	2.25 (2.21)
Nonamnesic	5.25 (2.12)	6.75 (1.58)	2.25 (1.49)	.13 (.58)
Simulating				
Amnesic	.21 (.41)	3.83 (2.50)	3.75 (2.49)	2.13 (2.09)

Note. Standard deviations appear in parentheses. Maximum number of events = 9. Top section of table adapted from McConkey, Sheehan, & Cross (1980). Reprinted from the February 1980 *British Journal of Social and Clinical Psychology.* Copyright 1980 by the British Psychological Society. Reprinted by permission. Bottom section of table adapted from McConkey and Sheehan (1981). Reprinted from the February 1981 *Journal of Abnormal Psychology.* Copyright 1981 by the American Psychological Association. Reprinted by permission.

highlights the distinctive experience of hypnotic (as contrasted with simulating and hypnotic nonamnesic) subjects.

Hypnotic amnesic subjects in both studies commented mainly on the difficulty that they were experiencing in recalling the hypnotic events. As one amnesic subject stated: "I can't really remember much of that . . . this is annoying because I've usually got a good memory, a photographic memory, but it's just a complete blank." Another hypnotic amnesic subject expressed it somewhat differently in saying: "I can't think of anything. I feel very objective, just sort of sitting here as though it's somebody else up there [on the screen]." In somewhat similar fashion, another subject commented: "I don't remember any of this. I don't remember it at all. It's like watching a television show that you've never seen before." In quite different fashion, however, another amnesic subject indicated that he had a memory of the hypnosis testing but that he didn't want to retrieve that memory: "I'm finding it hard to concentrate. It's sort of like all I have to do is to go where it all is. I just have to cross a little bridge or go around the corner or something to where all the recollection is. The effort to do that is just not worth it, you know. I just don't feel like putting in the effort."

The majority of hypnotic nonamnesic subjects, on the other hand, did not comment on the nature of their recall until viewing the posthypnotic amnesia item itself during the EAT. Generally, nonamnesic subjects shared the view of one subject who said: "There are some details I had forgotten but having seen it on the screen brought back everything." In similar fashion, another nonamnesic commented: "Before I couldn't remember things well, like everything was hazy but as I looked through the tape I could remember what I was feeling and can understand and remember it." Similarly, another nonamnesic subject indicated that the video tape clarified her memory of events: "It made me remember a few of the things that I'd forgotten and the thoughts that I had." These comments by subjects who were not amnesic for the events of hypnosis index the impact of EAT procedures in being able to revive subjects' memories or stimulate their recall of past (hypnotic) experiences.

Simulating amnesic subjects viewing the video-tape playback of their (simulated) hypnotic performance generally reported that they could not remember any of the events that they were viewing. Such a position by these subjects is completely in accord with the role demands of their social-psychological situation; simulators are uniquely placed in a situation where they are particularly highly motivated to respond appropriately according to whatever cues for hypnotic response exist in the total test situation (Sheehan, 1971b). Attempting to play a sophisticated role of pretense, some simulators in the context of the EAT expressed vague or generic memories of the hypnotic events. For instance, one simulator commented: "I can remember doing something with my hands, maybe this was it." However, simulating subjects faced with the EAT under conditions of posthypnotic amnesia generally minimized their comments about their hypnotic performance.

In terms of the type of comments made, hypnotic amnesic subjects often commented on their being able to recall the behavioral events being displayed on the video tape but not being able to recall the private experiences that accompanied those events during hypnosis. This distinction between the availability of memories of behavior versus experience was spontaneously mentioned by 37.5% of amnesic subjects in the study by McConkey, Sheehan, and Cross (1980) and 31.3% of amnesic subjects in the study by McConkey and Sheehan (1981). As one subject put it: "I can sort of remember this, but I can't remember the experience. I can remember [the hypnotist] doing it, but I can't remember how it felt." In somewhat similar fashion, another subject indicated: "I can remember this but it's not like I experienced it." This same distinction was made by subjects in differing ways. For instance, a third subject said: "I can remember it when it comes on the screen, but it seems like it's another part of me feeling the things." Another subject provided more detail when she commented: "All the words seem familiar but I can't remember the sensations of it. I sort of know these words, I think I've heard them before, but it doesn't seem like me there. Even when it happens, I have to believe it because it's there, but I can't sort of feel any of it. When I hear the voice I can sort of remember the words but I can't remember any of the sensations." Another amnesic subject commented in a similar vein: "I couldn't remember what had happened and when I saw it, it was just like new. I remember [the hypnotist's] voice but I can't remember what happened." Later, this same subject added: "A couple of things came back to me but I couldn't remember the feeling as much as the movement, you know, I couldn't remember how I felt. I couldn't really remember how I felt at the time, you know, my thoughts at the time." Other amnesic subjects made the distinction between behavioral and experiential memories in different ways: "I was sort of sitting here and I couldn't remember it all, some things I could remember when I saw them on the screen but I couldn't remember my feelings. I was just sitting here watching the tape." Also: "I can remember some of these things that happened but I can't remember how I felt. I can remember doing a couple of things, but not the feelings and thoughts while I was doing them."

In contrast, no simulating subject and only one nonamnesic subject reported this distinction; further, the nonamnesic subject made it clear that it happened only on one item. In reference to the arm-immobilization item, this subject indicated: "I can only vaguely remember [the hypnotist] telling me that. I sort of can't remember how it felt, how heavy it was. I can sort of remember trying to raise it up, but I can't remember how it felt." Clearly, this subject was partially amnesic for some of the hypnotic events. It is important to note that no simulator performed like hypnotic amnesic subjects in this respect. The cue demands of the hypnotic situation are very effectively indexed by the behavior of simulating subjects (Sheehan, 1973), and this difference found between the behavior of hypnotic and simulating subjects highlights the fact that the distinction between memories of behavior and experience commented on by hypnotic subjects is not based at all on the demand characteristics for appropriate response that exist in the test setting.

Reports by amnesic subjects also indicated that the degree of their recall while viewing the video tape of their hypnotic test session was severely limited. As one amnesic subject put it:

> I'd sort of be waiting until that [item] was finished to see what the next [item] was and as soon as [the hypnotist] would say one word, the key word, you know, then I'd remember the whole thing. Like when the hypnotist said the number 6, I could remember that whole item [the missing number item], but I had to wait until he said the key word in the next one before I could remember it, [and after the item passed] I couldn't remember it. It was sort of right in the back of my mind, but I couldn't reach it.

This subject, then, was unaware of an item until the appropriate cue was given by the hypnotist on the video tape, and she could then remember the particular task. Further, following the viewing of the item, she was aware of the memory of it but unable to access that memory. Other amnesic subjects also indicated an inability to anticipate recall, as it were: "I couldn't remember what was coming after [the item being viewed] but when it came I could remember it in some parts, but I couldn't remember the next task that was coming up, [and after that item had passed] it became part of the whole. I had a fair recollection of doing things once I had seen them." Somewhat similarly, another subject reported: "I couldn't think of anything except what was actually present on the screen."

Hypnotic amnesic subjects commented on the difficulty that they experienced in focusing on the events that they were viewing. As one subject put it: "It was very vague; it was as if I was trying to remember a dream and piece it all together." Similarly, another hypnotic amnesic subject commented: "I find it hard to concentrate on the tape; although I can watch it, it doesn't really mean anything to me." For amnesic subjects, then, there appeared to be a consistent inability to recall ahead of the particular item that they were viewing; there also was some evidence of the need for a particular cue to occur before they could remember the item being viewed.

The questioning of subjects during the end of the recall phase of the EAT indicated that amnesic subjects differed in the nature of their memories of the actual EAT session itself. Some subjects could fully recall the events of the EAT, but others indicated that they could not; their amnesia had expanded, as it were, to include the EAT session as a whole. As one subject commented during the end of the recall phase: "I don't know why, I can't really remember anything. I can't remember why, I mean, I mustn't have been watching very carefully, or something. I don't know, you know, I just couldn't tell you what happened on the video tape." Another subject indicated that she could remember some, but not all, of the events of the EAT when she commented: "I can only remember the things on the video tape that I discussed with [the inquirer]." For some amnesic subjects, then, their amnesia extended to the events of the EAT even though they had not been given suggestions to forget that period. No simulating or nonamnesic subjects reported being unable to remember the events of the EAT session itself.

CONCLUSION

In this chapter, an instrumental use of the EAT is presented by looking at the nature of posthypnotic amnesia as studied in the experimental setting. A major finding of the application of the EAT under laboratory test conditions for studying posthypnotic amnesia was that the amnesia is durable and persistent for some hypnotic subjects even when reality is intruded into their experiences by the viewing of a literal record of their hypnotic performance or when events are intruded that never actually happened.

The major finding from the program of research that we have reported in this chapter is that amnesia persists for some, but not all, susceptible hypnotic subjects. The data we have discussed, however, have been gathered entirely in the experimental context, and the chapter as a whole has a strong laboratory emphasis. We recognize that there is a need to validate these findings clinically and toward that end we have had a unique opportunity to do so. In a case brought to our attention, the EAT was used to test the durability of amnesia in a person diagnosed as a case of multiple personality, where three personalities presented themselves to the therapists who were involved. For this individual, amnesia for hypnotic events including performance on a learning task was induced in the dominant personality, and the EAT was then used to intrude reality. That intrusion was entirely unsuccessful, and the amnesia was maintained, although the session evoked a strong hostility reaction from the individual because she feared that the control she thought she possessed was now gone. The hostility, in a sense, validated the persistence of amnesia that we observed in the laboratory. Further data were collected to test whether the amnesia maintained itself in the other personalities. For these personalities, memory was tested by the consulting psychiatrist in charge of the case, and findings indicated that no recall of the learning that had occurred during hypnosis was evident in either of the two other personalities. Clinically speaking, then, evidence from this case supports the trend of the evidence we found in the experimental studies. The clinical data gathered here, however, interestingly challenge the reality of assumptions made in the literature on multiple personality about how one personality has more control of the recall of events as experienced than do others (see E. R. Hilgard, 1977, and Sutcliffe & Jones, 1962, for further discussion of multiple personality).

Other experimental findings of a more specific kind further help to define amnesia as a distinctive phenomenon. Hypnotic subjects in the studies we discuss, for example, reported amnesia for the viewing of the video tape as well as for the hypnotic testing. Further, during the EAT when recall was reported by amnesic subjects, it was often localized to a particular segment and dependent on the occurrence of a specific cue. Amnesic subjects generally reported a memory for the particular item that they were viewing after the hypnotist had employed a specific word or action that was integral to the hypnotic task and showed a general inability to recall ahead of the events being viewed.

A common finding across both studies was that some hypnotic amnesic subjects reported a memory for their hypnotic behavior but not for their hypnotic experiences when confronted with the video-tape record of their previous test session. Because no nonhypnotic subject we studied reported such a distinction, the differentiation of behavior and memories of experience that was made by some hypnotic subjects cannot be said to be an artifact of the social constraints for compliance in the laboratory test situation. It was as if the viewing of the video tape provided access to the behavioral aspects of hypnotic subjects' involvement but failed to provide effective access to the covert, experiential aspects of subjects' involvement. Therefore, it can be argued that the cues needed to provide access to the experiential memories were not, and could not, be supplied by information presented to subjects that was relevant only to their behavior. Behavior was directly shown by video tape, and experiences had to be inferred by subjects from their viewing of that information. That some hypnotic amnesic subjects were unable to comment on their experiences, even though they could recognize and comment on their behavior as they saw it on the screen, suggests an important distinction pertinent to the relationship between behavioral performance and experiential involvement in hypnosis. Findings suggest that different retrieval mechanisms may well be implicated in accessing behavioral and experiental memories. The basic phenomenon at issue is that some hypnotic subjects are able to acknowledge their behavior, but this does not necessarily facilitate recall of their hypnotic involvement in a private sense.

In summary, analyses of hypnotic subjects' performance through the application of the EAT under laboratory test conditions for studying posthypnotic amnesia brings us to conclusions similar to those we have arrived at in preceding chapters. Previously, the phenomenological analysis of hypnotic events that we have conducted focused more on specific cognitive processes that underlie hypnotic reactions than on the instrumental utility of the EAT in manipulating them.

Common themes again present themselves. There is a strong indication from our research into amnesia for idiosyncratic response, essential variability in hypnotic reaction, and strong individual differences in the way that reality information is processed. As in the previous chapters, the data argue the necessity of rephrasing contemporary issues relating to the function and nature of hypnotic phenomena, so as to acknowledge more fully the complexities and subtleties of hypnotic consciousness. Few would dispute the genuineness of amnesia as an experienced phenomenon, but the hypnotic literature has failed to date to come to grips with the complexity of process that is obviously involved, or to appreciate

fully even the individual character of subjects' responsiveness to amnesia suggestion in hypnosis. Among susceptible subjects, amnesia clearly manifests
itself in different ways, and the pursuit of the typical or representative amnesia
response does little justice to the variability that basically exists in susceptible
subjects' reactions. Central tendency responses to amnesia suggestion are mis-
leadingly indicated by standard scales of assessment that bypass within-group
variability and overlook the personal, subjective meaning to subjects of the
information that they receive in the hypnotic setting.

8 Cognitive Persistence: A Case Analysis

INTRODUCTION

Up to this point in the book we have examined the nature of a range of phenomena that are typically regarded as relevant to the standard scales of assessment that were reviewed in Chapter 2. For instance, in Chapter 4 we examined ideomotor response, a response that is normally regarded as a relatively easy and simple task to perform; Chapters 5, 6, and 7 then looked at more complex and cognitively oriented items that tapped deeper levels of hypnotic responsiveness.

Across all of the tasks that we have considered, however, there was strong and consistent evidence in support of our argument that we can fully interpret the meaning of hypnotic responsiveness only when it is considered in relation to the experience of the person doing the responding. This is not to deny the significance or importance of the behavior, but rather to assert that the full theoretical significance of the response in question cannot really be understood without measuring experience in a sensitive and in-depth manner. We have attempted to present data that speak to this position and have done so by reporting results from research that is oriented toward the intrinsic analysis of the EAT as an assessment device (see Chapters 4, 5, and 6 for details) as well as its use as a tool to manipulate stimulus test conditions in the laboratory setting (see Chapter 7). Important themes that have emerged through the data gathered in the previous chapters have been the idiosyncratic nature of hypnotic subjects' patterns of responding, the cognitive style-response task interface, and the degree to which the nature of the subject's involvement in the events of trance may shift within a single test situation as well as across different types of hypnotic response.

The present chapter reports a detailed case history of one highly susceptible subject whom we tested on a range of tasks over a period of time. We consider it important to present an in-depth account of one subject's responsiveness in order to illustrate as clearly as possible the degree of idiosyncrasy that may exist in an individual subject's hypnotic behavior. In reporting the case, we are data-oriented rather than concerned with reporting personal attributes and information about the subject whom we have studied. The data are the kind that we have discussed in previous chapters, but the case that we analyze illustrates the same themes in a clinically intensive way. Importantly, however, we wish to make the point that the phenomena emerging through intensive individual analysis are not easily classifiable in terms of those measured on standard scales of assessment that are currently available. We believe that the current scales are relevant and important, but they are in need of revision in order to recognize more clearly the subtlety and complexity of hypnotic consciousness that exist and that are illustrated so forcibly in the following case study.

This case study illustrates a distinctive and unusual imaginative talent at work. The history began when Subject F was asked by one of the authors (PWS) whether she would volunteer for a workshop demonstration in hypnosis. The hypnotist serving as the demonstrator for the workshop was a visiting hypnotherapist who was unknown to the subject and who simply wanted to demonstrate for the group that was present a range of standard techniques of hypnosis. The subject who had been scheduled for the workshop had failed to turn up and, because Subject F was known to us, she was asked to help out. At the time, we had no idea of Subject F's special aptitude for trance or the level of her susceptibility. Previous testing had been conducted with the HGSHS:A, and her response on that occasion had indicated only that she was a good, but not excellent, hypnotic subject and that she could easily experience some, but not all, of the standard phenomena of hypnosis.

The workshop session oriented itself around her response to a range of routine hypnotic test tasks that included arm levitation, arm stiffness, age regression, and amnesia. The induction of hypnosis was conducted through routine relaxation eye-closure instructions, after which the hypnotist counted the subject down into deep hypnosis by asking her to imagine scenes that were restful and relaxing. In the course of the session, the subject demonstrated that she was highly susceptible. She successfully responded to all of the hypnotic tasks that were given to her and obviously had no difficulty in doing so. She evidenced, for example, an age-regression response that was characterized by trance logic. When regressed to an early age, she lapsed at once into German. She had lived as a small child in Germany and now spoke fluently in German while understanding perfectly the hypnotist's instructions and questions to her in English (another example of the kind of phenomenon that we discussed in Chapter 5).

The case history that follows pursues rather distinctive effects of hypnotic suggestion. Subject F demonstrated a peculiar endurance or persistence of hypnotic behavior that was quite idiosyncratic. The phenomenon was first explored through the subject's own reporting of her experience, then through an analysis of her behavior in the laboratory setting, and finally through the application of the EAT, which indicated the phenomenon at work when it was altogether unsuspected by the hypnotist.

SUBJECT REPORT

The case history begins with Subject F coming to the first author 14 months after the workshop just described. She was concerned about the aftermath or sequelae of the session and wanted to talk her experiences through. At the time, she was also having difficulties understanding her reaction to hypnosis induced in a second workshop, which had taken place some months after the first one and in which she had participated in a demonstration of hypnotic analgesia. Her coming to the first author to talk about how she felt was quite spontaneous and unsolicited. He had no idea that anything was wrong, and what emerged from the subject's account of her experience became a fascinating illustration of hypnotic persistence. After listening to that account of what happened, he asked Subject F to write down her experiences in as much detail as possible. We begin, then, with her verbatim report of her experience, which sets the stage for tracking through the phenomenon of persistence. This report has been discussed elsewhere in relation to the analysis of imaginative processes in hypnosis (Sheehan, 1979d).

My first experience with hypnosis was when I read a notice in the Psychology Department: "Subjects wanted for hypnosis experiments." My curiosity was aroused and I decided to go along to see what it was all about. However, I arrived late and missed the introductory remarks of the HGSHS:A tape, and, consequently, I wasn't at all sure whether to cooperate or to resist the suggestions. Having misconceptions about hypnosis, I decided to resist. That was not so easy, however. Every now and then I found myself listening to the voice and I experienced considerable difficulty in resisting. It was as if part of me was drawn in by the voice and wanted to let go and do as he said, and I had to remind myself constantly that I wasn't going to be hypnotized, that I was going to resist. At the end of the session, I was confused; had I been hypnotized or not? How could I tell? I decided that I couldn't have been because I hadn't felt all that different and I certainly had not been asleep as the voice suggested, quite the contrary! To my surprise I was later told that I had scored 9 out of 12.

My next experience was nearly four years later, when I was asked unexpectedly to be a subject for the demonstration of hypnosis at a hypnosis workshop. This time I was willing to cooperate and decided to just let things happen. It was similar to that first experience in that I was drawn in by the voice but instead of resisting I seemed to repeat the hypnotist's words in my mind. He took me to a beach where 20 steps led down to the water and as we counted I went down. I could see that scene so vividly, it was as if I was really there. I enjoyed being there, it was warm and peaceful, but I didn't mind when he took me away from there and back to my school days. Going back to childhood was funny, it was like watching a film that is running too fast, the years flashed past so quickly that I couldn't really see anything, but stopped whenever he stopped them.

The hypnotist then told me that he was going to talk to the audience but it wouldn't disturb me, and that's just how it was. I was aware that he was talking to them about me, yet I felt so detached from it all, it didn't disturb me in the least.

I felt very relaxed and enjoyed it all so very much that I was disappointed when he said that he was going to count and bring me back, I didn't really want to. I remember thinking "that isn't fair, he said it would take about 30 minutes and now he is going to stop it already after only a few minutes." Then he simply counted and that didn't feel at all right. Everything inside me was calling out to him "No—you can't do that—you have to take me back to the beach," and as he counted I became more and more anxious, I wanted to come up the stairs again. I kept thinking, "why doesn't he take me back to the beach and up the stairs?" I was all churned up inside, yet seeing the video some time later I was absolutely amazed that I didn't show any outward signs of this inner struggle. I saw myself sitting there quite calmly, not moving or giving any indication of what was going on.

For some weeks after the session and for no apparent reason an image of the beach would flash into my mind and I would have a strong desire to go back up those stairs. This feeling and the image would last for a split second only, but it was quite strong. Even to this day, approximately 14 months later, I still get the feeling that I would like to come back up the stairs. It does not occur as frequently now or as strong, and I can dismiss it more rationally, but nevertheless it is still with me. I have even tried to visualize myself going up the stairs and I can do this very successfully, but the next time the image occurs, I am always back at the bottom of the stairs!

Some eight months later I took part in a workshop in hypnosis where members in small groups practiced pain-reduction techniques. After a baseline measure, a brief induction, and a specific technique, the person's arm was again placed in a bucket of ice water and the person rated himself from 1–10 for pain and suffering. The member hypnotizing me used a brief relaxation induction and suggestions of analgesia. I didn't feel nearly as detached as I did at the previous workshop, however, but was very much aware of everything. In fact, I remember thinking "I won't be able to stand that ice water again, that really hurt." Then my arm began to feel quite numb, with every stroke it really became more and more numb, I could hardly feel his hand touch my arm. When he placed my arm into the water I thought, "oh, oh, here it goes! I won't be able to stand this." But to my surprise it didn't even worry me; then, after a while my hand began to hurt a little, but my arm didn't hurt at all, I simply couldn't feel it. Then, as far as I remember, the hypnotist simply told me to wake up. I was somewhat bewildered; I knew I was awake, yet something didn't seem right, and my arm felt very numb. I recall saying, "what have you done to my arm, it's numb?" After a brief group discussion it was decided that he put me "under" again, and remove the suggestion. The hypnotist told me to relax, that I was hypnotized again and that upon opening my eyes my arm would feel normal.

Well, first of all, I didn't feel hypnotized the second time; it was much too quick, I felt, and secondly, he did not touch my arm again. He simply said it would feel normal again. Yet, when he induced the numbness he did it by stroking, saying that with every stroke my arm would become more and more numb. Whatever the reason, when I opened my eyes my arm still felt numb. Not as much, but still quite numb. Not wanting to make a fuss and thinking that it was perhaps the ice water anyway that made it feel numb, I decided not to say anything more. For the rest of the seminar, however, I kept rubbing my arm, thinking ''how much longer is it going to take, surely the effects of the ice water should be wearing off by now?''

The following day it was much better but still numb enough to annoy me. It was as if something inside me reminded me that my arm felt numb and it did. Thirty-six hours later my arm still felt numb, and I was beginning to get really annoyed and tried hard to be rational, saying things to myself like ''you are being silly, your arm doesn't feel numb, and you know it, be sensible. How can it be numb when all he did was stroke it, nothing else, how can that possibly make your arm numb? You are just imagining it, it's all in your head.'' The funny thing was that I agreed with all this, I could see and understand the logic of it and yet—my arm felt numb! It was as if that part of me that was responsible for the numb feeling either didn't take any notice of my reasoning or couldn't even hear me.

When, after 48 hours, I was still battling with myself, and it interfered even with my driving—I had to rest my arm on the car window because it felt too heavy and numb to hold the steering wheel—I decided that I had had enough. Imagination or real, I wasn't going to put up with it any longer. I didn't want to look foolish, however, and contact the chairman of the workshop, so I confided in a colleague who agreed to remove the suggestion. After an induction he took me back to the day of the workshop and suggested that there were two buckets, the ice bucket and another containing warm, soothing water. He then told me to take my numb arm out of the ice water and to place it in the other bucket, and as I did the warm water would bring the feeling back, that my arm would feel warm and comfortable just the way it normally felt. This experience was very real, I could see the room and the people, feel the warm water and the numbness leaving my arm. When I took my arm out of the bucket it felt good and no longer numb. The hypnotist then counted backwards and told me to wake up. That's when an extraordinary thing happened. I ''saw'' the room and the people in it superimposed on the wall. I couldn't believe my eyes and blinked a few times but the image remained. I could see the white tiled wall very clearly, I knew where I was, I was awake, but I saw the workshop room and the people in it right there on the wall. It was as if I or at least some part of me was still there in that room. It was most peculiar. When I mentioned it to the hypnotist he reinduced hypnosis and told me I was leaving the workshop room, that I was coming back to the present, that it was Monday and I was back in my room. When I opened my eyes everything was back to normal, the image had disappeared; there was only a white wall.

I was glad that everything had ended well, yet something odd has remained with me since that day. When I think back to that workshop I know that there was only one bucket—the ice bucket—I know exactly what transpired, yet when I visualize that day, I can ''see'' two buckets, the ice bucket and the warm water bucket. On one level I know what really happened, on another I don't. A part of me has been fooled, and I have a feeling that I can't reach that part; the two just can't seem to get together.

Comment

Subject F is clearly very susceptible to hypnosis, and the group administration of hypnosis that first tested for her susceptibility massively underestimated her hypnotic skills and capacities. Her verbatim report illustrates in very cogent fashion the particular relevance of imaginative processes to hypnosis. There is little doubt that the imaginative skills of the subject would be available to the subject in both the hypnotic and waking state, but clearly the hypnotic context marshaled those skills together in an altogether individual way. We have considered data elsewhere in this book that illustrate the importance of imagination and related processes (see especially Chapters 4 and 6), but here the illustration of those processes at work is considerably more dramatic.

It should be said at the outset that Subject F is sophisticated about psychology and about hypnosis and probably has particular expectations or preconceptions about hypnotic behavior that could well have influenced the detail of her hypnotic response. The persistence of the effects of suggestion, however, was not anticipated by her and is not documented in the hypnotic literature. In that sense, we can view her experience as a counterexpectational phenomenon (Evans, 1968) of hypnosis. The role of the hypnotic subject does not ordinarily encompass the existence of a response outside the hypnotic setting when the continuation of that response is not suggested by the hypnotist, although some data exist to the contrary (Perry, 1977c).

A number of features of Subject F's hypnotic response were not instructed by the hypnotist, although they were consistent with the nature of the tasks that were being administered. Her transparency report, for example, was not suggested and illustrates a feature of hypnosis that is rare in incidence and normally idiosyncratic to highly susceptible subjects (Orne, 1959; Sheehan, 1977). The most distinctive feature of the subject's pattern of response, however, was the persistence of the effects of suggestion. The hypnotist's instruction to her to go down the steps to experience deep hypnosis and to experience analgesia continued in their effects. In both cases, the influence of suggestion remained, although the hypnotist had instructed Subject F in a way that would normally have removed any effects of suggestion for other subjects. The hypnotist aroused images and fantasies that persisted in their effects, and the hypnotist needed to know the precise involvement of the subject in the events of trance in order to counteract them and suggest their removal.

What the subject experienced was not directly a consequence of the literal text of the hypnotist's instructions, and internal tensions were created in the subject that needed to be resolved or alleviated. That resolution was provided following hypnosis, once knowledge of the sequelae had been obtained (for discussion of the sequelae of hypnosis, see Coe & Ryken, 1979; J. R. Hilgard, 1974b). The original hypnotist had awakened Subject F in the normal way but did not take her back up the steps. The first author hypnotized her 14 months later and took her back up the same steps in fantasy that she had gone down before and which she so earnestly wanted to ascend. This time there were no sequelae to the induction of hypnosis; once Subject F had ascended the steps, she felt comfortable and relaxed. The tension was dissipated, and the persistent effects of suggestion no longer remained.

We now consider a laboratory investigation of the hypnotic responsiveness of Subject F. The session again demonstrated the existence of distinctive effects of suggestion, and again in unexpected and persistent ways. The session itself was oriented to the investigation of whether Subject F would illustrate the effects of suggestion that were comparable to the effects of real perceptual stimuli.

VALIDATION OF THE PERSISTENT EFFECTS OF SUGGESTION

Because of her marked susceptibility to hypnosis, Subject F was considered an especially appropriate subject for testing the hypothesis that effects paralleling the consequences of actual sensory stimulation can be observed in hypnosis. The weight of the evidence appears to be against the hypothesis that hypnosis can demonstrate the effects of sensory stimulation for hallucinated stimuli, but recent evidence has emerged suggesting that the McCollough (1965) effect might be a particularly appropriate phenomenon for stringent test of the notion. Finke and Schmidt (1977) attempted to induce the McCollough effect and reported that colored aftereffects associated with the effect could be observed for imagination conditions. They found an effect for imagined contours viewed against a physically present color patch (but not for imagined colors viewed against a physically present pattern of bars). Later work (Finke & Schmidt, 1978; see also Finke, 1980) further implicated the relevance of imagery ability, although their claims in this respect have been seriously challenged (Broerse & Crassini, 1980). For the imagined McCollough effect, the effect found was that high imagery subjects (i.e., those subjects demonstrating especially vivid imagery) showed a stronger aftereffect than those who were deficient in visual imagery ability.

For testing the McCollough effect in the standard perceptual test situation, an induction (adaptation) and test period are routinely involved. During the period of induction, subjects inspect stimulus pairs consisting of complementary colors (e.g., red and green). These stimuli are paired with orthogonal orientations (e.g., vertical and horizontal), and each member of the pair (e.g., green-vertical, red-horizontal) is viewed in alternation with the other for the full adaptation period. In the test period, achromatic test stimuli containing vertical and horizontal contours are shown, and subjects are asked what they see. In demonstration of the actual McCollough effect, subjects typically report that the test stimuli appear colored (e.g., the horizontal contours appear green and the vertical contours appear red). The colored aftereffect is orientation specific and opposite to the color paired with the orientation that is presented during the adaptation period. The McCollough phenomenon seems especially suitable for examination of the sensory hypothesis because very few subjects know of the effect, and hence their performances should be relatively uninfluenced by expectations about appropriate response.

In the test that was conducted (a detailed report of procedures and findings is provided by Sheehan, Crassini, & Murphy, 1979), the McCollough effect was studied under different sets of instructions where the order of instructions was counterbalanced in separate sessions. Subject F participated in each of three sessions, and the experiment represents an intensive investigation of her response to McCollough test conditions under real, hypnotic, and imagination instruction. In Session 1, Subject F was tested under hypnotic instruction and then tested again in the same session under imagery instruction. In Session 2, this order of instructions was reversed. In Session 3, the real conditions for test of the actual McCollough phenomenon were employed. The three sessions were conducted over a 2-week period, and the detailed procedures for the test of the McCollough phenomenon were as set out by McCollough (1965).

In Session 1 (hallucination, then imagination) a pattern of response was demonstrated that continued throughout the first and second sessions, and it was modified only when the real conditions for testing the McCollough effect were implemented in the final session. The subject gave color responses in both the hallucinated and imagination situation to the test stimuli, but her pattern of response suggested very strongly that the colors being reported to the imagined stimuli were responses that persisted from the hallucination test situation that was administered at the beginning of the first session. The responses of the subject in the second session showed that she carried over the same color responses to the vertical and horizontal stimuli as were shown in the first session, and these continued throughout the second session. Throughout, the color responses reported by the subject matched those given by the subject in the hallucination-adaptation period, and the phenomenon persisted with the strength of the effect being dissipated only when the actual McCollough effect was tested in the third session using real colored stimuli. Furthermore, the sensory effect was strongly evident in the third session just for the eye that had been stimulated, this finding being entirely consistent with the McCollough phenomenon as a real effect. The color effect in the first two sessions, however, transferred interocularly. Color reports consistent with the previous pattern of response as evident in the first two sessions continued to be demonstrated in the third session for the eye that was not actually stimulated.

The results of the experiment were not at all consistent with the sensory stimulation hypothesis. Hallucination and imagination conditions gave rise to the same color reports when each should have produced different results if actual sensory processes were influencing effects. The hallucination response that the subject gave in the adaptation period in the first session dominated the pattern of her responsiveness throughout the testing, and results demonstrated a peculiarly persistent cognitive-delusory response that was not anticipated in the testing. A report of the difficulty that the subject experienced during the imagination period cogently illustrates the phenomenon. In the imagination condition, which followed the hypnosis condition, the subject had definite difficulty in imagining the colors as they were requested by the experimenter. That difficulty, however, was experienced only when the color that the subject was requested to imagine was different from the color that had been hallucinated previously in the first part of the session. Asked to imagine red, when before she had hallucinated the stimulus as green, the subject reported: "Something seems to be wrong! The moment you say the color, I see a different color. You're not saying the color I see."

Comment

The persistent effects of suggestion that were apparent in the foregoing test paralleled those observed in relation to Subject F's participation in the workshop sessions, which led to the detection of sequelae that needed to be removed. Before, a routine fantasy situation imbedded by the hypnotist into the framework of suggestion remained influential over an extensive period of time. Here, an analogous finding was evident. In Session 1, the subject was adapted with alternating patterns of horizontal and vertical lines and asked to "fill in" (i.e., hallucinate) the space between horizontal bars with vivid red and the space between the vertical bars with vivid green. The hypnotist checked in each instance that the hallucinated color was present, and the subject showed evidence of uniformly strong hallucination response.

From this point on in the testing, whenever the subject reported a color to the actual test stimuli, vertical gratings were reported as green and horizontal gratings were reported as red. This pattern of response persisted during the subsequent testing up until Session 3 where, during test of the actual McCollough effect, vertical test gratings were reported as red and horizontal bars as green (or vice versa as appropriate to strict confirmation of the real McCollough phenomenon). In both the laboratory situation and the workshop sessions, then, it was as if the subject expected that the hypnotist would return to the original suggestion in order to work it through in relation to her personal experience with the instructions that she had been given. Just as the hypnotist needed to bring Subject F back up the stairs, he also needed to tell the subject not to see the color red (or green) any longer, even though she was presented with achromatic test stimuli and had been given no instructions that they ought to be seen as colored in any way. The subject had to be explicitly told, it seems, that vertical gratings would no longer be seen as green and horizontal gratings as red, no matter where or when they were experienced. In terms of the cognitive styles that we outlined in Chapter 3 and discussed in Chapters 4–6, the subject was in some respects cognitively tied, as it were, in a literal fashion to what the hypnotist was suggesting.

As we have argued elsewhere in this book, traditional methods of inquiry into the experience of hypnotic subjects do not elicit the in-depth information that is obviously relevant to the individual character of Subject F's response; they are not especially geared to the isolation or detection of experiential phenomena of an idiosyncratic kind. The section to follow discusses Subject F's reaction to a further hypnosis session in which unusual perceptions of hypnotic events were obviously present, but the hypnotist was unaware of their nature. Conflict was clearly indicated, but when the presence of conflict was known to the hypnotist, he was at a loss to detect the reason for the problem. Application of the EAT indicated the nature of the difficulty and suggested possible ways of resolving the dilemma that the subject was experiencing. The EAT was varied in procedure in this instance in order to meet the demands of the problem, and this adaptation illustrates one way of modifying the EAT for a particular purpose (other adaptations and modifications are discussed in Chapter 9). Consistent with the underlying assumptions of the technique, the adaptation employed the special capacities of the subject to reexperience imagined events in a way that could facilitate interpretative comment about the meaning of her experience.

IMPACT OF AN INADVERTENT SUGGESTION: EAT ANALYSIS

The following report describes a sequence of events that illustrates the application of the EAT to analysis of the persistence of the effects of suggestion, a phenomenon that threads through the different phases of this total case analysis. In this instance, a particular message about hypnotic response was inadvertently communicated by the hypnotist, and the EAT was used to resolve a unique dilemma that existed for both hypnotist and subject. The inadvertent suggestion was that Subject F would not be hypnotized unless she looked at the hypnotist's keys. The hypnotist, however, did not realize that this suggestion had been given, and the case history deals with the problems created for the subject by the fact that she could not experience hypnosis with other hypnotists, even when she wished. The history of events is compelling in that the subject's hypnotic aptitude is obviously marked, yet that aptitude could not be used until the appropriate suggestion had been given and the influence of the previous (inadvertent) communication removed. The case also presents us with a modification of the EAT, which can be used interpretively to explore clients' conflict areas in a subtle yet revealing way, a topic to which we turn in Chapter 9.

Inadvertent Communication of Suggestion

The problem reported in this case history arose during a hypnotic session involving the administration of two standard hypnotic test items. The induction of hypnosis was routine, and the session was being recorded for the purpose of producing a video tape of hypnosis.

The signal for induction was the sight of the hypnotist's keys; this stimulus had been used previously on other occasions (together with other stimuli) to induce hypnosis in Subject F both quickly and easily. Following induction, she was tested for arm lowering and hallucination. Prior to awakening, the hypnotist gave the subject the suggestion that she would not go into trance when she looked at just anybody else's keys—that she could not be hypnotized by every person who simply wanted to hypnotize her. This instruction was given so as to communicate that the subject should be a little cautious about slipping into trance with every person who attempted induction. However, Subject F took the suggestion to mean that she would not go into hypnosis unless she looked at the hypnotist's keys and his keys alone. The response of the subject was a literal one and was based on a misinterpretation of the communication of the hypnotist. The hypnotist terminated the hypnotic session in the mistaken belief that all suggestion effects had been removed and that the subject was completely free of the influence of everything that had happened in the session. This was clearly not so, as seen by future events.

Aftermath of Suggestion

Two weeks following this hypnotic session, Subject F participated in a workshop on hypnosis. There, two separate inductions were attempted by different hypnotists. The first author was the hypnotist in the session just described but was not a member of the workshop. Both inductions were totally unsuccessful, and Subject F became concerned about the fact she could not experience hypnosis; further, she could not understand the reason for the sudden lack of response. Nothing that was attempted with her in the workshop was successful, and the subject knew that something was obviously wrong and expressed her concern to the authors. At this stage, we could not offer any explanation and were puzzled by the inability of Subject F to experience hypnosis when she had displayed such obvious aptitude and abilities for doing so in the past.

It became obvious in discussing the concern with the subject, however, that she was experiencing spontaneous (unsuggested) amnesia for the period where the hypnotist finally removed all of the suggestions and where he showed her his keys, warning her that she should be cautious. Full amnesia for this final period was obviously intact, and Subject F was not herself aware of the final set of instructions that the hypnotist had given previously. This contributed to the confusion she was experiencing. At the same time, she also attended a talk where the author of the presentation reported that susceptible people find it easier to go to sleep. She reported at that time that she became aware of the difficulty she was experiencing with sleep—a difficulty she had never experienced before. She further reported that she had had trouble sleeping since the previous session had concluded. At this point, we resolved to rehypnotize Subject F and to explore her reactions by having her view a video tape of the session that had been conducted, which included her discussion of the session that she had completed. In this way, we thought she could subjectively review the events that immediately preceded the final instructions of the hypnotist and so help us move toward locating the cause of the stress that she was experiencing.

Rehypnosis

Subject F's reactions were first obtained to the video tape that had been recorded at the previous session. It was considered useful to have Subject F review the events that immediately preceded the final instructions of the hypnotist to see if perception of those events would prod her memory of the material that had been forgotten. By this time, Subject F had become quite agitated. Two previous inductions that had been attempted at a workshop had failed; in addition, she could no longer experience self-hypnosis. She stated that she now knew, for the very first time, the difference between experiencing hypnosis and not experiencing hypnosis and the difference between being hypnotized and being relaxed.

When the video tape was played it became obvious that the hypnotist's keys were relevant to the conflict that the subject was experiencing. When the keys were first shown on the screen the subject reported that she felt similar to the way she had felt at the workshop—uneasy and anxious—and when the hypnotist began talking (on tape) after putting the keys away the uneasy feeling went away. Again, when Subject F saw the hypnotist's keys just prior to awakening, she reported feeling uneasy. After the video tape had finished, Subject F expressed surprise and remarked, "Is that it? Was that all?" She was obviously still amnesic for the final reinduction when the hypnotist checked that all suggestions were removed and presented his keys for the last time to suggest she should be careful about entering hypnosis with anyone who attempted induction.

At this stage, the first author attempted hypnosis and used the standard eye-closure technique to induce trance, as had been done previously on many other occasions, but the attempt failed. Two further attempts using different methods also failed, and the subject reported that the more the hypnotist talked about hypnosis the more uneasy and anxious she felt. Considering the many successful sessions in the past when Subject F had been hypnotized to the deepest level of involvement by the first author, the present inability to enter hypnosis was remarkable. By now more than six different attempts had been made, two by other hypnotists, several attempts by the subject to induce self-hypnosis, and three attempts by the first author. All were unsuccessful.

The hypnotist asked at this point whether the problem had anything to do with his keys, to which the subject replied, "Keys? What's it got to do with keys?" The author then took his keys, asked the subject to look at them intently, and trance was induced immediately. The rapid induction to the keys confirmed the hypothesis that the subject had taken the hypnotist's instruction in the last session to mean that she would be hypnotized only with the hypnotist's keys and only when the hypnotist used them himself to induce trance. This inadvertent suggestion created an extremely effective and persistent block to all attempts to induce trance in any other way.

Still, the reason for the personal anxiety that was present was not apparent, and the EAT was introduced to help clarify the difficulty. An adaptation of the EAT that has been made for clinical purposes was adopted. The subject was asked to play back on film the events of the previous session, and instructions for hallucinatory EAT were delivered (see Chapter 9 for a verbatim text and further discussion of this particular adaptation). Our purpose was to clarify why the subject had developed amnesia for the events of the last session. The hallucinatory EAT revealed the nature of the problem. In the last hypnosis session, the hypnotist (PWS) had established a suggestion for positive hallucination involving a friend of the subject. That suggestion was removed by the hypnotist asking the subject to open her eyes and report that she could no longer see her friend sitting in the chair. This she did, and the hypnotist assumed that the suggestion was no longer effective.

Earlier, however, when the item was being tested the subject had engaged in a discussion with the hypnotist about her friend's contact lenses, and the subject noted at that time that they could be on the floor somewhere. During the session, the subject had initiated discussion of the contact lenses and had actually looked around the floor trying to find them. The hallucinatory EAT session revealed that the subject thought the contact lenses were still on the floor. This left the suggestion still operative, with the subject remaining in partial conflict. The spontaneous amnesia had occurred to help the subject deal with the conflict. The contact lenses on the floor meant that the friend (or "some part of her") was still there, but the subject had indeed looked at the chair and reported that she couldn't see her when the hypnotist had given instructions to lift the suggestion. The hallucination had been removed in part, but the subject still knew that her friend "was there in some way." Subject F expressed relief in the hallucinatory EAT because she was able to remember that the hallucination of her friend had been removed by the hypnotist. This realization, however, came only after she played back in imagery form the hypnotist telling her that her friend was no longer sitting in the chair. At this point, the hypnotist was also able to restructure his understanding of what had happened and to intervene in order to deal with the contact lenses by suggesting that they were no longer on the floor, just as her friend was no longer present. The hypnotist then took the opportunity to instruct the subject quite unambiguously that she would be hypnotized by other hypnotists only when she wanted to be. All mention of the keys was omitted, with the focus clearly placed on the subject becoming hypnotized only when she herself wanted to be hypnotized on any future occasion at which hypnosis was attempted.

Comment

This case illustrates in quite dramatic fashion the unsuggested features of hypnotic response that can occur in the hypnotic context. For Subject F, the influence of the hallucination was still partially operative, and the conflict that was created as a result was resolved inadequately by her through the development of spontaneous amnesia. The amnesia served to alleviate the stress of having to acknowledge that the friend was there when she really was not, but at the same time it prevented Subject F from resolving the conflict because the events lying behind it were forgotten. The situation was further complicated by the fact that an inadvertent suggestion that only the first author could hypnotize the subject in a particular way had persisted and was still operative.

Two validity checks were conducted on the effectiveness of the hallucinatory EAT in isolating the problem and pointing to the way to resolve it. First, immediately following this session Subject F was introduced to the second author (KMMcC), who then induced hypnosis by the standard method of eye closure. Here, for the first time since the conflict was established, induction was effortlessly achieved, and the subject entered deep trance. Second, 4 days after the session, Subject F commented spontaneously on the difficulty she had experienced earlier with sleeping. Deliberately, no attempt had been made to suggest a solution to this problem. It was interpreted as a residual effect of the conflict that had been established and, if removal of the conflict was successful, then the sleeping problem should disappear. Subject F reported that she was sleeping normally and felt relaxed and comfortable for the first time in months. No difficulty with sleeping has been reported by her since that time.

CONCLUSION

At a clinical level this case dramatically illustrates the impact of inadvertent suggestion and the unexpected persistence of suggested effects. Persistence of response characterized this particular subject in a very idiosyncratic way. In fact, the broad history of this subject's hypnotic involvement suggests that "persistence" is a major feature of her hypnotic responsiveness. The way this attribute displays itself, however, is often totally unexpected.

There are several important features of the pattern of responsiveness shown by this subject that seem worthy of comment. First, one notes the consistency with which the persistence of suggested effects was manifest across different task conditions and occasions of testing. Although the responsiveness that was evident was idiosyncratic in the sense that it could not be regarded as a routine illustration of hypnotic behavior or as a pattern of responsiveness that is tapped by standard scales of assessment, the behavior was coherent in the sense that the idiosyncratic manifestation of response replicated itself many times within the same subject. This would suggest to us that the essential variability of hypnotic response that we have highlighted so often in this book is indeed meaningful in that coherent patterns of responsiveness may be revealed in that variability. The data also tell us something important about the cognitive style-response task interface that we discussed in terms of data from a number of different groups of susceptible subjects in Chapters 3–6.

The case on which this chapter is based presents us with a marked display of imaginative talent that was brought to bear in distinctive ways on the suggestions that were received. Differing cognitive styles, however, were apparent within the one subject and were associated for the subject with the same test situation. For example, the hypnotist gave no instruction about the contact lenses of the hallucinated friend. This element of response clearly represents a cognitive construction by the subject of the events (see Chapters 3—6 for further discussion of this style). At the same time, however, the instructions that were received were processed in a literal enough way that the presence of the hallucinated contact lenses had to be removed before the effects of what the hypnotist had suggested could be lifted. Although the subject's imaginative involvement was effortful and was brought to bear in a highly individual way on the situation that was suggested, the subject was nevertheless dependent on the hypnotist's precise removal of events as she had perceived them. That dependence may implicate processes of rapport as well as cognitive style, and we recognize the possible dynamic factors that may have been involved. But the response pattern as a whole demonstrates a general pattern of coherence and illustrates the highly complex ways of processing suggestions that can be adopted by individual subjects who are extremely susceptible to hypnosis.

The research data that exists with respect to purposively uncancelled suggestions tells us that such effects of suggestion are confined to a relatively small number of susceptible subjects (Perry, 1977c). But, many reasons exist with this case for why the subject ought to have behaved in a routine way. The hypnotist at each of the three stages in the work that we have reported clearly did not expect any of the effects to persist, and his instructions were those that would normally be interpreted as indicating that all possible effects should be removed. The fact that there are no apparent cues that the persistence in question was required or expected in any way makes it difficult to argue for the effects observed here as subtle consequences of the instructions that the subject received. The idiosyncrasy of effects highlights yet again the relevance of accounting for minority response among susceptible subjects, a point that we have asserted frequently throughout this book. Not all good hypnotic subjects, for example, override the influence of previous perceptions (Dolby & Sheehan, 1977; Sheehan & Dolby, 1975), demonstrate hidden observer effects (E. R. Hilgard, 1977), illustrate trance logic (Sheehan, 1977), or breach amnesia (see Chapter 7).

Although the EAT presents itself as a technique that is peculiarly suited to illustrating hypnotic phenomena and so facilitates a more complete understanding of hypnotic behavior and experience, the case that was discussed illustrates how the EAT may be used in ways that are different from the standard procedures outlined in Chapter 3. Such modifications may be used to isolate relevant and significant aspects of experience related to specific purposes and problems, and such an approach may be critical to the understanding of conflict and anxiety associated with clinical difficulties. In this instance, a hallucinatory form of the EAT helped to illustrate the personal nature of the conflict that was present and allowed appropriate suggestions to be given to the subject so as to ameliorate the problem. The success of the authors' clinical strategy was confirmed both by the subject's readiness to enter hypnosis again (with an independent hypnotist) after hypnotic responsiveness had been blocked altogether, and by the ease with which the subject could now sleep comfortably after she had reported extensive difficulty. Once hypnotically responsive again, Subject F's sleeping pattern reverted to normal; the case, however, does not explore the possible dynamic factors involved, nor does it allow one to separate out how much the subject's knowledge of possible links between susceptibility and behavioral effects could have contributed to what occurred.

In vividly illustrating the nature and significance of a phenomenological approach to the study of hypnosis, this case raises definite questions about the ways in which the assessment procedures that we have developed may be generalized to the clinical setting and how they might be modified to meet specific purposes. We now discuss ways in which the EAT can be changed to suit a range of objectives. We wish to recognize, however, that the procedures we have set out in Chapter 3 should be regarded as the standard ones and represent to us the optimal way of learning about the experience of hypnotized individuals.

9 Modified Applications of the EAT

INTRODUCTION

Data reported in the previous chapters have indicated that the Experiential Analysis Technique (EAT) in its original format of video-tape playback of hypnotic events has yielded important and meaningful information about the nature of the phenomenal experience of hypnotic subjects. The data also suggest that this type of information is not readily yielded through the use of more traditional and routine techniques of inquiry into the hypnotic experiences of highly responsive individuals (see Chapter 3). Although no one technique or methodology is suitable for examining all of the questions that clinicians or researchers need to address (Sheehan & Perry, 1976), the strategies that do exist can be usefully varied. From this perspective, a number of modifications and adaptations of the EAT have been developed and applied to allow for the investigation of a wide range of issues relevant to the experience of hypnosis (see also Chapters 7 and 8). In this chapter, we address the issue of the modification and application of the EAT so that we can usefully investigate specific issues in both clinical and experimental situations.

Initially, we discuss the use of hallucinatory or imaginary, rather than actual, video-tape playback of the hypnotic events as a way of providing pertinent information about subjects' or clients' hypnotic experiences. (This is the technique that we applied to study some aspects of the case discussed in Chapter 8). In this chapter, we further outline the technique and highlight how the clinical application of this modification may yield information concerning therapeutically relevant experiences of clients who are being treated by hypnosis as an adjunctive therapy. We then turn to the research use of this modification and present an individual case study in which the nature of the experimental subject's hypnotic experience was investigated through the application of this hallucinatory playback technique. In the research context, we also use the hallucinatory playback method to compare the reactions of hypnotic and nonhypnotic subjects. Finally, we consider an adaptation of the original video-tape version of the EAT to provide a more structured or directive situation for examining hypnotic experiences, and we discuss the data yielded by this use of structured questioning during subjects' viewing of the video-tape playback of their hypnotic session. This chapter, then, considers a variety of ways in which the basic procedures for the EAT that were outlined in Chapter 3 may be modified or altered so as to suit the specific purposes of the investigator or practicing clinician. We first consider an experiential analysis of clinical hypnotic events.

EXPERIENTIAL ANALYSIS
OF CLINICAL HYPNOTIC EVENTS

The logic underlying the use of the EAT in the clinical hypnosis context fits within a framework that attunes us to an understanding of the processes at work that bring about therapeutic change. An approach that stresses the various abilities and aptitudes of individual clients highlights in particular the relevance of imagination processes to response in the hypnotic situation (Bowers, 1976; E. R. Hilgard, 1979a; Sheehan, 1979a). According to this view, clinical hypnosis essentially provides a context in which the therapist requests the client to engage in imaginative behavior in order to facilitate therapeutic change. In doing so, the situation provides a focus for the investigation of the relationship between attitudes, emotions, and motivations in shaping the final behavior of the total functioning person.

Many (e.g., Ahsen, 1977; Leuner, 1977) argue cogently that the processes of imagination should be used directly in the therapeutic endeavor and that an understanding of the role of affect and motivations relates to the extent to which imagery may be facilitative in the process of cure. Although the positive use of imaginative processes is clearly enhanced by the clinical hypnosis context, evidence also indicates that the reporting of hypnotized persons may quite accurately reflect the reality features of their situation. That is, hypnotic persons' verbal reports may reflect both fantasy and reality events at one and the same time; this was evidenced, for instance, in the reports of subjects discussed in Chapters 5 and 6. A major aspect of the therapeutic context is that information is needed concerning the interactions of motives and cognitions. As these interactions are often illustrated through the processes of imagination and have clear therapeutic benefits, it is a problem for assessment to detect them and index their particular therapeutic relevance (Sheehan, 1979d). One of the major clinically relevant inferences drawn from our applications of the EAT is that hypnotized persons are not simply to be regarded as passive recipients of instructions from the hypnotist. Rather, the data tell us that not only do many susceptible persons actively interpret the instructions that they receive, but they also imbed them into their own preferred fantasies. Further, even while hypnotized, they are often aware of conflict between different aspects of their experience. Reports appear to demonstrate the influence of expectancies and need states on the nature of their ideation and, in this important sense, there are definite implications for the use of inquiry techniques that encourage imagery as a means of focusing on the personal nature of the client's response.

The EAT was designed initially to be based on the video-tape playback of the hypnotic session in the presence of an independent inquirer. Although there is no necessary impediment to the use of video-tape equipment in the therapeutic setting, it is not normally incorporated into that situation. Further, the presence of an independent person functioning as an inquirer into clinically relevant factors of a person's experiences during therapeutic hypnosis may be counterindicated by the particular therapy program that has been scheduled; the intrusion of others can inhibit the therapeutic process.

The EAT can be adapted for use in the clinical setting in a way that takes account of the synthesizing or constructive aspects of subjects' fantasy potential and allows for the hypnotist-therapist to adopt the role of inquirer as well. The technique is essentially the EAT as we used it in Chapter 8; it employs hallucinatory or imaginary, rather than actual, video-tape playback of the events of the hypnotic session. Here the hypnotist (therapist) serves as the inquirer, and the clients in trance are given the suggestion that they watch a hallucinatory playback of the events of the hypnotic session as it unfolds in their mind's eye. In its application clients are instructed to keep watching the scene and to stop it when they want to comment, letting the hypnotist know when they are doing this so that he or she can then adopt the role of inquirer. There seems no reason to believe that a person in this situation would not be able to give some commentary on his or her experience, especially when such experience has clinical importance or relevance. Further, the use of the viewing of a hallucinatory playback provides clients with the opportunity to place themselves at a distance so that the therapeutic events can be commented on with a possible degree of detachment, thus avoiding some of the risks that can be associated with self-confrontation techniques in therapy (see Gur & Sackeim, 1978). Importantly, the material yielded by the application of the hallucinatory playback technique may direct the therapist to areas in which clarification of issues or further therapy is needed. Specifically, the major utility of this adaptation is the provision of information about the subjective reactions of hypnotized clients to clinical interventions, therefore allowing the hypnotist-therapist to refine his or her therapeutic assumptions and approach.

Procedurally speaking, either when the client is still experiencing hypnosis or when the client is rehypnotized following therapy, an EAT session can be conducted by the hypnotist-inquirer. In this regard, care should be taken to insure that the inquiry session is perceived by clients not as a direct part of the therapy intervention itself, but rather as an opportunity for them to undertake a role of reviewing their experiences with the therapeutic intervention. Instructions given by the hypnotist-inquirer at the beginning of the EAT session can be as follows:

> Now that you are deeply relaxed and deeply hypnotized once more, I want you to listen carefully to what I say. During your hypnotic session you probably felt and thought a lot of things that you didn't say aloud. The mind generally works faster than the voice, and so there were probably times when you didn't have the time to say all that you wanted. Also, perhaps you just didn't want to mention some of the things earlier, or else you might have just had some vague ideas that you couldn't get into words at that time.
>
> In a moment I am going to get you to see your hypnosis session in your mind. You'll easily see it all happening, just like a film, and, as you watch this film in your mind's eye, you'll find that many thoughts and feelings will come back to you. Whenever you recall something about the film you'll find that you will be able to stop it and tell me about your thoughts.
>
> I want you now to think about all that you did just a little while ago during hypnosis from the moment I told you to close your eyes until the moment I told you to wake up. I want you to think vividly, in your mind's eye, to hallucinate the whole session right from the beginning to the end. Just let it roll through your mind like a film, just exactly as it was for you, like a film unwinding and showing you the whole hypnosis session.
>
> I want you to stop the film whenever you want to comment on any of your experiences, anything at all, just stop it. You can do this easily by lifting up the index finger of your right hand. This will stop the film and also it will let me know that you are going to comment on an experience that you are recalling. Stop the film whenever you want to comment on anything.
>
> Do you understand now? Now just let the film roll exactly as it happened during hypnosis. Whenever you want to say something just lift your finger, anything at all. Let's start now, just let the film roll.

As clients comment during the hallucinatory playback of the events, the therapist can inquire into their reports by using, for instance, the probes for the EAT that we have outlined in Chapter 3. In the clinical setting, the therapist may also find that more directive questioning is appropriate in the context of a client's particular problem. Apart from the fact that it can be employed without the technology of video tape or an independent inquirer, the major utility of this version of the EAT is the provision of information about the reactions of the hypnotized individual to the clinical hypnotic intervention, therefore allowing the hypnotist-therapist to refine his or her working assumptions and strategies. During this application of the EAT, the hypnotist is the inquirer and retains the status of therapist—these two roles (inquirer and therapist) necessarily intermesh; however, the therapist should not deny the client the opportunity of personally directing and interpreting his or her experiences with hypnosis. And when the hypnotist plays the role of the inquirer and the client is still hypnotized at the time of EAT testing, then it should be recognized that particular effects may be associated with the hallucinatory version of the EAT, as compared with the standard version of the technique (see Chapter 3).

Material gathered by the application of this mode of inquiry needs to be analyzed closely for the clinically relevant information it contains; in particular, the material needs to be assessed in terms of the information that it holds regarding events that will foster the therapeutic impact of hypnosis. We now consider an application of the EAT that was modified to employ hallucinatory playback. Salzman (1982) employed this clinical adaptation of the EAT as a means of probing whether anxiety or stress of some kind existed for the client during clinical hypnosis. One of the difficulties encountered in clinical hypnosis (as in other modes of therapy) is the patient's resistance to disclosing information or thoughts that may be in conflict with the therapist's instructions, and the specific intent of Salzman's (1982) use of the technique was to facilitate the emergence of data that were relevant to the client's progress. Clinical hypnotic subjects may well be experiencing thoughts that, if elicited, could aid the therapeutic process and help to define more quickly the problems that exist. Nevertheless, trying to elicit all points of concern is a very lengthy procedure, and Salzman (1982) attempted to overcome this problem by asking clients to focus on specific areas of concern. This approach not only reduced the amount of time needed but also implicitly acknowledged the client's ability to identify relevant material for the therapist to consider.

Specifically, subsequent to the hypnotherapy session but prior to awakening, clients were instructed to visualize a television screen and to review the hypnosis session they had just been through by watching it on the television screen. Further, they were told that if anything that the hypnotist had said or if any of their thoughts had made them anxious (either as a result of things discussed during this session or from other thoughts that might have occurred), or if there had been anything left unfinished during the session, then they should lift the index finger of their right hand. If the client responded by raising his or her right index finger while reviewing the hypnotherapy session, the problem was discussed, and appropriate therapeutic procedures were subsequently employed in order to resolve the difficulty. The client was then instructed to continue reviewing the session from the point at which the previous problem had been identified. When the client reported having reviewed the entire session, he or she was then awakened.

During application of the EAT, the majority of subjects responded once; on no occasion was there more than one response to each playback. These data can be understood by close analysis of the instructions that clients were given. The point of this application is that the hypnotist left clients with a contingent response.

obviously have the cognitive potential for exploring a wide variety of material, some of which may be anxiety-provoking and/or important to the therapeutic process.

We now consider the application of the hallucinatory playback version of the EAT in the experimental (as opposed to the clinical) context. The case study that we discuss is one in which the modified version of the EAT was applied as a way of attempting to explore the age-regression response of a highly responsive female subject.

HALLUCINATORY PLAYBACK: A CASE STUDY

The example we present usefully contrasts with the data presented previously on age regression (see Chapter 5). In the following case, when the subject was regressed to 1 year of age and administered hidden observer instructions, she interpreted those instructions as allowing her to describe her age-regressed experience rather than indicating that she should respond fully in terms of the reality of the situation in which she was actually placed. Another interesting facet of this case was that this subject appeared to behave incongruously by speaking English but at the same time denying that she could either speak or understand English. This case contrasts with the kinds of observations about age-regressed behavior that we detailed in Chapter 5. This case study involved two sessions. In Session 1, the idiosyncratic response to age regression was first witnessed and recorded (this session provides the most meaningful contrast with the reactions of subjects described in Chapter 5) and, in Session 2, the hallucinatory playback version of the EAT was applied as a means of exploring the phenomenology underlying this subject's personal experience of age regression.

Session 1

The verbatim transcript of the interaction between the hypnotist (H) and the subject (S) for the initial hypnotic age-regression experience follows.

> **H:** Now you're going back further into the past, much younger, younger and smaller. Becoming a little girl, back past the age of 4, becoming younger and smaller, back past the age of 2, becoming younger and smaller, right back to the age of 1, you're 1 year old. What's your name?
>
> **S:** [No response]
>
> **H:** Do you know your name?
>
> **S:** Uhmm.
>
> **H:** How old are you?
>
> **S:** Uhmm, 1.
>
> **H:** There may be another part of you that can tell me about the experience you're

having at this time. If there is, I want that part of you to tell me about the experience when I put my hand on your shoulder. If there isn't, you won't say anything at all when I put my hand on your shoulder. [Hypnotist places hand on shoulder.]

S: Me and Mama are together, on the sofa.

H: You and your Mama are together.

S: Sitting.

H: Just sitting, whereabouts?

S: In the living room.

H: In the living room. What city is that?

S: Kuopio.

H: What are you talking about?

S: Don't know.

H: Don't know. Can you speak English?

S: No.

H: Can you understand English?

S: No.

H: Can your Mama speak English?

S: No.

H: What language can you speak?

S: Finnish.

H: Can your Mama speak Finnish?

S: Yeah.

H: Is there anything you'd like to say to your Mama?

S: No.

H: What's she saying to you?

S: Don't know.

H: Don't know. Okay, now I'd like you to grow right back up.

Comment. The interesting point to observe here is that, in contrast to those cases that we discussed in Chapter 5, this subject did not speak Finnish during her age-regressed experience even though she maintained that she could speak only that language. The logical contradiction apparent in her behavior is different in style from those that we commented on previously, and this fact again stresses the importance of recognizing the variation in response that exists among highly susceptible subjects. In considering examples of trance logic, we need to consider carefully the factors that may have influenced the particular shape that the logically incongruous response takes. For instance, the degree of emotional involvement of the subject with the age-regressed experience was seen to be influential in shaping the response of those subjects that we considered previously (see Chapter 5), and it may have been that this particular subject was not very emotionally involved in her experience. Thus, she did not speak Finnish but was rather taking more of an observer's view of the age-regressed experience (hence communicating in English).

In discussing this experience with the subject, however, another influential factor became apparent. The subject explained that throughout her experience of age regression she "felt as if [she] should have been speaking Finnish," but was speaking English because she knew that the hypnotist (KMMcC) could not speak Finnish and she was cognitively translating her replies in order to "stay in contact with [the hypnotist]." That is, when viewed from the subject's own perspective, it becomes apparent that she considered that she should speak English in order to maintain her rapport with the hypnotist. She was acting in a quite logical manner so that both she and the hypnotist could maintain their respective roles and level of involvement in the hypnotic experience. This example highlights the fact that a close analysis of the factors that influence apparent tolerance of logical incongruity would seem to be always necessary in order to determine the strategies that subjects or clients employ and that reflect the distinctive nature of their processing of suggestions. Clearly, these strategies sometimes query the appropriateness of the labels we adopt to classify their hypnotic responses.

Following our analysis of this particular subject's experience, we decided to test her again in order to determine whether similar reactions would occur and, if so, whether they could be understood in similar terms. Further, in the second session with this experimental subject, we employed the hallucinatory playback version of the EAT as a way of tapping potentially important factors influencing the subjective and objective reactions to the age-regressed situation.

Session 2

The verbatim transcript of the second hypnotic age-regression testing and of the application of the hallucinatory EAT is as follows.

> **H:** Now I just want you to think back, back in time, right back, back to the time when you were 5 years old. Think right back to the time when you were 5 years old, 5 years of age. Further and further, right back when you were a little girl, right back, further and further, right back to when you were 5 years of age. Tell me about the scene. What's going on?
>
> **S:** Oh, I'm in the kindergarten. I brought my doll with me—it's got a blue dress.
>
> **H:** What's your doll's name?
>
> **S:** It hasn't got a name—I got it from my aunty.
>
> **H:** What's your aunty's name?
>
> **S:** Hazel. I think she brought it home from Paris.
>
> **H:** Is it your favorite doll?
>
> **S:** Yeah. I took it to the kindergarten because they said you could bring one doll with you.

H: Did the other people bring dolls?

S: I can't, I don't know.

H: How long have you been at kindergarten?

S: Oh, it started this year.

H: You started this year.

S: Yeah.

H: What year is it?

S: Oh, I don't know really.

H: You don't know, okay. What do you do after kindergarten is finished?

S: Sometimes I have to go to the shop for Mum.

H: What do you buy at the shop?

S: Meat, and we play at the back of the house, there's a big hangar.

H: Who do you play with?

S: Oh, the other kids from the same house. We live on the second floor with my two brothers.

H: What are their names?

S: Viney and Youssef.

H: Are they bigger than you?

S: No, they're smaller and sometimes I put Youssef in the carriage and push him around.

H: Who's your best friend?

S: Oh, downstairs there lives a girl, her name is Maria. She's older than me, but we sometimes go and play. They've got lots of toys, and they've got TV too.

H: Okay, that's fine. Now I want you to go back further, further, and further into the past. Go back to when you were 1 year old, 1 year old, further and further, 1 year old, right back, 1 year of age. Tell me about it.

S: Uhmm, there's nobody else, just me and Mum. We're not living . . . we're living in a different house. I don't know what it looks like.

H: What are you doing, you and Mama?

S: Oh, nothing much.

H: Is she talking to you?

S: No, I can't see.

H: Can you hear her?

S: No, I can't hear her. I can see her face. I can see her, but I can't hear her.

H: How old are you?

S: I don't know, I'm small. I can see the carriage where they put me.

H: The carriage.

S: Yeah, when they take me out, they put me in this carriage, and they push me around.

H: Do you like that carriage?

S: Yeah.

H: Do you know that really you're not 1 year old, that really you're at the university? Do you know that?

S: Uhmm, yeah.

H: How old are you?

S: Uhmm, 22.

H: Can you still see the carriage?

S: Yeah, yeah, I'd like to be there.

H: You'd rather be there?

S: It's a long, long way.

H: Can you be there and be here at the same time?

S: Yeah, I can see there when I'm here.

H: Okay, just go right back there now, right back with the carriage when you were 1 year of age. Are you back there?

S: Mmmm.

H: Okay, just enjoy that for a moment. Now I want you to grow right back up, to 22 years of age, back to the university. How old are you now?

S: Uhmm, 22.

H: Okay, that's fine. Now listen carefully. You're deeply relaxed and deeply hypnotized, and I want you to do something for me. I want you to think about all that we've done, all that we've done, to see it happen again, to watch it happen in your mind, to see it happen again. Just let the whole session roll through your mind like you were watching a film in your mind. I want you to stop the film whenever you want to comment on any of your experiences. I want you to watch the film go through your mind and tell me about anything you want to tell me about, anything at all. To stop that film, all you have to do is to lift that finger up. Okay, let the film roll.

S: When you were saying I was getting younger, I was going sort of deeper, I could feel it.

H: What were the sorts of feelings like when you were going deeper and deeper?

S: Oh, like I was going some place, like a place I didn't know. Going some place I didn't know, just letting go, and I could sort of physically feel it inside.

H: Did you feel that you were going there alone?

S: Oh, I wanted you to keep talking so that I wouldn't be there alone.

H: Okay, that's fine. Okay, let the film roll on.

S: I wanted to stay there when I was 5 because I could remember quite a lot of that.

H: About being at the kindergarten.

S: Yeah, and playing in the back yard there.

H: What were the sorts of things that you wanted to tell me about? Were there other things?

S: I could see the house and what it looked like, and I went swimming with Mama and the kids.

H: Okay, let the film roll on.

S: And then, ah, there came this big gap from 5 to 1. I just sort of jumped from 5 to 1. There was nothing I could relate to along the way. Like 3 years, being 3, I couldn't get anything from there. Before 5, I haven't got clear pictures.

H: Okay, let the film roll on a little.

S: I didn't get anything, I didn't get any clear images from being 1 like I did from being 5. Can't even see them, not real well.

H: What sort of thoughts were going through your mind when you were 1?

S: Oh, all the time I was just sort of thinking of Mama, and looking at her.

H: Could you hear her say something?

S: Oh no, she didn't say anything. But then I had to come back here again and be old, and it was really hard. I really struggled and sort of tried to go away, because I felt like I was still there, but I had to tell you, ah, how old I was. But one part of me was still back there.

H: What about the part of you that came back, how did that feel?

S: Oh, it wasn't really real. I mean, I knew my age and I knew I was sitting in this room, but I couldn't really think of the university or anything as big as that. It's just a small part that came back and told you that, you know, I'm 22 and could I go back.

H: So that part wanted to go back to the other part that was a year old?

S: Yeah.

H: Okay, now just let the film roll along.

S: On the second time I came back, I left everything behind and I came, you know, all of me came back.

H: What was the difference between the first time when part of you came back and the second time when all of you came back?

S: Well, the first time I still had some of these pictures, and I could see them and maybe I was there, but the second time I just sort of left it there, and forgot it, and I was thinking of sitting here now.

H: What was it that I said that made those two times different?

S: The second time I had to come back slowly and sort of think it, and the first time I had to sort of jump.

H: So the first time you had to do it quickly to answer the question.

S: Yes.

H: And the second time you could just come back.

S: Yes.

H: Okay, that's fine. Let the film roll on a bit more.

S: I can't see anything. It's finished.

H: It's finished. Okay, that's fine. Comfortably relaxed, relaxed and hypnotized [once more], quite relaxed. The film's finished now.

Comment.   The data from this case analysis demonstrate the subtle impact of the factors that may influence the hypnotic responses of highly susceptible subjects. In this instance, multiple levels of awareness by the subject appeared to be evidenced during the EAT. These multiple cognitive perspectives seemed especially active when the hypnotist intruded the reality of the situation into the subject's experience of age regression. For this subject a forced awareness of the nature of her actual, rather than suggested, situation had an obvious and meaningful impact on her experience, and this point is in accord with the data presented earlier (see Chapter 6) that highlight the high sensitivity of hypnotic subjects to reality influences during their experiences of age regression. In the present case, the application of the hallucinatory playback adaptation of the EAT also pointed to the specific phenomenal events that had meaning for the subject herself, and parallels can be seen here with the data from the clinical study discussed earlier in this chapter. Close analysis of the comments made by the subject indicates that, as in the previous hypnotic session, her degree of emotional involvement in the age regression as well as her level of rapport with the hypnotist were highly influential in shaping her reactions to the hypnotist's instructions for age regression (see Chapter 5 for a fuller discussion of these and other factors that shape age-regression response). Finally, it is important to note that focused idiographic investigations of this kind can provide information concerning the nature of the hypnotic experience and can suggest meaningful hypotheses, which can be subsequently operationalized and tested with a larger number of subjects. The relationship between degree of emotional involvement and nature of age-regressed experience is one such case in point.

In testing any hypothesis concerning hypnosis, there is a great deal of value in comparing the responses of hypnotically responsive and unresponsive subjects (see Sheehan & Perry, 1976, for a detailed discussion of this point). Consequently, we now consider an application of the hallucinatory EAT with both hypnotic and nonhypnotic subjects. The value of this particular comparison lies specifically in analyzing the extent to which the comments made by subjects are based either in the nature of their experience with hypnotic testing or in the influences that the inquiry technique itself brings to bear on their reports. The condition of simulation (Orne, 1959; see also Chapter 7) employs nonhypnotic subjects who are especially attuned to respond in a way that the assessment procedure dictates and, consequently, this group was employed in our study of the hallucinatory playback of hypnotic events.

HALLUCINATORY PLAYBACK AND SIMULATION

In order to examine closely the nature and use of the hallucinatory playback adaptation of the EAT, we employed real, susceptible and simulating, insusceptible subjects. Application of the hallucinatory technique to these groups provided data for nonhypnotic as well as hypnotic subjects. Clinical applications of the hallucinatory playback technique have suggested that subjects do not comment as much during hallucinatory playback as they do during the standard video-tape playback. For this reason, our study involved a relatively large number of subjects in order to obtain a reasonable amount of data for analysis. Further, because the use of the hallucinatory playback technique has not been explored systematically, the cues associated with it and the specific impact of these cues need to be delineated and defined. The condition of simulation employed in the study is a quasi-control technique that effectively determines the nature of the cues in the hypnotic situation (Orne, 1959, 1972), which was also adopted in our experimental analysis of hypnotic amnesia (see Chapter 7). Specifically, simulation aimed to establish the nature of the cue demands being conveyed by the use of the hallucinatory playback technique and provided an index of the overall demand characteristics that could potentially operate to influence the reports of real hypnotic subjects when the technique is applied.

Here, we report unpublished data based on 50 real, susceptible subjects (42 female and 8 male) of mean age 21.06 years ($SD = 5.36$) and 50 simulating, insusceptible subjects (23 female and 27 male) of mean age 25.02 years ($SD = 1.10$) who were undergraduate psychology students at the University of Queensland. Subjects were preselected on the 12-item HGSHS:A; the mean HGSHS:A score for real, susceptible subjects was 9.70 ($SD = .86$) and for simulating, insusceptible subjects was 1.82 ($SD = 1.10$).

Subjects were instructed initially by an experimenter prior to their hypnotic testing by the hypnotist, who was blind to their subject grouping (real or simulating). The initial experimenter instructed subjects according to the exact procedures of the real-simulating model of hypnosis (Orne, 1959, 1972). The experimenter briefly discussed with susceptible subjects the nature of their previous hypnotic experience, but no instructions were given as to the type of behavior they should display during the hypnotic session. Simulating, insusceptible subjects, on the other hand, were told to convince the hypnotist that they were deeply susceptible to hypnosis by using whatever cues were available, that the hypnotist did not know which subjects were pretending, and to maintain their pretense until they returned to the initial experimenter following the hypnotic session.

When subjects met the hypnotist, he administered a range of hypnotic test items and then instructed subjects to review their hypnotic experiences through a hallucinatory playback of the events. The instructions for this (see earlier for the verbatim text) informed subjects that they would see their hypnosis session in their minds just like a film and that they should stop the film whenever they wanted to comment on any of their experiences. Whenever subjects stopped the hallucinatory playback and reported on their recall of the hypnotic events, the hypnotist explored the nature of their hypnotic experiences by using the kinds of probes outlined in Chapter 3 that were designed to encourage subjects to describe their feelings and personally reflect upon their experiences.

Review of Evidence

Verbatim transcriptions were made of each subject's comments during the hallucinatory playback, and these records were scored for the number of times

TABLE 9.1
Mean Number of Stops Made by Hypnotic and Simulating
Subjects During Recall of Hypnotic Events

| Events | Subject Grouping | |
	Hypnotic (n = 50)	Simulating (n = 50)
Hypnotic induction	.22 (.42)	.18 (.44)
Moving hands apart	.34 (.48)	.18 (.39)
Mosquito hallucination	.24 (.43)	.16 (.37)
Arm rigidity	.18 (.39)	.16 (.37)
Dream	.18 (.39)	.16 (.42)
Arm immobilization	.10 (.30)	.14 (.34)
Negative visual hallucination	.34 (.48)	.16 (.37)
Age regression	.32 (.47)	.32 (.47)
Color hallucination	.60 (.49)	.44 (.50)
Identity delusion	.56 (.58)	.44 (.50)
Total	3.10 (2.00)	2.36 (1.72)

Note. Standard deviations appear in parentheses.

subjects stopped the playback to report on their hypnotic experiences and the number of words they spoke in commenting on the events. The results for these two indices are listed in Tables 9.1 and 9.2, respectively, for each of the hypnotic events that were studied. With respect to the number of times subjects stopped their hallucinatory playback, hypnotic subjects stopped significantly more than did simulating subjects on the negative visual hallucination item, $t(98) = 1.80$, p

TABLE 9.2
Mean Number of Words Spoken by Hypnotic and Simulating
Subjects During Recall of Hypnotic Events

| Events | Subject Grouping | |
	Hypnotic (n = 50)	Simulating (n = 50)
Hypnotic induction	10.78 (24.40)	5.80 (15.35)
Moving hands apart	15.68 (35.68)	4.95 (17.29)
Mosquito hallucination	5.84 (13.96)	2.14 (5.52)
Arm rigidity	7.16 (17.78)	4.14 (11.59)
Dream	7.74 (21.36)	8.28 (34.95)
Arm immobilization	4.08 (15.20)	4.44 (17.59)
Negative visual hallucination	12.60 (22.56)	3.00 (8.09)
Age regression	19.16 (37.08)	10.30 (20.77)
Color hallucination	49.16 (74.43)	18.68 (33.07)
Identity delusion	33.62 (55.05)	18.84 (40.90)
Total	164.56 (166.17)	80.78 (127.81)

Note. Standard deviations appear in parentheses.

Essentially, the message to the client was that if anxiety or stress of some kind was experienced during the session, then the client should stop the playback. That is, the client was allowed some initative but was also given a specific purpose or direction by the therapist's instruction. Viewed in this way, it is clear that the data that emerge are potentially relevant to the nature of the client's problem and to the progress of therapy. The relatively low rate of clients' response (usually no more than one stop per session), however, suggests that the clinical context may meaningfully influence response output. It may well be, for instance, that a high rate of response by clients could have implied that lots of things were going wrong with therapy and that a low rate of response was thus more acceptable; that is, one response to the EAT per session could be related to a clinical response-set effect—stressing, of course, that this technique of assessment has artifacts associated with it as do other forms of assessment that we reviewed in Chapter 2.

Variations in the qualitative response of the clients to the EAT were also evident in Salzman's (1982) study. One client, for instance, reported being unable to visualize the television screen during her first session and so reviewed the session verbally; however, on subsequent occasions, she was able to visualize the session. A second client reported that she was unable to visualize the screen but could nevertheless hear the material that was discussed during the therapy session. Interestingly, when visualizing the session on the television screen, clients reported varying levels of involvement with the therapist. Whereas some clients reported seeing themselves sitting in the chair with the therapist at his desk, others saw only themselves, and others reported seeing only the therapist. This variation in clients' reporting of themselves, the hypnotist, or themselves with the hypnotist may well reflect different perceptions of their level of involvement with the therapist, which was subsequently reflected in their different imagery accounts (for data bearing on other aspects of rapport, see Chapter 6).

Whenever clients responded, they indicated a concern that had not been discussed explicitly during the hypnotherapy session, and the discussion of these concerns at times had a substantial impact on the client's well-being. During hallucinatory playback, for instance, Salzman (1982) reports that one patient indicated she often experienced cramps in her legs, which immobilized her when she was walking, and that this had been going through her mind during hypnosis. Although this client had been receiving medical care for approximately 2-years for neurotic problems, she had failed to mention cramps during this entire period. Following discussion of this concern, a vascular problem was diagnosed and treated. In this case, the identification of a medical problem through the use of hallucinatory playback helped to resolve a severe case of agoraphobia. In summary, this example highlights the importance of understanding that hypnotic subjects may be actively involved with thoughts and emotions that are somewhat detached from their transactions with the therapist. During hypnosis, subjects

$< .05$ (1-tailed), as well as overall, $t(98) = 1.94$, $p < .05$ (1-tailed). With respect to the number of words subjects spoke in commenting on their hypnotic experiences, hypnotic subjects demonstrated significantly greater verbal output on the moving hands apart item, $t(98) = 1.89$, $p < .05$ (1-tailed), the mosquito hallucination item, $t(98) = 1.73$, $p < .05$ (1-tailed), the negative visual halluci-natic.. item, $t(98) = 2.80$, $p < .05$, and the color hallucination item, $t(98) = 2.62$, $p < .05$, as well as overall, $t(98) = 2.80$, $p < .05$. That is, during the hallucinatory playback of the hypnotic events, hypnotic subjects stopped the playback and talked more about the session than did simulating, insusceptible subjects on some, though not all, events.

Subjects differed markedly in the degree to which they were spontaneously willing to stop the hallucinatory playback to comment on their experience. For instance, the variation shown in the number of stops (ranging from 0–7 for hypnotic subjects and 0–8 for simulating subjects) illustrates the individual way in which subjects responded to the technique. Results also suggest that the nature of the hypnotic items affects the quality of verbal output. The two nonstandard items that occurred toward the end of the session received substantial comment by subjects, whereas many subjects did not comment at all on the standard items that they had experienced earlier in the session. The effect no doubt illustrates the fact that this and other inquiry techniques involving the recall of events that are sequenced in time could be influenced more by events occurring at one time period during a session than at another.

Table 9.3 sets out the number of hypnotic and simulating subjects who commented on each of the hypnotic events; Tables 9.4 and 9.5, respectively, set out the mean number of stops made and the mean number of words spoken by these subjects. In terms of the number of stops made, hypnotic and simulating subjects

TABLE 9.3
Number of Hypnotic and Simulating Subjects Who
Commented on Hypnotic Events

	Subject Grouping	
Events	Hypnotic	Simulating
Hypnotic induction	11	8
Moving hands apart	17	9
Mosquito hallucination	12	9
Arm rigidity	9	8
Dream	9	7
Arm immobilization	6	7
Negative visual hallucination	18	8
Age regression	16	16
Color hallucination	31	22
Identity delusion	26	22
Total	47	41

TABLE 9.4
Mean Number of Stops Made by Hypnotic and Simulating
Subjects Who Commented on Hypnotic Events

	Subject Grouping	
Events	Hypnotic	Simulating
Hypnotic induction	1.00 (.00)	1.13 (.35)
Moving hands apart	1.00 (.00)	1.00 (.00)
Mosquito hallucination	1.00 (.00)	1.00 (.00)
Arm rigidity	1.00 (.00	1.00 (.00)
Dream	1.00 (.00)	1.14 (.38)
Arm immobilization	1.00 (.00)	1.00 (.00)
Negative visual hallucination	1.00 (.00)	1.00 (.00)
Age regression	1.00 (.00)	1.00 (.00)
Color hallucination	1.00 (.00)	1.00 (.00)
Identity delusion	1.08 (.27)	1.00 (.00)
Total	3.30 (1.90)	2.88 (1.45)

Note. Standard deviations appear in parentheses.

did not differ appreciably; most subjects commented only once on any hypnotic event. In terms of the number of words spoken, hypnotic subjects commented significantly more than did simulating subjects on the age regression, $t(28) = 2.12$, $p < .05$, and color hallucination, $t(51) = 1.94$, $p < .05$ (one-tailed) items, as well as overall, $t(86) = 2.32$, $p < .05$; on most of the hypnotic items, however, these hypnotic and simulating subjects commented to a similar degree.

Application of the hallucinatory playback adaptation of the EAT yielded rele-

TABLE 9.5
Mean Number of Words Spoken by Hypnotic and Simulating
Subjects Who Commented on Hypnotic Events

	Subject Grouping	
Events	Hypnotic	Simulating
Hypnotic induction	49.00 (29.30)	36.25 (19.70)
Moving hands apart	46.12 (49.06)	27.56 (33.63)
Mosquito hallucination	22.83 (20.21)	12.67 (6.93)
Arm rigidity	39.78 (21.86)	25.88 (17.23)
Dream	43.00 (32.98)	59.14 (80.41)
Arm immobilization	39.67 (29.02)	31.57 (38.94)
Negative visual hallucination	35.00 (25.26)	18.75 (10.96)
Age regression	59.88 (43.47)	32.19 (25.64)
Color hallucination	79.29 (81.12)	42.45 (38.67)
Identity delusion	64.65 (62.07)	42.82 (53.18)
Total	175.06 (165.94)	98.51 (134.98)

Note. Standard deviations appear in parentheses.

vant qualitative data. The material of the subjects' recall was thus analyzed for the information that it revealed concerning the nature of the experiences that subjects reported as well as the nature of their responses to the specific hypnotic test items that were employed. Analyses focused on: (1) global ratings of the material reported by subjects; (2) selection of case material to illustrate processes underlying the various hypnotic events. Qualitative analyses pointed to important differences occurring between hypnotic and nonhypnotic subjects.

Two raters, blind as to subjects' real or simulating identity, scored the transcripts of the material in terms of whether it: (1) indicated that subjects' hypnotic experience involved personalized experiences or whether it was a hypnotic experience that closely followed that suggested by the hypnotist (i.e., idiosyncratic vs. literal response); (2) focused more on describing the nature of subjects' experiences rather than on describing their behavior (i.e., experience vs. behavior).

Both raters made global ratings on each of these two dimensions for all 100 subjects; Rater 1 rescored 10 randomly chosen subjects in order to index his intrarater reliability. The raters agreed in 84% of the cases on the idiosyncratic-literal dimension and in 85% of the cases on the experience-behavior dimension. Rater 1 agreed with himself in 90% of the cases on both dimensions.

Table 9.6 presents the number of hypnotic and simulating subjects whose material was rated as indicating an idiosyncratic or literal response to the suggested hypnotic events. Chi-square analysis of these data yielded a significant effect, X^2 (1) = 3.53, p < .05 (one-tailed). Whereas the recall of hypnotic subjects was rated as characterized by both idiosyncratic and literal response to the suggested events, the recall of simulators was rated as being illustrative mainly of literal response. Arguably, simulators may not have reported idiosyncratic experiences because they cannot experience the suggested hypnotic events in any genuine sense, but the important fact is that they chose not to describe events in an individual way when that option for responding was clearly available to them.

The process of individuation, or the idiosyncratic perception of the response to hypnotic suggestions, has been discussed a number of times in this book (see

TABLE 9.6
Number of Hypnotic and Simulating Subjects Whose Recall was
Rated as Indicating Idiosyncratic or Literal Hypnotic Responses

Subject Grouping	*Hypnotic Response Rating*	
	Idiosyncratic	*Literal*
Hypnotic	21 (15)	29 (35)
Simulating	10 (6)	40 (44)

Note. Ratings of Rater 2 appear in parentheses. Raters agreed in 84.00% of cases.

Chapters 3, 4, 5, 6, and 8), and such a focus highlights the importance of recognizing that meaningful variations in patterns of reaction occur among subjects of a similar level of high hypnotic ability. The previous data that we have considered on this matter, however, have emphasized the reactions of highly responsive subjects. Present data importantly reveal appreciable differences between hypnotic and nonhypnotic subjects, which indicate that individuation is not a cue-related feature of hypnotic response. The data further imply that the nature of the hypnotic experience is much more heterogeneous among highly susceptible subjects than it is among low susceptible subjects.

Although hypnotic subjects may display similar behavior, quite diverse phenomenal events may underlie their performance. Consequently, we investigated the degree to which hypnotic and nonhypnotic subjects commented on either their experience or their behavior during hypnosis (for an elaboration of the significance of this distinction, see Chapter 7). Table 9.7 presents the number of real and simulating subjects whose material was rated as being descriptive of either their hypnotic experience or their hypnotic behavior. Chi-square analysis of these data also yielded a significant effect, $X^2(1) = 13.09$, $p < .01$. Whereas hypnotic subjects were generally rated as describing their hypnotic experiences, simulating subjects were rated as describing the behavior that they displayed during hypnotic testing. In this regard, it is important to stress that simulators do not have response alternatives defined for them. Given the role of simulation, there is nothing to prevent them from commenting on their (faked) hypnotic experience; that is, simulators need not have commented only on the behavior that they displayed given the demands of their particular role.

A somewhat similar observation between the responses of hypnotic and nonhypnotic subjects was made in Chapter 7 where data showed that hypnotic subjects who were experiencing amnesia and were placed in a situation of forced confrontation with the events for which they were amnesic reported that they could recall their behavioral reactions but not the experiences underlying those reactions to the hypnotic events; nonhypnotic subjects, on the other hand, simply did not comment on underlying experiences at all. Together with those data (see

TABLE 9.7
Number of Hypnotic and Simulating Subjects Whose Recall was Rated
as Describing Either Their Experience or Behavior
During Hypnotic Testing

	Description Rating	
Subject Grouping	Experience	Behavior
Hypnotic	32 (28)	18 (22)
Simulating	13 (8)	37 (42)

Note. Ratings of Rater 2 appear in parentheses. Raters agreed in 85.00% of cases.

Chapter 7), present findings highlight the fact that the phenomenology of events is especially significant for the hypnotic subject; highly susceptible subjects tend to focus on experiential, rather than behavioral, descriptions of their hypnotic testing when they are questioned about it.

Nature of Hypnotic Events

We now consider the information that was provided by subjects during their hallucinatory playback of the hypnotic events in order to determine what was revealed about the nature of those hypnotic events. A common theme throughout this book has been the wide range of individual responses that hypnotic subjects make following suggestions by the hypnotist, and this theme is also apparent in the present data. The information that was provided by the hallucinatory playback of the hypnotic events reinforces many of the points that we have made elsewhere in this book. Accordingly, we have selected illustrative case material dealing with hypnotic induction and ideomotor response (see also Chapter 4), identity delusion and age regression (see also Chapter 5), and hypnotic dreams and hallucinations (see also Chapter 6). Each of these broad types of hypnotic events is considered in turn, and abstracted material is presented in order to focus on the findings that emerged concerning both hypnotic phenomena and process.

Hypnotic Induction and Ideomotor Response.   During the induction, hypnotic subjects often commented on particular nonsuggested effects that occurred. For instance, one hypnotic subject commented: "When you said my neck and chest were getting heavy, I could feel my neck getting much heavier than the rest of me, [and] I thought I was going to topple over, [but] it didn't seem to matter." In somewhat similar fashion, another hypnotic subject commented: "When you were counting from 1 to 20, I got this sensation throughout my whole body like I get in a nightmare I used to have. I felt as though my whole body just swelled up, but [after the counting] the feeling just sort of passed." Both of these subjects experienced nonsuggested, personalized effects during the hypnotic induction that, nevertheless, did not appear either to interfere with or facilitate the induction process. Simulating subjects, on the other hand, were quite constrained in their comments about the induction, saying, for instance: "I just felt very sleepy and tired" or "My eyelids were very heavy. I felt really out of it." That is, the comments of simulators stressed predictable consequences of the instructions that the hypnotist had delivered.

With ideomotor items, there was often evidence of involuntariness or goal-directed fantasy (see Chapter 4 for a discussion) in the experiences reported by hypnotic subjects. One hypnotic subject, for instance, commented about the moving hands apart item: "When my arms were straight out in front and the palms facing each other, I didn't expect them to feel as if they were going away from each other, and it was strange when they did"; this subject also decided that because her hands moved apart as if by themselves then, "Hypnosis must be working." Involuntariness was also evident in the report of the hypnotic subject who commented, "When my hands were facing each other, it was very strong, like an antimagnet. I could feel it and I tried to push my hands back together, [but when I tried] it repelled them more." Similarly, another hypnotic subject indicated that: "When my arms were straight out in front of me and a force was pushing them apart, I just couldn't control them, they just kept moving apart." Some hypnotic subjects, however, reported the use of constructive images and goal-directed fantasies to facilitate the suggested experiences; for instance, one subject reported that she "was imagining that there was a north–south magnet on either side [of her hands]." Simulating subjects generally reported that there was "just an invisible force pushing [the hands] apart" or that their "hands started moving apart." That is, simulators stayed close to descriptions of the events based on the instructions provided by the hypnotist and showed less evidence of (faked) constructive imaginative play.

Identity Delusion and Age Regression.   The identity-delusion suggestion involved subjects assuming the identity of an acquaintance. The reactions of hypnotic subjects to this suggested event highlighted the degree to which they can involve their personal feelings in the hypnotic testing and, in this sense, is similar to the experience of age regression. One hypnotic subject, for instance, reported assuming the identity of her husband who had accidentally died some months earlier: "When you asked me to assume an identity, that was pretty painful, because my husband got killed last year in a car accident, and I'm still having hassles accepting it; it's still a big hassle at the moment."

Somewhat similarly, another hypnotic subject reported assuming the identity of a person whom she feared: "Changing into [that person], that face, it was really scary. I had a feeling of being trapped inside [him] and that was terribly frightening." Some hypnotic subjects, on the other hand, reported assuming the identity of people whom they loved or admired and commented that it was a personally rewarding experience for them to experience that effect. One subject, for instance, reported assuming the identity of a friend "who I like and want to be like. I felt like I was sitting the way she sits and felt an air of confidence just like her." No simulator reported assuming the identity of someone who could be said to be personally meaningful to them and generally indicated that they assumed the identity of a person who was familiar to them. Together with the data from Chapter 5, these findings again highlight the role of emotional processes and level of personal involvement in determining the experience and behavior of highly susceptible hypnotic subjects.

Similar processes were apparent in subjects' experience of age regression where the degree to which hypnotic subjects can personalize their hypnotic experiences was very evident. Rather than literally following the hypnotist's suggestion to experience the fifth grade, some hypnotic subjects reported experiencing past events that held a high degree of personal relevance. For instance, as one subject commented: "I was trying to think of something in fifth grade, but I preferred grade six."

Subjects sometimes saw anomalies in their regressed experience and commented on these by saying, for instance: "When I was in grade five again, it struck me as very funny, I was shrinking, but somehow it was like I didn't quite make it all the way. I felt small, but knew that I wasn't." This comment parallels closely those presented in Chapter 5. In general, simulating subjects simply reported that they were at school participating in a task set by their teacher. For instance, one simulating subject reported that he was "in class reciting French verbs"; another simply commented that she was "at school and writing down [her] name."

Hypnotic Dreams and Hallucinations.   With respect to the hypnotic dream experience, one hypnotic subject reported a negative reaction in that she "started to get dizzy, and dreamt that she was going round and round, and the feeling of spinning wouldn't stop." This was clearly a nonsuggested effect that was nevertheless vividly experienced by the subject. Another hypnotic subject reported, "I was amused by the dream. I saw [a stage hypnotist] and I was annoyed and amused at the same time. I was annoyed by the things that he was doing to his subjects." This subject clearly dreamt in accordance with the suggestion of the hypnotist but also added a personal interpretation of what he saw as the inappropriate use of hypnosis for purposes of entertainment. Simulating subjects again were more constrained in their reports of the dream item. For instance, one subject reported: "When it came to the dream, I was dreaming that I was being hypnotized and the chair was so warm. The warmth of the chair was the main thing in the whole dream."

Individuation was apparent again in hypnotic subjects' descriptions of their experience in the mosquito hallucination item. One hypnotic subject, for instance, illustrated this by commenting: "I didn't feel the mosquito on my hand, it was on my arm, it was annoying. I was also annoyed that it was in the wrong place." Somewhat similarly, the partial responding of subjects to hypnotic suggestions was highlighted by one hypnotic subject's comment that: "When you mentioned the mosquito, I couldn't see the mosquito, and when you told me that it landed on my hand, I couldn't feel it, but I started to hear it. It was as if it was in the air, I could hear it buzzing."

There were also indications of involuntariness in the responses of hypnotic subjects to the mosquito hallucination item. For instance, one hypnotic subject commented that he "was trying hard to hear [the mosquito] but wasn't hearing it very well, and was surprised when [his] hand reacted [to the mosquito]." Simulating subjects commented far more in strict accordance with the text of the suggestion given by the hypnotist by making statements such as: "The mosquito bit my hand." "The mosquito was there, but it did not bite me." "There was a mosquito on my hand and it was going to sting me so I shooed it away.'' ''The mosquito was on my hand, but he went before I could catch him.''

In summary, then, our application of the hallucinatory playback version of the EAT with hypnotic and simulating subjects in the experimental setting provided information on the impact of the technique with separate groups of hypnotic and nonhypnotic subjects. Findings clearly indicated the utility of the technique as a means of inquiring into the experiences of subjects in the sense that they displayed a wide variety of individual reactions. Hypnotic and nonhypnotic subjects were reliably distinguished in terms of the information that was elicited by application of the technique. Further, the technique yielded information that highlighted again the complexity and heterogeneous nature of the phenomenal events experienced by highly responsive hypnotic subjects, a heterogeneity that implicates particular processes at work for some hypnotic subjects and not for others.

So far in this chapter, we have considered a modification of the standard EAT by using hallucinatory, rather than video-tape, playback of hypnotic events. The applications of this method have indicated that this modification was useful in the clinical situation; it provided meaningful information concerning the age-regressed experience of an experimental case study and yielded important differences between hypnotic and nonhypnotic subjects. Other modifications and adaptations of the standard video-tape playback version of the EAT are, of course, possible. In using the hallucinatory playback EAT, for example, Salzman (1982) delineated and structured the events upon which his patients could comment.

This use of a structured and directive inquiry is quite different from the inquiry method that we advocated for the video-tape version of the technique (see Chapter 3). However, given the special needs of clinicians and researchers to focus at times on specific issues, argument can be made for the use of a more structured version of the technique. We now consider in more detail the logic that underlies such an adaptation as well as some data provided by an application of a more directed inquiry version of the video-taped playback EAT.

STRUCTURED INQUIRY AND THE EAT

The primary focus of the EAT is on the examination of individual differences in response to hypnotic phenomena among hypnotizable individuals. Consequently, we developed the EAT as a relatively unstructured, nondirective method of inquiry in order that subjects may speak for themselves with minimal cueing from the experimenter (see Chapter 3). Our logic for this approach was based on the notion that if subjects are allowed to speak only when they have been asked a direct question the experimenter may obtain the information that he or she wants but may not elicit the information that is actually needed to understand the phenomena and processes at work. That is, when subjects simply reply to directive questioning, relevant information may be obtained. But when subjects are allowed to make spontaneous comment, the experimenter may gain access to information that, in the long run, is infinitely richer and more rewarding. It needs to be acknowledged, however, that when subjects are allowed to direct their own comments, much irrelevant information may also come forward.

There is no guarantee, for instance, that complete data on the issues under scrutiny will be obtained, and not all subjects will volunteer information on their subjective experience and cognitive processing for every aspect of their hypnotic testing. Therefore, it can be argued that in some situations subjects should be systematically questioned in a structured fashion. Laurence (1979, 1980; see also Laurence & Perry, 1981) employed such an adaptation of the EAT in a detailed analysis of the cognitive patterns of highly susceptible subjects.

Specifically, Laurence (1979) used a structured adaptation of the EAT as the basis of a directive inquiry into the hypnotic experiences of a small group of highly responsive subjects. Subjects were tested on a range of difficult hypnotic items, and following the hypnotic session an independent experimenter interviewed subjects using a structured version of the EAT. Structure was provided by the inquirer controlling the video-tape playback and directly questioning subjects when particular hypnotic events were viewed. In this way it was possible to obtain standardized interview data on all aspects of testing that were relevant to the issues under examination. The EAT material was then scored to focus on dimensions relating to whether subjects employed cognitive effort in the construction of a response or whether the response seemed to be involuntary.

Laurence (1979) correctly notes that much of the complexity of the hypnotized subjects' experience is lost by structuring the inquiry session in this way and limiting the analysis to questions concerning specific dimensions. That is, although a multiplicity of factors helps to shape the response of highly hypnotizable subjects, the influence of many of them can be missed when the EAT is applied in a structured fashion because focus is on obtaining complete data on only those dimensions relevant to the immediate interests of the experimenter.

With respect to the dimension of effort versus involuntariness (see also Chapters 4 and 6), considerable variation was evident among the subjects in terms of their reports about the items. Across items relating to age regression, missing number delusion, glove analgesia, and the hidden observer, subjects varied in terms of whether they reported that the experiences happened following cognitive effort or apparently involuntarily. It appears that the processes of effort and apparent involuntariness were a major aspect of the experience underlying subjects' reactions in Laurence's (1979) study. This information was yielded through the application of a structured version of the EAT and is consistent with findings presented elsewhere in this book; the variability in the degree to which subjects reported effort or involuntariness across the different hypnotic test items is consistent, for instance, with data presented in Chapters 4 and 6.

Findings suggest a need for further close analysis of the way in which subjects perceive their role in responding to different hypnotic items. For instance, subjects may consciously bring cognitive effort to bear on hypnotic test items when those items require it, but may consider that they are responding involuntarily when the hypnotic test items are such that effort is expended only at a nonconscious level.

Overall, the data yielded by Laurence's (1979) application of a structured adaptation of the EAT indicate the richness and diversity of experiences that occur for highly responsive hypnotic subjects, and this finding is consistent with other data that we have presented. Much of these data have been provided by the use of sensitive inquiry techniques, and if the usual objective scoring procedures had been used in isolation, then many of the present findings would have gone unnoticed (Laurence, 1979). Modes of assessment that focus on behavioral performance (see Chapter 2 for a full review) do, of course, yield important information about subjects' reactions to hypnosis, but the use of techniques that attempt to index the personal significance of hypnotic subjects' experience provide necessary information about the hypnotic phenomena and the cognitive processes that shape them. In fact, the conscientious and systematic application of inquiry techniques that are sensitive to the private experiences of subjects will ultimately provide a sound data base for a more adequate conceptualization of hypnosis (see Chapter 10).

CONCLUSION

In this chapter, we have considered the use of various modifications and adaptations of the EAT in both the clinical and the experimental situation. The data that have been yielded have provided information concerning the impact of the techniques as well as extending our knowledge about the factors that influence the behavior and experience of highly susceptible subjects. With respect to the impact of the modifications on the information obtained, the data provided by Salzman (1982) and Laurence and Perry (1981) suggest that imposing structure on the inquiry session has a somewhat inhibiting influence on the degree to which subjects will report on their experiences.

Each of Salzman's (1982) patients commented only once during the EAT, and this may well have been because the structure that was supplied implicitly communicated that further comment would probably indicate that their therapy was not progressing in optimal fashion; that is, in asking his patients to comment on those aspects that caused them anxiety. Salzman probably minimized his patients' comments, although he gathered information that appeared relevant to their therapeutic progress. Similarly, Laurence and Perry's (1981) subjects generally restricted their comments to the material that was indicated as being relevant by the inquirer, and in so doing potentially relevant and important information was probably lost. Laying aside this inhibiting and restricting aspect of imposing structure, however, the data obtained by Laurence (1979) were directly relevant to the notions under scrutiny and indicated that structured inquiry can be valuable as long as one recognizes the limitations of such an approach.

In terms of the processes that were isolated by the application of the adaptations of the EAT that we have considered in this chapter, it is important to note that the level of susceptibility of subjects was generally insufficient to explain the differences that were observed in their reports about their experiences. Appeal must ultimately be made to factors other than level of aptitude for hypnosis. Throughout this book (see especially Chapters 3–7), we have seen that subjects of a similar level of hypnotic aptitude often respond in quite different fashion experientially; factors relating to emotional involvement, rapport, and cognitive style, for instance, need to be considered in order to understand fully the phenomena being observed. Our analyses of age regression in this chapter as well as in Chapter 5 indicated the important role that subjects' level of emotional involvement may play; the degree of rapport that the subject has with the hypnotist may also play a part in shaping the nature of the age-regressed experience.

In similar fashion, the degree to which subjects idiosyncratically interpret suggestions from the hypnotist was as evident for hypnotic subjects in our clinical and experimental modifications of the EAT as it was in those applications of the standard EAT discussed in Chapters 3–6. The point serves to highlight the fact that variations in cognitive evaluation of and response to hypnotic suggestions will occur among subjects of a similar level of hypnotizability, no matter what substantial differences there are in the detail of the inquiry techniques that are adopted. Further, the heterogeneity of cognitive styles that we have witnessed seems again to reflect the influence of the different types of hypnotic tasks in which subjects are asked to engage themselves (see also Chapters 3 and 6). Finally, in this respect, it is important to note that the relevance of the cognitions that subjects employ in order to experience suggested effects has been consistently highlighted by a variety of applications of different versions of the EAT.

10 Overview and Conclusions: Toward the Understanding of Phenomena and Process

MAJOR THEMES

The aim of this chapter is to draw together the themes that have emerged throughout the preceding chapters and to discuss some of the implications they convey for our understanding of hypnotic phenomena and the processes that explain them. Throughout this book we have emphasized the value of assessing the phenomenological meaning of the experience of the hypnotic subject and accordingly have focused in detail on the application of a technique of assessment (the EAT) developed by us to examine the subject's or client's own observations about their experience when the events of hypnosis are made available to them via video-tape playback or imagery-induced recall. The EAT has been used both instrumentally and intrinsically as a means to elicit data with respect to a variety of hypnotic phenomena, and in Chapters 4–8 we attempted to describe and evaluate specific hypnotic phenomena that cover a range of items, many of which currently appear on standard hypnotic scales of assessment.

The phenomenological framework that the EAT has imposed on the data has given the book both a cognitive and subject-oriented bias. We have, however, adopted the phenomenological framework and discussed it in detail as a useful means of exploring phenomena and process in more detail than has been done previously in other texts about hypnosis. This framework of thinking is not the only orientation one may (or even should) adopt in studying hypnotic responsiveness, but it seems to us to illustrate the diversity and richness of hypnotic behavior and experience especially well. It serves to focus thoughtfully on individual differences in response, is sensitive to the relevance and significance of the whole person viewed as an organism influenced by skills and the situation in which he or she is placed, and searches for the meaning of qualitative (not just quantitative) aspects of hypnotic performance. Finally, the phenomenological method recognizes more explicitly than do other forms of assessment the fact that subjective information is primary datum on the meaning of hypnosis and its phenomena.

In this final chapter we draw together a number of important themes that have emerged from our consideration of the various hypnotic phenomena and processes that we have discussed in the earlier chapters. We then consider some relevant concepts from modern cognitive psychology and how these concepts help us to understand some aspects of hypnosis. Like other investigators (e.g., Neisser, 1979), we consider that hypnosis researchers have not made sufficient effort to incorporate the achievements of contemporary psychology into their work, and one aim of this chapter is to encourage moves in that direction. We also offer summary comment on the status of verbal reports when investigating hypnosis (and other phenomena) because much of the approach that we have advanced here is dependent on an informed and judicious interpretation of subjects' introspections and reports. Finally, we outline some relevant empirical and conceptual issues that can be drawn on the basis of the data that we have presented.

Seven interrelated and recurrent themes can be distinguished in our discussions of hypnotic phenomena. Specifically, we have emphasized: (1) the individuality of hypnotic response; (2) its essential variability; (3) its complexity; (4) the relevance of considering the interactions between subject aptitudes or skills and the tasks that are being performed in hypnosis; (5) modes of cognitive responding on hypnotic tasks; (6) the hypnotic subject as an active participant or respondent; and (7) the adequacy of traditional criteria for the assessment of the meaning of hypnotic responsiveness.

Individuality

Data gathered for the multiple independent groups of susceptible subjects that we have considered in the preceding chapters have revealed strong idiosyncrasy of hypnotic response. Susceptible subjects organize their behavior and respond in terms of the way they perceive the events to which they are exposed, and response to suggestion frequently cannot be understood adequately without recourse to knowing the way in which the suggestions have been perceived in the first instance. This idiosyncrasy of response on the part of hypnotic subjects is what we have indexed by the process of individuation, and it is highlighted by distinctive ways in which the processing of suggestion may occur. To fully understand hypnotic phenomena, we consider that focus must be more pointedly placed on particular patterns of behavior and experiences occurring in specific contexts of hypnotic testing. Traditional assessment has tended to emphasize the central tendencies of response among hypnotic subjects (see Chapter 2) and as a result has tended to lose sight of the within-group variances that frequently occur among deeply susceptible subjects. Standard techniques of assessment are not oriented adequately enough toward the measurement of specificity or individuality and, although they serve a useful purpose in the assessment of overall hypnotic responsiveness, they need to be supplemented by other forms of assessment that capture subjects' hypnotic reactions in far richer detail. In moving in this direction, we should think of expanding our current vocabulary for categorizing types of hypnotic response, and individuality needs to be addressed as an actual problem. Indeed, a major thrust of this book has been toward that end.

Variability

Together with the individuality of hypnotic responsiveness, equal focus should be placed on the essential diversity and variability that exists among the forms of hypnotic response that susceptible subjects may manifest. There are many sources for the differences that can occur. Data cited in this book and published elsewhere now clearly confirm that there are different types of susceptible subjects and that their performance in the hypnotic setting illustrates contrasting cognitive and motivational orientations to hypnotic tasks. For example, not all good hypnotic subjects override the influence of previous perceptions (Dolby & Sheehan, 1977; Sheehan & Dolby, 1975) or preconceptions (Sheehan, 1971a, 1980), demonstrate hidden observer effects (E. R. Hilgard, 1977), illustrate trance logic (Sheehan, 1977; see also, Chapters 5 and 9), or respond to uncancelled suggestions (Perry, 1977b, 1977c; see also Chapter 8). Strong individual differences both in response style and the degree and nature of hypnotic involvement exist among susceptible subjects. Data suggest that the most appropriate way of acknowledging this complexity of hypnotic response is to recognize and pursue the interactive mix that occurs among subjects' aptitude for hypnosis, level of imaginative and absorbed involvement, motivated cognitive commitment to the task at hand, and the social interactional features (e.g., cue demands and rapport) that define the social character of the test situation in which the hypnotic subjects are placed. People do appear to have characteristic ways of processing and responding to the information that they receive, and a more detailed understanding of the differences that occur is integral to a full understanding of phenomena and process.

Complexity

The interactions that occur among modes of processing and involvement, aptitude for trance, and task constraints are complex and require precise definition. Our argument is that this definition depends critically on the way in which hypnotic subjects perceive the meaning of the communications of the hypnotist and the overall setting in which they are placed. The data we have presented in Chapters 4–8 with respect to the interactions between the trait and skill capacities of the subject and the treatment conditions under which those skills are studied suggest that qualitative, phenomenologically oriented assessment reveals more of the complexity that exists than do other alternative forms of assessment. The framework within which we have considered phenomena in the preceding chapters has led us to redefine phenomena (see, e.g., Chapters 5 and 9 for a discussion of trance logic behavior in this respect) as well as to reevaluate the processes that have been argued in the past to explain them (see Chapter 7 for a discussion of amnesia in this light). In addressing the complexity of the interactions that occur between skill and task, however, it is important to recognize that where skill is implicated it may not only be defined in terms of aptitude for trance, but may also be defined in terms of style of attentional and cognitive processing, an issue taken up again later in the chapter.

Trait-Task Interactions

Many data exist to tell us that aptitude for hypnosis is a critical factor in determining the nature of response that hypnotized subjects will display (e.g., E. R. Hilgard, 1965, 1977; see also Sheehan & Perry, 1976). Only very few subjects, for instance, can eliminate pain or discomfort entirely and report feeling nothing when analgesia suggestions are given after they have placed their hand and forearm in circulating ice water (E. R. Hilgard, 1977). The data also tell us that subjects who report age regression and hallucinations and illustrate logical incongruity are typically those who have a relatively marked degree of aptitude for trance. The regularity of these occurrences of individual differences in responsiveness and the reliable demonstration of hypnotic effects that are associated with them leads us to have confidence in the conclusion that hypnotizability is a relatively stable trait. Recent evidence on the modifiability of hypnosis (Diamond, 1974, 1977) has challenged this inference, but there is presently no evidence to show that insusceptible subjects can alter their performance to demonstrate all of the phenomena that we have reviewed in Chapters 5-8 (see also Perry, 1977a). The nature of the kind of skills or capacities that define hypnotizability has long eluded researchers in hypnosis, but, as we discussed in Chapter 4, the evidence would suggest that aptitude for imagination and related skills such as absorption are strong contenders for the most obvious sources of influence. Results gathered from Tables 6.1-6.4, for example, tell us that the two dimensions of imagery and absorption discriminated positive responders particularly well and correlated highly with one another.

But just as one may focus on the skills, attributes, or person characteristics of the susceptible, hypnotizable subject, so one may emphasize the influence of the hypnotic test situation as a setting in which the subject is asked to respond and which involves a host of variables of a social psychological nature. The views of Barber (1969, 1972), Sarbin and Coe (1972, 1979), and Spanos (1981), in particular, have focused on the role of situational influences and have ascribed major weight to social interactional and attitudinal variables among the network of factors that determine hypnotic response. It is important at the outset to fit the respective influence of trait and situation in proper perspective, and to do so we make general comment on the trait-situation debate.

In general, trait theory—for our purposes, this means theorizing that focuses on the relative stability of aptitude factors such as hypnotizability—acknowledges that situations and settings will have an impact (see Epstein, 1979). There are few who would support the notion of complete consistency across hypnotic test situations in arguing for the way in which hypnotizability works. Although the skills that are implicated in determining hypnotic responsiveness are not situation free, one needs to recognize that the impact of situations (i.e., the task and social constraints operating in the hypnotic setting) are viewed differently in a trait and an interactionist account of hypnotic functioning. The trait account assumes that the rank order of individuals with respect to hypnotic aptitude will be maintained across test situations; the interactionist account shifts the focus to give far greater weight to situational factors and asserts that there is no reason to assume that trait influences will be manifest in a fashion that is relatively stable or that preserves the rank ordering across situations (Endler & Magnusson, 1976).

The true meaning of the term "relatively stable" is not adequately appreciated in the hypnotic literature, and hypnotic performance is frequently assumed to be stable across settings that vary considerably in their social complexity. As argued elsewhere in more detail (Sheehan, 1979c; see also Chapter 1) such a position is naive. It is person-in-context that shapes behavior and experience and, if individual differences in hypnotic susceptibility clearly exist, their importance is not at all diminished by also recognizing that the social characteristics of the hypnotic setting will interact dynamically with these characteristics to shape the detail of subjects' final hypnotic response. Hypnotic responsiveness is not only a function of susceptibility; it is also a function of the social-influence nature of the tasks that hypnotic subjects are requested to perform and the broad social character of the setting or context in which that behavior occurs. The question to ask is not which source of influence (trait or situation) is more influential than the other in hypnosis, but to isolate those conditions where situations are more likely to exert powerful effects and those conditions where person variables are more likely to be influential (Mischel, 1977).

An interactionist stance is not incompatible with the notion of hypnosis as an altered or alternate state, which we described as useful in Chapter 1. Assuming that hypnosis involves such a state, it is conceivable that some persons may achieve or attain that state more easily in some situations than in others by virtue of particular trait characteristics or styles of cognitive processing that they adopt. From this perspective, the primary problem for research is to differentiate the consequences of the three components: trait, situation, and state. The advantage of the state concept as we have described it is that it orients us to look for distinctive differences between hypnotized and unhypnotized subjects, especially as those differences are associated with qualitative shifts in experience. Importantly, this approach stresses the essential variability of response that exists among hypnotic subjects themselves, which has been highlighted empirically throughout this book.

Within this interactionist model of explanation it is important to determine the patterns of consistency that adhere to susceptible subjects' performance. Although outcomes will vary with ability, it is also critical to note that the behavior and reported experience of subjects do differ in meaningful ways according to the contextual constraints that are placed on the hypnotized subject. We consider that one of the important and useful ways of ordering the outcomes that occur in hypnosis is through attempts to classify individual subjects' cognitive modes of responding to the situational demands placed on them. As for aptitude for trance, however, the cognitive modes of responding of susceptible subjects and the styles of processing that accompany them can be expected to interact with the situations in which the subjects are placed.

Cognitive Modes of Responding

Our data point to the occurrence of reliably judged patterns of individual differences in reported hypnotic experience (see Chapters 4–8), and these suggest to us the value of formulating specific styles in the ways susceptible subjects process and cognitively respond to hypnotic suggestion. We share with Wardell and Royce (1978) the view of cognitive style as a dimension that functions as a moderator variable: "in the 'recruitment' of those abilities and/or affective traits that are involved in a situation [p. 475]." Cognitive style is a process variable that provides us with a useful device for structuring real differences that exist in the way hypnotic subjects respond. The data forcefully suggest that much is to be gained from analyzing hypnotic responsiveness in terms of style variables because the peculiar property of "style" as a concept is that it aims to shed light on patterns of individual variation in response. Witkin (1978) notes that the concept of individual diversity is inherent or integral to the cognitive style approach or framework of thinking, the assumption being that cognitive styles guide the formation of patterns of behavior and experience in subjects that are compatible with preferred modes of cognitive functioning. In essence, the data reported in Chapters 4–8 suggest to us that style as a process variable usefully organizes the individual differences that occur in a way that emphasizes patterns of meaningful and lawful associations that express the essential diversity and complexity of hypnotic reaction.

The notion of cognitive style first appeared as part of a loose collection of research efforts focused around the value of the perceiver in perception, and the concept further grew in importance from the explicit study of individual differences in perceiving (Witkin, 1978). Since that time, the notion of style has been extended to the study of interpersonal behavior, learning, perceptual constancy, memory, autonomic nervous system function, defense mechanisms, dreaming, childrearing, laterality, and moral judgment (Witkin, 1978), and it is significant that hypnosis is one of the areas that has not been permeated by the concept. Nevertheless, the compatibility of the concept of cognitive style with the study of hypnotic phenomena seems evident for several reasons other than the fact that it is oriented especially toward the study of individual differences. As we have stressed throughout this book, many hypnotic subjects present themselves as active cognizers, working to process suggestions in ways that they see appropriate, and the notion of style expresses clearly the degree of cognitive activity that some hypnotic subjects bring to bear in their response to suggestions. It also focuses on particular types of response rather than on aggregate scores, which conceal the presence of individuality. Finally, the notion of style recognizes the importance of context in the final shaping of response and moves us away from too much reliance on the competence or efficiency of response; style to us expresses less the achievement of success than the ways taken to achieve that success.

The criteria for the formulation of style have been outlined clearly by Witkin (1978) and others (e.g., Wardell & Royce, 1978), and their formal relevance to the study of hypnosis can be asserted tentatively. Cognitive style is a process variable that can be considered to reflect the ways in which subjects move toward positive hypnotic response. It expresses a pervasive dimension of individual functioning in the sense that it points to lawful patterns of variability that are predictable for susceptible subjects. We have focused in our research work on three styles or modes of cognitive functioning: concentrative, independent, and constructive. The data tell us that these modes of functioning can be rated reliably from subjects' verbal reports via the EAT and emerge consistently in subjects' responses across a range of hypnotic test tasks.

The list of possible styles is far from exhaustive and, as stated earlier, no claim is made for personality types of subjects, but rather for the operation of relatively distinct styles of cognition that appear to interact with task complexity so as to determine the precise nature of the response to suggestions that subjects will demonstrate. Data in Chapters 3-6 tell us that stability is not generated for particular hypnotic subjects from one task to another, but rather particular patterns of cognitive response are associated with specific hypnotic tasks (e.g., the concentrative style emerged for a structured hallucination task more obviously than for a less structured hypnotic dream suggestion; see Chapter 6); overall, the coherence in the data was compelling. Consistency of cognitive functioning was seen in Chapter 8, for example, where strong regularity in the data existed across a range of different test situations. Styles of processing are not independent but related, although styles such as the cognitive-constructive mode of functioning are separate from other styles in the degree of imaginative involvement that subjects may display (see Chapter 6 for a discussion of the role of imagery in relation to this style).

As Wardell and Royce (1978) note, it is not known whether cognitive style constructs represent mutually distinct processes or whether each is distinct from the other, and this point seems relevant to the study of hypnosis and its phenomena. Although cognitive styles in hypnosis appear to have some generality, future research must decide the extent to which the styles are, in fact, related and the degree to which highly susceptible subjects will shift or modify their modes of functioning in accordance with different situational demands. Such a shift, for instance, was observed in Chapter 8 where constructive and concentrative modes of functioning were evident in the same subject (Subject F), despite the overall coherence of the data and the repetitive display of cognitive persistence.

Considering the utility of the style construct for ordering the essential variability of hypnotic reaction, it is surprising that the notion of style has not been fully examined in the context of hypnosis. Research in hypnosis has been conducted on field independence and tolerance for unrealistic experience, as well as other styles (Klein, Gardner, & Schlesinger, 1962; Morgan, 1972; Roberts, 1965). A relationship with hypnotizability has been found for field independence (Morgan, 1972), and some correlations exist for sharpening and broad category width (Goldberger & Wachtel, 1973), but, generally, the data have been unrewarding. Recent research has also formulated the notion of coping cognitions, which recognizes explicit patterns of individual differences in response among hypnotic subjects (see Spanos, 1981; Spanos et al., 1979). However, the concept of style has never been applied to the analysis of fine-grained patterns of differences in susceptible subjects' performance across a range of hypnotic test tasks.

But for all its usefulness, it should be recognized that the concept of style is limited. For example, it does not embrace the complexity of hypnotic reaction adequately enough as a single concept, and it is not yet clear what predicts the use of a particular style. Further, the definitions of styles do not convey adequately enough the implications for other relevant processes such as rapport and emotional mood. The data tell us, for example, that reliable individual differences in cognitive style occur (see Chapters 3 and 5) and that rapport and emotion are also relevant (see Chapters 4, 5, and 9), but the evidence has not been gathered to indicate how different process variables such as rapport and emotion interact with stylistic features of cognitive processing to pattern the regularity of hypnotic subjects' responses.

The active nature of much of the cognizing that occurs in hypnosis expresses an essential feature of hypnotic responsiveness that flows in principle from the adoption of an interactionist model of explanation. This feature reflects the extent to which susceptible subjects become involved in cognitively processing their perceptions of a test situation. We now offer brief comment on this sixth major theme before concluding this section by discussing the implications of our data for evaluating scales of assessment.

The Hypnotic Subject as an Active Participant

The interactions that occur among task or setting constraints and aptitude variables such as propensity for trance and style of cognitive responding are complex and dynamic in character. A reciprocal relationship probably exists among trait variables, situation, and behavior. The active nature of this process is formally recognized by us in the process of individuation and perhaps most explicitly in the style of cognizing we have classified as constructive. Subjects operating under a constructive mode of cognition receive the suggestions of the hypnotist and work upon them cognitively, as it were, to solve the task at hand by departing from the text of the suggestion in a frequently imaginative fashion in order to respond in ways that they see as being appropriate. A hypnotist may in turn attempt to handle the subject's reaction by communicating in tune with the subject's chosen way of responding. The flexibility afforded by such an account of the hypnotist's reaction is argued most persuasively perhaps by those who advocate the adoption of clinical forms of assessment of hypnotic responsiveness (see Chapter 2 for their review). Susceptible individuals can differ markedly in the ways in which they construct their response to suggestions, and hypnotists may interact with their attempted constructions in quite different ways. Of course, observers (including the hypnotist) can misperceive the meaning of a subject's reaction if they remain unaware of the nonsuggested aspects of the subject's experience (see Chapters 4 and 7).

An approach that comes close to formalizing this feature of hypnotic responsiveness is Spanos' (1981) account of hypnosis as a problem-solving situation in which hypnotic subjects cognize actively to become attuned to variations in context and modify their interpretations and enactments accordingly. Spanos has presented evidence to suggest, for instance, that highly susceptible subjects will attempt to meet their implicit expectations of response by selectively employing coping strategies that lead them to the desired results; they will also modify their imaginative activities to meet those expectations. But such an account, although recognizing explicitly the active kinds of cognizing that may occur in hypnosis, fails to address the essential diversity of hypnotic reaction by exploring the different patterns of cognitive processing that appear necessary to explain the variable ways in which subjects may respond hypnotically. Of course, the same can be argued for the majority of test instruments designed to measure or assess hypnotic responsiveness in the laboratory and/or clinical setting, to which we now turn.

Criteria for Assessment

The approach we have adopted in this book stresses the type of response that susceptible subjects demonstrate rather than the "scale score" that subjects achieve. This emphasis, for the most part, is contrary or antithetical to the majority of standard objective tests of hypnotic responsiveness that are available to the researcher and the clinician. Standard objective tests stress success across a range of designated tasks. Although some behavioral measures attempt to recognize the diversity of hypnotic reaction, our emphasis on individuality focuses on the special relevance of phenomenological modes of assessment such as depth scales, Shor's (1979) phenomenological method, and the EAT. We stress, however, that these instruments of measurement need to be supplemented by alternative modes of assessment such as scales that have been designed to benefit from a focus on objective patterns of response and standardized conditions of administration. But objective tests alone are insufficient to define the phenomena of hypnosis in their full complexity.

Specific trait and situation interactions are implicated by what susceptible subjects do and experience, and standard techniques are not sufficiently oriented in and of themselves to account for the degree of specificity and individuality of response that exists. Perhaps this is most clearly illustrated in our analysis of trance logic (see Chapters 5 and 9) where classification of response as tolerance of incongruity really failed to account for the fact that the waking subject (asked to retrace the events of trance immediately) did not at all view the behavior that occurred as incongruous; the results suggested that the categories of the observing hypnotist were quite inappropriate to classify the exact nature of the response that was observed.

Our study of hypnosis indicates that the mental abilities, perceiving, reasoning, and emotive responses of susceptible subjects are organized into a complex system of functioning and that subtle decisions are made by hypnotic subjects that guide them toward what they see as appropriate response. The essential error made by routine scales of assessment (however useful they are) is that similar behavior does not necessarily indicate that the same experience or involvement by the subject has occurred. If one accepts the experience of hypnotic subjects as primary datum about hypnosis then the scores on such tests fail to convey the full meaning of hypnotic phenomena and may even disguise or distort it. That meaning can best be understood by considering the hypnotic subject as an active, sentient organism who uses the information that is available in a variety of ways. We now consider some particular features of cognition that may ultimately help explain the problems and issues that relate to the processes of hypnosis and the full participation of the subject in the task of responding hypnotically.

INFORMATION PROCESSING IN HYPNOSIS

Like any other cognitive event, hypnosis basically involves the processing of information by the individual within a particular social context. From the viewpoint of contemporary psychology, information processing can be conceptualized in terms of a control processor that is responsible for planning and sustaining action in relation to the broad goals of the individual, and monitoring functions that serve to scan and maintain alertness with what is occurring in the environment. These two components are integrally related. Further, the assumption of the modal model of information processing (see Murdock, 1974) is that cognition involves a sequencing of discrete stages (e.g., short-term and long-term memory) that differ in their capacity for information, the way information is represented, and how information is used; these stages have different accessing characteristics, with the control processor determining what stage is operating at any particular time.

One of the major lessons of information-processing accounts of cognition (see Anderson, 1980; Glass, Holyoak, & Santa, 1979, for a discussion of such accounts) is that individuals are viewed most appropriately as active rather than passive recipients and processors of information. For example, research has consistently highlighted the constructive nature of perceptual and cognitive processes (see Bruner, 1973; Davidson, 1980; Neisser, 1967, 1976). The input that comes to us is integrated and coordinated in such a way as to give that information the meaning we desire; we attend to some parts but ignore or modify other parts.

Despite the fact that information-processing concepts seem relevant to hypnosis in this respect, there are major gaps in our knowledge about the way that information is processed in hypnosis. We believe that the cross-fertilization of findings from cognition and hypnosis research will be useful in helping us understand the adaptation of the whole functioning person to the hypnotic situation. In fact, in order to understand fully the data that characterize hypnotic events (as reported in Chapters 4–8), one needs to sort through in a systematic way the complexities of subjects' experiences that their verbal reports indicate. Information-processing concepts may help in this regard. To that end, it is useful to highlight recent data concerning: (1) attention and divided consciousness; (2) the notion of top-down processing as relevant to hypnosis; and (3) the relation between thought (fantasy) and reality. Each of these issues is raised by the data presented throughout this book, and we review here their importance and summarily tie them to recent literature in the general area of human cognition.

Attention and Divided Consciousness

Attentional processes clearly are relevant to the understanding of hypnosis. For example, Shor (1959) talks of the loss of generalized reality-orientation as attention becomes focused on the world as suggested by the hypnotist, and E. R. Hilgard (1977) has built a sophisticated account of hypnosis around a theory based on modification of monitoring controls where hypnotic consciousness is divided and information becomes concealed from awareness. Tasks for establishing hypnotizability that are incorporated in the scales used by investigators have also been discussed as specifically reflecting attentional competence (Davidson & Goleman, 1977).

To date, most of the empirical support for the relevance of attention, in particular, has come from the analysis of the correlates of hypnotizability or from the examination of differences in the pattern of performance of high and low susceptible subjects. Support for the specific relevance of attention comes from the work of Van Nuys (1973), Graham and Evans (1977), Karlin (1979), Tellegen and Atkinson (1974), Spanos, Rivers, and Gottlieb (1978), and Spanos, Stam, Rivers, and Radtke (1980). Van Nuys found that subjects who were better equipped to concentrate during meditation, as defined by fewer thought intrusions, were more highly susceptible to hypnosis and demonstrated a significant negative correlation between number of intrusive thoughts reported by subjects during a meditative exercise and their degree of susceptibility to hypnosis. This negative correlation was replicated by Spanos et al. (1978, 1980), but this research also demonstrated that meditation practice is a prerequisite for obtaining the effect. Graham and Evans investigated the association between hypnotizability and performance on an attention deployment task (random number generation) and found a relationship; they concluded that high susceptible subjects redistribute attention more easily than less susceptible subjects, and others have reported data that are in essential agreement. Karlin (1979), for instance, predicted that individuals who were successful at a difficult attentional task would also succeed on cognitive hypnotic test items, and this hypothesis was confirmed. Tellegen and Atkinson (1974) further demonstrated a consistent and appreciable relationship between hypnotizability and self-report measures of absorption, which was a trait they defined as the capacity to engage one's total attention imaginatively (see Chapter 4 for a discussion). This same relationship was evident in our research reported in Chapter 6, and a moderate correlation between absorption and hypnotizability has also been reported by others (e.g., Spanos et al., 1979, 1980).

The majority of these studies stress narrowly defined attentional competence. For instance, research focuses on how well susceptible subjects can perform on single, specific tasks that are demanding of their attention. The recent work by Spanos (1981) has moved away from that focus to a broader, more process-orientated account of cognitive functioning in hypnosis by analyzing the notion that amnesia involves inattention to the material that is to be remembered (for an independent discussion of the relevance of selective inattention to the study of mechanisms behind hypnotic phenomena, such as amnesia and hallucinations, see Blum & Barbour, 1979). Spanos conceptualizes amnesia in terms of attention deployment and claims that its occurrence is determined by what subjects ignore and attend to during their testing. He rejects the notion that amnesia is automatic for hypnotized subjects. The evidence is emerging in relation to this account of amnesia; there is support, for instance, for the position that some susceptible subjects will breach amnesia when pressure to attend is placed upon them (see Chapter 7). However, data from Chapter 7 indicate that this process is not uniform and that when subjects are confronted directly with the material to be remembered some susceptible subjects still persist in their forgetting. The EAT is a situation where the cues for attention are optimal for test of the persistence of amnesia, and the data presented in Chapter 7 suggest that an account of amnesia in terms of effortful inattention cannot fully explain the phenomena that occur and that we discuss.

The theoretical assumptions behind contemporary research in the field are that the subject who is susceptible to hypnosis is capable of attending to what the hypnotist is suggesting while ignoring irrelevant stimuli. Much unattended input is registered without conscious perception and only influences the subject in what is said and done at an unconscious level, unless special techniques are used to bring that material to the surface (see E. R. Hilgard, 1977, for their detailed exposition and Chapter 5 for their application). However, such an account does an injustice to the cognitive skills of the susceptible person as manifest in the data we have considered in this book. The evidence suggests (see Chapter 6) that much reality information enters consciousness readily and frequently.

We believe that a plausible way of considering the data at hand is to argue that susceptible individuals are skilled at detecting and processing multiple sources of information and can respond on the basis of both reality and suggested events at the same time when it becomes necessary to do so. The necessity for doing so depends on the salience of the information, and susceptible individuals may be practiced enough at discriminating between real and suggested events that the meaning of the two kinds of events is readily understood in arriving at some appropriate response.

The issue of shifts and divisions in consciousness is an especially difficult one to address, and we discussed the problem only very briefly in Chapter 1. It obviously occurs, although some (e.g., Broadbent, 1971) would argue that attention is only effectively directed to a single activity at a time and that multiple tasks (e.g., attending to reality sources of input and processing suggestions) require either a rapid alternation of attention or automatic processing of one of the tasks. Certainly, subjects experience events at times by alternating attention between them, but the evidence tells us that this is not always the case. The fact that tasks can be executed easily through the simultaneous processing of input in consciousness has been demonstrated forcibly by Spelke, Hirst, and Neisser (1976) and Hirst, Spelke, Reaves, Caharack, and Neisser (1980).

Working closely with individual subjects, these investigators first demonstrated that practiced individuals can do cognitive tasks as effectively and rapidly together as they can do them alone (Spelke et al., 1976). Hirst et al. (1980) then proceeded to test the hypothesis that subjects in the earlier study alternated awareness rapidly rather than attended to different inputs simultaneously (without loss of efficiency). This study refuted the notion that there are fixed limits to attentional capacity, with results failing to support either the view that input was processed automatically on the second task or that awareness alternated rapidly between tasks. Collectively, the work demonstrates that division of attention can be defined in terms of simultaneous directed activity and that attention is based on the development with practice of situation-specific skills. Performance on multiple cognitive tasks relates closely to the subject's knowledge about the set of tasks at hand, and skills in coping with them are clearly relevant to an understanding of the nature of attentional performance.

Looking at the relevance of this research to hypnosis and to some of the major cognitive processing implications of the EAT data, our results suggest that susceptible subjects are frequently able to differentiate reality stimuli from suggested sources of input, and they can both attend to the suggestions of the hypnotist while at the same time process reality information that is relevant and significant to their response. There is no evidence from the subjects' reports in our studies that they always alternated the two sources of information in consciousness or that one source of information (reality) was for the most part concealed and processed automatically. The research of Spelke, Hirst, and their associates indicates that the ability to attend to different sets of events at one and the same time is not peculiar to susceptible subjects alone, and the case for simultaneous processing of real and suggested events by hypnotic subjects obviously represents a talent or skill that is not unique.

For too long a period of time, the study of hypnosis has failed to emphasize the cognitive and attentional skills of the susceptible person in broad perspective. Indeed, consciousness itself can be readily conceptualized as the exercise of the learned skill of saying what we are doing and experiencing (Fingarette, 1969). The consciousness of the hypnotic subject is complex, and the hypnotic subject is more cognitively proficient than what the hypnotic literature has to date allowed for. Close study of divisions in attention has only just begun, and we are still far from reconciling the experimental results from hypnotic and nonhypnotic paradigms. But the data that do exist hint provocatively at the relevance and significance of what yet needs to be explained.

The theory that has addressed the complexity of divided consciousness most explicitly in conceptual detail is that proposed by E. R. Hilgard (1977). This theory states that hypnosis modifies the hierarchical relations of the susceptible person's cognitive substructures, and it posits that processing is concealed from consciousness by alterations and modifications in the system of monitoring. An amnesialike barrier determines what is available and what is not, and techniques such as the hidden observer can remove that barrier and release information that was previously inaccessible. Application of such techniques provides, as Hilgard states, evidence on the fractionation of the monitoring function.

However, the theory has been criticized (Neisser, 1979) as describing separate consciousnesses as if they were separate persons and for divided attention not being treated: ''as something accomplished by a single skilled individual [p. 100].'' Certainly, the EAT data suggest more evidence of cognitive skill and more simultaneous directed activity in consciousness than this account of cognitive functioning based on dissociation would seem to allow, though as E. R.

Hilgard (1977) points out much research needs to be done to determine how much of the normal monitoring function is retained in hypnosis and how much the detachment of the central monitor is sustained. For Hilgard, also, the hypnotic subject is an active agent who formulates plans and makes decisions, but the theory of dissociation suggests the subject is more deceived about the causes of his or her behavior than appears, in fact, to be the case.

Top-Down Processes

In the general area of cognition research, a basic distinction that appears to be relevant to understanding the cognitive processes underlying hypnosis is that between bottom-up and top-down processes (for discussions of this distinction see Anderson, 1980; Glass et al., 1979). The former is illustrated by a process where perception is constructed out of features of the stimulus input and where the outcome of a lower step in the process is not affected by a higher step. To take Glass et al.'s example, we first discriminate between the light and dark areas of this page; next, the dark areas are encoded as figures and the light areas as ground; finally, letter shapes are discriminated individually from each other. In this example, the steps in processing can be ordered from lower to higher on the basis of the sequence in which the visual input is transformed; higher steps play no role in the processing associated with lower ones. Top-down processing, however, is different and would seem more relevant to the way in which some hypnotic subjects process the input that they receive. With this kind of processing, the output of a lower step is influenced by the outcome of a higher one; expectations, for example, may come to alter the perceptual process. When test conditions are not defined clearly, as frequently occurs in hypnosis, top-down processes may then come into play.

The relevance to hypnosis of such processes at work is illustrated by the research of Sheehan and Dolby (1975) and Dolby and Sheehan (1977) who found that ambiguous stimuli were processed by subjects in terms of their expectancy of what the hypnotist wanted, rather than by the structural properties of the stimulus that was being presented. In this instance, susceptible hypnotic subjects reported seeing an ambiguous wife/mother-in-law figure as old, rather than young, when they were led to believe that old was the most appropriate response to give. The effect was strong and durable, and it replicated across different testing conditions and subgroups of subjects. In top-down processing, it is difficult to specify precisely when higher outcomes influence lower ones and to differentiate the influence of the components in the processing system defined by expectations, attitudes, and motivations. However, the distinction helps explain what hypnotic subjects do and illustrates the relevance of contemporary constructs of information-processing theory to an understanding of the complexity of the consciousness of the hypnotic subject.

Also related to this understanding is the degree to which hypnotized individuals construct, test, and monitor the various suggested and reality events that impinge upon them. One of the characteristics that susceptible hypnotic subjects display is the ability to process real and suggested events simultaneously, and one may ask what degree of interference or confusion this creates. The issues in the nonhypnotic literature of reality testing (e.g., Perky, 1910; Segal, 1971) and reality monitoring (e.g., Johnson & Raye, 1981; Raye & Johnson, 1980) seem to reflect concepts in this respect that aid an understanding of hypnosis, and we turn finally in this section to discuss some of the relevant literature.

The Relation Between Thought (Fantasy) and Reality

The relationship between thought and reality has been a persistent theme in both the imagery and memory literature. Although the data tell us that it is generally easy to discriminate between internal and external sources of information, the extent to which such events can interfere with each other is evident from classical and more recent work that has analyzed the structural association between imagery and perception (see Finke, 1980; Kosslyn, 1980, for reviews). In her classic investigation of the similarity of imagery and perception, Perky (1910) instructed subjects to imagine different items in the center of a window; unknown to the subjects, faint replicas of the items to be imaged were projected onto the window. When subjects reported their imagery, although their descriptions were essentially those of the projected, externally present stimuli, most subjects indicated that what they were describing was based solely on their internally generated imaginings. Perky's (1910) demonstration that low-intensity visual stimuli can be confused with mental images has been partially replicated in several studies (see Segal, 1971, 1972, for a review of these studies).

The similarity between mental images and physically present objects or events (see Finke, 1980, for a discussion) has been examined more recently in a number of quite novel ways. Comparison has been made of subjects' responses to imaged or real events that subjects know are either imaged or physically present. Evidence from this research has shown that estimates of both imaged and observed object size are related to an object's actual size (Moyer, Bradley, Sorensen, Whiting, & Mansfield, 1978); the time required to detect parts of an imaged object decreases with increasing part size (Kosslyn, 1975, 1976); and the time it takes to scan between objects that are imaged after being observed is proportional to the actual physical distance between the objects (Pinker & Kosslyn, 1978). Research has also been extended to demonstrate that memories for imagined and perceived events can be confused (Johnson, Raye, Wang, & Taylor, 1979). For instance, in their concept of reality monitoring Johnson and Raye (1981) argue that the processes that one should especially note are those that people use in deciding whether information initially had an internal or external source. The evidence from a series of studies (see Johnson & Raye, 1981, for a review) indicates that, although there are reasonably good decision criteria that individuals can use in order to decide whether an event was internally or externally based, there is room for error. Hence, argument can perhaps be made that, for some susceptible subjects at least, hypnosis may lead to a shift in the decision criteria about which events are externally or internally based.

Among psychologists examining the relationship between imaginal thought and reality, those working outside the area of hypnosis have emphasized either fantasy or reality at the expense of the other. Those working within the area of hypnosis, however, have consistently underestimated the impact of reality. We conclude the present section by returning to our data to reinforce this point.

Theorizing in hypnosis largely has accepted the view that the influences of reality fade in hypnosis as subjects lose their everyday orientation to their surrounding environment and accept the world as structured for them by what the hypnotist suggests (e.g., Shor, 1959, 1962). Reality may be registered without perception, and the processing of reality features can become automatic (see Bowers, 1976; E. R. Hilgard, 1977). The general impact of our data, however, is that a considerable amount of information appears to enter consciousness from sources that are not the focus of attention.

One of the most compelling features of the experience of hypnotic subjects as revealed by the EAT in our exploration of hypnotic phenomena is the extent of reality awareness that occurs in hypnosis. Our explorations of ideomotor response, age regression, hallucination, dreaming, and amnesia were replete with instances of subjects commenting on the real state of affairs or the environment outside the framework of suggestion established by the hypnotist; this happened at the same time they were attempting to process the suggestions they received and were working toward an acceptable response. The monitoring of reality information in hypnosis raises profoundly important questions about the consciousness of the hypnotic subject. We may ask how influential the information is; what confusion or interference it creates; whether the hypnotic subject switches rapidly from one source of attention to another, deals with one source automatically while the other is attended to, or processes the two kinds of information (suggested and real) contemporaneously. At an introspective level, the data appear persuasive. There is little evidence in the case of age regression (see, e.g., Chapter 5, Case 3) that monitoring of reality information necessarily interferes with the processing of the suggestion that is the main focus of attention. Our subject experienced vivid and compelling regression while at the same time was seemingly aware of reality features of his environment such as the uncertainty the hypnotist might have about his being left or right handed. The data we have collected imply that critical reality information often combines with other sources of information (viz., suggestion) and is processed concurrently; this is consistent with our notion of the hypnotic subject as an active participant in the events of hypnosis.

The answer to many of the issues raised by these concepts that attempt to broaden the theoretical domain of hypnosis appears to reside in close and detailed analysis of the cognitive events that subjects report are occurring during hypnosis. Recognizing that the data we have collected and theorized about depend critically on the status of verbal reports, we now summarily evaluate them. We review their status, outline the factors that affect them, and attempt to draw out some of the implications of the procedures we have adopted in Chapters 4–8 for determining their accuracy.

VERBAL REPORTS
AND LIMITING FACTORS

Verbal reports are frequently criticized as totally unreliable and as revealing nothing of scientific value about the processes that underlie them. We attempted to discount this view in Chapter 1 where we argued that they have the kind of status that justifies considering them as relevant and significant for the understanding of hypnotic processes. Earlier we discussed Nisbett and Wilson's (1977) view that individuals report falsely rather than truthfully most of the time and that, if accurate verbal reports do occur, then they can be regarded as incidental because individuals correctly adopted a priori causal theories about their behavior. There are data to suggest that Nisbett and Wilson's claims should lead us to be cautious about using verbal reports. They showed, for instance, that subjects verbalizing retrospectively (in a mixture of contexts) about their reasons for behaving in the way that they did were no more accurate than independent observers who attempted to isolate the relevant situational factors that determined their response.

Ericsson and Simon (1980; see also, Smith & Miller, 1978), however, have drawn attention to the fact that Nisbett and Wilson (1977) failed to analyze thoroughly the conditions under which their conclusions held and that the studies they report did not provide optimal conditions for recovering information; for example, the probes that Nisbett and Wilson reported on were not the most appropriate ones. Still, Nisbett and Wilson's arguments alert us to the potential limitations of verbal reports, especially when suitable conditions of inquiry are not adopted.

The factors that may affect reports are many and varied, and it is necessary to delineate procedures for soliciting them carefully so that appropriate inquiry questions are used and potential biases are minimized, wherever possible. Subjects may vary considerably, for instance, in the degree to which they are able to reflect upon the specific cognitive steps they go through in processing the suggestions received. Subjects recalling their experiences of hypnotic testing may also be more aware of parts of a hypnotic session than of others and recall their experience only on the basis of memory fragments. They may also remember specific components of their hypnotic performance and construct their experience of the session as a whole from that memory. Alternatively, they may draw on their general knowledge of appropriate hypnotic response and recall their experiences in ways that are not entirely faithful to the actual cognitive processes that they employed in performing the tasks in the session itself. The video display of events in the EAT, however, exposes subjects directly to multiple aspects of their hypnotic performance, and the aid to recall that is thereby introduced can have the consequence that they will draw less from memory about what they think happened, than from their recall of events that actually occurred. The presence of strong cues for recall should limit the tendency to fill in gaps in memory with guesses about appropriate experience. However, the EAT situation is vulnerable to incompleteness of recall as are other forms of retrospective assessment. It is clear, for instance, that under standard conditions of relatively unstructured probing subjects do not recall all of the information available to them. And directing subjects to respond specifically on certain aspects of their performance serves to accentuate the problem. Attempts to structure the EAT inquiry and its modified hallucinatory form (see Chapter 9) show that subjects will report less than they would otherwise on other aspects of their experience and behavior if asked to report specifically on issues that are of special interest to the inquirer. It seems that, when spoken to, clients and subjects say less than they could. This fact puts the clinician in something of a dilemma. He or she may wish to probe particular areas of conflict or anxiety, but verbal output on other matters is likely to be limited as a result.

A particular risk with verbal reports in the field of hypnosis is that when subjects come to report on different aspects of their personal experience their reporting can be affected by the nature of the attribution that they make concerning the source of the experience. As Spanos (1981) indicates, reports of effortless experiencing can be conceptualized as reflecting attributions that subjects draw about the reasons for their behavior: While effortful forgetters might attribute their recall difficulties to their self-generated behavior (e.g., "I did it."), effortless forgetters may attribute their difficulties to events that are external to them (e.g., "It happened to me."). Inasmuch as subjects may thus create for themselves illusions about what they are experiencing, care must be taken to minimize expectations or preconceptions about appropriate response. The EAT helps to meet this problem, in part, through the provision of optimal cues for detailed recall, but the possibility of errors introduced by false attributions that affect the nature of verbal reports can be studied in other ways—namely, through employing comparison groups of control (or quasi-control) subjects whose performance is based exclusively on guesswork about the most appropriate responses to provide.

Care is obviously needed in collecting verbal reports for the reasons we have indicated. Frequently, they are problematic in character, and thus one needs to detail closely procedures that enhance their accuracy. As Ericsson and Simon (1980) suggest, we need to distinguish between procedures in which the verbal reporting directly reflects the information that is stored and procedures that expose information to contaminating factors such as inference and abstraction. Some specific guidelines may help.

A major relevant issue is the directness of probing, an issue we discussed in some detail in Chapters 3 and 9. The data indicate that interpretive probing cannot be relied upon to produce results that reflect subjects' actual thought processes, especially when the probing encourages the subject to speculate or theorize (Nisbett & Wilson, 1977). Inquiry questions that elicit types of information that subjects do not have direct access to or questions that force subjects to guess or draw inferences about the reasons for their behavior pose considerable risks, and, as we have noted, the investigator or practicing clinician needs to balance such risks carefully against the value of inquiring about specific areas of concern.

Another relevant issue is the nature of the material being recalled. Thought episodes such as those characterized by hypnosis are difficult to recall fully unless the reports about the experiences concerned are collected shortly after the experiences themselves take place. Inquiry, then, must be close in time to when the events occur in order to provide a relatively detached account of the thought processes that are involved. The EAT in this respect needs to follow shortly after the time when the events of hypnosis are recorded.

Finally, we return again to the issue of attention. Ericsson and Simon (1980) present a cogent case for the argument that inaccurate reports are most likely to result when verbal reports are requested about nonattended information. Requesting information that was never directly heeded forces subjects to infer rather than remember their mental processes. Therefore, requests for comment should gain in accuracy when the events for recall are presented in a concrete and attention-getting way. The direct aid to recall provided by our standard version of the EAT (see Chapter 3 for its description) is an important procedural feature that is likely to be related to the technique's accuracy. This sets it apart from other phenomenologically oriented modes of inquiry where direct aids to recall are not provided.

The potential limitations of verbal reports as data bring us directly to discuss the research implications of the evidence we have presented in the preceding chapters. The processes implicated by verbal report data require careful and precise validation. Although the richness of the data makes it easy to speculate about the processes involved, it is research that will ultimately decide whether those speculations are justified or not.

ISSUES FOR RESEARCH

The major consideration in formulating directions for future research is the need to explore in specific fashion the nature of the interactions that exist among aptitude for hypnosis, situational (including task) constraints, style of cognition, and degree and type of hypnotic involvement. The nature of subjects' involvement in the events of trance is shaped in turn by such factors as rapport and emotion (for an explication of their relevance, see Chapter 5), but the nature of that interaction is uncertain, as is their association with subjects' preferred modes of cognitive responding. Subjects also shift in their modes of cognizing about the information that they receive, and they demonstrate several styles that may be potentially related. For instance, data from Chapter 6 demonstrate that some tasks are more prone to reflect particular styles than others, and the interactive mix between hypnotic task and style of processing seems an especially fruitful focus for research.

Aptitude for hypnosis is insufficient to account for the essential variability of hypnotic reaction, but it is a major determinant of effects nevertheless, and its exact contribution remains to be investigated further. It is clear that subjects require a high degree of aptitude to perform standard hypnotic tasks of the kind we have analyzed in Chapters 5–8, but future research needs to address the problem of determining its significance for particular types of hypnotic response in a way that will eventually predict individuality of response.

Theoretically speaking, research needs to address much more pointedly than it has done to date the changes in subjects' monitoring system that occur in hypnosis and the potential capacity of the hypnotic subject for simultaneous directed activity that involves the processing of both reality and suggested information. If the hypnotized subject is at once attending to the hypnotist and processing suggestions, while at another level constructing for himself or herself an explanation of what is going on, it is to the second stream of consciousness that the notion of cognitive style may be more relevant (Tilden, 1979). The conditions under which preferred modes of cognitive functioning operate and their relationship to response outcomes have not yet been researched systematically, nor has the relevance of cognitive style to top-down processing, which appears to characterize a number of important aspects of hypnotic performance. Finally, as Davidson (1980) states, when we speak of individual differences in cognitive and attentional style, we could well be attempting to isolate relatively enduring biocognitive structures that affect information in particular and idiosyncratic ways. The structural basis of individual differences in cognitive processing, then, presents itself as an important, but neglected, area of research.

The processes of attention should clearly be a major focus of research, and a number of issues other than the ones we have highlighted should be pursued. Evidence tells us, for instance, that absorption and hypnotizability are appreciably related, and the relevance of attention to absorption is well established theoretically (J. R. Hilgard, 1970; Tellegen & Atkinson, 1974). But when attention is focused at the request of the investigator, high-absorption subjects as compared with low-absorption subjects initially show lowered levels of performance (for a detailed analysis of this effect in relation to relaxation performance for waking subjects, see Qualls & Sheehan, 1981a, 1981c). Data indicate that the imaginative involvement of highly absorbed subjects needs to be maintained by their own efforts rather than at the instruction of others (Qualls & Sheehan, 1981b, 1981d). Following the implications of this evidence, it seems plausible to argue that the way in which the experience of the absorbed hypnotic subject is generated will play an equally important role in determining just how the processes of attention will aid or abet hypnotic performance.

Turning to issues more relevant to method, a major focus for research inquiry is the impact of the hypnotist-inquirer on the data that are revealed. We have been very much subject oriented in our analysis of phenomena and process, and it remains to be seen what influence those persons other than the subject will have on the kinds of information that phenomenologically based techniques of assessment can provide. Research has shown that individual differences in styles of cognizing are related meaningfully to extent of verbal output (for a discussion of the dimension of field dependence–independence, see Witkin, 1978), and it seems reasonable to assert that such differences will be functionally related to variation in the structure of the questioning that inquirers (or therapists) conduct. It is the essence of an interactionist approach to the study of behavior that subjects' reactions influence the behavior of others toward them and consequently affect the responses that result. The reciprocal nature of the processes of interaction thus seems an especially pertinent area for detailed inquiry.

Specific types of inquiry questions may suit the cognitive style of particular subjects or clients, and the task of replying may fall better to some kinds of subjects than to others. Certainly, strong individual differences in verbal productivity occurred for the application of the EAT and its modifications, and independent evidence suggests that verbalizing output may be affected under conditions in which subjects are placed under high cognitive load (Ericsson & Simon, 1980); therefore, variability in the completeness of verbal reporting may be meaningfully related to processing characteristics of the hypnotizable person. Consistency and completeness of verbal reporting may be analyzed in relation both to the personality structure and cognitive characteristics of the subject, as well as in relation to the procedures that are adopted by the hypnotist-inquirer. And the topics for research that we are suggesting also seem relevant to standard modes of postexperimental inquiry and to application of the EAT.

Finally, it is important to stress the value of validating the findings from our research on groups of nonhypnotic subjects. Chapters 6, 7, and 9 discussed in some detail the reactions of insusceptible simulating subjects in order to ascertain whether the effects found for susceptible subjects replicated in groups that were optimally attuned to respond to the social psychological constraints of the test situation. Future work should extend the domain of comparison groups that we have used (for the range that is available, see Sheehan & Perry, 1976) to include subjects who are both susceptible to hypnosis and insusceptible to hypnosis and who have high aptitude for imagination. If, for instance, the differences that were sustained between hypnotic and simulating subjects in Chapters 7 and 9 (where hypnotic subjects were distinguished by their recall of behavior vs. experience) replicated for independent groups of nonhypnotic subjects, then one would gain important additional evidence confirming the distinctive cognitive processing that we have argued is associated with hypnotic amnesia. Research of this kind would also help to answer the important question of whether cognitive abilities of the kind we have discussed generalize from hypnotic to waking consciousness. We have premised many of our conclusions about process on the assumption that such generalization will occur. In-depth analysis of the moment-to-moment mental life of waking subjects (e.g., Witz, 1978) reveal many of the same kinds of processes as shown in our studies of hypnotic subjects, and the skills of attention that we suggested underlie hypnotic performance are clearly evident among nonhypnotic subjects as well (see, e.g., Hirst et al., 1980; Spelke et al., 1976).

In our attempts to explore both phenomena and process, it is evident that the options for research are as diverse as the data that give rise to their consideration. The notion of cognitive style, for example, has no imperial hold on the domain of hypnosis, and future research may well limit its utility and point to ways in which other concepts may be of greater value in accounting for the complexity and variability of hypnotic response. We now offer summary comment on our position and draw out more explicitly the major thrust of our approach.

CONCLUDING COMMENTS

We began this book by discussing the usefulness of the concept of consciousness and the scientific status of the statements that individuals offer about it. We considered that the notion of consciousness was important to the study of hypnosis both in its clinical and experimental applications and that the term ''alternate state'' was perhaps better suited to acknowledging its complexity than other constructs. We then searched through the available modes of assessment for a technique of measurement that was sensitive to the richness and diversity of hypnotic phenomena, which we felt could be used to explore the nature of both hypnotic phenomena and process in intensive detail. The Experiential Analysis Technique (EAT) was the mode of assessment that we adopted to pursue that goal, and it was applied across a relatively broad spectrum of hypnotic tasks to illustrate hypnotic consciousness at work. For the most part, our emphasis has been on susceptible subjects' reactions to suggestion, and we chose to explore hypnotic phenomena most intensively in those subjects whose talents and skills appeared best suited to manifest them.

Hypnosis is seen by us as providing a context in which susceptible subjects work toward appropriate response as they perceive it by actively processing the information that they receive. Suggestions create situations that elicit the display of the subject's talents, with the hypnotist guiding rather than directing the subject toward the goal of successful hypnotic response, which they are positively motivated to produce. The conditions of hypnotic testing facilitate qualitative shifts in cognitive functioning, and the concept of altered (or alternate) state is useful for incorporating the extent of change that seems evident for some hypnotic subjects, although Sheehan (1979c) points out that the: "very ease of that assimilation reflects the risk of overgeneralization and the breadth of the concept's explanatory power [p. 238]." The special utility of the concept of altered state appears to us to lie in the extent to which it orients or directs the investigator to search for distinctive (but not unique) differences between hypnotic and nonhypnotic subjects, particularly as those differences are associated with qualitative shifts in experience among hypnotic subjects themselves. It is important to stress, however, that the state of awareness of the hypnotic subject necessarily intereacts with situational factors associated with the hypnotic context, subjects' aptitude for hypnosis and preferred modes of cognition, the degree of hypnotic involvement, attentional skill, and other subject characteristics. In this book, we have focused on the notion of cognitive style, in particular, as a useful device for classifying the essential variability of hypnotic reaction, a facet of hypnosis that we feel has been relatively unexplored by others.

The cognitive-style approach stands apart from other approaches in the scope of what is encompasses and in its focus on person-situation interactions (Petersen & Scott, 1975; Witkin, 1978). As Witkin states, it is basically concerned with individuality and with variability among people rather than with differences viewed in a narrow sense. Particular situational variables (e.g., the nature of the hypnotic test task) may determine the actual behavior that emanates from a subjects' use of a specific cognitive style, and mobility in their use emphasizes an important source of diversity. The data tell us that individuals who use a style as it suits the hypnotic situation at hand may well show considerable variation in their response. Hypnotic subjects work through suggestions to an acceptable solution; but some subjects are more inventive, imaginative, and constructive in their efforts than others who appear tied to a greater extent to the literal text of what the hypnotist is suggesting. The problem-solving nature of the hypnotic experience is indexed in part by the extent to which input from suggestions appears to be processed by the subject together with cognitions about reality features of his or her environment. We know that the hypnotic subject never loses touch with reality (otherwise, how could the hypnotized person easily awake?), but the precise nature of the processing that defines the handling of such information represents to us one of the most intriguing aspects of hypnotic performance as revealed by the evidence that we have collected. The data gathered from the verbal reports of subjects via application of the EAT are consistent with the view that genuine divisions in consciousness are accomplished in hypnosis, but the processing of separate streams of information that derive from perception of reality and suggestion needs to be explored much more intensively.

Current theorizing in the field is inclined to argue that the hypnotic subject becomes selectively attuned to suggestion while other information is concealed from consciousness. However, the sophisticated nature of the cognizing of susceptible subjects as revealed by the EAT data implies that hypnotic consciousness should be viewed much more in terms of susceptible subjects demonstrating higher order attention skills. We do not wish to argue that there is no registration without perception. That process is extremely well documented and argued forcibly elsewhere (Bowers, 1976; Sheehan & Perry, 1976). Rather, we wish to argue that the extent of higher order cognizing has been underemphasized to date in contemporary accounts of the consciousness of the hypnotized subject. It appears that susceptible subjects can skillfully extract meaning from what the hypnotist is suggesting and from features of their environment such as their personal identity, past history, and other events occurring outside the framework of suggestion established by the hypnotist. Discriminations between reality and suggested information that the hypnotic subject makes may at times be easy because hypnotic subjects are usually well practiced at experiencing the effects of trance (naturally occurring or suggested) and at the same time adapting to and interacting with the everyday world around them. The fact that attention seems more directed than we have acknowledged in the past does not at all suggest that viewpoints focusing on the automaticity of response or occurrence of dissociation are untenable. But the data do imply that such theories have underestimated the fluidity of barriers that exist between the different streams of awareness and the higher order nature of cognizing that occurs when input from unattended consciousness breaks into conscious awareness. The presence or absence of dissociation is not at issue so much as the degree of dissociation that is maintained consistently through time in hypnosis and the nature of hypnotic consciousness that displays it.

Our theorizing about the nature of hypnotic consciousness is speculative and must obviously await the judgment of future research on the kinds of issues that we have outlined. We are aware, for instance, of the potential limitations of verbal reports and the need to pursue patterns of regularity in hypnotic performance through the adoption of alternative modes of assessment. Methods, however, need to be diverse in the search for phenomena. Phenomenological modes of assessment can and should be used together with more objective standardized modes of measurement, clinical testing, and natural observation. One of the special advantages in adopting such multiple sets of procedures is that their application guarantees more valid investigation. The use of different procedures of observation strongly increases the chances that phenomena will richly manifest themselves. If essential diversity exists in hypnosis, we need to adopt enough procedures of the right kind to demonstrate it.

References

Abelson, R. P. Script processing in attitude formation and decision making. In J. S. Carrol & J. W. Payne (Eds.), *Cognition and social behavior*. Hillsdale, N.J.: Lawrence Erlbaum Associates, 1976.

Abelson, R. P. Psychological status of the script concept. *American Psychologist*, 1981, *36*, 715–729.

Ahsen, A. *Psycheye: Self-analytic consciousness*. New York: Brandon House, 1977.

Anderson, J. R. *Cognitive psychology and its implications*. San Francisco: Freeman, 1980.

Angyal, A. *Foundations for a science of personality*. Cambridge, Mass.: Harvard University Press, 1941.

Archer, J., & Kagan, N. Teaching interpersonal relationship skills on campus: A pyramid approach. *Journal of Counseling Psychology*, 1973, *20*, 535–540.

Arnold, M. B. On the mechanism of suggestion and hypnosis. *Journal of Abnormal and Social Psychology*, 1946, *41*, 107–128.

As, A. Hypnotizability as a function of nonhypnotic experience. *Journal of Abnormal and Social Psychology*, 1963, *66*, 142–150.

As, A., & Lauer, L. W. A factor-analytic study of hypnotizability and related personal experiences. *International Journal of Clinical and Experimental Hypnosis*, 1962, *10*, 169–181.

Ascher, L. M., Barber, T. X., & Spanos, N. P. Two attempts to replicate the Parrish–Lundy–Leibowitz experiment on hypnotic age regression. *American Journal of Clinical Hypnosis*, 1972, *14*, 178–185.

Atkinson, R. C., & Shiffrin, R. M. The control of short-term memory. *Scientific American*, 1971, *224*, 82–90.

Bandura, A. Self-efficacy: Toward a unifying theory of behavioral change. *Psychological Review*, 1977, *84*, 191–215.

Bandura, A. The self system in reciprocal determinism. *American Psychologist*, 1978, *33*, 344–358.

Banyai, E. I., & Hilgard, E. R. A comparison of active-alert hypnotic induction with traditional relaxation induction. *Journal of Abnormal Psychology*, 1976, *85*, 218–224.

Barber, T. X. The afterimages of "hallucinated" and "imagined" colors. *Journal of Abnormal and Social Psychology*, 1959, *59*, 136–139.

267

Barber, T. X. Hypnotic age regression: A critical review. *Psychosomatic Medicine*, 1962, *24*, 286–299. (a)

Barber, T. X. Toward a theory of "hypnotic" behavior: The "hypnotically induced dream." *Journal of Nervous and Mental Disease*, 1962, *135*, 206–221. (b)

Barber, T. X. Measuring "hypnotic-like" suggestibility with and without "hypnotic induction"; psychometric properties, norms, and variables influencing responses to the Barber Suggestibility Scale (BSS). *Psychological Reports*, 1965, *16*, 809–844.

Barber, T. X. *Hypnosis: A scientific approach*. New York: Van Nostrand, 1969.

Barber, T. X. Suggested ("hypnotic") behavior: The trance paradigm versus an alternative paradigm. In E. Fromm & R. E. Shor (Eds.), *Hypnosis: Research developments and perspectives*. Chicago: Aldine-Atherton, 1972.

Barber, T. X., & Calverley, D. S. The relative effectiveness of task motivating instructions and trance-induction procedure in the production of "hypnotic-like" behaviors. *Journal of Nervous and Mental Disease*, 1963, *137*, 107–116.

Barber, T. X., & Ham, M. W. *Hypnotic phenomena*. Morristown, N.J.: General Learning Press, 1974.

Barber, T. X., Spanos, N. P., & Chaves, J. F. *Hypnosis, imagination, and human potentialities*. New York: Pergamon, 1974.

Barber, T. X., & Wilson, S. C. Hypnosis, suggestions, and altered states of consciousness: Experimental evaluation of the new cognitive-behavioral theory and the traditional trance-state theory of "hypnosis." *Annals of the New York Academy of Sciences*, 1977, *296*, 34–47.

Barber, T. X., & Wilson, S. C. The Barber Suggestibility Scale and the Creative Imagination Scale: Experimental and clinical applications. *American Journal of Clinical Hypnosis*, 1978–1979, *21*, 84–108.

Barrett, D. The hypnotic dream: Its relation to nocturnal dreams and waking fantasies. *Journal of Abnormal Psychology*, 1979, *88*, 584–591.

Barry, H., MacKinnon, D. W., & Murray, H. A., Jr. Studies on personality: A. Hypnotizability as a personality trait and its typological relations. *Human Biology*, 1931, *13*, 1–36.

Battista, J. R. The science of consciousness. In K. S. Pope & J. L. Singer (Eds.), *The stream of consciousness: Scientific investigations into the flow of human experience*. New York: Plenum Press, 1978.

Bell, G. *A phenomenological study of hypnosis using the Experiential Analysis Technique*. Unpublished honors thesis, University of Queensland, 1978.

Bentler, P. M., & Roberts, M. R. Hypnotic susceptibility assessed in large groups. *International Journal of Clinical and Experimental Hypnosis*, 1963, *11*, 93–97.

Bernheim, H. *Hypnosis and suggestion in psychotherapy*. New Hyde Park, N.Y.: University Books, 1888. (Reprinted 1964.)

Binet, A. *On double consciousness: Experimental psychological studies*. Chicago: Open Court Publishing Co., 1905.

Binet, A., & Fere, C. *Animal magnetism* (English translation). New York: Appleton, 1888. (Originally published in French, 1886.)

Bitterman, M. E., & Marcuse, F. L. Autonomic response in posthypnotic amnesia. *Journal of Experimental Psychology*, 1945, *35*, 248–252.

Blum, G. S., & Barbour, J. S. Selective inattention to anxiety-linked stimuli. *Journal of Experimental Psychology: General*, 1979, *108*, 182–224.

Bowers, K. S. Hypnotic behavior: The differentiation of trance and demand characteristic variables. *Journal of Abnormal Psychology*, 1966, *71*, 42–51.

Bowers, K. S. The effect of demands for honesty on reports of visual and auditory hallucinations. *International Journal of Clinical and Experimental Hypnosis*, 1967, *15*, 31–36.

Bowers, K. S. Situationism in psychology: An analysis and critique. *Psychological Review*, 1973, *80*, 307–336.

Bowers, K. S. *Hypnosis for the seriously curious*. Monterey, Cal.: Brooks/Cole, 1976.

Bowers, K. S. Do the Stanford scales tap the "classic suggestion effect"? *International Journal of Clinical and Experimental Hypnosis*, 1981, *29*, 42-53.

Bowers, P. Hypnotizability, creativity and the role of effortless experiencing. *International Journal of Clinical and Experimental Hypnosis*, 1978, *26*, 184-202.

Bowers, P. G., & Bowers, K. S. Hypnosis and creativity: A theoretical and empirical rapprochement. In E. Fromm & R. E. Shor (Eds.), *Hypnosis: Developments in research and new perspectives*. Hawthorne, N.Y.: Aldine, 1979.

Bradley, F. O. A modified interpersonal process recall technique as a training model. *Counselor Education and Supervision*, 1974, *14*, 34-39.

Brady, J. P., & Rosner, B. S. Rapid eye movements in hypnotically induced dreams. *Journal of Nervous and Mental Disease*, 1966, *143*, 28-35.

Braid, J. The physiology of fascination and the critics criticized. Manchester: Grant, 1855. Reprinted in M. M. Tinterow (Ed.), *Foundations of hypnosis: From Mesmer to Freud*. Springfield, Ill.: Thomas, 1970.

Bramwell, J. M. *Hypnotism* (Rev. ed.). New York: Julian, 1903.

Brenneman, H. A. *Peer descriptions during hypnotic age regression*. Paper presented at the 30th Annual Meeting of the Society for Clinical and Experimental Hypnosis, Asheville, North Carolina October 1978.

Broadbent, D. E. *Decision and stress*. London: Academic Press, 1971.

Broerse, J., & Crassini, B. The influence of imagery ability on colour aftereffects produced by physically present and imagined induction stimuli. *Perception & Psychophysics*, 1980, *28*, 560-568.

Bruner, J. S. *Beyond the information given*. New York: Norton, 1973.

Bugelski, B. R. Words and things and images. *American Psychologist*, 1970, *25*, 1002-1012.

Campbell, R. J., Kagan, N., & Krathwohl, D. R. The development and validation of a scale to measure affective sensitivity (empathy). *Journal of Counseling Psychology*, 1971, *18*, 407-412.

Cantor, N., & Kihlstrom, J. F. (Eds.). *Personality, cognition, and social interaction*. Hillsdale, N.J.: Lawrence Erlbaum Associates, 1981.

Carkhuff, R. R., & Berenson, B. G. *Beyond counseling and psychotherapy*. New York: Holt, Rinehart & Winston, 1967.

Cheek, D. B. Use of rebellion against coercion as mechanism for hypnotic trance deepening. *International Journal of Clinical and Experimental Hypnosis*, 1959, *7*, 223-227.

Coe, W. C. The credibility of posthypnotic amnesia: A contextualist's view. *International Journal of Clinical and Experimental Hypnosis*, 1978, *26*, 218-245.

Coe, W. C., Basden, B., Basden, D., & Graham, C. Posthypnotic amnesia: Suggestions of an active process in dissociative phenomena. *Journal of Abnormal Psychology*, 1976, *85*, 455-458.

Coe, W. C., Baugher, R. J., Krimm, W. R., & Smith, J. A. A further examination of selective recall during hypnosis. *International Journal of Clinical and Experimental Hypnosis*, 1976, *42*, 13-21.

Coe, W. C., & Ryken, K. Hypnosis and risks to human subjects. *American Psychologist*, 1979, *34*, 673-681.

Coe, W. C., & Sarbin, T. R. An alternative interpretation to the multiple composition of hypnotic scales: A single role relevant skill. *Journal of Personality and Social Psychology*, 1971, *18*, 1-8.

Collison, D. R. Hypnotherapy in asthmatic patients and the importance of trance depth. In F. H. Frankel & H. S. Zamansky (Eds.), *Hypnosis at its bicentennial: Selected papers*. New York: Plenum, 1978.

Connors, J., & Sheehan, P. W. The influence of control comparison tasks and between—versus within—subjects effects in hypnotic responsivity. *International Journal of Clinical and Experimental Hypnosis*, 1978, *26*, 104-122.

Cooper, L. M. Hypnotic amnesia. In E. Fromm & R. E. Shor (Eds.), *Hypnosis: Developments in research and new perspectives*. Hawthorne, N.Y.: Aldine, 1979.

Cooper, L. M., & London, P. The development of hypnotic susceptibility: A longitudinal (convergence) study. *Child Development*, 1971, *42*, 487–503.

Cooper, L. M., & London, P. The Children's Hypnotic Susceptibility Scale. *American Journal of Clinical Hypnosis*, 1978–1979, *21*, 170–185.

Crasilneck, H. B., & Michael, C. M. Performance on the Bender under hypnotic age regression. *Journal of Abnormal and Social Psychology*, 1957, *54*, 319–322.

Crebolder, R. J. *A study of the utility of the Experiential Analysis Technique as a subjective method of inquiry into hypnosis*. Unpublished honors thesis, University of Queensland, 1980.

Curran, J. D., & Gibson, H. B. Critique of the Stanford Hypnotic Susceptibility Scale: British usage and factorial structure. *Perceptual and Motor Skills*, 1974, *39*, 695–704.

Danish, S. J., & Brodsky, S. L. Training of policemen in emotional control and awareness. *Psychology in Action*, 1970, *25*, 368–369.

Danish, S. J., & Kagan, N. Measurement of affective sensitivity: Toward a valid measure of interpersonal perception. *Journal of Counseling Psychology*, 1971, *18*, 51–54.

Davidson, R. J. Consciousness and information processing: A biocognitive perspective. In J. M. Davidson & R. J. Davidson (Eds.), *The Psychobiology of consciousness*. New York: Plenum Press, 1980.

Davidson, R. J., & Goleman, D. J. The role of attention in meditation and hypnosis. A psychobiological perspective on transformations of consciousness. *International Journal of Clinical and Experimental Hypnosis*, 1977, *25*, 291–308.

Davis, L. W., & Husband, R. W. A study of hypnotic susceptibility in relation to personality traits. *Journal of Abnormal and Social Psychology*, 1931, *26*, 175–182.

Debetz, B., & Stern, D. B. Factor analysis and score distributions of the HIP: Replication by a second examiner. *American Journal of Clinical Hypnosis*, 1979, *22*, 95–102.

Deckert, G. H., & West, L. J. The problem of hypnotizability: A review. *International Journal of Clinical and Experimental Hypnosis*, 1963, *11*, 205–235.

Diamond, M. J. Modification of hypnotizability: A review. *Psychological Bulletin*, 1974, *81*, 180–198.

Diamond, M. J. Hypnotizability is modifiable: An alternative approach. *International Journal of Clinical and Experimental Hypnosis*, 1977, *25*, 147–166.

Diment, A. D. *Some aspects of nonsuggested experience in hypnosis*. Unpublished honors thesis, Macquarie University, 1974.

Dolby, R. M., & Sheehan, P. W. Cognitive processing and expectancy behavior in hypnosis. *Journal of Abnormal Psychology*, 1977, *86*, 334–345.

Domhoff, B. Night dreams and hypnotic dreams: Is there evidence that they are different? *International Journal of Clinical and Experimental Hypnosis*, 1964, *12*, 159–168.

Easton, R. D., & Shor, R. E. Information processing analysis of the Chevreul pendulum illusion. *Journal of Experimental Psychology: Human Perception and Performance*, 1975, *1*, 231–236.

Easton, R. D., & Shor, R. E. An experimental analysis of the Chevreul pendulum illusion. *Journal of General Psychology*, 1976, *95*, 111–125.

Ekehammer, B. Interactionism in modern personality from a historical perspective. *Psychological Bulletin*, 1974, *81*, 1026–1048.

Elstein, A. S., Kagan, N., Shulman, L., Jason, H., & Loupe, M. J. Methods and theory in the study of medical inquiry. *Journal of Medical Education*, 1972, *47*, 85–92.

Endler, N. S., & Magnusson, D. Toward an interactional psychology of personality. *Psychological Bulletin*, 1976, *83*, 956–974.

Epstein, S. The stability of behavior: 1. On predicting most of the people much of the time. *Journal of Personality and Social Psychology*, 1979, *37*, 1097–1126.

Erickson, M. H. Development of apparent unconsciousness during hypnotic reliving of a traumatic experience. *Archives of the Neurological Psychiatrist*, 1937, *18*, 1282–1288.

Ericsson, K. A., & Simon, H. A. Verbal reports as data. *Psychological Review*, 1980, *87*, 215–251.

Evans, F. J. Recent trends in experimental hypnosis. *Behavioral Science*, 1968, *13*, 477–487.

Evans, F. J. Phenomena of hypnosis: 2. Posthypnotic amnesia. In G. D. Burrows & L. Dennerstein (Eds.), *Handbook of hypnosis and psychosomatic medicine*. Amsterdam, The Netherlands: Elsevier/North Holland, 1980.

Eysenck, H. J., & Furneaux, W. D. Primary and secondary suggestibility: An experimental and statistical study. *Journal of Experimental Psychology*, 1945, *35*, 485–503.

Fellows, B. J., & Creamer, M. An investigation of the role of 'hypnosis', hypnotic susceptibility and hypnotic induction in the production of age regression. *British Journal of Social and Clinical Psychology*, 1978, *17*, 165–171.

Field, P. B. An inventory scale of hypnotic depth. *International Journal of Clinical and Experimental Hypnosis*, 1965, *13*, 238–249.

Field, P. B. Some self-rating measures related to hypnotizability. *Perceptual and Motor Skills*, 1966, *23*, 1179–1187.

Field, P. B. Humanistic aspects of hypnotic communication. In E. Fromm & R. E. Shor (Eds.), *Hypnosis: Developments in research and new perspectives*. Hawthorne, N.Y.: Aldine, 1979.

Fingarette, H. *Self deception*. London: Routledge & Kegan Paul, 1969.

Finke, R. A. Levels of equivalence in imagery and perception. *Psychological Review*, 1980, *87*, 113–132.

Finke, R. A., & Schmidt, M. J. Orientation-specific color aftereffects following imagination. *Journal of Experimental Psychology: Human Perception and Performance*, 1977, *3*, 599–606.

Finke, R. A., & Schmidt, M. J. The quantitative measure of pattern representation in images using orientation-specific color aftereffects. *Perception & Psychophysics*, 1978, *23*, 515–520.

Foulkes, D., & Vogel, G. Mental activity at sleep-onset. *Journal of Abnormal Psychology*, 1965, *70*, 231–243.

Frankel, F. H. Scales measuring hypnotic responsivity: A clinical perspective. *American Journal of Clinical Hypnosis*, 1978–1979, *21*, 208–218.

Friedlander, J. W., & Sarbin, T. R. The depth of hypnosis. *Journal of Abnormal and Social Psychology*, 1938, *33*, 453–475.

Frischholz, E. J., Tryon, W. W., Fisher, S., Maruffi, B. L., Vellios, A. T., & Spiegel, H. The relationship between the Hypnotic Induction Profile and the Stanford Hypnotic Susceptibility Scale, Form C: A replication. *American Journal of Clinical Hypnosis*, 1980, *22*, 185–196.

Gebhard, J. W. Hypnotic age-regression: A review. *American Journal of Clinical Hypnosis*, 1961, *3*, 139–168.

Gidro-Frank, L., & Bowersbuch, M. K. A study of the plantar response in hypnotic age regression. *Journal of Nervous and Mental Disease*, 1948, *107*, 443–458.

Gill, M. M. Hypnosis as an altered and regressed state. *International Journal of Clinical and Experimental Hypnosis*, 1972, *20*, 224–237.

Gill, M. M., & Brenman, M. *Hypnosis and related states*. New York: International Universities Press, 1961.

Glass, A. L., Holyoak, K. J., & Santa, J. L. *Cognition*. Reading, Mass.: Addison-Wesley, 1979.

Globus, G. G., Maxwell, G., & Savodnik, I. *Consciousness and the brain*. New York: Plenum Press, 1976.

Goldberger, N. I., & Wachtel, P. L. Hypnotizability and cognitive controls. *International Journal of Clinical and Experimental Hypnosis*, 1973, *21*, 298–304.

Gordon, R. An investigation into some of the factors that favour the formation of stereotyped images. *British Journal of Psychology*, 1949, *39*, 156–167.

Graham, C., & Evans, F. J. Hypnotizability and the deployment of waking attention. *Journal of Abnormal Psychology*, 1977, *86*, 631–638.

Graham, C., & Leibowitz, H. W. The effect of suggestion on visual acuity. *International Journal of Clinical and Experimental Hypnosis*, 1972, *20*, 169–182.

Graham, K. R., & Patton, A. Retroactive inhibition, hypnosis, and hypnotic amnesia. *International Journal of Clinical and Experimental Hypnosis,* 1968, *16,* 68–74.

Greenberg, B. S., Kagan, N., & Bowes, J. Dimensions of empathic judgment of clients by counselors. *Journal of Counseling Psychology,* 1969, *16,* 303–308.

Grzegorek, A. E., & Kagan, N. A study of the meaning of self-awareness in correctional counselor training. *Criminal Justice and Behavior,* 1974, *1,* 99–122.

Gur, R. C., & Sackeim, H. A. Self-confrontation and psychotherapy: A reply to Sanborn, Pyke, and Sanborn. *Psychotherapy: Theory, Research and Practice,* 1978, *15,* 258–265.

Hammer, A. G. *Some effects of the hypnotic state.* Paper presented at the 7th International Congress of Hypnosis and Psychosomatic Medicine, Philadelphia, July 1976.

Hammer, A. G., Evans, F. J., & Bartlett, M. Factors in hypnosis and suggestion. *Journal of Abnormal and Social Psychology,* 1963, *67,* 15–23.

Hammer, A. G., Walker, W. L., & Diment, A. D. A nonsuggested effect of trance induction. In F. H. Frankel & H. S. Zamansky (Eds.), *Hypnosis at its bicentennial: Selected papers.* New York: Plenum Press, 1978.

Hartson, D. J., & Kunce, J. T. Videotape replay and recall in group work. *Journal of Counseling Psychology.* 1973, *20,* 437–441.

Hatfield, E. C. The validity of the LeCron method of evaluating hypnotic depth. *International Journal of Clinical and Experimental Hypnosis,* 1961, *9,* 215–221.

Hilgard, E. R. Lawfulness within hypnotic phenomena. In G. H. Estabrooks (Ed.), *Hypnosis: Current problems.* New York: Harper & Row, 1962.

Hilgard, E. R. *Hypnotic susceptibility.* New York: Harcourt, Brace & World, 1965.

Hilgard, E. R. Altered states of awareness. *Journal of Nervous and Mental Diseases,* 1969, *149,* 68–79.

Hilgard, E. R. The domain of hypnosis: With some comments on alternative paradigms. *American Psychologist,* 1973, *23,* 972–982.

Hilgard, E. R. Toward a neodissociation theory: Multiple cognitive controls in human functioning. *Perspectives in Biology and Medicine,* 1974, *17,* 301–316.

Hilgard, E. R. Hypnosis. *Annual Review of Psychology,* 1975, *26,* 19–44.

Hilgard, E. R. Neodissociation theory of multiple cognitive control systems. In G. E. Schwartz & D. Shapiro (Eds.), *Consciousness and self-regulation: Advances in research* (Vol. 1). New York: Plenum Press, 1976.

Hilgard, E. R. *Divided consciousness: Multiple controls in human thought and action.* New York: Wiley, 1977.

Hilgard, E. R. The Stanford Hypnotic Susceptibility Scales as related to other measures of hypnotic responsiveness. *American Journal of Clinical Hypnosis,* 1978–1979, *21,* 68–83.

Hilgard, E. R. Consciousness and control: Lessons from hypnosis. *Australian Journal of Clinical and Experimental Hypnosis,* 1979, *7,* 103–116. (a)

Hilgard, E. R. *A saga of hypnosis: Two decades of the Stanford Laboratory of Hypnosis research, 1957–1979.* Unpublished manuscript, Stanford University, 1979. (b)

Hilgard, E. R. Consciousness in contemporary psychology. *Annual Review of Psychology,* 1980, *31,* 1–26.

Hilgard, E. R. Hypnotic susceptibility scales under attack: An examination of Weitzenhoffer's criticisms. *International Journal of Clinical and Experimental Hypnosis,* 1981, *29,* 24–41.

Hilgard, E. R., & Cooper, L. M. Spontaneous and suggested post-hypnotic amnesia. *International Journal of Clinical and Experimental Hypnosis,* 1965, *13,* 261–273.

Hilgard, E. R., Crawford, H. J., Bowers, P., & Kihlstrom, J. F. A tailored SHSS:C, permitting user modification for special purposes. *Intentional Journal of Clinical and Experimental Hypnosis,* 1979, *27,* 125–133.

Hilgard, E. R., Crawford, H. J., & Wert, A. The Stanford Hypnotic Arm Levitation Induction and Test (SHALIT):A six minute hypnotic induction and measurement scale. *International Journal of Clinical and Experimental Hypnosis,* 1979, *27,* 111–124.

Hilgard, E. R., & Hilgard, J. R. *Hypnosis in the relief of pain*. Los Altos, Cal.: Kaufmann, 1975.

Hilgard, E. R., & Hommel, L. S. Selective amnesia for events within hypnosis in relation to repression. *Journal of Personality*, 1961, *29*, 205–216.

Hilgard, E. R., Lauer, L. W., & Morgan, A. H. *Manual for Stanford Profile Scales of Hypnotic Susceptibility*. Palo Alto, Cal.: Consulting Psychologists Press, 1963.

Hilgard, E. R., Sheehan, P. W., Monteiro, K. P., & Macdonald, H. Factorial structure of the Creative Imagination Scale as a measure of hypnotic responsiveness: An international comparative study. *International Journal of Clinical and Experimental Hypnosis*, 1981, *29*, 66–76.

Hilgard, E. R., & Tart, C. T. Responsiveness to suggestions following waking and imagination instructions and following induction of hypnosis. *Journal of Abnormal Psychology*, 1966, *71*, 196–208.

Hilgard, E. R., Weitzenhoffer, A. M., Landes, J., & Moore, R. K. The distribution of susceptibility to hypnosis in a student population: A study using the Stanford Hypnotic Susceptibility Scale. *Psychological Monographs*, 1961, *75*, 1–22.

Hilgard, J. R. *Personality and hypnosis: A study of imaginative involvement*. Chicago: University of Chicago Press, 1970.

Hilgard, J. R. Imaginative involvement: Some characteristics of the highly hypnotizable and nonhypnotizable. *International Journal of Clinical and Experimental Hypnosis*, 1974, *22*, 138–156. (a)

Hilgard, J. R. Sequelae to hypnosis. *International Journal of Clinical and Experimental Hypnosis*, 1974, *22*, 281–298. (b)

Hilgard, J. R. Imaginative and sensory-affective involvements in everyday life and in hypnosis. In E. Fromm & R. E. Shor (Eds.), *Hypnosis: Developments in research and new perspectives*. Hawthorne, N.Y.: Aldine, 1979.

Hilgard, J. R., & Hilgard, E. R. Assessing hypnotic responsiveness in a clinical setting: A multi-item clinical scale and its advantages over single-item scales. *International Journal of Clinical and Experimental Hypnosis*, 1979, *27*, 134–150.

Hirst, W., Spelke, E. S., Reaves, C. C., Caharack, G., & Neisser, U. Dividing attention without alternation or automaticity. *Journal of Experimental Psychology: General*, 1980, *109*, 98–117.

Holt, R. R. Beyond vitalism and mechanism: Freud's concept of psychic energy. *Science and Psychoanalysis*, 1967, *11*, 1–40.

Howard, M. L., & Coe, W. C. The effects of context and subjects' perceived control in breaching posthypnotic amnesia. *Journal of Personality*, 1980, *48*, 342–359.

James, W. *Principles of psychology* (Vol. II). New York: Holt, 1890.

Jason, H., Kagan, N., Werner, A., Elstein, A., & Thomas, J. B. New approaches to teaching basic interview skills to medical students. *American Journal of Psychiatry*, 1971, *127*, 1404–1407.

John, E. R. A model of consciousness. In G. E. Schwartz & D. Shapiro (Eds.), *Consciousness and self-regulation: Advances in research* (Vol. 1). New York: Plenum Press, 1976.

Johnson, L. S. Self-hypnosis: Behavioral and phenomenological comparisons with heterohypnosis. *International Journal of Clinical and Experimental Hypnosis*, 1979, *27*, 240–264.

Johnson, M. K., & Raye, C. L. Reality monitoring. *Psychological Review*, 1981, *88*, 67–85.

Johnson, M. K., Raye, C. L., Wang, A. Y., & Taylor, T. H. Fact and fantasy: The roles of accuracy and variability in confusing imaginations with perceptual experiences. *Journal of Experimental Psychology: Human Learning and Memory*, 1979, *5*, 229–240.

Johnson, R. F., Maher, B. A., & Barber, T. X. Artifact in the "essence of hypnosis": An evaluation of trance logic. *Journal of Abnormal Psychology*, 1972, *79*, 212–220.

Julesz, B. *Foundations of cyclopean perception*. Chicago: University of Chicago Press, 1971.

Jung, C. G. *Psychological types*. London: Kegan Paul, Trench, Trubner & Co., 1923.

Kagan, N. Can technology help us toward reliability in influencing human interaction? *Educational Technology*, 1973, *13*, 44–51.

Kagan, N. *Influencing human interaction*. East Lansing, Mich.: Instructional Media Center, Michigan State University, 1975. (a)

Kagan, N. Influencing human interaction—eleven years with IPR. *The Canadian Counselor*, 1975, *9*, 74–97. (b)

Kagan, N., Krathwohl, D. R., & Miller, R. Stimulated recall in therapy using videotape—A case study. *Journal of Counseling Psychology*, 1963, *10*, 237–243.

Kagan, N., & Schauble, P. G. Affect simulation in interpersonal process recall. *Journal of Counseling Psychology*, 1969, *16*, 309–313.

Kagan, N., Schauble, P. G., Resnikoff, A., Danish, S. J., & Krathwohl, D. R. Interpersonal process recall. *Journal of Nervous and Mental Disease*, 1969, *148*, 365–374.

Kaiser, H. F., & Caffrey, J. Alpha factor analysis. *Psychometrika*, 1965, *30*, 1–14.

Karlin, R. A. Hypnotizability and attention. *Journal of Abnormal Psychology*, 1979, *88*, 92–95.

Kety, S. S. A biologist examines the mind and behavior. *Science*, 1960, *132*, 1861–1870.

Kiddoo, K. P. *Personality, cognitive style, and imagination-related behaviors*. Paper presented at the 85th Annual Meeting of the American Psychological Association, San Francisco, August 1977.

Kihlstrom, J. F. Models of posthypnotic amnesia. *Annals of the New York Academy of Sciences*, 1977, *296*, 284–301.

Kihlstrom, J. F. *Accessibility of material covered by posthypnotic amnesia via retrieval of semantic memories*. Paper presented at the 30th Annual Meeting of the Society for Clinical and Experimental Hypnosis, Asheville, North Carolina, October 1978. (a)

Kihlstrom, J. F. Context and cognition in posthypnotic amnesia. *International Journal of Clinical and Experimental Hypnosis*, 1978, *26*, 246–267. (b)

Kihlstrom, J. F., & Evans, F. J. Recovery of memory after posthypnotic amnesia. *Journal of Abnormal Psychology*, 1976, *85*, 564–569.

Kihlstrom, J. F., & Evans, F. J. Residual effect of suggestions for posthypnotic amnesia: A reexamination. *Journal of Abnormal Psychology*, 1977, *86*, 327–333.

Kihlstrom, J. F., & Evans, F. J. Memory retrieval processes during posthypnotic amnesia. In J. F. Kihlstrom & F. J. Evans (Eds.), *Functional disorders of memory*. Hillsdale, N.J.: Lawrence Erlbaum Associates, 1979.

Kihlstrom, J. F., Evans, F. J., Orne, E. C., & Orne, M. T. Attempting to breach posthypnotic amnesia. *Journal of Abnormal Psychology*, 1980, *89*, 603–616.

Kihlstrom, J. F., & Shor, R. E. Recall and recognition during posthypnotic amnesia. *International Journal of Clinical and Experimental Hypnosis*, 1978, *26*, 330–349.

Kingdon, M. A. A cost/benefit analysis of the interpersonal process recall technique. *Journal of Counseling Psychology*, 1975, *22*, 353–357.

Klein, G. S., Gardner, R. W., & Schlesinger, H. J. Tolerance for unrealistic experiences: The study of the generality of a cognitive control. *British Journal of Psychology*, 1962, *53*, 41–55.

Klinger, E. Modes of normal conscious flow. In K. S. Pope & J. L. Singer (Eds.), *The stream of consciousness: Scientific investigations into the flow of human experience*. New York: Plenum Press, 1978.

Knox, V. J., Morgan, A. H., & Hilgard, E. R. Pain and suffering in ischemia: The paradox of hypnotically suggested anesthesia as contradicted by reports from the "hidden observer." *Archives of General Psychiatry*, 1974, *30*, 301–316.

Kosslyn, S. M. Information representation in visual images. *Cognitive Psychology*, 1975, *7*, 341–370.

Kosslyn, S. M. Can imagery be distinguished from other forms of internal representation: Evidence from studies of information retrieval times. *Memory & Cognition*, 1976, *4*, 291–297.

Kosslyn, S. M. *Image and mind*. Cambridge, Mass.: Harvard University Press, 1980.

Kupper, H. I. Psychic concomitants in wartime injuries. *Psychosomatic Medicine*, 1945, *7*, 15–21.

Larsen, S. *Strategies for reducing phobic behavior*. Unpublished doctoral dissertation, Stanford University, 1965.

Laurence, J-R. *Cognitive patterns in hypnosis*. Unpublished honors thesis, Concordia University, 1979.

Laurence, J-R. *Duality and the reports of the "hidden observer."* Paper presented at the 88th Annual Meeting of the American Psychological Association, Montreal, September 1980.

Laurence, J-R., & Perry, C. The "hidden observer" phenomenon in hypnosis: Some additional findings. *Journal of Abnormal Psychology,* 1981, *90,* 334–344.

Lavoie, G., Sabourin, M., & Langlois, J. Hypnotic susceptibility, amnesia, and IQ in chronic schizophrenia. *International Journal of Clinical and Experimental Hypnosis,* 1973, *21,* 157–168.

LeCron, L. M. A study of age regression under hypnosis. In L. M. LeCron (Ed.), *Experimental hypnosis: A symposium of articles on research by many of the world's leading authorities.* New York: Macmillan, 1948.

LeCron, L. M. A method of measuring the depth of hypnosis. *Journal of Clinical and Experimental Hypnosis,* 1953, *1,* 4–7.

Leuner, H. Guided affective imagery: An account of its development. *Journal of Mental Imagery,* 1977, *1,* 73–92.

Levine, J., & Ludwig, A. M. Alterations in consciousness produced by combinations of LSD, hypnosis, and psychotherapy. *Psychopharmacologia,* 1965, *7,* 123–137.

Levitt, E. E., & Chapman, R. H. Hypnosis as a research method. In E. Fromm & R. E. Shor (Eds.), *Hypnosis: Developments in research and new perspectives.* Hawthorne, N.Y.: Aldine, 1979.

Lewin, K. *Field theory in social science: Selected theoretical papers.* New York: Harper, 1951.

Liébeault, A. A. *Le sommeil provoqué et les etats analogues.* Paris: Doin, 1889.

Lieberman, J., Lavoie, G., & Brisson, A. Suggested amnesia and order of recall as a function of hypnotic susceptibility and learning conditions in chronic schizophrenic patients. *International Journal of Clinical and Experimental Hypnosis,* 1978, *26,* 268–280.

Loewenfeld, L. *Der hypnotismus.* Wiesbaden: Bergamann, 1901.

London, P. *Children's Hypnotic Susceptibility Scale.* Palo Alto, Cal.: Consulting Psychologists Press, 1963.

London, P., & Cooper, L. M. Norms of hypnotic susceptibility in children. *Developmental Psychology,* 1969, *1,* 113–124.

Ludwig, A. M. Altered states of consciousness. In C. Tart (Ed.), *Altered states of consciousness: A book of readings.* New York: Wiley, 1969.

Marsh, C. A framework for describing subjective states of consciousness. In N. E. Zinberg (Ed.), *Alternate states of consciousness.* New York: Free Press, 1977.

McCollough, C. Color adaptation of edge-detectors in the human visual system. *Science,* 1965, *149,* 1115–1116.

McConkey, K. M. *Reality and suggestion in hypnosis.* Unpublished doctoral dissertation, University of Queensland, 1979.

McConkey, K. M., & Sheehan, P. W. Inconsistency in hypnotic age regression and cue structure as supplied by the hypnotist. *International Journal of Clinical and Experimental Hypnosis,* 1980, *28,* 394–408.

McConkey, K. M., & Sheehan, P. W. The impact of videotape playback of hypnotic events on posthypnotic amnesia. *Journal of Abnormal Psychology,* 1981, *90,* 46–54.

McConkey, K. M., Sheehan, P. W., & Cross, D. G. Posthypnotic amnesia: Seeing is not remembering. *British Journal of Social and Clinical Psychology,* 1980, *19,* 99–107.

McConkey, K. M., Sheehan, P. W., & Law, H. G. Structural analysis of the Harvard Group Scale of Hypnotic Susceptibility, Form A. *International Journal of Clinical and Experimental Hypnosis,* 1980, *28,* 164–175.

McConkey, K. M., Sheehan, P. W., & White, K. D. Comparison of the Creative Imagination Scale and the Harvard Group Scale of Hypnotic Susceptibility, Form A. *International Journal of Clinical and Experimental Hypnosis,* 1979, *27,* 265–277.

McDonald, R. D., & Smith, J. R. Trance logic in tranceable and simulating subjects. *International Journal of Clinical and Experimental Hypnosis,* 1975, *23,* 80–89.

McKeachie, W. J. Psychology in America's bicentennial year. *American Psychologist,* 1976, *31,* 819-833.

Mischel, W. The interaction of person and situation. In D. Magnusson & N. S. Endler (Eds.), *Personality at the crossroads: Current issues in interactional psychology.* New York: Wiley, 1977.

Mischel, W. On the interface of cognition and personality: Beyond the person-situation debate. *American Psychologist,* 1979, *34,* 740-754.

Monteiro, K. P., Macdonald, H., & Hilgard, E. R. Imagery, absorption, and hypnosis: A factorial study. *Journal of Mental Imagery,* 1980, *4,* 63-82.

Morgan, A. H. Hypnotizability and "cognitive styles": A search for relationships. *Journal of Personality,* 1972, *40,* 503-509.

Morgan, A. H., & Hilgard, J. R. The Stanford Hypnotic Clinical Scale for Adults. *American Journal of Clinical Hypnosis,* 1978-1979, *21,* 134-147. (a)

Morgan, A. H., & Hilgard, J. R. The Stanford Hypnotic Clinical Scale for Children. *American Journal of Clinical Hypnosis,* 1978-1979, *21,* 148-169. (b)

Moss, C. S. *The hypnotic investigation of dreams.* New York: Wiley, 1967.

Moss, C. S. Review of Children's Hypnotic Susceptibility Scale. In O. K. Buros (Ed.), *Personality tests and reviews.* Highland Park, N.J.: Gryphon Press, 1970.

Moyer, R. S., Bradley, D. R., Sorensen, M. H., Whiting, J. C., & Mansfield, D. P. Psychophysical functions for perceived and remembered size. *Science,* 1978, *200,* 330-332.

Murdock, B. B., Jr. *Human memory: Theory and data.* Hillsdale, N.J.: Lawrence Erlbaum Associates, 1974.

Murphy, M. A. M. *Reality and strength of posthypnotic amnesia: A study employing the Experiential Analysis Technique.* Unpublished honors thesis, University of Queensland, 1980.

Nace, E. P., Orne, M. T., & Hammer, A. G. Posthypnotic amnesia as an active psychic process: The reversibility of amnesia. *Archives of General Psychiatry,* 1974, *31,* 257-260.

Nash, M. R., Johnson, L. S., & Tipton, R. D. Hypnotic age regression and the occurrence of transitional object relationships. *Journal of Abnormal Psychology,* 1979, *88,* 547-555.

Neisser, U. *Cognitive psychology.* New York: Appleton Century Crofts, 1967.

Neisser, U. *Cognition and reality: Principles and implications of cognitive psychology.* San Francisco: Freeman, 1976.

Neisser, U. Is psychology ready for consciousness? *Contemporary Psychology,* 1979, *24,* 99-100.

Nemiah, J. C. Dissociative amnesia: A clinical and theoretical reconsideration. In J. F. Kihlstrom & F. J. Evans (Eds.), *Functional disorders of memory.* Hillsdale, N.J.: Lawrence Erlabum Associates, 1979.

Nisbett, R. E., & Wilson, T. D. Telling more than we know: Verbal reports on mental processes. *Psychological Review,* 1977, *84,* 231-259.

Obstoj, I., & Sheehan, P. W. Aptitude for trance, task generalizability, and incongruity response in hypnosis. *Journal of Abnormal Psychology,* 1977, *86,* 543-552.

O'Connell, D. N. An experimental comparison of hypnotic depth measured by self-ratings and by an objective scale. *International Journal of Clinical and Experimental Hypnosis,* 1964, *12,* 34-46.

O'Connell, D. N. Selective recall of hypnotic susceptibility items: Evidence for repression or enhancement? *International Journal of Clinical and Experimental Hypnosis,* 1966, *14,* 150-161.

O'Connell, D. N., Shor, R. E., & Orne, M. T. Hypnotic age regression: An empirical and methodological analysis. *Journal of Abnormal Psychology,* 1970, *76* (Monograph Issue No. 3, Pt. 2).

Orne, M. T. The mechanisms of hypnotic age regression: An experimental study. *Journal of Abnormal and Social Psychology,* 1951, *46,* 213-225.

Orne, M. T. The nature of hypnosis: Artifact and essence. *Journal of Abnormal and Social Psychology,* 1959, *58,* 277-299.

Orne, M. T. Hypnotically induced hallucinations. In L. J. West (Ed.), *Hallucinations.* New York: Grune & Stratton, 1962.

Orne, M. T. On the mechanisms of posthypnotic amnesia. *International Journal of Clinical and Experimental Hypnosis*, 1966, *14*, 121-134.

Orne, M. T. Demand characteristics and the concept of quasi-controls. In R. Rosenthal & R. L. Rosnow (Eds.), *Artifact in behavioral research*. New York: Academic Press, 1969.

Orne, M. T. On the simulating subject as a quasi-control group in hypnosis research: What, why, and how. In E. Fromm & R. E. Shor (Eds.), *Hypnosis: Research developments and perspectives*. Chicago: Aldine-Atherton, 1972.

Orne, M. T. *On the concept of hypnotic depth*. Paper presented at the 18th International Conference of Applied Psychology, Montreal, August 1974.

Orne, M. T. The construct of hypnosis: Implications of the definition for research and practice. *Annals of the New York Academy of Sciences*, 1977, *296*, 14-33.

Orne, M. T., & Evans, F. J. Inadvertent termination of hypnosis with hypnotized and simulating subjects. *International Journal of Clinical and Experimental Hypnosis*, 1966, *14*, 61-78.

Orne, M. T., & Hammer, A. G. Hypnosis. *Encyclopaedia Brittanica* (Vol. 15). Chicago: Benton, 1974.

Orne, M. T., Hilgard, E. R., Spiegel, H., Spiegel, D., Crawford, H. J., Evans, F. J., Orne, E. C., & Frischholz, E. J. The relation between the Hypnotic Induction Profile and the Stanford Hypnotic Susceptibility Scales, Forms A and C. *International Journal of Clinical and Experimental Hypnosis*, 1979, *27*, 85-102.

Orne, M. T., & McConkey, K. M. Toward convergent inquiry into self-hypnosis. *International Journal of Clinical and Experimental Hypnosis*, 1981, *29*, 313-323.

Orne, M. T., & O'Connell, D. N. Diagnostic ratings of hypnotizability. *International Journal of Clinical and Experimental Hypnosis*, 1967, *15*, 125-133.

Overton, D. A. State-dependent learning produced by addictive drugs. In S. Fisher & A. M. Freedman (Eds.), *Opiate addiction: Origins and treatment*. Washington, D.C.: Winston, 1973.

Parrish, M., Lundy, R. M., & Liebowitz, H. W. Effect of hypnotic age regression on the magnitude of the Ponzo and Poggendorff illusions. *Journal of Abnormal Psychology*, 1969, *74*, 693-698.

Perky, C. W. An experimental study of imagination. *American Journal of Psychology*, 1910, *21*, 422-452.

Perry, C. Is hypnotizability modifiable? *International Journal of Clinical and Experimental Hypnosis*, 1977, *25*, 125-146. (a)

Perry, C. W. Uncancelled hypnotic suggestions: The effects of hypnotic depth and hypnotic skill on their posthypnotic persistence. *Journal of Abnormal Psychology*, 1977, *86*, 570-574. (b)

Perry, C. Variables influencing the posthypnotic persistence of an uncancelled hypnotic suggestion. *Annals of the New York Academy of Sciences*, 1977, *296*, 264-273. (c)

Perry, C. *Cognitive patterns in hypnosis*. Paper presented at the 88th Annual Meeting of the American Psychological Association, Montreal, September 1980.

Perry, C. W., & Chisholm, W. Hypnotic age regression and the Ponzo and Poggendorff illusions. *International Journal of Clinical and Experimental Hypnosis*, 1973, *21*, 192-204.

Perry, C., Gelfand, R., & Marcovitch, P. The relevance of hypnotic susceptibility in the clinical context. *Journal of Abnormal Psychology*, 1979, *88*, 592-603.

Perry, C. W., & Laurence, J-R. Hypnotic depth and hypnotic susceptibility: A replicated finding. *International Journal of Clinical and Experimental Hypnosis*, 1980, *28*, 272-280.

Perry, C. W., & Sheehan, P. W. Aptitude for trance and situational effects of varying the interpersonal nature of the hypnotic setting. *American Journal of Clinical Hypnosis*, 1978, *20*, 256-262.

Perry, C. W., & Walsh, B. Inconsistencies and anomalies of response as a defining characteristic of hypnosis. *Journal of Abnormal Psychology*, 1978, *87*, 574-577.

Peters, J. E. *Trance logic: Artifact or essence in hypnosis*. Unpublished doctoral dissertation, Pennsylvania State University, 1973.

Peters, J. E., Dhanens, T. P., Lundy, R. M., & Landy, F. S. A factor analytic investigation of the

Harvard Group Scale of Hypnotic Susceptibility, Form A. *International Journal of Clinical and Experimental Hypnosis*, 1974, *22*, 377–387.

Peterson, C., & Scott, W. A. Generality and topic specificity of cognitive styles. *Journal of Research in Personality*, 1975, *9*, 366–374.

Pettinati, H. M., & Evans, F. J. Posthypnotic amnesia: Evaluation of selective recall of successful experiences. *International Journal of Clinical and Experimental Hypnosis*, 1978, *26*, 317–329.

Piaget, J. Piaget's theory. In P. Mussen (Ed.), *Carmichael's manual of child psychology* (Vol. 1). New York: Wiley, 1970.

Pinker, S., & Kosslyn, S. M. The representation and manipulation of three-dimensional space in mental images. *Journal of Mental Imagery*, 1978, *2*, 69–84.

Podmore, F. *From Mesmer to Christian Science: A short history of mental healing.* New Hyde Park, N.Y.: University Books, 1964. (Originally published, 1909.)

Posner, M. I., & Klein, R. M. On the functions of consciousness. In S. Kornblum (Ed.), *Attention and performance* (Vol. 4). New York: Academic Press, 1973.

Posner, M. I., & Snyder. C. Facilitation and inhibition in the processing of signals. In P. M. A. Rabitt & S. Dornic (Eds.), *Attention and performance* (Vol. 5). New York: Academic Press, 1975.

Pribram, K. H. Problems concerning the structure of consciousness. In G. G. Globus, G. Maxwell, & I. Savodnik (Eds.), *Consciousness and the brain.* New York: Plenum Press, 1976. (a)

Pribram, K. H. Self-consciousness and intentionality: A model based on an experimental analysis of the brain mechanisms involved in the Jamesian theory of motivation and emotion. In G. E. Schwartz & D. Shapiro (Eds.), *Consciousness and self-regulation: Advances in research* (Vol. 1). New York: Plenum Press, 1976. (b)

Qualls, P. J., & Sheehan, P. W. Electromyograph biofeedback as a relaxation technique: A critical appraisal and reassessment. *Psychological Bulletin*, 1981, *90*, 21–42. (a)

Qualls, P. J., & Sheehan, P. W. Imagery encouragement, absorption capacity, and relaxation during electromyograph biofeedback. *Journal of Personality and Social Psychology*, 1981, *41*, 370–379. (b)

Qualls, P. J., & Sheehan, P. W. Role of the feedback signal in electromyograph biofeedback: The relevance of attention. *Journal of Experimental Psychology: General*, 1981, *110*, 204–216. (c)

Qualls, P. J., & Sheehan, P. W. Trait-treatment interactions: Reply to Tellegen. *Journal of Experimental Psychology: General*, 1981, *110*, 227–231. (d)

Radtke-Bodorik, H. L., Planar, M., & Spanos, N. P. Suggested amnesia, verbal inhibition, and disorganized recall for a long word list. *Canadian Journal of Behavioral Science*, 1980, *12*, 87–97.

Rappaport, D. Cognitive structures. In *Contemporary approaches to cognition: University of Colorado Symposium.* Cambridge, Mass.: Harvard University Press, 1957.

Rasch, G. *Probabilistic models for some intelligence and attainment tests.* Copenhagen: Nielsen & Lydiche, 1960.

Raye, C. L., & Johnson, M. K. Reality monitoring vs. discriminating between external sources of memories. *Bulletin of the Psychonomic Society*, 1980, *15*, 405–408.

Reed, G. Everyday anomalies of recall and recognition. In J. F. Kihlstrom & F. J. Evans (Eds.), *Functional disorders of memory.* Hillsdale, N.J.: Lawrence Erlbaum Associates, 1979.

Reiff, R., & Scheerer, M. *Memory and hypnotic age regression: Developmental aspects of cognitive function explored through hypnosis.* New York: International Universities Press, 1959.

Reyher, J. Clinical and experimental hypnosis: Implications for theory and methodology. *Annals of the New York Academy of Sciences*, 1977, *296*, 69–85.

Roberts, M. R. Attention and cognitive controls as related to individual differences in hypnotic susceptibility. *Dissertation Abstracts International*, 1965, *25*, 4261.

Ruch, J. C. Self-hypnosis: The result of heterohypnosis or vice versa? *International Journal of Clinical and Experimental Hypnosis*, 1975, *23*, 282–304.

Ruch, J. C., Morgan, A. H., & Hilgard, E. R. Measuring hypnotic responsiveness: A comparison of the Barber Suggestibility Scale and the Stanford Hypnotic Susceptibility Scale, Form A. *International Journal of Clinical and Experimental Hypnosis*, 1974, *22*, 365-376.

Ryan, M., & Sheehan, P. W. Reality testing in hypnosis: Subjective versus objective effects. *International Journal of Clinical and Experimental Hypnosis*, 1977, *25*, 37-51.

Sacerdote, P. *Induced dreams*. New York: Vantage Press, 1967.

Salzman, L. K. A clinical modification of the Experiential Analysis Technique. *Australian Journal of Clinical and Experimental Hypnosis*, 1982. (May issue).

Sanders, R. S., & Reyher, J. Sensory deprivation and the enhancement of hypnotic susceptibility. *Journal of Abnormal Psychology*, 1969, *74*, 375-381.

Sarbin, T. R. Mental age changes in experimental regression. *Journal of Personality*, 1950, *19*, 221-228.

Sarbin, T. R., & Coe, W. C. *Hypnosis: A social psychological analysis of influence communication*. New York: Holt, Rinehart & Winston, 1972.

Sarbin, T. R., & Coe, W. C. Hypnosis and psychopathology: Replacing old myths with fresh metaphors. *Journal of Abnormal Psychology*, 1979, *88*, 506-526.

Sarbin, T. R., & Slagle, R. W. Hypnosis and psychophysiological outcomes. In E. Fromm & R. E. Shor (Eds.), *Hypnosis: Research developments and perspectives*. Chicago: Aldine-Atherton, 1972.

Schneck, J. M. Clinical and experimental aspects of hypnotic dreams. In M. V. Kline (Ed.), *Clinical correlations of experimental hypnosis*. Springfield, Ill.: Thomas, 1963.

Schuyler, B. A., & Coe, W. C. A physiological investigation of volitional and nonvolitional experience during posthypnotic amnesia. *Journal of Personality and Social Psychology*, 1981, *40*, 1160-1169.

Schwartz, G. E., & Shapiro, D. (Eds.). *Consciousness and self-regulation: Advances in research* (Vol. 1). New York: Plenum Press, 1976.

Segal, S. J. Processing of the stimulus in imagery and perception. In S. J. Segal (Ed.), *Imagery: Current cognitive approaches*. New York: Academic Press, 1971.

Segal, S. J. Assimilation of a stimulus in the construction of an image: The Perky effect revisited. In P. W. Sheehan (Ed.), *The function and nature of imagery*. New York: Academic Press, 1972.

Shallice, T. The dominant action system: An information-processing approach to consciousness. In K. S. Pope & J. L. Singer (Eds.), *The stream of consciousness: Scientific investigations into the flow of human experience*. New York: Plenum Press, 1978.

Sheehan, P. W. A shortened form of Betts' Questionnaire upon Mental Imagery. *Journal of Clinical Psychology*, 1967, *23*, 386-389.

Sheehan, P. W. Countering preconceptions about hypnosis: An objective index of involvement with the hypnotist. *Journal of Abnormal Psychology Monograph*, 1971, *78*, 299-322. (a)

Sheehan, P. W. A methodological analysis of the simulating technique. *International Journal of Clinical and Experimental Hypnosis*, 1971, *19*, 83-99. (b)

Sheehan, P. W. Hypnosis and the manifestations of "imagination." In E. Fromm & R. E. Shor (Eds.), *Hypnosis: Research developments and perspectives*. Chicago: Aldine-Atherton, 1972.

Sheehan, P. W. Analysis of the heterogeneity of "faking" and "simulating" performance in the hypnotic setting. *International Journal of Clinical and Experimental Hypnosis*, 1973, *21*, 213-225.

Sheehan, P. W. Incongruity in trance behavior: A defining property of hypnosis? *Annals of the New York Academy of Sciences*, 1977, *296*, 194-207.

Sheehan, P. W. Clinical and experimental hypnosis: Toward rapprochement. *Australian Journal of Clinical and Experimental Hypnosis*, 1979, *7*, 135-146. (a)

Sheehan, P. W. Hypnosis and the processes of imagination. In E. Fromm & R. E. Shor (Eds.), *Hypnosis: Developments in research and new perspectives*. Hawthorne, N.Y.: Aldine, 1979. (b)

Sheehan, P. W. Hypnosis considered as an altered state of consciousness. In G. Underwood & R.

Stevens (Eds.), *Aspects of consciousness: Psychological issues* (Vol. 1). London: Academic Press, 1979. (c)

Sheehan, P. W. Imagery processes and hypnosis: An experiential analysis of phenomena. In A. A. Sheikh & J. T. Shaffer (Eds.), *The potential of fantasy and imagination*. New York: Brandon Press, 1979. (d)

Sheehan, P. W. Factors influencing rapport in hypnosis. *Journal of Abnormal Psychology,* 1980, *89,* 263–281.

Sheehan, P. W., Crassini, B., & Murphy, M. *Persistence in cognitive effect: A case study.* Unpublished manuscript, University of Queensland, 1979.

Sheehan, P. W., & Dolby, R. M. Artifact and Barber's model of hypnosis: A logical-empirical analysis. *Journal of Experimental Social Psychology,* 1974, *10,* 171–187.

Sheehan, P. W., & Dolby, R. Hypnosis and the influence of most recently perceived events. *Journal of Abnormal Psychology,* 1975, *84,* 331–345.

Sheehan, P. W., & Dolby, R. M. Motivated involvement in hypnosis: The illustration of clinical rapport through hypnotic dreams. *Journal of Abnormal Psychology,* 1979, *88,* 573–583.

Sheehan, P. W., & McConkey, K. M. Australian norms for the Harvard Group Scale of Hypnotic Susceptibility, Form A. *International Journal of Clinical and Experimental Hypnosis,* 1979, *27,* 294–304.

Sheehan, P. W., McConkey, K. M., & Cross, D. Experiential analysis of hypnosis: Some new observations on hypnotic phenomena. *Journal of Abnormal Psychology,* 1978, *87,* 570–573.

Sheehan, P. W., McConkey, K. M., & Law, H. G. Imagery facilitation and performance on the Creative Imagination Scale. *Journal of Mental Imagery,* 1978, *2,* 265–274.

Sheehan, P. W., Obstoj, I., & McConkey, K. Trance logic and cue structure as supplied by the hypnotist. *Journal of Abnormal Psychology,* 1976, *85,* 459–472.

Sheehan, P. W., & Perry, C. W. *Methodologies of hypnosis: A critical appraisal of contemporary paradigms of hypnosis.* Hillsdale, N.J.: Lawrence Erlbaum Associates, 1976.

Shor, R. E. Hypnosis and the concept of the generalized reality-orientation. *American Journal of Psychotherapy,* 1959, *13,* 582–602.

Shor, R. E. The frequency of naturally occurring "hypnoticlike" experiences in the normal college population. *International Journal of Clinical and Experimental Hypnosis,* 1960, *8,* 151–163.

Shor, R. E. Three dimensions of hypnotic depth. *International Journal of Clinical and Experimental Hypnosis,* 1962, *10,* 23–28.

Shor, R. E. The three-factor theory of hypnosis as applied to the book-reading fantasy and to the concept of suggestion. *International Journal of Clinical and Experimental Hypnosis,* 1970, *28,* 89–98.

Shor, R. E. *Inventory of Self-Hypnosis, Form A.* Palo Alto, Cal.: Consulting Psychologists Press, 1978.

Shor, R. E. A phenomenological method for the measurement of variables important to an understanding of the nature of hypnosis. In E. Fromm & R. E. Shor (Eds.), *Hypnosis: Developments in research and new perspectives.* Hawthorne, N.Y.: Aldine, 1979.

Shor, R. E., & Easton, R. D. A preliminary report on research comparing self- and hetero-hypnosis. *American Journal of Clinical Hypnosis,* 1973, *16,* 37–44.

Shor, R. E., & Orne, E. C. *Harvard Group Scale of Hypnotic Susceptibility, Form A.* Palo Alto, Cal.: Consulting Psychologists Press, 1962.

Shor, R. E., & Orne, E. C. Norms on the Harvard Group Scale of Hypnotic Susceptibility, Form A. *International Journal of Clinical and Experimental Hypnosis,* 1963, *11,* 39–47.

Shor, R. E., Orne, M. T., & O'Connell, D. N. Psychological correlates of plateau hypnotizability in a special volunteer sample. *Journal of Personality and Social Psychology,* 1966, *3,* 80–95.

Singer, J. L. Ongoing thought: The normative baseline for alternate states of consciousness. In N. E. Zinberg (Ed.), *Alternate states of consciousness.* New York: Free Press, 1977.

Smith, E. R., & Miller, F. S. Limits on perception of cognitive processes: A reply to Nisbett and Wilson. *Psychological Review*, 1978, *85*, 355–362.

Spanos, N. P. Goal-directed fantasy and the performance of hypnotic test suggestions. *Psychiatry*, 1971, *34*, 86–96.

Spanos, N. P. Hypnotic responding: Automatic dissociation or situation-relevant cognizing? In E. Klinger (Ed.), *Imagery: Concepts, results and applications*. New York: Plenum Press, 1981.

Spanos, N. P., Ansari, F., & Stam, H. J. Hypnotic age regression and eidetic imagery: A failure to replicate. *Journal of Abnormal Psychology*, 1979, *88*, 88–91.

Spanos, N. P., & Barber, T. X. "Hypnotic" experiences as inferred from subjective reports: Auditory and visual hallucinations. *Journal of Experimental Research in Personality*, 1968, *3*, 136–150.

Spanos, N. P., & Barber, T. X. Cognitive activity during "hypnotic" suggestibility: Goal-directed fantasy and the experience of non-volition. *Journal of Personality*, 1972, *40*, 510–524.

Spanos, N. P., & Barber, T. X. Toward a convergence in hypnosis research. *American Psychologist*, 1974, *29*, 500–511.

Spanos, N. P., & McPeake, J. D. Involvement in suggestion-related imaginings, experienced involuntariness and credibility assigned to imaginings in hypnotic subjects. *Journal of Abnormal Psychology*, 1974, *83*, 687–690.

Spanos, N. P., & McPeake, J. D. Cognitive strategies, reported goal-directed fantasy, and response to suggestion in hypnotic subjects. *American Journal of Clinical Hypnosis*, 1977, *20*, 114–123.

Spanos, N. P., Radtke-Bodorik, H. L., Ferguson, J. D., & Jones, B. The effects of hypnotic susceptibility, suggestions for analgesia and the utilization of cognitive strategies on the reduction of pain. *Journal of Abnormal Psychology*, 1979, *88*, 282–292.

Spanos, N. P., Radtke-Bodorik, H. L., & Stam, H. J. Disorganized recall during suggested amnesia: Fact not artifact. *Journal of Abnormal Psychology*, 1980, *89*, 1–19.

Spanos, N. P., Rivers, S. M., & Gottlieb, J. Hypnotic responsivity, meditation and laterality of eye movements. *Journal of Abnormal Psychology*, 1978, *87*, 566–569.

Spanos, N. P., Rivers, S. M., & Ross, S. Experienced involuntariness and response to hypnotic suggestions. *Annals of the New York Academy of Sciences*, 1977, *296*, 208–221.

Spanos, N. P., Spillane, J., & McPeake, J. D. Cognitive strategies and response to suggestion in hypnotic and task-motivated subjects. *American Journal of Clinical Hypnosis*, 1976, *18*, 252–262.

Spanos, N. P., Stam, H. J., Rivers, S. M., & Radtke, H. L. Meditation, expectation and performance on indices of nonanalytic attending. *International Journal of Clinical and Experimental Hypnosis*, 1980, *28*, 244–251.

Spelke, E., Hirst, W., & Neisser, U. Skills of divided attention. *Cognition*, 1976, *4*, 215–230.

Sperry, R. Mental phenomena as causal determinants in brain function. In G. Globus (Ed.), *Brain and conscious experience*. New York: Plenum Press, 1976.

Spiegel, H. *Manual for Hypnotic Induction Profile*. New York: Soni Medica, 1974.

Spiegel, H., & Bridger, A. A. *Manual for Hypnotic Induction Profile*. New York: Soni Medica, 1970.

Spiegel, H., Shor, J., & Fishman, S. An hypnotic ablation technique for the study of personality development. *Psychosomatic Medicine*, 1945, *7*, 273–278.

Spiegel, H., & Spiegel, D. *Trance and treatment: Clinical uses of hypnosis*. New York: Basic Books, 1978.

Stern, D. B., Spiegel, H., & Nee, J. C. M. The Hypnotic Induction Profile: Normative observations, reliability and validity. *American Journal of Clinical Hypnosis*, 1978–1979, *21*, 109–133.

St. Jean, R., & Coe, W. C. Recall and recognition memory during posthypnotic amnesia: A failure to confirm the disrupted-search hypothesis and the memory disorganization hypothesis. *Journal of Abnormal Psychology*, 1981, *90*, 231–241.

Stewart, C. G., & Dunlap, W. P. Functional isolations of associations during suggested post-hypnotic amnesia. *International Journal of Clinical and Experimental Hypnosis*, 1976, *24*, 426–434.

Stoyva, J., & Kamiya, J. Electrophysiological studies of dreaming as the prototypes of a new strategy in the study of consciousness. *Psychological Review*, 1968, *75*, 192–205.

Straus, R. A. A naturalistic experiment investigating the effects of hypnotic induction upon Creative Imagination Scale performance in a clinical setting. *International Journal of Clinical and Experimental Hypnosis*, 1980, *28*, 218–224.

Stross, L., & Shevrin, H. A comparison of dream recall in wakefulness and hypnosis. *International Journal of Clinical and Experimental Hypnosis*, 1967, *15*, 63–71.

Sullivan, H. S. *The interpersonal theory of psychiatry.* New York: Norton, 1953.

Sutcliffe, J. P. "Credulous" and "skeptical" views of hypnotic phenomena: A review of certain evidence and methodology. *International Journal of Clinical and Experimental Hypnosis*, 1960, *8*, 73–101.

Sutcliffe, J. P. "Credulous" and "skeptical" views of hypnotic phenomena: Experiments in esthesia, hallucination, and delusion. *Journal of Abnormal and Social Psychology*, 1961, *62*, 189–200.

Sutcliffe, J. P., & Jones, J. Personal identity, multiple personality, and hypnosis. *International Journal of Clinical and Experimental Hypnosis*, 1962, *10*, 231–269.

Sutcliffe, J. P., Perry, C. W., & Sheehan, P. W. Relation ot some aspects of imagery and fantasy to hypnotic susceptibility. *Journal of Abnormal Psychology*, 1970, *76*, 279–287.

Sutcliffe, J. P., Perry, C. W., Sheehan, P. W., Jones, J. A., & Bristow, R. A. *The relation of imagery and fantasy to hypnosis* (Progress Report on NIMH Project M-30950). Washington: United States Public Health Service, 1963.

Tart, C. T. Hypnotic depth and basal skin resistance. *International Journal of Clinical and Experimental Hypnosis*, 1963, *11*, 81–92.

Tart, C. T. The hypnotic dream: Methodological problems and a review of the literature. *Psychological Bulletin*, 1965, *63*, 87–99.

Tart, C. T. Types of hypnotic dreams and their relation to hypnotic depth. *Journal of Abnormal Psychology*, 1966, *71*, 377–382.

Tart, C. T. Psychedelic experiences associated with a novel hypnotic procedure, mutual hypnosis. *American Journal of Clinical Hypnosis*, 1967, *10*, 65–78.

Tart, C. T. Self-report scales of hypnotic depth. *International Journal of Clinical and Experimental Hypnosis*, 1970, *18*, 105–125.

Tart, C. T. Measuring the depth of an altered state of consciousness, with particular reference to self-report scales of hypnotic depth. In E. Fromm & R. E. Shor (Eds.), *Hypnosis: Research developments and perspectives.* Chicago: Aldine-Atherton, 1972. (a)

Tart, C. T. States of consciousness and state-specific sciences. *Science*, 1972, *176*, 1203–1210. (b)

Tart, C. T. *States of consciousness.* New York: Dutton, 1975.

Tart, C. T. Discrete states of consciousness. In P. R. Lee, R. E. Ornstein, C. Tart, A. Deikman, & D. Galin (Eds.), *Symposium on consciousness.* New York: Viking Press, 1976.

Tart, C. T. Quick and convenient assessment of hypnotic depth: Self-report scales. *American Journal of Clinical Hypnosis*, 1978–1979, *21*, 186–207.

Tart, C. T. Measuring the depth of an altered state of consciousness, with particular reference to self-report scales of hypnotic depth. In E. Fromm & R. E. Shor (Eds.). *Hypnosis: Developments in research and new perspectives.* Hawthorne, N.Y.: Aldine, 1979.

Tart, C. T. A systems approach to altered states of consciousness. In J. M. Davidson & R. J. Davidson (Eds.), *The psychobiology of consciousness.* New York: Plenum Press, 1980.

Tart, C. T., & Hilgard, E. R. Responsiveness to suggestions under "hypnosis" and "waking imagination" conditions: A methodological observation. *International Journal of Clinical and Experimental Hypnosis*, 1966, *14*, 247–256.

Taylor, A. *The differentiation between simulated and true hypnotic regression by figure drawings.* Unpublished masters thesis, The City University of New York, 1950.

Taylor, S. E. Developing a cognitive social psychology. In J. S. Carroll & J. W. Payne (Eds.), *Cognition and social behavior.* Hillsdale, N.J.: Lawrence Erlbaum Associates, 1976.

Tellegen, A. On measures and conceptions of hypnosis. *American Journal of Clinical Hypnosis,* 1978-1979, *21,* 219-237.

Tellegen, A., & Atkinson, G. Openness to absorbing and self-altering experiences ("absorption"), a trait related to hypnotic susceptibility. *Journal of Abnormal Psychology,* 1974, *83,* 268-277.

Tellegen, A., & Atkinson, G. Complexity and measurement of hypnotic susceptibility: A comment on Coe and Sarbin's alternative interpretation. *Journal of Personality and Social Psychology,* 1976, *33,* 142-148.

Thorne, D. E., & Hall, M. V. Hypnotic amnesia revisited. *International Journal of Clinical and Experimental Hypnosis,* 1974, *22,* 167-178.

Tilden, J. *Analysis of modes of consciousness in hypnosis: A case for the relevance of cognitive style.* Unpublished manuscript, University of Queensland, 1979.

True, R. M. Experimental control in hypnotic age regression states. *Science,* 1949, *110,* 583-584.

True, R. M., & Stephenson, C. W. Controlled experiments correlating electroencephalogram, pulse, and plantar reflexes with hypnotic age regression and induced emotional states. *Personality,* 1951, *1,* 252-263.

Van Noord, R. W., & Kagan, N. Stimulated recall and affect simulation in counseling: Client growth reexamined. *Journal of Counseling Psychology,* 1976, *23,* 28-33.

Van Nuys, D. Meditation, attention, and hypnotic susceptibility: A correlational study. *International Journal of Clinical and Experimental Hypnosis,* 1973, *21,* 56-69.

Walker, N. S., Garrett, J. B., & Wallace, B. Restoration of eidetic imagery via hypnotic age regression: A preliminary report. *Journal of Abnormal Psychology,* 1976, *85,* 335-337.

Wallace, B. Restoration of eidetic imagery via hypnotic age regression: More evidence. *Journal of Abnormal Psychology,* 1978, *87,* 673-675.

Ward, R. G., Kagan, N., & Krathwohl, D. R. An attempt to measure and facilitate counselor effectiveness. *Counselor Education and Supervision,* 1972, *11,* 179-186.

Wardell, D. M., & Royce, J. R. Towards a multi-factor theory of styles and their relationships to cognition and affect. *Journal of Personality,* 1978, *46,* 474-505.

Watkins, J. G. Review of Children's Hypnotic Susceptibility Scale. In O. K. Buros (Ed.), *Personality tests and reviews.* Highland Park, N.J.: Gryphon Press, 1970.

Weitzenhoffer, A. M. *General techniques of hypnotism.* New York: Grune & Stratton, 1957.

Weitzenhoffer, A. M. Review of The Children's Hypnotic Susceptibility Scale. *American Journal of Clinical Hypnosis,* 1963, *5,* 336-337.

Wetizenhoffer, A. M. Hypnotic susceptibility revisited. *American Journal of Clinical Hypnosis,* 1980, *22,* 130-144.

Weitzenhoffer, A. M., & Hilgard, E. R. *Stanford Hypnotic Susceptibility Scale, Forms A and B.* Palo Alto, Cal.: Consulting Psychologists Press, 1959.

Weitzenhoffer, A. M., & Hilgard, E. R. *Stanford Hypnotic Susceptibility Scale, Form C.* Palo Alto, Cal.: Consulting Psychologists Press, 1962.

Weitzenhoffer, A. M., & Hilgard, E. R. *Stanford Profile Scales of Hypnotic Susceptibility: Forms I and II.* Palo Alto, Cal.: Consulting Psychologists Press, 1963.

Weitzenhoffer, A. M., & Hilgard, E. R. *Revised Stanford Profile Scales of Hypnotic Susceptibility, Forms I and II.* Palo Alto, Cal.: Consulting Psychologists Press, 1967.

Weitzenhoffer, A. M., & Sjoberg, B. M. Suggestibility with and without "induction of hypnosis." *Journal of Nervous and Mental Disease,* 1961, *132,* 204-220.

Werner, A., & Schneider, J. M. Teaching medical students interactional skills. *New England Journal of Medicine,* 1974, *290,* 1232-1237.

White, R. W. Two types of hypnotic trance and their personality correlates. *Journal of Psychology*, 1937, *3*, 265–277.

White, R. W. A preface to the theory of hypnotism. *Journal of Abnormal and Social Psychology*, 1941, *36*, 477–505.

Williamsen, J. A., Johnson, H. J., & Eriksen, C. W. Some characteristics of posthypnotic amnesia. *Journal of Abnormal Psychology*, 1965, *70*, 123–131.

Wilson, S. C., & Barber, T. X. The Creative Imagination Scale as a measure of hypnotic responsiveness: Applications to experimental and clinical hypnosis. *American Journal of Clinical Hypnosis*, 1978, *20*, 235–249.

Witkin, H. A. *Cognitive styles in personal and cultural adaptation*. Worcester, Mass.: Clark University Press, 1978.

Witz, K. (Ed.) *Case studies in visual imagery*. (Vol. 1). Urbana, Ill.: University of Illinois Press, 1978.

Woody, R. H., Krathwohl, D. R., Kagan, N., & Farquhar, W. W. Stimulated recall in psychotherapy using hypnosis and video tape. *American Journal of Clinical Hypnosis*, 1965, *7*, 234–241.

Yates, A. J. Hypnotic age regression. *Psychological Bulletin*, 1961, *58*, 429–440.

Young, P. C. Hypnotic regression—fact or artifact? *Journal of Abnormal and Social Psychology*, 1940, *35*, 273–278.

Zamansky, H. S. Suggestion and countersuggestion in hypnotic behavior. *Journal of Abnormal Psychology*, 1977, *86*, 346–351.

Zinberg, N. E. The study of consciousness states: Problems and progress. In N. E. Zinberg (Ed.), *Alternate states of consciousness*. New York: Free Press, 1977.

Author Index

Numbers in *italic* denote bibliographic information.

Subject Index